Donated by
Ian Thomson

Not for loan

ECONOMIC IMPACT OF EU MEMBERSHIP ON ENTRANTS

Economic Impact of EU Membership on Entrants

New Methods and Issues

Edited by

Richard E. Baldwin

Graduate Institute of International Studies (GIIS), Geneva and CEPR

and

Aymo Brunetti

State Secretariat for Economic Affairs, Berne and University of Basel, Switzerland

KLUWER ACADEMIC PUBLISHERS

BOSTON / DORDRECHT / LONDON

A C.I.P. Catalogue record for this book is available from the Library of Congress.

ISBN 0-7923-7574-2

Published by Kluwer Academic Publishers,
P.O. Box 17, 3300 AA Dordrecht, The Netherlands.

Sold and distributed in North, Central and South America
by Kluwer Academic Publishers,
101 Philip Drive, Norwell, MA 02061, U.S.A.

In all other countries, sold and distributed
by Kluwer Academic Publishers,
P.O. Box 322, 3300 AH Dordrecht, The Netherlands.

Printed on acid-free paper

Printed in the Netherlands.

TABLE OF CONTENTS

PREFACE

As part of its EU strategy, the Swiss government commissioned several research projects covering the most important aspects of economic integration. Given the interesting results and the wealth of methods used in these studies we decided to organize a conference on the topic of "The Economic Impact of EU Membership on Entrants: New Methods and Issues". The idea was to use the work on Switzerland as a case study for discussing modern approaches on how to assess the economic effects of joining an integration zone. This seemed to us to be a topic of considerable interest for the rising number of prospective EU-member countries. The response was very favourable with many eminent scholars agreeing to contribute. The conference took place in Lausanne, Switzerland in October 1999 and the papers submitted together with the discussions are published in this volume. We would like to acknowledge the financial support of the Swiss State Secretariat for Economic Affairs and to thank the University of Lausanne for providing the venue facilities for the conference. Many persons helped in the preparation of the conference and this volume but we would like to especially mention Marc Surchat who provided substantial input for the conference and Walter Brodmann who very efficiently reviewed and finalized the manuscript.

The Editors

RICHARD E. BALDWIN AND AYMO BRUNETTI

THE ECONOMIC IMPACT OF EU MEMBERSHIP ON ENTRANTS: NEW METHODS AND ISSUES

INTRODUCTION

What a transformation Europe has witnessed in the past 15 years. A ruthless observer in 1985 could have described the European Economic Community as a glorified customs union held together by an irreproducible mix of idealism, pretension, agriculture subsidies and guilt. Just a decade and a half latter, the European Union has achieved a depth and vigour of regional economic integration that surpasses all contemporary and historical efforts and it seems intent on pursuing ever-deeper integration. At the same time, the EU economy has recovered some of the economic dynamism it enjoyed in the 1950s and 1960s, and this has created a political-economic 'gravitational' force that is attracting a queue of applicants. Between 1985 and 1995, 6 new members joined the incumbent 9, and membership talks are underway with another dozen nations. Beyond this perhaps another 10 to 20 nations are contemplating EU applications.

This volume focuses on the entrants rather than the EU. Specifically it centres on the issues surrounding the likely economic impact that EU membership has on joining nations, with the main emphasis on new issues and methods. Given the significantly greater level of economic integration that now exists in the EU, accession brings up a host of issues that either did not arise or were of secondary importance during earlier enlargement waves. For instance, EU membership now entails eventual membership in the monetary union. This raises a series of new issues such as interest rate convergence, exchange rate stability and the loss of sovereignty over monetary policy. Additionally, these macro issues interact with micro issues such as export performance, capital formation and foreign direct investment (FDI). Migration, unemployment and foreign direct investment are further issues that acquire a magnified importance for the prospective entrants. Lastly, the vast majority of prospective entrants are small nations and the EU is by now an economic superpower. This radical size difference poses a series of challenges for economists.

About half the chapters in this volume focus on the Swiss case that constitutes, in many ways, a natural experiment. Switzerland, with its long history of European integration and its market orientation, provides the researcher with wealth of data that is missing for many of the other nations contemplating EU membership. The unique role of the Swiss franc in the international financial system also makes the EMU and macro issues central to Swiss concerns. Nevertheless, exchange rate issues and questions related to changes in the monetary independence of small European nations contemplating EU membership have a wide relevance to all prospective entrants.

1. *NEW WORK IS NEEDED*

While there is hardly a dearth of work on the economics of EU enlargement, a disproportionate share of this focuses on the EU rather than the entrants. While understandable -- it is naturally more attractive to write about the impact on the EU with its 370 million citizens than on an entrant with a population of 5-15 million -- the fact that upwards of 20 nations are seeking accession suggests that more works on the entrants is now essential. Of course, the entrants differ widely. No single collection of studies could address all the important issues. This volume, therefore, focuses on issues that are likely to have importance for many entrants. These include:

- EMU-related issues, such as:
  - Macro-micro interactions
  - Migration
- Trade/Micro Issues
  - FDI
  - Tax reforms, especially changes in the VAT
  - Labour Market Issues
- Small Economy Concerns

There is no clear cut method of addressing such issues since the economics profession is a long way from the "grand unified theory" of economic activity. Instead, a range of methods is used. These included:

- Computable general equilibrium models used to calculate the impact of microeconomic reforms -- both trade and tax policy -- on the general economy.
- Structural macroeconomic models for forecasting the short and medium-term consequences of integration.
- Sociological and discrete choice empirical models to predict demographic issues like immigration or factors that are important in the localisation of firms.

2. *SUMMARY OF THE INNOVATIVE CONTRIBUTIONS*

The chapters in this volume advance the research frontier in several ways. Many of the studies adopt the computable general equilibrium (CGE) approach and here important progress is made. The papers consider innovative ways of including growth effects, location effects and labour market effects. They also explore the problems of CGE modelling when the regions used are of vastly different economic size. On the macro side, the chapters present several innovations mainly focusing on the budgetary, interest rate, exchange rate and monetary policy aspects of EU membership. Consider these in turn.

2.1. The CGE approach

The European Commission has mainly used CGE models for estimating impacts of reforms. CGE models are sufficiently rich to capture many detailed aspects of the working of markets. They can also offer some insights about the distributions of benefits and costs among different groups of the population and different sectors. CGE models have also the ability to show precisely which reforms will bring along the most benefits, which gives valuable information whether such reforms should be undertaken independently of joining the EU.

Given the importance of the CGE approach, almost half the chapters in this volume are concerned with such analysis. In the Handbook of International Economics, Baldwin and Venables (1995) classify the microeconomic effect of integration into 'allocation effects' (i.e. the classic static effects allowing for both perfect competition with constant returns and imperfect competition with increasing returns), 'location effects' (i.e. the impact on the geographical allocation of economic activity), and 'accumulation effects' (i.e., growth effects stemming from the accumulation of technology, physical capital, or human capital). Recently, the research frontier of CGE analysis has been expanding mainly in the direction of location and accumulation effects, and the chapters in this volume contribute to both developments.

2.1.1. Dynamic aspects of integration in CGE models

The dynamic aspects of CGE models -- especially issues concerning the impact of integration on national capital stocks and FDI -- is still an area in which a good deal of progress is needed. The chapters by Jim Markusen, Tom Rutherford and David Tarr, by Jean-Marie Grether and Tobias Müller and by Renger van Nieuwkoop and Andre Müller focus on this set of issues.

Markusen, Rutherford and Tarr, which analyses the impact of FDI in producer services, concentrates on the liberalisation of imports of services in Russia and its impact on FDI and growth. The framework of this analysis is however sufficiently large so that the method could be applied to any country and any sector quite easily. The key to the result is the specification of the production function where imported services are an intermediary good complementary to other services. It is argued that by definition services provided by foreign firms consist mostly in managerial, financial, informational and technical services, which are intensive in skilled labour. Although they need a local presence, they are particular in the sense that they can not be supplied locally with the same quality, as they require an accumulated knowledge that is often lacking in developing countries. By liberalising the import of services, and thus allowing an almost infinite supply of skilled labour, countries encourage domestic and foreign direct investments, which are complimentary. This in turn stimulates economic growth and the welfare of most voters. The model shows that the impact on unskilled labour is non-linear and ambiguous. Furthermore, the impact on providers of local services, which are a substitute to imported services, can be negative for a while. However, with time the quality of services provided by local firms improves and becomes competitive with those provided by international firms. In fact, in a vintage model, local service providers who have the ability to acquire foreign technologies without loosing their prior investment gain immediately. The government' choices are clear between protecting local providers and services or promoting economic growth.

The chapter by *Grether and Müller* is innovative in several ways. The key to growth effects in dynamic CGE model is to determine how integration affects the equilibrium capital stock in an economy. Most dynamic CGE models rely on very simple rules for determining the equilibrium physical capital stock and thus for determining the medium-term growth effects that occur as the economy approaches its new equilibrium capital stock. Specifically, models either rely on a constant savings rate, or they assume that the capital stock adjusts to restore capital's reward to a 'normal' level (see Baldwin and Francois, 1999 for a more complete discussion). Grether and Müller go beyond this, introducing for the first time the Blanchard (1995) approach to intertemporally optimal savings behaviour. The key equation here relates an endogenous savings rate to the levels of two types of wealth -- human capital and physical capital. While the details are complex, the result is that the authors are able to allow tax policy (e.g. the VAT rate) to influence savings and investment behaviour. This brings up the second innovation which is that they allow for changes in trade policy and fiscal policy to interact. The third important innovation concerns assumptions that are necessary to consider the impact of integration between a very small and very large area (CGE models intrinsically have difficulties with large size asymmetries). The final innovation concerns foreign assets. Grether and Müller include earnings from foreign investments and this allows them to show that the benefits of unlimited free movement of capital. Although these effects are quite hard to estimate, they have probably been so far quite underestimated. The ongoing revolution on the European capital market might be a first sign of such an effect.

The application chosen by Grether and Müller is a CGE model designed to study the economic consequences of the EU-membership of Switzerland. The study allows for numerous aspects of integration, including the budgetary costs of joining the EU and the implications for the Swiss tax policy, potential immigration, a lowering of non-tariff barriers, the adoption of the common external tariff and of the common agricultural policy, and finally joining the EMU. Although this covers most of the reforms, the list is probably not comprehensive. Finally Grether and Müller propose to include earnings from foreign investments which allows them to show that the benefits of unlimited free movement of capital, although they are quite hard to estimate, have probably been so far quite underestimated. The ongoing revolution on the European capital market might be a first sign of such an effect.

Van Nieuwkoop and Müller also present a CGE model to analyse the microeconomic benefits of integration. Their research builds on their existing models and they incorporate it into a global model. The most innovative aspect of their model is its focus on transportation issues. Specifically, they estimated more precisely the gains from the transit agreement between Switzerland and the EU, which is expected to lower transportation costs. They also analyse alternative ways of using the additional income raised through the adaptation of the Swiss VAT rate to 15% (it is now less than half that rate). As such, it provides a first estimation of the potential benefit of a corresponding tax reform in Switzerland. Of course, many of the potential entrants will have to significantly modify their tax structure to conform to EU membership requirements. This aspect of the paper is therefore a welcome advance in CGE analysis.

2.1.2. Location effects in CGE models

Much of the public debate on European integration revolves around fears that freer trade will cause industrial 'delocation', namely the shifting of manufacturing activities from one region or nation to another. These fears are many and often inconsistent. Rich nations fear delocation to low-wage nations, poor nations fear delocation to highly industrialised nations, small countries fear delocation to large countries, and non-members fear delocation to EU members. The theory of international trade has recently made important advances in capturing the links between integration and location. This so-called 'new economic geography literature' (see the overview by Fujita, Krugman and Venables 1999) is now working its way into CGE analysis and two of the chapters in this volume contribute to this important effort. Before turning to these two contributions, a general introduction of the economic geography models is in order.

The so-called economic geography literature focuses on two types of models: the Krugman model based on footloose labour sometimes called the core-periphery model and the model based on vertically-linked industries introduced by Venables (see Fujita, Krugman and Venables 1999 for specifics). The hallmark of these models is that agglomeration forces tend to encourage concentration of industrial activity via 'circular causality.' That is to say, spatial concentration itself creates an environment that encourages spatial concentration.

Both variants feature demand-linked and cost-linked circular causality. In the footloose-labour model, a shock to the distribution of firms triggers two distinct cycles of circular causality. The first views migrants as consumers. When firms move, workers follow and this migration leads to expenditure shifting that makes demand in the receiving region large and demand in the sending region smaller. Since firms prefer, *ceteris paribus*, to be in the big market, expenditure-shifting leads to more production shifting, and the demand-linked cycle repeats. The second cycle views migrants as workers. Production shifting lowers the price index in the 'receiving' country (since fewer goods need to be imported) and raises it in the 'sending' country. Assuming migration equalises real wages, the initial shock will lower the receiving nation's nominal industrial wage relative to that of the sending nation. This 'cost shifting' or change in industrial competitiveness encourages more delocation to the receiving nation, so the cost-linked cycle repeats. Both of these cycles create agglomeration forces that favour geographic concentration of all economic activity in one region.

In the vertically linked industry model, firms use the output of other firms as intermediate inputs. Thus, production shifting alters the international demand pattern (viewing other firms as customers) and alters the international cost pattern (viewing other firms as suppliers). As in the Krugman model, two distinct but closely related processes of circular causality encourage agglomeration. Since labour mobility is negligible in Europe, often even between regions within a nation, the Venables model is generally preferred in European applications.

The basic point of these models is that as trade costs come down, forces emerge that encourage further concentration of economic activity where economic activity is already concentrated. This, in principle, could be bad news for the nations aspiring to join the EU, they are economically small compared to the EU.

Baldwin, Forslid, Haaland and Midelfart-Knarvik propose a calibrated model aimed at gauging location effects of EU enlargement on non-members, especially those in Central and Eastern European countries (CEECs). This is of interest in three ways. First, it allows one to judge whether the theoretical predictions generated by very simple theory models hold up in a more realistic, more complete model. Second, they propose a set of technological innovations that help to incorporate economic-geography features into CGE models. Third, the actual simulation results from their suggested 14-sector, 10-region model broadly confirm the theoretical predictions, but the effects are much more nuanced than those suggested by the simple theory models. In particular, they find that tighter European integration has a significant impact on Central and an Eastern European country, but the impact on the other regions of the world is rather small. They also find that the simple models of economic geography analysing European integration miss important elements. The most important of these are comparative advantage and real trade costs. In some industries, for example, leather, CEEC industries do suffer, but in others, for example textiles, the CEEC industries gain.

The chapter by *Francois* takes a different look at the location and integration issue. His study examines the importance of factor mobility within a nation for the location effects of economic integration across nations. The economic geography literature, and its manifestations in the CGE modelling literature (such as Baldwin, Forslid, Haaland and Midelfart-Knarvik above), puts most of its emphasis on the importance of trading cost. Francois, however, finds that the flexibility with which resources can be shifted between sectors within a nation have a critical impact on the ultimate location effects. By implication, he argues that structural reforms within nations are intimately linked to the impact of European integration. Of course, this is hardly a new point at a political level, but this is an area where the pronouncements of political leaders are far ahead of the state of economists' knowledge. Francois's study is therefore a welcomed first step towards quantifying and studying the connections at a more detailed level.

2.2. The structural macro model approach

"In the long run, we are all dead," quipped Keynes in response to classical economists who focused exclusively on models that assumed continuous market clearing. This aphorism aptly highlights one of the major shortcomings of CGE models. By assuming markets are constantly in equilibrium, CGE models do not show in a convincing way the transition toward a new long-term equilibrium. For the transition-process, so-called structural macroeconomic models are able to give a clearer picture of the immediate outcome of a change in economic policy. Such models are complementary to CGE models, because they have limits in predicting the evolution of relative prices, the structural sectoral shifts, the microeconomic gains of more efficient markets and so on. In this sense they depend on results previously supplied by CGE models in order to give proper predictions. But, when they take those results as inputs, macroeconomic models are able to figure out how the economy is going to get there in a more realistic fashion.

Structural macro models provide especially valuable input for decision-maker and politicians because the short-run effects of long-run policies have a persistent habit of ending their political lives well short of the "long run".

2.2.1. Impact of budgetary, interest rate and exchange rate changes

Four chapters in this volume employ structural macro models to shed light on the impact of European integration on potential entrants. A particularly innovative aspect of these studies is their focus on the transition to EMU. There exists a considerable literature on EMU's impact on the welfare of a country. However, discussion of the transition to EMU is often left aside. For all eventual members of the EMU, the transition towards the single currency will imply important changes as the disciplinary effect of fixed exchange rate and loss of monetary autonomy started to bite. Here, the Swiss case is interesting in its uniqueness. Switzerland has historically enjoyed nominal interest rates that were significantly below those of the deutschemark bloc, so EMU membership will entail a long-term interest rate rise (in contrast to the drop experienced by nations such as Ireland and Italy).

Three of the four chapters, namely those by Simmons-Süer and Himmel, by Stalder, and by Bärlocher study the impact of three types of macroeconomic shocks. Changes in the interest rate implied by EMU membership, changes implied by fixed exchange rates, and the budgetary effect of membership. The Swiss case provides the focus of the applications.

Simmons-Süer and Himmel work with a macro model of the Swiss economy that is similar in spirit to the one-good Mundel-Flemming model augmented to include investment demand that is driven by a Tobin's q model of investment, and a Phillips curve that is vertical in the long run. The authors note that the lack of microeconomic structure implies that integration has virtually no positive economic effects stemming from a more efficient allocation of resources. They therefore view their study as focusing on the macroeconomic costs of EU membership, rather a full blown cost-benefit analysis. Using this model, the authors find that in the 'long-run' the increase in interest rates and the net transfer to the EMU is estimated to have large negative effects on the Swiss economy. In the short-term, the negative impact is even more strongly negative, with a substantial slow down or even a recession predicted.

Stalder shows that there is much more involved in the transition to EMU as one would think at first. First expectations of membership play a major role in the phase preceding the entry into the EMU. If interest rates are lower than the EU average, then one should expect a weakening of the national currency before the accession. Second, it would be wrong to assume that exchange rates are going to stay fixed if the country is not going to join a monetary system. Switzerland has experienced a regular appreciation in the real value of the Swiss franc until recently. This is consistent with lower interest rates in financial markets. So, by merging its currency with the Euro, Switzerland would avoid a rampant appreciation of its currency, which in the long-term would be beneficial.

Bärlocher studies the fiscal impact of an EU membership, which, in the case of Switzerland, is net transfer to the EU. Its impact on the welfare of Swiss household would be even more negative, as it unleashes a fiscal reaction which is unfavourable to economic development. It is the transfer by itself which is so problematic, whereas the model shows that the increase in the VAT does not have a strong influence on economic activity, as long as it is redistributed back to Swiss households.

2.2.2. Impact of the loss of monetary autonomy

Many countries are proud of their national currency, so asking citizens to give up their money for an unknown future is politically challenging. This is especially true in the Swiss case, since the Swiss National Bank has an enviable reputation of adroit macroeconomic management.

Other studies in this conference have highlighted microeconomic benefits from a unique currency, as well as how to manage the transition period toward unification. The paper by *Genberg and Kadareja* tackles a very different issue with a highly innovative approach. A key question is whether the Swiss economy would be better managed by guarding its independence, or by joining the single currency. The Genberg-Kadareja methodology considers simulations of thousands of different business cycles (based on historical shocks) under two types of monetary policy rules. In the first, Switzerland purses an independent monetary policy rule, with the particular policy reaction rule is estimated from historical data. In the second, Swiss monetary policy is set by fixing the exchange rate to the euro (i.e. it is set by the European Central Bank). The authors' judgement criteria takes account of the objectives of low inflation and stable economic activity. The results are astonishing. They find that a monetary union between Switzerland and the EU would have a positive impact on the stability of most macroeconomic variables, except marginally on the stability of some price indexes. This implies that although monetary independence looks like a good idea as it gives a country some additional policy choices, it is not absolutely necessary. This result is particularly relevant for a small country like Switzerland which is so much integrated (in economic terms, even though not officially) in European markets.

2.3. Labour market issues

A very important aspect of European integration concerns the impact on labour markets. Two chapters in this volume tackle these issues.

Keuschnigg presents a CGE model with an endogenous unemployment rate. This model constitutes an important advance in CGE modelling -- by allowing endogenous non-market clearing based on a search model -- in addition to directly addressing labour market issues. With a matching process for hiring on the labour market, which is integrated into a general equilibrium model, he derives a structural unemployment rate. With this innovation, he can answer questions like: "How would a liberalisation affect the unemployment rate?" and "Will the EU expansion increase the unemployment?" Such questions could not be answered with most CGE models, because most of them assumed away unemployment. Many would fear that more liberalisation would mean a higher unemployment. The paper shows the opposite. While this is certainly not the last contribution on this topic (many more aspects of European labour markets might be incorporated into CGE models), the major outcome of the model is sensible and welcome. Namely, the chapter finds that unemployment is not only independent of trade, but can be lowered with the economic benefits of liberalisation. While this result is not entirely novel in political circles, the paper makes an important contribution by showing the inner working of why this result obtains.

CGE and structural macroeconomic models are the two major types of predictive models available. The last paper in the volume presents a sociological/empirical approach to the important topic of migration.

It has long being assumed that migration was mainly explained by economic forces. In particular the immigration from developing countries to the most advanced economies is set to continue at an accelerating rate. On this background the results presented by *Straubhaar* are interesting as they show that when income differences are in a reasonable range there does not exist a considerable inflow of lower skilled workers. In those cases migration operates on relatively small distances and follows the natural evolution of the labour market. But income, as long as differences are not too pronounced, is not a major motivation in comparison to the easiness in finding a job or cultural factors. In Europe, allowing free movement of labour has not resulted in any substantial long-distance migration, but has improved the functioning of labour market especially at borders. As Switzerland is a small country, it is bound to benefit from this additional flexibility and has no reason to fear any surge in immigrants coming from countries that are not its immediate neighbours. Actually, it has been long observed than even inside some big countries the unemployment rate could differ substantially among different regions without unleashing any considerable internal migration. So, if a convergence in employment conditions has been observed at the European level and inside many countries, it was due more probably to the diffusion of technological knowledge and to free trade than to the free movement of labour. Straubhaar even shows that in the Swiss case, immigrants of some European nationalities returning to their country of origin even if the unemployment rate is higher there. The study also brings along a second result: long-distance migration in Europe is now mostly by high-skilled workers and intra-firm migration. This type of migration improves the diffusion of technologies and economic growth and it is known to benefit the social security system without generating cultural frictions. In other words every country caring about its own self-interest should welcome this type of migration, even if it generates a healthy competition to local skilled workers, who are anyway the most likely to adapt successfully to it.

REFERENCES

Baldwin, R. and A. Venables (1995), Regional Economic Integration, in Grossman, G. and K. Rogoff (eds.), Handbook of International Economics, Volume III, Amsterdam: Elsevier.

Baldwin, R. and J. Francois (1999), Dynamic Issues in Commercial Policy Analysis, Cambridge University Press.

Blanchard, O. (1995), Debts, Deficits and Finite Horizons, Journal of Political Economy, 93, p. 223-247.

Fujita, M., P. Krugman and A. Venables (1999), The Spatial Economy: Cities, Regions and International Trade, Cambridge: MIT Press.

JEAN-MARIE GRETHER
TOBIAS MÜLLER

SORTING OUT THE EFFECTS OF SWITZERLAND'S ACCESSION TO THE EU: A SIMULATION ANALYSIS*

1. INTRODUCTION

A long and still active debate surrounds the desirability for Switzerland to join the EU. Should the application be reactivated? Should it be for full or "partial" membership? If the controversies surrounding the debate have political, historical and economic roots, it is fair to say that much of the debate is concerned about the economic effects. Will any increased efficiency gains be sufficient to compensate for the transfer that will have to accompany membership? What will be the effects of increased migration or the possible adoption of the euro? It is clear that with all the likely effects coming into play it is necessary to sort out their respective importance. A natural way to do so is simulation analysis, which is specifically designed to this purpose. This is what we set out to do in this paper.

The accession of Switzerland to the European Union (EU) would imply important changes in many areas, some expected to raise welfare, others to lower it. On the one hand, most observers expect the Swiss economy to gain from the abolition of tariff barriers between Switzerland and the EU, the reduction of non tariff barriers (NTBs), the adoption of the Common Agricultural Policy (CAP) and the abolition of migration quotas. On the other hand, Switzerland's contribution to the EU's budget would represent an important cost. Finally, the welfare consequences of the adoption of the common external tariff, tax reforms (increase in VAT to minimum EU levels and reduction in direct taxes), and the suppression of the interest rate differential (in case of EMU membership) are less obvious to anticipate. This paper attempts to give orders of magnitude of these effects using a three-region (Switzerland, the EU and the rest of the world) simulation model.

Although the issue of European integration has been analyzed extensively for other countries, the Swiss case raises interesting policy issues, which distinguish it from other European countries. First, after the Swiss rejected participation in the European Economic Area (EEA) in 1992, the Swiss government adopted a series of measures aimed at bringing Swiss regulations closer to European ones, thereby

* This paper grew out of a research project funded by the Swiss federal government. We thank Jaime de Melo for his detailed comments, Gabrielle Antille, Marc Bacchetta, and Daniel Morales for their helpful suggestions and Rolando Alcala, Samuel Guillet and José Ramirez for excellent research assistance.

R.E. Baldwin and A. Brunetti (eds.), Economic Impact of EU Membership on Entrants, 1–26.

reducing technical barriers to trade. It can thus be expected that Switzerland would gain less from full EU membership than EU countries did from the Single Market Program (SMP), insofar as technical barriers were larger among EU countries at the start of the SMP. Second, country size is likely to matter, as one would expect "small" countries to gain more by integrating with a large block than countries of comparable size gain by integrating with each other. Third, Swiss VAT rates are far below the minimum European level, which means that EU membership necessitates important fiscal reforms. Fourth, Switzerland experiences substantially lower interest rates than other European countries. This advantage is bound to disappear if Switzerland participates in the EMU.

The simulation model has been designed with these issues in mind, which explains its main characteristics. Ex-post (econometric) estimates of the impact of the SMP are used whenever possible as a benchmark for parameter values, but they have been adjusted for the unilateral measures taken by the Swiss government after 1992. The problem of asymmetry of size between Switzerland and the EU is also addressed. In the case of differentiated products, it is unrealistic to assume that a small country produces the entire range of varieties of a good. Thus we account for the existence of noncompeting imports in each imperfect competition sector in Switzerland, and for the fact that Swiss firms may have substantial market shares for the varieties they export to the EU. Finally, savings and investment decisions are explicitly modeled, taking into account the role of international capital mobility. This is an important issue for Switzerland, where net foreign assets account for a large proportion of total financial wealth. Moreover, the endogenization of savings allows to capture in a meaningful way the interest rate increase that would follow Switzerland's participation in the EMU or the shift from direct to indirect taxation, which would arise in Switzerland in case of EU membership.

The remainder of the paper is structured as follows: Section 2 presents a brief overview of the domains in which Switzerland's accession to the EU would lead to substantial changes. The principal features of the model are described in section 3. Simulations are presented in section 4, results in section 5, and final comments in section 6.

To anticipate the results, it turns out that EU accession without monetary union leads to a net welfare gain of 1%-1.2% of Swiss GDP. This may seem rather small in comparison with other studies using the same type of dynamic simulations. Gross gains are larger though, as the contribution of Switzerland to the EU budget generates by itself a welfare loss of more than 1% of GDP. The additional adoption of the euro allows to double the net welfare gain, basically through an increase in wealth, but at the cost of a contraction of GDP.

2. THE SCOPE OF INTEGRATION

This section briefly describes the domains in which European integration policy is likely to develop its strongest effects for Switzerland. It considers first the "traditional aspects" of trade in goods and services, and then moves to other fields, such as migration, fiscal and monetary policy.

2.1. *Trade in goods and services*

Apart from agricultural and food products, tariff protection is usually weak in Switzerland. Moreover, since the conclusion of a free-trade agreement with the European Community in 1972, Swiss tariffs on European imports are already lower than on imported goods from the rest of the world. Thus, although EU membership would mean the adoption of the common external tariff, it is not going to affect strongly the structure of Swiss tariffs on non-agricultural goods.

Tariff and non-tariff protection is a lot more widespread in the case of agricultural goods and food products, which were not covered by the 1972 free-trade agreement,.

In the past fifteen years, and along with Nordic States, Switzerland has typically recorded the highest protection levels in the OECD as measured by the production-subsidy equivalent (OECD, 1998). The adoption of the Common Agricultural Policy (CAP) in the case of EU accession would thus imply drastic changes in the protection of the agricultural and food products.

Other important changes can be expected in the case of non-tariff barriers (NTBs). Ex-post studies of the SMP suggest that their elimination through customs deregulation and regulatory harmonization led to a reduction of 1.5-2.5% of commercialization costs (Single Market Review, 1998). The reduction of NTBs is welfare-increasing because it means both a reduction in resource waste and a strengthening of competition in oligopolistic sectors. However, following the rejection of the EEA in 1992, Swiss authorities have embraced a number of unilateral reforms that have considerably reduced the level of technical barriers to Swiss-EU trade (systematic adaptation of Swiss technical prescriptions to those of the main trading partners and adoption of the "Swisslex" program in 1994 which brings parts of Swiss law closer to EEA law). Therefore, in case of Swiss accession to the EU, these effects are likely to be smaller than those experimented in the SMP.

2.2. *Migration, fiscal adjustment and EMU*

While the effects of integration in goods and services can be expected to be similar to those experienced by other countries recently joining the EU, three aspects require a more specific treatment: migration, fiscal adjustment and the EMU. We have tried to capture these effects in the modeling assumptions about the labor market, wealth accumulation and tax instruments.

Starting with migration, European integration would imply free labor movement between Switzerland and the EU (the transition period is not considered here as we focus on long run effects). Given the present wage differentials, Straubhaar (1999) estimates that net immigration flows could add up to 1%-1.5% of the resident population in the long run. The impact on the wage structure will depend on the skill composition of migrants. Recent surveys from the Statistical Federal Office reveal that entrepreneurs complain about the lack of skilled workers, suggesting that the "pull-effect" would be particularly strong for skilled migrants.

Second, to become a member of the EU, Switzerland will have to make a contribution to the European budget which has been officially estimated at 0.88% of GNP. This transfer would be financed by an increase in the VAT rate from 10% (the projected level in the absence of EU membership) to the European minimum level (15%). This would generate enough additional resources to consider a reduction in the income tax (direct federal taxation) without affecting the Swiss federal deficit.

Third, if Switzerland were to join the euro-zone, additional gains would come from the elimination of transaction costs and exchange rate uncertainty. As only two currencies are at stake, these gains would be plausibly smaller than those estimated for the euroland countries (between 0.25% and 0.5% of GDP according to the EC Commission). Moreover, the elimination of the exchange risk would drive to zero the interest rate differential between Switzerland and the EU, which is estimated by Bärlocher et al. (1999) to 0.7% over the long run (adjusted for exchange rate appreciation).

Finally, although EU membership is the official long run goal of the Swiss government, an intermediate step would be achieved in the short run were the bilateral agreements ratified by the Swiss government. These agreements, concluded in January 1999, consist mainly in a reduction of NTBs and free labor mobility gradually introduced between Switzerland and the EU[1].

3. THE MODEL

The model includes three regions of unequal size, Switzerland, the EU and the Rest of the World (RW), and 26 sectors, with the main industrial sectors modeled in imperfect competition and increasing returns to scale[2]. The benchmark year is 1995 (1996 for data on tariff equivalents). Because of the importance of budgetary transfers to the EU in case of membership, the model includes a balanced government budget. In light of the evidence, from both econometric and simulation studies, we assume that domestic labor supply is exogenous.[3]

3.1. The asymmetry problem

The particular situation of Switzerland – a small country with two big partners – requires careful modeling on two counts. On the one hand, in sectors with perfect competition, we assume, as usual, that goods (or services) are differentiated by country (or region) of origin and destination. The problem with this "Armington" assumption in an asymmetric multi-region model is that the small country faces relatively inelastic export demand. It is well known that in such a model, the small

---

[1] They also include other liberalization measures (for public procurement, civil aviation and some agricultural products) whose impact is not considered in the simulations because of lack of data and/or relevance at the aggregate level.

[2] Perfect competition and constant returns to scale are assumed in agriculture and services, where evidence regarding scale economies is scarce (eg. Zweifel (1993) for services).

[3] As de Melo and Tarr (1992) show in a simulation model of the US, introducing labor-leisure choice affects only very slightly the welfare outcome of trade liberalization.

country's terms of trade changes induced by trade liberalization are unrealistically strong and tend to dominate welfare effects (Brown, 1987). To avoid this problem, we assume very high elasticities of substitution (or transformation) between domestic and foreign goods in the two large regions (EU and RW).

On the other hand, in imperfect competition sectors, we assume that goods are differentiated at the firm level. On its own, this assumption would lead to an underestimation of the (calibrated) market power of Swiss firms, because at the usual levels of aggregation, goods from small countries have minuscule market shares in large regions. This is unrealistic because, say, a Swiss producer of specialized textile machines is not competing, in the real world, with foreign car producers. Therefore, in the model, each sector is subdivided into sub-sectors, assuming that only a small (exogenous) share of the product range of each sector is produced in Switzerland, whereas in the EU and RW the whole product range is covered. This hypothesis ensures that Swiss firms have significant market power in their market segment.

3.2. *Input demand*

Now turn to the structure of production and the derived demands for inputs. Note that demand for the different labor skill levels (four in Switzerland, two in the EU and RW) plays an important role in particular in the analysis of migration. Separability assumptions on the production function are depicted in figure 1. As in most models, value added and intermediate inputs are combined using a Leontief aggregation function. In order to capture the empirical fact that capital and skilled labor are complements, whereas capital and unskilled labor are substitutes,[4] the different skill levels of labor enter the cost function twice: higher skill levels enter predominantly "Labor composite (1)", which is complementary to capital, lower skill levels mostly enter "Labor composite (2)", which is a substitute to capital.

3.3. *Imperfect competition and integration*

In (sub-)sectors with imperfect competition, each firm is assumed to produce its own variety of a good. Dropping subscripts for industries and firms (varieties), the total cost function for a firm in country (region) c can be written as follows:

$$TC_c = MC_c(PVA_c, PIT_c)\,(q_c + fc_c) \qquad (1)$$

where q_c is the firm's output, fc_c fixed cost, and MC_c, marginal cost,. The latter is function of a price index of value added, PVA_c, and of a price index of intermediate inputs, PIT_c, corresponding to the structure of production shown in figure 1. As we focus on long-run effects, we assume free entry for firms by imposing a zero-profit condition (we do not address the integer issue).

[4] For a survey of this issue, see Hamermesh (1993).

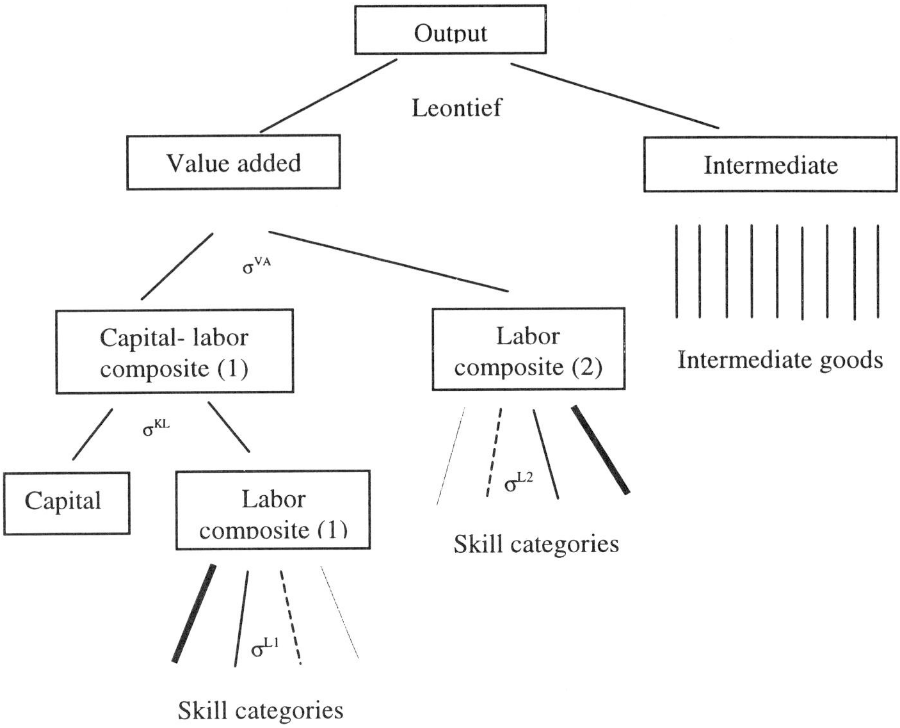

Figure 1. Structure of the production function

We assume Cournot competition between firms. As markets are assumed to be segmented, firms fix different prices for each country (or region). Profit maximization by a firm in country c yields the following markup equations:

$$\mu_{cd} = [(1\text{-}t_c)P_{cd}\text{-}MC_c] \;/\; [(1\text{-}t_c)P_{cd}], \tag{2}$$

where μ_{cd} is the markup, P_{cd} the producer price of a firm in country c selling to country d and t_c the output tax rate. Firms perceive correctly the structure of preferences, which is represented by a nested CES utility function. As depicted in figure 2, this structure can be interpreted as a multiple-stage budgeting process[5].

In the status quo (figure 2(a)), consumers perceive Switzerland and the EU as different regions, due to differences in regulations and technical standards. With integration, goods from Switzerland and from the EU are assumed to become closer substitutes, since they are perceived as originating from a same region (figure 2 (b)). Moreover, to reflect the fact that standardization of products would be reinforced in

[5] Producers are assumed to have identical preferences with respect to their choices of intermediate inputs.

Switzerland by EU membership, it is assumed that, prior to integration, $\sigma^{CH}<\sigma^{V}$. These changes in preferences increase the (perceived) price elasticity of demand and reduce mark-ups.

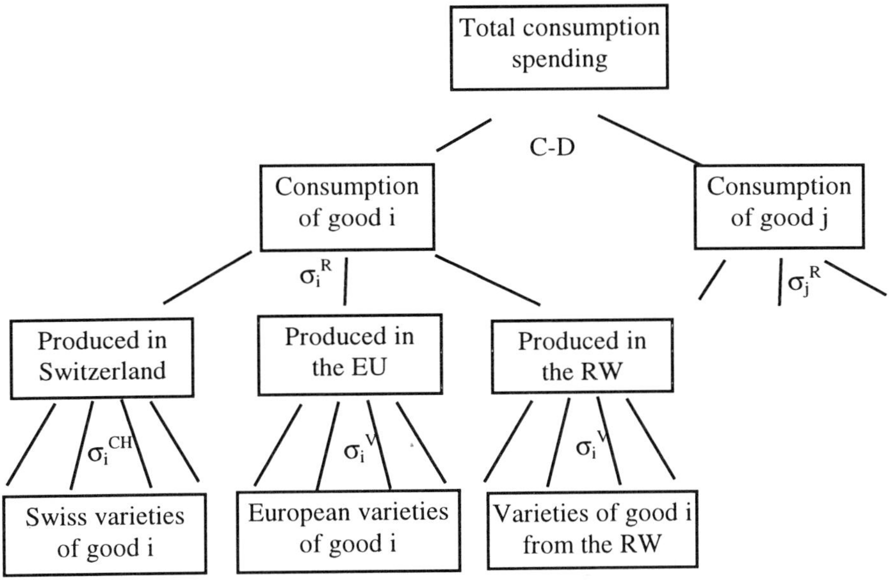

Figure 2a. Structure of preferences in the status quo

It can be shown that, for a good produced in country c and sold in country d, the resulting change in markup is given by (see Grether and Müller (1999b) for details):

$$\begin{cases} -\left(1-\dfrac{1}{n_c}\right)\left(\dfrac{1}{\sigma^{CH}}-\dfrac{1}{\sigma^{V}}\right)-\dfrac{1-s^{r}_{cd}}{n_c}\left(\dfrac{1}{\sigma^{R}}-\dfrac{1}{\sigma^{V}}\right) & \text{if } c=d=Switzerland \\ -\dfrac{1-s^{r}_{cd}}{n_c}\left(\dfrac{1}{\sigma^{R}}-\dfrac{1}{\sigma^{V}}\right) & otherwise \end{cases} \quad (3)$$

where n_c is the number of firms (varieties) and s^{r}_{cd} is the share of products from country c in country d's consumption of products from a "region" r. There are two regions: "Europe" (including EU and Switzerland) and "Other countries" (including RW). For example, if c=EU and d=Switzerland, s^{r}_{cd} represents the market share of EU products in total sales in Switzerland of EU and Swiss products. Note that markups of firms producing in the RW are not affected by Switzerland's accession to the EU, since $s^r_{cd} = 1$ for c=RW.

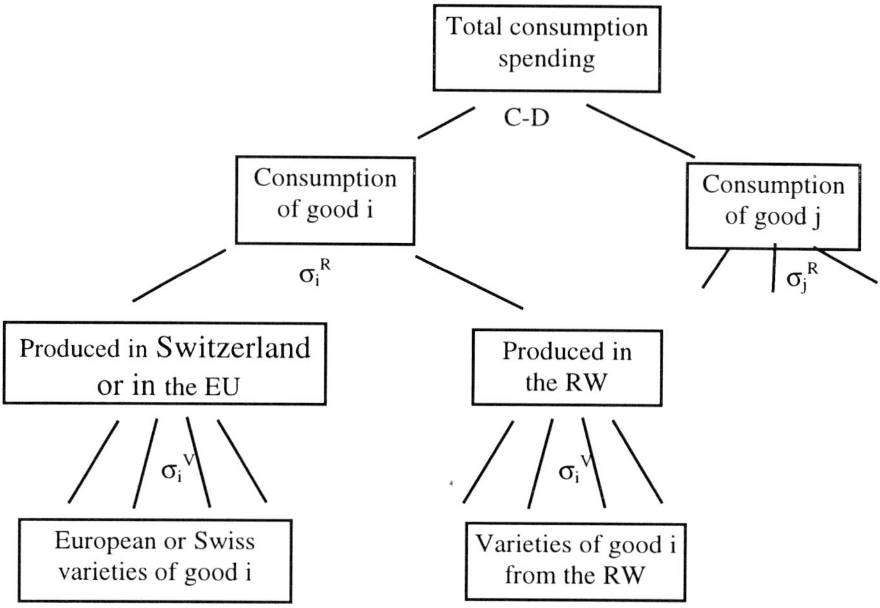

Figure 2b. Structure of preferences after integration

The main idea of the calibration procedure is to use the econometric estimates of the fall in markup generated by the Single Market Program. To account for Switzerland's unilateral harmonization efforts, only 50% of the original estimates of Allen et al (1997) were taken into account. This information is combined with the usual estimates of scale economies (see table A1 in the Appendix). Values for σ^R, σ^V and σ^{CH} are then calibrated from equation (3) and the zero-profit condition, using for s^r_{cd} base-year values (see Grether and Müller (1999b) for details).

3.4. *Determination of wealth and capital stock*

Investment and savings, and thus the aggregate stocks of capital and wealth, are modeled in a dynamic framework; but only the long-run (steady state) equations are used in the numerical model[6]. In the presentation below, we focus on the supply and demand of capital, dropping country subscripts unless necessary (for details, see Grether and Müller, 1999b).

In the steady state, and in the absence of adjustment costs, the value of total demand for capital is given by:

$$V = \Sigma_i P^I_i K_i. \tag{4}$$

where P_i^I is the price of the investment good (shadow price of capital) and K_i is the desired level of capital stock in sector i. The latter is derived from the usual equality between the marginal product and the rental rate of capital, $\partial f_i/\partial K_i = (r + \delta_i) P_i^I$ (where f_i is the production function, r the real interest rate and δ_i the depreciation rate).

Savings result from intertemporal optimization by a representative individual with finite life expectancy. Following the "perpetual youth" model proposed by Blanchard (1985), it can be shown that, at the steady state, total nonhuman wealth A (the stock of savings) is linked to human wealth H (the present value of labor income, net of taxes and social security contributions, and untaxed net transfer income) through a "savings rate", s, as follows:

$$A = s\,H, \qquad s = [\sigma^t (1 - t^D)\, r - \sigma^t \theta] \,/\, [\sigma^t \theta + \gamma - \sigma^t (1 - t^D)\, r] \tag{5}$$

where σ^t is the intertemporal elasticity of substitution, t^D the income tax rate, θ the rate of time preference and γ the inverse of life expectancy.

Neglecting the costs of transition, the steady state level of welfare depends on aggregate consumption, which is a positive function of both human and nonhuman wealth. Thus, given (5), the accumulation of nonhuman wealth acts as a human-wealth "multiplier".

A graphical representation of capital market equilibrium is given in figure 3. The downward-sloping long-run demand curve for capital (V) is derived from equation (4), while the upward-sloping domestic capital supply (A) is given by equation (5). In the base case it is assumed that the country is small and capital perfectly mobile, so that the interest rate is given by its world level, r*. The difference between capital supply and demand, at the world interest rate, corresponds to the stock of net foreign assets ($A_0^*=A_0-V_0$). We also simulate a version of the model without capital mobility, where the real interest rate is endogenous in each country and net foreign assets are fixed at the initial (calibrated) level.

[6] Building an intertemporal CGE model with rational expectations (see Keuschnigg and Kohler (1997)) would have necessitated important simplifications of the model which were not justifiable in the present context.

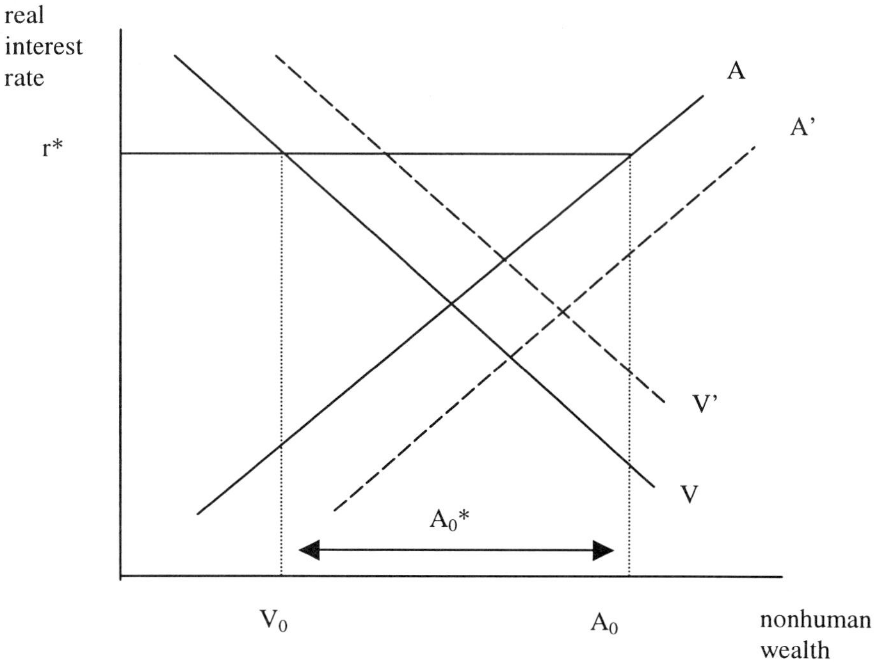

Figure 3. Capital market equilibrium

Figure 3 helps to illustrate the difference between our approach and other steady state models where the savings function is not spelled out explicitly (Baldwin et al., 1995, Harrison et al., 1994). In these models, where net foreign assets are set to zero, it is implicitly assumed that the savings function is a horizontal line, at r*. Let us imagine a policy change, such as a reduction in NTBs, which shifts both curves to A' and V'. In the « traditional » approach, only the shift from V to V' matters ; it is driven by the increase in capital demand at a given interest rate. By contrast, in the present model, human wealth ultimately determines both nonhuman wealth and the steady state welfare level ; welfare changes are predominantly driven by labor demand, since labor supply is perfectly inelastic.

3.5. *Data and calibration*

The data used for the calibration of the model stems from different sources (see Müller and Grether (1999) for details). The 1990 social accounting matrix for Switzerland was updated to 1995. VAT tax rates were calculated using direct information from fiscal authorities. For the two other regions (EU, RW), we used the GTAP database, version 4, which is also for 1995 (McDougall et al., 1998). The two data sources were reconciled by retaining, for Swiss imports and exports, data provided by the Swiss customs authorities. However, tariff data refer to 1996 for

Switzerland and the EU, because the changes following the Uruguay Round agreement were only introduced in mid-1995. As European data, which come from the Integrated Data Base (IDB) of the WTO, correspond to MFN rates, they were corrected to reflect the free-trade agreement between the EU and Switzerland. Protection data on the agricultural and food sectors are taken from OECD (1998), as described in Grether and Müller (1999a). The calibration procedure is standard, apart from the imperfect competition and savings parameters described above. Substitution elasticities are listed in table A1 in the Appendix.

4. SIMULATIONS

The impact of integration is decomposed into a number of simulations which are described below and aimed to capture the various dimensions discussed in section 2. Each simulation is identified with an acronym, whether it is an individual simulation, as those listed in table 1, or a cumulated one, as those defined in table 2.

4.1. Price measures

The first simulation to be considered is the adoption of the common external tariff by Switzerland for all commodities except agricultural and food products (*TARIFF*). This is performed by suppressing all tariffs on Swiss-European trade and by replacing the ad valorem Swiss tariffs on imports from the RW by their European equivalents. Because the changes following the Uruguay Round agreement were only gradually introduced in 1995, tariff data refer to 1996 for all partners. Due to the EU-EFTA free trade agreement, Swiss tariffs are lower on imports from the EU than on imports from the RW (see last two columns of table 3).

No such agreement exists for agricultural and food products, which are subject to a separate simulation capturing the impact of the Common agricultural policy (*AGR*). The logic of the simulation, namely a discriminatory elimination of trade barriers, is the same as for *TARIFF*. However, instead of tariffs, a broader measure of protection is used for those sectors where it was available. It is the ad valorem equivalent of the domestic support elaborated by the OECD on the basis of a comparison between the domestic and the international price (OECD, 1998). In general, these measures reflect a degree of tariff and non-tariff protection which is substantially larger in Switzerland than in other OECD countries[7].

[7] Protection data is for 1996, which means that both European and Swiss agricultural reforms adopted since then are not taken into account. Moreover, due to data availability, variations in direct payments are not contemplated

Table 1. Individual simulations

Acronym	Description
TARIFF	*Customs union (except agricultural and food products)* • Elimination of tariffs between SWI and EU • Application of common external tariff on Swiss imports from the RW
AGR	*Common agricultural policy* • Elimination of tariffs between SWI and EU • Application of common external tariff on Swiss imports from the RW • Replacement of Swiss production subsidy equivalents by European ones.
NTB	*Reduction of non-tariff barriers (NTBs)*[a] • Overland transport agreement (0.3% of exports value)) • Mutual recognition of regulations (0.18% of exports value) • Border costs between SWI and EU (second column of table 3) • Transport costs between SWI and EU (third column of table 3)
DESG	*Market desegmentation* • Increase in the substitutability between products (consistent with 50% of the fall in mark-up estimated by Allen et al, 1997)
MIGR	*Free movement of persons* • 100'000 additional immigrants (1.4% of resident population)
TRF	*Net transfer* • Net transfer to the EU (0.88% of GNP)
VAT15	*VAT adjustment* • Increase of VAT from 10% to 15% • Accommodating decrease of income taxes
DINT	*Interest rate differential* • Elimination of the 0.75% interest rate differential
TRS	*Transaction costs* • Reduction of transaction costs (0.66% of exports value)

SMR: Single Market Review
SWI: Switzerland
[a] Estimates derived from Müller and van Nieuwkoop (1999) for the overland transport agreement, otherwise from Single Market Review (1998).

Table 2: Cumulated simulations

	Acronym	Simulations
Market integration	*INT*	*NTB+DESG*
Fiscal consequences	*FISC*	*TRF+VAT15*
Monetary union	*EMU*	*DINT+TRS*
EU accession (without EMU)	*ACC*	*TARIFF+AGR+MIGR+INT+FISC*
EU accession (with EMU)	*ACC+EMU*	*ACC+EMU*
Bilateral agreements	*BIL*	*INT-B*[a]*+MIGR*

[a] Integration is weaker in this case: there is no reduction of border costs nor transports costs; the reduction of NTBs due to mutual recognition only amounts to 10% of SMR estimates; the increase in substitutability between products is consistent with 25% of the fall in mark-up estimated by SMR.

4.2. NTBs

Other aspects of market integration are captured by two simulations reflecting the reduction of non-tariff barriers (NTBs) on the one hand, the increase in product substitutability on the other hand. Regarding NTBs, the first reduction to be considered is the one that might result from the increase in the maximum weight authorized for heavy goods vehicles (the "40-tonners' agreement") and from the implementation of the "New Transalpine Railway" net. According to Müller and van Nieuwkoop (1999), this should lead to a cost reduction representing 0.3% of the value of exports. A further reduction in NTBs can be expected from the mutual recognition of tests, certificates and approvals in accordance with standards. In the EU case, this gain has been estimated at 0.5% of export value by ex post studies (Single Market Review, 1998), but given the unilateral harmonization efforts of Switzerland since 1993, only 10% of this figure has been applied in the present study[8]. Also taken into consideration is the recognition of the equivalence of national regulations, in accordance with the "Cassis de Dijon" principle. As this principle approximately covers a quarter of intra-EU trade, it is assumed here that this harmonization should bring an additional 25% of the 0.5% figure mentioned above. Other gains would come from the reduction of border controls, as illustrated by the second column of table 4. which reports the results of ex post studies for the EU. However, since it is estimated that a rough 50% of these gains were already reaped with the SMP, in the Swiss case, we only selected 50% of the original values. Finally, transport, banking and insurance costs related to trade should also come

[8] This gain is assumed to be identical across all goods sectors.

down. Here it is assumed that Switzerland would benefit from the same gains as those reported ex post for Germany, which appear in the third column of table 4.

An additional consequence of standardization and mutual recognition of tests is to increase the substitutability between domestic and foreign products, thus reinforcing competition between producers. This "market desegmentation" effect is captured in the *DESG* simulation by an increase in product substitutability on the demand side. This modification of the structure of preferences is calibrated on the decrease in price-cost margins identified by ex-post studies of the SMR. However, in order to take into account the gradual rapprochement between Swiss regulations and European ones, only half of the reported decrease in price-cost margins has been used for calibration.

The corresponding figures are reported in the fourth and fifth column of table 4. As this desegmentation effect is indissociable from the reduction of NTBs, this simulation is never run independently, but jointly with *NTB*, in the cumulated simulation representing market integration (*INT*).

4.3. Migration

The impact of the free labor movement (*MIGR*) is simulated by an increase of 1.4% of the population, corresponding to 100'000 additional immigrants. The skill composition of immigrants is assumed to be identical to that of the resident population. An alternative simulation is also run, where the share of the highest skill category among the migrants is three times its corresponding level in the resident population.

4.4. Fiscal consequences

Fiscal consequences of EU-membership (*FISC*) are represented by two simulations. On the one hand, Switzerland's annual contribution to the EU budget is estimated at 0.88% of GNP (*TRF*). On the other hand, value-added tax rates have to adjust from 10% to the minimum European level of 15% (*VAT15*). The net impact of these measures on public budget is neutralized by a corresponding variation (in fact a decrease) of the direct income tax.

Table 3. Parameters used in the simulations (percentages)

	Reduction of non-tariff barriers (*NTB*)		Reduction of price-cost margins [c]	Ad valorem tariffs on imports [d] (*TARIFF*)	
	border costs [a]	Transport costs [b]	(*DESG*)	from the EU	from the RW
Agriculture	0.60	0.04			
Electricity, gas, water	0.45	0.06		0.85	0.90
Meat and dairy products	0.82	0.08			
Other food products	0.82	0.08	-1.25	15.23	11.26
Beverages and tobacco	0.82	0.08	-1.25	12.70	19.78
Textiles	0.82	0.08		0.31	3.19
Clothing	0.82	0.08	-0.49	2.09	9.48
Wood	0.82	0.08	-1.70	0.08	0.77
Paper	0.82	0.08	-1.70	0.06	0.94
Leather	0.82	0.08		0.58	1.78
Chemicals, plastics	0.45	0.07	-2.78	0.06	0.48
Non metal products	0.77	0.08	-1.83	0.09	0.81
Metals	0.80	0.08	-1.70	0.08	0.53
Machinery	1.37	0.10	-0.72	1.06	1.64
Electronics	1.10	0.09	-2.46	0.20	0.40
Commerce	0.50	0.08			
Transport	1.25	0.08			
Communication	1.25	0			
Bank and insurance	1.25	0			
Other services (private)	0.50	0			

[a] percentage of the value of exports, corresponding to 50% of the original estimates by Single Market Review (1998).

[b] percentage of the value of exports, corresponding the estimates for Germany by Single Market Review (1998).

[c] (for imperfect competition sectors only) percentage of producer price corresponding to 50 % of the original estimates by Allen et al (1997).

[d] tariffs on non agricultural imports, own calculations based on 1996 data provided from Direction Générale des Douanes.

4.5. Monetary union

Finally, in case of the adoption of the euro (*EMU*), the elimination of the exchange rate risk is simulated by the elimination of the interest rate differential (*DINT*), which is estimated at 0.75% in the status quo scenario. Moreover, the reduction of transaction costs and uncertainty associated with the single currency is captured by a further reduction of NTBs by 0.66% of the value of exports (*TRS*)[9].

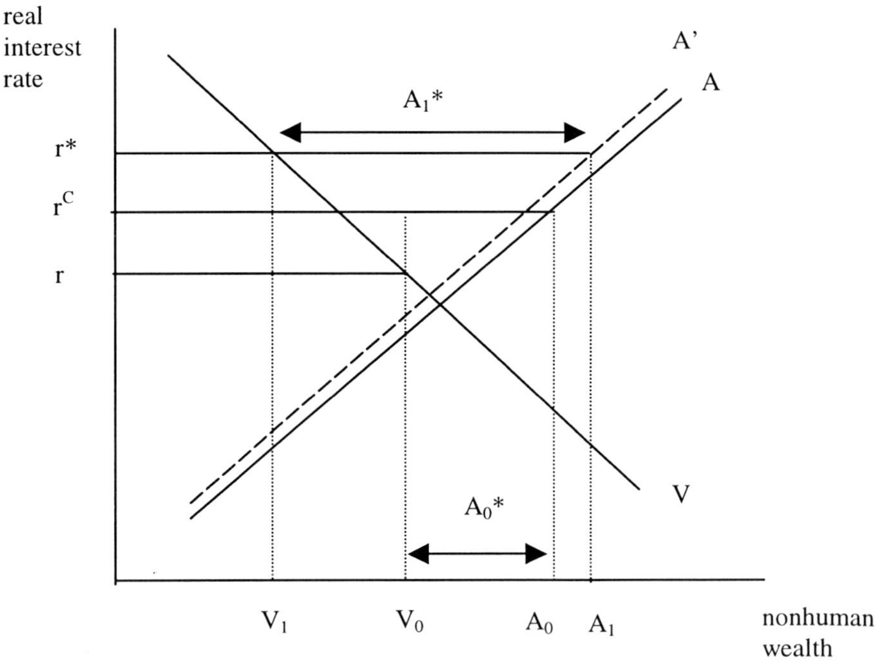

Figure 4: Effects of real interest rate convergence

The *DINT* simulation deserves further explanation. Since we do not account explicitly for risk in the model, the setup of this simulation is rather *ad hoc* and it is not strictly comparable to the others since the starting point differs. We assume indeed that in the status quo scenario there is a wedge between the domestic (Swiss) interest rate, r, and the European interest rate, r^* (see figure 4). As Swiss residents own domestic and foreign assets, the consumer interest rate (which matters for the savings decision), r^C, is a weighted average of these two. Thus, in the status quo firms face a different interest rate (r) from consumers (r^C); this determines the stock of net foreign assets in the status quo (A_0^*). With EU membership the interest rate

[9] This comes from the lower bound estimates of the EC Commission (1990), which is 0.25% of GDP, applied to the share of bilateral trade with the EU in Swiss GDP (38.1%).

differential disappears, and $r^C = r = r^*$. Hence the rental rate of capital increases, which diminishes the demand for capital (from V_0 to V_1) and exerts a downward pressure on wages. As a consequence of the latter, the capital-supply schedule shifts to the left (A'). However, the variation of capital supply has an ambiguous sign since the increase in r^C encourages savings. Because of the important fall in demand for capital, it is very likely that the stock of net foreign assets rises to A_1^*.

All the previous simulations may be combined to estimate the effects of EU accession without (*ACC*) or with the adoption of the euro (*ACC+EMU*). An alternative integration scenario is also considered, where Switzerland would only ratify the bilateral agreements negotiated with the EU in 1999 (*BIL*). In this case, simulations are limited to free labor mobility and a softened version of market integration (*INT-B*): reduction of NTBs only covers the overland transport agreement and 10% of SMR estimates regarding mutual recognition of regulations (against 35% in the EU accession case), while the fall in mark-up considered in the *DESG* simulation is 25% of SMR estimates (against 50% in the EU accession case).

5. RESULTS

In this section, results are generally expressed in terms of percentage change with respect to a "status quo" situation where Switzerland is supposed not to undertake any unilateral reform, maintaining its policies as they were in 1995[10]. The only exception is the welfare indicator, which is measured as the (permanent) increase of the disposable income of resident households as a percentage of initial GDP. To facilitate comparisons with other studies, we report results from different versions of the model. Our preferred version includes an endogenous capital stock and perfect international capital mobility (K-MOB).[11] The second version assumes that capital is perfectly immobile (K-IMM). Finally, a static version of the model (STAT) is used to identify efficiency gains.[12] We first comment aggregate results and then discuss the outcome of specific simulations.

5.1. Aggregate results

As shown by the second column of table 4, it turns out that EU accession (without monetary union) generates a net increase in welfare equivalent to 1.2% of GDP. This outcome reflects the combined effect of all the simulations described in section 4 (model version K-MOB). Results obtained with the two other variants of the model appear in the third and fourth columns of table 4.

---

[10] To simulate the "status quo", the VAT rate is raised from 7% to 10% in order to reflect, according to government estimates, the need for extra financing of social security spending.

[11] Estimating an intertemporal model of the current account for Switzerland, Höfert (1998) arrives at the conclusion that the hypothesis of perfect capital mobility cannot be rejected. This result is consistent with Feldstein's (1996) argument that small countries have lower savings retention rates than large countries.

[12] In the static version of the model, the aggregate capital stock is exogenous. Capital is mobile between sectors and the rental rate of capital adjusts to bring capital demand into line with fixed supply.

With version K-IMM, the net welfare gain remains similar (1.0% of GDP) but the increase in the capital stock and investment is nearly three times as big as with K-MOB. This is due to the impossibility to clear the excess supply in the capital market through a purchase of foreign assets. Consequently, the real interest rate has to drop, which generates an important increase in the capital stock.

These calculations are based on the comparison between two steady states, and therefore neglect the costs generated by reduced consumption during the transition period. Hence, our welfare indicator has to be considered as an upper bound, and is complemented with an alternative - lower bound - estimate from the static version of the model. As illustrated by the fourth column of table 4, static welfare gains amount only to 0.5% of GDP. Therefore, in this model, most welfare gains of European integration in the long run result from capital accumulation, not from better resource allocation.

Table 4: Aggregate results for EU accession (ACC) (Welfare change as a percentage of GDP)

	ACC			alternative scenarios (capital perfectly mobile)	
	Capital Perfectly mobile	Capital perfectly immobile	static model	BIL	ACC +EMU
GDP	2.9	3.7	2.5	2.0	2.2
GNP	3.3	3.6	2.4	2.2	3.8
Welfare of residents (% of GDP)	1.2	1.0	0.5	1.0	2.5
Investment	1.4	3.9	-.-	2.4	-1.5
Exports to EU	14.5	16.9	16.1	1.7	12.2
Exports to RW	-1.7	0.6	-0.5	-1.0	-9.9
Imports from the EU	15.5	16.4	15.2	2.2	15.9
Imports from the RW	-22.2	-21.8	-22.4	0.0	-21.7
Capital stock	1.0	3.4	-.-	2.0	-2.1
Wage – university	0.2	3.9	-0.8	0.8	-4.0
Wage – superior education	0.1	1.8	-0.3	0.5	-2.6
Wage – apprenticeship	-0.5	0.8	-0.9	0.5	-2.3
Wage – compulsory school	-1.4	-0.4	-1.7	0.5	-2.5
Real interest rate	0.0	-8.5	-.-	0.0	17.5
Net foreign assets	10.2	-.-	-2.1	5.4	46.4
Real exchange rate	-2.1	-1.7	-.-	-0.2	-3.7
Terms of trade	1.2	1.2	1.2	0.2	2.5

Alternative integration scenarios are also considered. The penultimate column of table 4 shows that the bilateral agreements, although far more limited in their scope, would lead to a net aggregate welfare gain which is fairly comparable to the EU accession case. This suggests that the additional elements brought by the EU accession scenario lead to losses as well as gains in terms of welfare, as can be verified through the decomposition presented in table 5. The last column of table 4 reveals a substantial increase in welfare (2.5% of GDP) in the case of EU accession with monetary union. However, this is mainly due to a "wealth effect", as the increase in the real interest rate leads both to a reduction of the capital stock and an increase in net foreign assets.

Table 5: Decomposition of welfare changes (% of GDP)
(capital perfectly mobile / results from static model in parentheses)

Simulation	Acronym	Welfare changes
• Customs union	*TARIFF*	0.1 (0.1)
• Common agricultural policy	*AGR*	0.6 (0.7)
• Market integration	*INT*	1.2 (0.5)
of which: reduction of NTBs	*NTB*	0.9 (0.4)
• Free movement of persons	*MIGR*	0.6 (0.1)
• Fiscal consequences	*FISC*	-1.5 (-1.0)
of which: net transfer	*TRF*	-1.6 (-1.0)
• Monetary union	*EMU*	1.1
of which: interest rate differential	*DINT*	0.9

5.2. *Customs union and agriculture*

The adoption of the common tariff structure on non-agricultural imports (*TARIFF*) leads only to a weak increase in aggregate welfare (0.1% of GDP). However, its impact on trade flows is important, particularly on imports (those from the rest of the world decrease by 20.6%, while those from Europe rise by 6.2%, see table A2 in the Appendix). On the whole, this suggests that trade creation effects are almost exactly compensated by trade diversion effects as far as aggregate welfare is concerned.

Although the basic logic of the simulation (discriminatory elimination of trade barriers and adoption of the European protection structure) is the same for agricultural and food products (*AGR*), the impact on aggregate welfare is more substantial (0.6% of GDP). This appears surprising given the small size of Swiss agriculture with respect to the rest of the economy. It reflects the importance of the distortions introduced by protection in these sectors, remembering that our indicator, based on price differences at the border, captures the incidence of tariff and non-tariff barriers[13]. This net welfare gain is mainly due to improved resource allocation, as results from the static variant of the model turn out to be of the same magnitude.

5.3. *Market integration*

The reduction of NTBs favors Swiss-European trade at the expense of trade with the RW (which decreases approximately by 1.5%). A standard argument from trade theory would lead one to expect that trade diversion cannot be welfare decreasing as no tariff revenue is involved. However, this doesn't need to be the case here, because of the presence of numerous distortions. It turns out that aggregate welfare rises by 0.9% of GDP. Associated with this reduction of NTBs is the increase in substitutability between products, which increases competitive pressure and is calibrated to reproduce 50% of the fall in mark-up estimated by EU ex-post studies. When this market desegmentation effect is added to the NTB simulation (*INT*), the welfare gain reaches 1.2% in the K-MOB version, as opposed to 0.5 % in the STAT case. Note from table 6 below that the effective decrease in mark-up is smaller than the one used in the calibration (fourth column of table 3). This is due to the rationalization process driven by increased competitive pressure: a number of firms disappear and, irrespective of the change in the output of the sector, the individual firm's production level increases. It is this concentration process that mitigates the fall in mark-up.

5.4. *Free movement of persons*

Regarding migration, the most striking feature of the simulation (*MIGR*) is the dynamic gains that amplify the positive welfare impact in the static model. Following the entry of 100'000 additional immigrants, the increase in capital productivity induces capital formation which hinders wages from falling. In the standard case of perfect mobility of capital, investment increases by 1.9%, and factor prices remain at their initial level.[14]

In the *MIGR* simulation, the immigrants' skill-structure is assumed to be identical to the resident population's. In an alternative simulation, we assume that the share of the highest skill category (university level) is three times larger than in the resident population. This leads to a sharp reduction of the wage rate of the highest skill category (-5.2%) and to an increase of the wage rate of the other skill levels. At the same time, investment increases more than in *MIGR* (0.5% instead of 0.2%), due to the complementarity between capital and high-skill labor.

[13] A more disaggregated version of the model (Grether and Müller, 1999a), with 17 agricultural and food sectors, led to a still stronger net welfare gain (1.3% of GDP), reflecting the high dispersion of protection across sectors.

[14] If capital is perfectly immobile internationally, the increase in investment is still larger (2.7%), as the real interest rate decreases, and with it the user cost of capital. This decrease in the interest rate is caused by positive externalities from immigration: as it is assumed that the same level of public services can be maintained without additional costs, the larger population allows a lower income tax per capita, thus increasing disposable income and savings. Thus, in this case, real wages go up following immigration.

Table 6. Market integration in imperfect competition sectors (INT) (percentages)

Sector	Mark-up[a]	Number of firms	Output of the firm	Output of the sector
Other food products	-0.9	-8.4	10.2	0.9
Beverages and tobacco	-0.9	-15.7	20.0	1.2
Clothing	-0.7	-16.1	10.8	-7.1
Wood	-1.4	-20.1	25.4	0.2
Paper	-1.3	- 9.9	10.6	-0.3
Chemicals, plastics	-2.0	- 6.2	8.7	1.9
Non metal products	-1.3	-13.0	14.5	-0.4
Metals	-1.2	-16.1	14.1	-4.3
Machinery	-0.6	- 5.6	4.8	-1.1
Electronics	-1.7	- 8.2	11.4	2.3

[a] Mark-up defined as a percentage of producer price.

5.5. *Fiscal consequences*

Switzerland's contribution to the EU budget (0.88% of its GNP), which is financed by an increase of VAT from 10% to 13% (*TRF*), leads to an important net welfare loss (-1.6% of GDP). The direct impact of the transfer is reinforced by a secondary burden in the form of a deterioration of the terms of trade (-0.3%). Moreover, there is a contraction of the supply of capital, which leads to a further loss in disposable income through a decrease in net foreign assets (alternatively, if capital is perfectly immobile internationally, the decrease in capital supply leads to an increase in the real interest rate with the same adverse impact on welfare).

A further increase in VAT (from 13% to 15%) will be necessary for Switzerland to comply with the EU minimum rates. It is assumed that the extra government revenue is used to reduce the rate of direct taxation (from an average rate of 18.8% to 17.9%), to net out the impact on the public deficit. Adding this simulation to the former (FISC, which includes the transfer) does not lead to any significant change in the welfare loss. However, the decrease in net foreign assets almost disappears. This is due to the well-known effect that switching from direct to indirect taxation promotes saving[15].

[15] Another effect of the increase in VAT is to reduce incentives to invest in sectors which are excluded from the VAT base, thus leading to a further decrease in the stock of capital.

5.5. *Monetary Union*

The strongest effect of the adoption of the euro by Switzerland is simulated here by the elimination of the interest rate differential (*DINT*), as the exchange risk, the assumed cause of this differential, disappears. An increase of 0.75% of the interest rate has a dramatic impact on the capital market. On the one hand, the capital stock decreases (and so does GDP). On the other hand, the supply of capital increases, which leads to a strong increase in net foreign assets (more than 30%). It is this "wealth effect" which basically explains the net steady-state welfare gain of 0.9% of GDP, although domestic production, measured by GDP, decreases by 1.1%.

Another effect of this simulation is to worsen the inequality of income distribution, as labor income decreases and capital income rises. Finally, the complete simulation (EMU) also includes the reduction of transaction costs resulting from the adoption of a single currency (TRS). As could be expected, this slightly improves the net welfare gain, along the same lines as the reduction of NTBs, which is identically modeled.

6. CONCLUSIONS

The main objective of this paper has been to include all the relevant dimensions of integration in a CGE model to assess the impact of EU membership for Switzerland. Combining the impact of the reduction of tariff and non-tariff barriers, the entry of immigrants, tax reform and the contribution to the EU budget, EU accession leads to a net increase in domestic welfare of 1.2% of GDP when capital is perfectly mobile internationally (1.0% if it is immobile). This may appear as a weak effect in comparison with other estimates using the same type of simulation model (see Baldwin and Venables, 1995). However, it must be noted that, unlike other studies, this figure takes account of the budgetary transfer of Switzerland to the EU (0.9% of GDP). Moreover, the magnitude of the impact was far from obvious *a priori* given that Switzerland had already undertaken an important unilateral rapprochement with the EU while, at the same time, small countries are known to benefit more from integration.

Although more limited in scope, the bilateral agreements turn out to lead to a net welfare gain which is quite similar to the EU accession case. This is surprising, as EU membership is more profitable than the bilateral agreements on several counts (stronger reduction in NTBs and liberalization of agricultural trade). However, these positive effects are counterbalanced by the negative impact of the financial transfer to the EU budget, while the discriminatory reduction in tariffs generates as much trade creation as trade diversion in terms of welfare.

More gains could be expected from monetary union. If Switzerland were to join the euro-zone as well as the EU, the net welfare gain from integration would roughly double. However, this would be obtained at the cost of a substantial increase in the cost of capital, and a strong decrease in labor remuneration, thus exacerbating distributional conflicts. The results from this last simulation should be taken with a grain of salt. They are based on the disappearance of the interest rate differential, as the elimination of the exchange risk is assumed to induce perfect substitutability between Swiss and European assets. Even if the assumption of perfect capital mobility seems more realistic in the Swiss case than for many other countries, alternative interpretations of the imperfect substitutability between assets could be explored, such as informational asymmetries or "safe haven" effects, although their inclusion in a simulation model is far from obvious.

The other results also deserve a number of qualifications. First, positive effects from market desegmentation may have been underestimated. An original procedure of the paper has been to calibrate the change in the structure of preference (reflecting harmonization of norms) on the basis of the observed decrease in mark-up by ex-post studies of the SMP. Once applied, this technique led to surprisingly low estimates of the impact of standardization. Again, one may explain this weak effect by our decision to downscale the SMP impact because of Switzerland's past efforts to comply with EU rules. Another part of the explanation may come from the modeling of imperfect competition: imposing the zero profit condition generates behaviors that mimic perfect competition too much to reflect pro-competitive effects. An interesting extension of this part of the analysis would thus be to model the collusion between firms, along the lines of Mercenier and Schmitt (1996).

Second, welfare gains are expressed in terms of differences between two steady states. This has the clear advantage of taking account of the dynamic gains from integration, but the equally clear disadvantage of failing to include the loss from reduced consumption due to capital accumulation during the transition period. Baldwin (1992) shows that, on the margin, induced capital formation (which is the source of dynamic output effects) only translates into dynamic welfare gains if the social return to capital exceeds the private return. Thus our welfare results must be interpreted as upper bounds of the true welfare effects, suggesting that another avenue of future research would be to rely on a more elaborate version of the model including the adjustment path of consumption. The unsolved challenge is to succeed in introducing these improvements in the model without having to sacrifice the detailed treatment of sectors and of firms' behavior.

REFERENCES

Allen, C., M. Gasiorek and A. Smith (1997), Trade Creation and Trade Diversion, Single Market Review, subseries IV, volume 3, European Communities.

Baldwin, R.E. (1992), Measurable Dynamic Gains from Trade, Journal of Political Economy, 100, p.162-174.

Baldwin, R.E. and A.J. Venables (1995), Regional Economic Integration, in: Grossman, G. and K. Rogoff (eds.), Handbook of International Economics, Volume III, Amsterdam: Elsevier.

Baldwin, R. E., R. Forslid and J. Haaland (1995), Investment Creation and Investment Diversion: Simulation Analysis of the Single Market Programme, NBER Working Paper 5364.

Bärlocher, J., B. Schips and P. Stalder (1999), Makroökonomische Auswirkungen eines EU-Beitrittes der Schweiz, série Contributions à la politique économique, Office fédéral du développement économique et de l'emploi, Berne.

Blanchard, O. J. (1985), Debt, Deficits, and Finite Horizons, Journal of Political Economy, 93, p. 223-247.

Brown, D. K. (1987), Tariffs, the Terms of Trade and National Product Differentiation, Journal of Policy Modeling, 3, p. 503-526.

EC Commission (1990), One Market, one Money, European Economy, vol. 44.

Feldstein, M. (1994), Tax Policy and International Capital Flows, Weltwirtschaftliches Archiv, 130, p. 675-697.

Grether, J.-M. and T. Müller (1999a), Long-Run Effects of the Common Agricultural Policy of Switzerland: A Simulation Analysis, mimeo, LEA, University of Geneva.

Grether, J.-M. and T. Müller (1999b), Modeling Switzerland's Accession to the EU: a Decomposition of the Economic Costs and Benefits, mimeo, LEA, University of Geneva.

Hamermesh, D. S. (1993), Labor Demand. Princeton University Press, Princeton.

Harrison, G., T. Rutherford and D. Tarr (1994), Product Standards, Imperfect Competition and Completion of the Market in the European Union, PR Working Paper 1293, The World Bank, Washington D.C.

Höfert, A. (1998), Wie gross ist die Kapitalmobilität zwischen der Schweiz und dem Ausland ? Ergebnisse einer intertemporalen Betrachtung der Schweizer Ertragsbilanz, Konjunktur, 9/98, Konjunkturforschungsstelle ETH Zürich.

Keuschnigg, C. and W. Kohler (1997), Dynamics of Trade Liberalization, in: Francois, J. F. and K. A. Reinert (eds.), Applied Methods for Trade Policy Analysis, Cambridge University Press.

Laxton, D., P. Isard, H. Faruqee, E. Prasad and B. Turtelboom (1998), MULTIMOD Mark III : The Core and Steady-State Models, IMF Occasional Paper 164.

McDougall, R.A., A. Elbehri, and T.P. Truong (1998), Global Trade Assistance and Protection: The GTAP 4 Data Base, Center for Global Trade Analysis, Purdue University.

De Melo, J. and D. Tarr (1992), A General Equilibrium Analysis of US Foreign Trade Policy, Cambridge: MIT Press.

Mercenier, J. and N. Schmitt (1996), On Sunk Costs and Trade Liberalization in Applied General Equilibrium, International Economic Review, 37, p. 553-572.

Müller, A. and R. van Nieuwkoop (1999), EU-Integration der Schweiz: wirtschaftliche Auswirkungen, BWA-Schriftenreihe, Beiträge zur Wirtschaftspolitik, Bern.

Müller, T. and J.-M. Grether (1999), Effets à long terme de l'intégration de la Suisse à l'Europe, BWA-Schriftenreihe, Beiträge zur Wirtschaftspolitik, Bern.

OECD (1998), Politiques agricoles des pays de l'OCDE: Mesure du soutien et informations de base, OCDE, Paris.

Single Market Review (1998), Aggregate Results of the Single Market Program, Subseries VI, Vol. 5, European Communities.

Smith, A. and A.J. Venables (1988), Completing the Internal Market in the European Community: Some Industry Simulations, European Economic Review, 32, p. 1501-25.

Straubhaar, T. (1999), Integration und Arbeitsmarkt: Auswirkungen einer Annäherung der Schweiz an die Europäische Union, BWA-Schriftenreihe, Beiträge zur Wirtschaftspolitik, Bern.

Zweifel P. (ed.) (1993), Services in Switzerland: Structure, Performance and Implications of European Economic Integration, Springer Verlag, Berlin.

Table A1. Calibrated parameters

A) Supply parameters				
Elasticities of substitution				
· between capital and labor (1), (σ^{VA})				1.2
· between capital-labor (1) and labor (2), (σ^{KL})				0.4
· between labor qualification categories (1), (σ^{L1})				0.4
· between labor qualification categories (2), (σ^{L2})				1.2
Elasticity of transformation (perfect competition sectors)				
· between domestic and exported goods in Switzerland				2.0
· between domestic and exported goods in the EU/RW				∞
B) Demand parameters				
Elasticities of substitution: global				
· intertemporal (σ^{t})		0.25		
between domestic and imported goods (perfect competition sectors):				
		Switzerland	EU/RW	
· agriculture and food (σ^{R}_{1})		2.5	100	
· industry and services (σ^{R}_{2})		3.0	100	
Elasticities of substitution in imperfect competition sector:				
sector:	CDR[a]	σ^{R}	σ^{V}	σ^{CH}
Other food products	0.08	8.4	19.5	15.6
Beverages and tobacco	0.04	5.7	38.4	25.8
Clothing	0.03	10.3	41.4	29.6
Wood	0.05	3.6	25.8	17.9
Paper	0.11	6.3	12.6	10.3
Chemicals, plastics	0.10	7.3	13.3	9.5
Non metal products	0.08	7.6	21.6	15.3
Metals	0.05	6.2	25.2	17.5
Machinery	0.07	13.2	21.1	18.2
Electronics	0.05	9.1	27.8	16.1

See figures 1 and 2 for a description of the parameters.
[a] Cost disadvantage ratio (share of fixed costs in total cost)

Table A2. Accession to the EU (ACC) – capital perfectly mobile (variations in %)

	TARIFF	NTB	INT	MIGR	TRF	FISC	AGR	ACC
GDP	0.0	0.6	1.1	1.6	-0.5	-0.6	0.7	2.9
GNP	0.0	0.7	1.3	1.7	-0.7	-0.5	0.7	3.3
Welfare of residents (% of GDP)	0.1	0.9	1.2	0.6	-1.6	-1.5	0.6	1.2
Investment	0.1	0.8	1.4	1.9	-1.2	-1.4	-0.3	1.4
Exports to EU	2.2	4.8	4.2	0.7	3.5	3.1	3.7	14.5
Exports to RW	-2.6	-5.8	-6.4	0.7	4.0	3.5	3.9	-1.7
Imports from the EU	6.2	4.6	3.7	1.5	-0.6	-0.6	4.7	15.5
Imports from the RW	-20.6	-6.4	-6.7	1.6	-0.7	-0.7	2.3	-22.2
Capital Stock	-0.1	0.6	1.1	1.6	-1.1	-1.4	-0.2	1.0
Wage – university	0.1	1.2	2.2	0.0	-3.0	-4.4	2.3	0.2
Wage – superior education	0.3	1.1	1.6	0.0	-2.6	-3.9	2.2	0.1
Wage – apprenticeship	0.2	0.9	1.3	0.1	-2.6	-3.9	1.7	-0.5
Wage – compulsory school	0.3	0.8	1.1	0.1	-2.7	-3.9	1.0	-1.4
Real interest rate	0.0	0.0	0.0	0.0	0.0	0.0	0.0	0.0
Net foreign assets	0.4	3.7	4.7	3.9	-3.8	-0.1	0.4	10.2
Real exchange rate[1]	-0.1	-0.7	-0.8	0.0	-1.9	-3.2	2.1	-2.1

[1] real appreciation if negative

JAMES MARKUSEN
THOMAS F. RUTHERFORD
DAVID TARR

FOREIGN DIRECT INVESTMENT IN PRODUCER SERVICES*

1. SCOPE OF THE PAPER

Any paper on services typically either chooses to define services or to ignore the question and assume that we all know what we are talking about. The first option is a swamp, and in seminars authors who chose this route seldom get beyond section one. The second route is almost as bad, but at least the authors may make it to the model before the inevitable question arises.

In the present paper, we may be able to escape the need to provide a general definition of services, since we are going to look at a rather limited range of activities. Therefore, perhaps the reader will allow us to get away with a sort of definition by example. Later in the paper we then adopt a circular definition in the formal model: services are what are labeled in the model as services.

The types of activities we are interested in include the following: (1) managerial services, which improve organizational and decision-making efficiency. (2) engineering services, which improve technical efficiency and product quality. (3) financial services (not actual trade in capital) which provide expertise in financial management and decision making. (4) marketing services which improve firms' abilities to sell or purchase other goods and services. (5) information services in which the buyer receives some type of information or knowledge not just listed.

We believe these types of services represent a substantial share of the GDP of modern economies. Based on national income statistics, all services are about 60 percent of GDP in OECD countries, and are about 50 to 55 percent of GDP in middle income countries. Business services (which is perhaps a rough indicator of the types of services on which we focus in this paper) are about one-third of the total of all services. See UNCTAD (1994, tables A.1 and B.1).

* Financial support from the World Bank is gratefully acknowledged. The views expressed are those of the authors and do not necessarily reflect those of the World Bank. This paper is a much shorter version of Markusen, Rutherford, and Tarr (1999). Please see that version for more complete derivations of the theory, and for dynamic extensions in which skilled workers are endogenous.

R.E. Baldwin and A. Brunetti (eds.), Economic Impact of EU Membership on Entrants, 27–39.

Many routine services, such as cleaning services have been left off this list quite deliberately. While unskilled-labor-intensive services might be quantitatively important, they are not generally traded internationally. Firms incur costs of doing business abroad, and as such must have advantages over domestic firms. Thus we will disregard a wide range of routine services, and concentrate on the list just presented.

Several concepts emerge from this list. First, these services are not necessarily synonymous with a firm or indeed sold as a final product at all. A new airline might be called a service, but the firm's ability to run it efficiently and safely is what we are interested in, not the planes themselves (which could be purchased or leased by any domestic firm or individual). Our services are thus generally intermediate inputs.

Second, the services we are interested in generally involve an exchange of knowledge, which has been accumulated by the seller through previous investments. This implies two separate characteristics: the services of interest here are (a) intensive in skilled labor and other knowledge-based assets, and (b) involve some sort of scale economies: once painfully or slowly learned, knowledge can be supplied at low marginal cost.

Third, these services are generally customized to some extent, solving particular problems of the buyer, and they are not generally good substitutes for the services of other firms. Thus there is firm-level product differentiation. There may also be differentiation by firm nationality: two US management consulting firms may be better substitutes for one another than a US firm is for a Russian firm.

Finally, our services generally require a personal presence in a country or at least personal contact and discussions between the service provider and the client. This is not so important from the point of view of theory as it is for policy. In particular, restrictions on goods trade only affect service trade indirectly, while restrictions on foreign investment and the movement of business personnel have major, direct impacts. Note in particular that insofar as many services of interest are intensive in knowledge capital or knowledge-based assets, firms may insist on proprietary control of these assets to prevent their dissipation. Laws and regulations prohibiting foreign investment may thus rule out "trade" in many services; i.e., firms may only be willing to provide their services internally within the firm, not through arm's length contractual arrangements.

In summary then, we are interested in services have the following general characteristics:

(a) intermediate goods
(b) intensive in skilled labor and other knowledge capital
(c) produced with increasing returns.
(d) differentiated by firm and possibly by firm nationality
(e) subject to high or prohibitive transactions costs from barriers to foreign ownership, movement of business personnel, etc.

"Imported" services with these characteristics offer a number of important advantages to developing or transition economies. First, they may complement rather than substitute for domestic producer services, the differentiated-product characteristic just mentioned. Second, they economize on scarce domestic skilled labor which is then freed for other uses, the factor-intensity property noted above. This second property suggests that imported producer services might harm domestic skilled labor and its accumulation in the long run. But combined with the first "complements" property, this is far from obvious as we shall show below.

Third, imported services allow countries to obtain in the present expertise that is not otherwise available and would take considerable time and/or resources to develop, the scale economies property. In a static model, this could be captured by simple scale economies with fixed costs in terms of skilled labor, or in a dynamic model by a learning-by-doing or investment process which requires a time lag between skilled-labor inputs and service output.

Fourth, imported services may provide crucial missing inputs which allow a country to produce and export goods in which the country has a natural comparative advantage except for the missing input. This has the potential for huge surplus value. The Arabian gulf may have had huge oil supplies, but expertise was required to bring it to market. A few hundred million dollars worth of foreign expertise likely had a return of many billions of dollars.

The purpose of this paper is to take several steps toward incorporating the types of producer services just discussed into applied general equilibrium models. The first step in this process is to adopt a formal theoretical approach. Our formulation will build on existing work, including Markusen (1989), Francois (1990a,b), and Stibora and de Vaal (1995).

We feel that these template models should provide a useful starting point for the analysis of these issues in future applications with real data. Before proceeding, we will mention of a couple of interesting results which may induce the reader to continue. First, we use a static model to show that liberalization of rules to permit inward FDI in producer services may imply that these services are general-equilibrium complements to domestic skilled labor, even though they appear to substitute for domestic skilled labor in a partial-equilibrium sense. Second, allowing inward FDI in producer services may significantly affect the pattern of trade in goods. As in the "key input" argument above, these services may reverse the direction of trade, permitting the host country to successfully export advanced products.

The order of the paper is as follows. In the next section we lay out the basic theoretical model and some simplifying assumptions.. Section 3 presents a number of implementational issues involved in the analysis, and section 4 describes some of the results of numerical simulations. Section 5 concludes.

2. MODELLING TRADE AND FDI IN PRODUCER SERVICES

Our basic approach will be to model producer services as intermediate inputs. These intermediate inputs will be differentiated from one another and may also be differentiated according to whether or not they are produced domestically or by foreign firms. Both types of services are produced with increasing returns to scale due to fixed costs.

There will be two final goods, X and Y, and two primary factors, S and L. S will denote skilled labor and L will denote all other factors, aggregated into a composite factor to simplify the model. S and L are in fixed aggregate supply and immobile between countries. The production function for Y is written in Cobb-Douglas form to facilitate comparison with X, but its elasticity of substitution is a choice parameter in the numerical model.

$$Y = S_y^{\alpha_y} L_y^{(1 - \alpha_y)}$$

Services (Z_x) are an intermediate input into X production. There are domestic services firm producing inputs ZD and foreign firms producing inputs ZM.

$$X = S_x^{\alpha_x} L_x^{\beta_x} Z_x^{(1 - \alpha_x - \beta_x)}$$

Later, in some illustrative simulations, we will assume that in direct S and L requirements, X is skilled-labor intensive relative to Y, in the sense that $\alpha_x > \alpha_y$. Z_x is a CES function of ZD and ZM, each of which is in turn a CES function of the individual ZD and ZM varieties, zd_i and zm_j respectively.

$$Z_x = (ZD^{\gamma} + ZM^{\gamma})^{1/\gamma}$$

$$ZD = \left[\sum_i^{nd} zd_i^{\delta} \right]^{1/\delta} \qquad ZM = \left[\sum_j tonm\ zm_j^{\varepsilon} \right]^{1/\varepsilon}$$

where nd and nm are the number of domestic and imported service varies (synonymous with the number of firms) respectively.

Domestic intermediate inputs ZD are produced using skilled labor and the composite factor. Imported services ZM are produced from imports and domestic skilled labor and composite factor. These imports will be denoted V. zd_i and zm_i are produced with a fixed and a variable cost.

Because of the two components of cost, it is normal to express technologies for these differentiated goods by a cost function rather than by a production function. Let CD and CM be the cost function for producing individual domestic and foreign varieties. cd and cm represent unit variable cost functions and fd and fm represent the fixed costs functions for domestic and foreign varieties respectively. Let r be the price of S, w be the price of L, and p_v be the price of V. Cost functions for domestic and foreign intermediates are thus:

$$C^D(r, w, zd) = cd(r, w)\, zd + fd(r, w)$$

$$C^M(r, w, p_v, zm) = cm(r, w, p_v)\, zm + fm(r, w, p_v)$$

Let n_d and n_m as variables refer to the number of domestic and foreign service firms active in equilibrium. Recalling that the derivatives of cost function with respect to the price of factor *i* is the input demand for factor *i*, the market clearing equations for *S* and *L* can then be written as:

$$L = L_y + L_x + n_d C_w^D + n_m C_w^M$$

$$S = S_y + S_x + n_d C_r^D + n_m C_r^M$$

in which C_w^j and C_r^j represents the partial derivatives of unit cost for firm type $j \in \{D, M\}$ with respect to the unskilled wage rate and the rental price of skilled labor, respectively. (By Shephard's lemma, these are the compensated demand functions).

The demand side of the economy consists of a representative consumer, who derives income from factor supplies and possibly from tax revenues (net of subsidies). Let subscripts *c* and *p* distinguish consumption and production of *X* and *Y*. Preferences of the representative consumer are given by

$$U = U(X_c, Y_c)$$

The model is closed with a trade balance condition that requires that net exports of *X* and *Y* equal net payments for foreign services. Let *px,** and *py,** denote the world prices of *X* and *Y* (which may differ from domestic prices if there are taxes or subsidies).

Trade balance is given by:

$$p_x^*(X_p - X_c) + p_y^*(Y_p - Y_c) + p_v^* V = 0$$

where the demand for foreign services is given by the number of foreign services times the derivative of the cost function for a given foreign service with respect to the cost of imports::

$$V = n_m C_{p_v}^M$$

We make several assumptions to simplify the interpretation of results. The first is generally referred to as large-group monopolistic competition. It implies that the markup of services over marginal cost is constant. The ratio of price to marginal cost is simply 1/ε.

Equilibrium for a symmetric group of service firms (*zm* or *zd*) is found as the solution to two equations and two unknowns. One equation is the individual firm's optimization condition, marginal revenue equals marginal cost. A second condition arising from the free-entry condition is that price equals average cost. This condition determines the number of firms in equilibrium.

At this point, we will make an assumption which simplifies the interpretation of results. We assume that *cm* and *zm* have the same functional form, including elasticities of substitution and factor intensities. The consequence of this assumption, combined with the constant markup, is that *zm* is then a constant, and *ZM* increase or decreases through the addition or subtraction of varieties, not through changes in the scale of any variety that is produced. Corresponding comments apply to *zd* and *ZD*.

ZM and *ZD* can therefore be written as:

$$ZD = n_d^{1/\delta} zd \qquad ZM = n_m^{1/\varepsilon} zm$$

Since production expands by new firms only, *ZD* and *ZM* exhibit increasing returns to scale in inputs and are homogeneous of degree $1/\delta > 1$ and $1/\varepsilon > 1$ respectively. This of course implies that Z_x has increasing returns; note in the special case in which $\gamma = \delta = \varepsilon$ and $zm = zd$, that Z_x can be written as:

$$Z_x = (n_d + n_m)^{1/\gamma} zi \qquad zi = zm = zd$$

in which case domestic and imported firms, while differentiated, are perfect substitutes at the margin.

A final set of assumptions needed to complete the model formulation relate to the specification of the external sector, and in particular the endogeneity of prices. For our purposes, we will begin with a "small country assumption", that prices to our country are fixed. It is clear what this means with respect to *X* and *Y*, but less clear with respect to foreign producer services. We assume that there are a large number of potential foreign firms in production in the rest of the world. A fixed cost is needed to enter the domestic market (*fm*). Foreign firms will enter up to the point where the local markup revenues cover this fixed cost. In other words, the domestic market has no "world" effect on the number of multinationals. This assumption would generally not hold in a "large-country case", with firm level scale economies. In such a model, excess markup revenues contribute to firm-level fixed costs, and the number of multinational firms becomes endogenous to policy changes in one country (Markusen and Venables, 1998, 2000).

3. IMPLEMENTATION ISSUES

Before presenting some results, we present a brief discussion of some important practical issues.

3.1. *Initially - inactive activities*

Often AGE models avoid initial calibrations in which there are no initially-inactive production activities or trade links. Or, if there is an initially inactive trade link (aircraft exports from Sri Lanka to the US), the link is omitted from the model: i.e., an inactive link is always inactive.

In our case, this is not an appropriate procedure. We very much want to consider initial situations in which FDI is prohibited in a sector, and liberalization opens the closed sector. In a complementarity framework this is not a technical difficulty. The difficulty is economic. We would like to know how profitable the excluded activity would be if the barrier were removed. This will obviously be very quantitatively important to the results, which can range from zero (the barrier was redundant, the activity is not profitable with no barrier) to extremely high values. But there are no easily obtainable data for the "shadow price" of these restrictions. Survey evidence from multinational firms might be one source of information.

3.2. *Firm-level production differentiation*

We have no good estimates of the extent to which the outputs of firms in a given sector are good or poor substitutes for one another. Note that in the large-group monopolistic-competition model, the degree of production differentiation is closely related to scale economies, or more precisely the elasticity of scale (average cost over marginal cost). Thus if one were to take the model seriously, one could use possible data on scale economies to estimate the elasticity of substitution among different firms. This estimate will of course be of considerable importance to the results: a lower elasticity of substitution implies higher "aggregate scale economies".

3.3. *Differentiation by region of origin*

If we really believe that the essence of production differentiation is firm-level only, and that firms are symmetric but imperfect substitutes for one another, then the three parameters γ, δ, and ε in (3) and (4) should be identical. But is it really believable that the elasticity of substitution between two Russian management consulting firms is the same as the elasticity of substitution between one Russian and one American firm? In the model presented here we will assume that $\delta = \varepsilon$, but that this number is greater than or equal to γ. Substitution across firm type (domestic and foreign) is less than or equal to substitution within a type.

3.4. *Multiple equilibria*

Models with scale economies are non-convex and may display multiple equilibria. In this specific case there is typically a "bad" equilibrium in which none of the increasing-returns good is produced: at zero output, productivity is so low that price (while possibly quite high) is less than average cost. This is of course interesting from a certain point of view, and it has important policy implications in that developing countries may get stuck in a bad equilibrium. We have often found such equilibria in experimenting with "toy" models.

Assumptions which tend to eliminate multiple equilibria, particularly the "bad" equilibria with an IRS activity slack, could be referred to as "convexifying" assumptions. In our case, these could include (i) specific factors of production in different sectors, (ii) large factor-intensity differences among sectors, (iii) low elasticities of factor substitution within sectors, (iv) a rising foreign supply price of services (analogous to a specific factor in the foreign country), and (d) firm-type product differentiation.

In order to see the role of the last assumption, refer back to equation (13) which assumes strictly firm-level product differentiation. Although the point is not widely appreciated in the theoretical literature, there is a sense in which one foreign service is a perfect substitute for a domestic service. Decreasing n_m by one is perfectly matched by increasing n_d by one. This is only indirectly recognized in the theory literature where it is acknowledged that the identical nature of individual products doesn't matter, only the total number. But in our case it matters a lot. If the technologies for producing a domestic and foreign service are not that different, and they are collectively a small part of total GDP, then we can get bang-bang solutions in which small change in relative costs shift us from only *ZD* begin produced to only *ZM* being produced or vice versa. This has indeed occurred in our simulations, and we discovered that this extreme substitutability can be dampened by setting γ less than $\delta = \varepsilon$. But this may also be justified by economic arguments as noted above.

4. SIMULATION RESULTS

Table 1 shows some simulation results from the static model. In these calculations, the elasticity of substitution among services of one firm type (domestic or multinational) is set at 5 while the elasticity of substitution between firm types is set at

The model is benchmarked such that key variables have the values of one or zero initially. The first column of Table 1 shows results when imports of *V* are banned and hence *ZM* is zero. The country exports *Y* and imports *X*, and there is no trade in *V* (trade balance requires that the last three entries in a column sum to zero). The prices for skilled and unskilled labor are real prices, the nominal price divided by the consumer price index.

The second column of Table 1 gives the price of V as 100% of domestic cost. What this means is that we have chosen a price for V such, as the initial prices with imports of V banned, the cost of producing one *zm* is such that the entering *zm* firm would just break even. In other words, the cost of *V* for an entering *zm* producer is equal to the costs of addition labor that an existing zd producer incurs: the costs of domestic factors that *V* economizes on are just equal to the cost of V. Nevertheless, Table 1 shows that there is a strong productivity and welfare boost even at this price for *V*. An entering zm producer confers an „externality" effect on *zd* producers raising q_{zd} for a given p_{zd}. Entry of more *zd* and/or *zm* firms in column 2 (100%) confers a pure variety or productivity effect; i.e., in a competitive model without scale economies this second column would be identical to the first. The second column in fact shows a welfare increase of 3%. When one *zm* producer can enter at zero profits, no entry may be an equilibrium, but it is „unstable" and there is another equilibrium with significant entry and welfare benefits.

One of the most interesting results is that the real wage of skilled labor rises by 7.0%. This is an effects suggested earlier, in which the substitution effect away from domestic skilled labor (*V* economizes on domestic skilled labor in producing *ZM*) is outweighed by a scale effect. Imported services produce a sort of productivity effect that lowers the cost of final output and increases the *X*-sector's direct demand for skilled labor. A final interesting result in the second column is change in the trade pattern. Imports of X are eliminated due to the economy's increased ability to produce it domestically, and trade consists of a small export of *Y* to pay for imported *V*.

As the price of *V* falls, these results are amplified. This lower price for *V* may be economically reasonable, insofar as foreign multinationals have made large sunk investments and are willing to supply *V* at a low marginal cost when competing with one another. The number of domestic service firms continues to fall as the price of *V* falls, but this fall in demand for domestic skilled labor is outweighed by the scale effect in *X* production so that the real wage of skilled labor continues to rise. In the right-hand column of Table 1, the skilled-labor wage has risen by 41% while the real wage of the composite factor has fallen by 4%. These results are particularly dramatic is we want to think of *V* as largely consisting of imported skilled workers: they are clearly a general-equilibrium complement to domestic skilled labor.

Note the reversal of the pattern of trade in goods in the right-hand two columns of Table 1. When *V* is sufficiently cheap, the country imports *Y* and exports *X*. Finally, we might draw attention to the very large changes in welfare in Table 1. The model is calibrated so that imported services *ZM* have only a 10% value share in *X* production at the initial price of 1.0 for *V*, and *V* has only a 40% value share in producing *ZM*. Thus *V* has a 4.0% value share in *X* initially. Yet a fall in the cost of *V* to 20% of its initial value produces a 14.6% increase in welfare, a result that is due to scale/variety effect.

Earlier, we noted that the entry of a new service producer confers a positive productivity boost or „externality" on existing producers. To put it somewhat differently, a well-known result in this type of model is that the number of firms in market equilibrium is below the optimal number. In Figure 2, we therefore present results when we impose a tax/subsidy on imported V. Figure 2 uses column five of Table 1 (Price of V is 40%), and welfare changes are measured relative to the no-tax reference point (i.e., 1.07 in Table 1 is the basis for equivalent variations in income depicted in Figure 2). Figure 2 shows that the optimal tax on V is in fact negative, the optimum is a subsidy of about 25%. The welfare improvement from such a subsidy is not large, but the idea is simply to show that there is no case in this model for a positive rent-shifting tariff as there typically is in models where the differentiated goods are final goods. A related result is found in Lopez-de-Silanes, Markusen, and Rutherford (1994), where the authors find that the optimal tariff on auto parts imported into Mexico is negative. For theoretical foundations of this problem, see Markusen (1989, 1990).

5. CONCLUSIONS

Although there is a clear trend among developing countries to liberalize their policies with respect to inward foreign direct investment (UNCTAD, 1995, 272-275), many developing countries continue to impose restraints on FDI in general and in services in particular. These policies may be motivated by the fear that foreign service providers will harm the domestic skilled workers that provide these services in domestic firms. For example, examination of the commitments on services of WTO members in their GATS schedules reveals that 32 countries (mainly in Africa and Latin America) have scheduled „horizontal restrictions" that require foreign firms to use and train domestic skilled workers. In many cases these restraints may impede the foreign firm from importing the specialized people it would desire.

In this paper we have examined the impact of the liberalization of policies to allow the formation of foreign firms that provide intermediate services. The foreign service providers import an input (which we interpret as a composite of foreign skilled labor and specialized technology), and economize on the use of domestic skilled labor compared to domestic firms that provide the substitute service.

We examined this issue with a comparative static model and showed that liberalization could lead to large gains in GDP, depending on parameter assumptions. These are very large gains relative to what we might expect from a comparative static model. The source of these large gains is that additional intermediate service firms increase the productivity of the final goods sector that uses these firms services as intermediate inputs. More service firms allow final goods producers to use better or more appropriate firms that more closely meet their needs.

One of the more interesting results of the comparative static model is that the real wage of domestic skilled labor increases with liberalization of policies against foreign service providers, and the more foreign firms there are in the domestic market the more the real wage of domestic skilled workers increases. Thus, despite the fact that foreign firms import an input (V) and thereby use domestic skilled labor less intensively than domestic firms, additional foreign firms benefit domestic skilled labor. The reason is that additional foreign firms lower the cost of the intermediate service product in final goods production and thereby increase the relative importance of the final good sector (X), which uses services relatively intensively. Thus, in a general equilibrium sense, domestic skilled labor and the specialized foreign input V are complements. One possible interpretation of this result is that the policies of certain developing countries discussed above that restrain the import of foreign inputs or force foreign multinationals to use domestic skilled factors in place of foreign inputs may not only result in lost national income, but may hurt the factor of production they are designed to assist.

Table 1. Simulations for various prices of V, the imported input for FDI in services (skilled labor, blueprints, patents, etc.)

VARIABLES	PRICE OF V (units of foreign exchange)*					
	+ inf	1.00	0.80	0.60	0.40	0.20
Welfare	1.00	1.03	1.03	1.05	1.07	1.15
Real wage of skilled labor	1.00	1.07	1.07	1.11	1.14	1.41
Real wage of composite factor	1.00	0.99	1.01	1.00	1.02	0.96
No. of domestic service firms	1.00	0.45	0.35	0.24	0.11	0.08
No. of foreign service firms	0.00	0.51	0.67	0.98	1.42	2.70
Net imports of X	1.00	0.00	0.00	-0.42	-0.63	-2.97
Net imports of Y	-1.00	-0.26	-0.32	0.00	0.11	2.17
Net imports of V	0.00	0.26	0.32	0.42	0.52	0.81

* To interpret the price of V, a price of 1.0 means that the cost of producing a foreign service ist calibrated to exactly equal the cost of producing a domestic service. Yet welfare nevertheless increases due to a complementarity effect (see text)

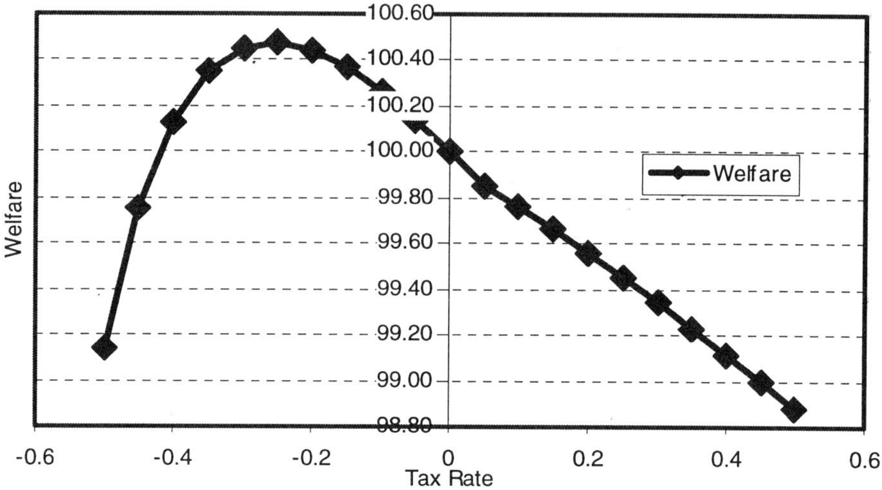

Figure 1. Welfare as a function of a tax on V (price of V 40% in Table 1, welfare renormalized to 100 at t = 0)

REFERENCES

Francois, J. F. (1990a), Trade in Producer Services and Returns due to Specialization under Monopolistic Competition, Canadian Journal of Economics, 23, p. 109-124.

Francois, J. F. (1990b), Producer Services, Scale, and the Division of Labor, Oxford Economic Papers , 42, p. 715-729.

Lopez-de-Silanes, F., J. R. Markusen and T. Rutherford (1994), Complementarity and Increasing Returns in Imported Intermediate Inputs, Journal of Development Economics, 45, p. 101-119.

Markusen, J. R. (1989), Trade in Producer Services and in Other Specialized Intermediate Inputs, American Economic Review, 79, p. 85-95.

Markusen, J. R. (1990), Derationalizing Tariffs with Specialized Intermediate Inputs and Differentiated Final Goods, Journal of International Economics, 28, p. 375-384.

Markusen, J. R, and A. Venables (1998), Multinational Firms and the New Trade Theory, Journal of International Economics, 46, p. 183-204.

Markusen, J. R. and A. J. Venables (2000), The Theory of Endowment, Intra-Industry, and Multinational Trade, Journal of International Economics.

Markusen, J. R., T. F. Rutherford and D. Tarr (1999), Foreign Direct Investment in Services and the Domestic Market for Expertise, World Bank Working Paper.

Rutherford, T. F. and D. Tarr (1999), Blueprints, Spillovers and the Dynamic Gains from Trade Liberalization in a Small Open Economy, in R. Baldwin (ed.), Dynamic Analysis of Commercial Policy, Cambridge University Press.

Rutherford, T. F. (1999), Applied General Equilibrium Modeling with MPSGE as a GAMS Subsystem: An Overview of the Modeling Framework and Syntax, Computational Economics.

Rutherford, T. F. (1995), Extensions of {GAMS} for complementarity problems arising in applied economics, Journal of Economic Dynamics and Control, p. 1299 - 1324.

Stibora, J. and A. de Vaal (1995), Services and Services Trade: A Theoretical Inquiry, Amsterdam: Tinbergen Institute.

United Nations Conference on Trade and Development (1994), Liberalizing Trade in Services: A Handbook, New York and Genva: United Nations.

United Nations Conference on Trade and Development, Division on Transnational Corporations and Investment (1995), World Investment Report 1995, New York and Geneva: United Nations.

JEAN-MARIE GRETHER

FOREIGN DIRECT INVESTMENT IN PRODUCER SERVICES

A Comment

It is hard to overestimate the importance of foreign direct investment (FDI) for developing and transition economies. In recent decades, FDI flows have experimented a dramatic increase, not only between industrialized countries, but also towards less developed ones. In spite of the failure of the MAI negotiations, these flows have been promoted by the TRIPS and GATS agreements, and also by deliberate fiscal policies welcoming FDI in host countries. Benefits from these are generally expected to be large, not only because of increased availability to foreign capital, but also, and perhaps more fundamentally, because FDI is believed to be a major channel of technological transfer. However, apart from competition issues that this paper does not address, the precise mechanisms through which foreign technology benefit to host countries are still a matter of debate, with the underlying fear that multinational corporations (MNCs) operate in technological enclaves, apart from the local economy. Moreover, there is a widespread concern among policy makers that FDI may be detrimental to the local skilled labor force, as MNCs tend to rely on specialized imported labor services.

This paper provides an original theoretical framework to deal with these issues, focusing on the impact of FDI in business services. It is first based on a static model. Foreign ownership is not explicitly modeled, but assumed to be reflected in the availability of a specialized input, V, which may correspond to foreign experts, blueprints, or whatever other factor contributing to the subsidiary's advantage over its domestic competitors. Services are differentiated across firms and origin, and used in the production of a final good X. The other final good, Y, whose production does not require services as intermediate inputs, is relatively intensive in unskilled labor with respect to good X. Both final goods are traded and produced under perfect competition. The host country is assumed to be small and relatively poorly endowed in skilled labor. FDI in services is initially banned, then authorized, through a progressive decline in the price of V.

Although these are well known analytical tools, it is, to my knowledge, the first time they are implemented in this way. Apart from building a bridge between the trade, services and FDI literature, the basic contribution is to put into light the origin of the welfare gains for the host country. When the first foreign-produced intermediate input becomes available, the increase in variety boosts up the marginal revenue of the local services producers, leading to more entry of (foreign and/or local) firms until a new equilibrium is reached. As a result, there is an overall

R.E. Baldwin and A. Brunetti (eds.), Economic Impact of EU Membership on Entrants, 41–43.

increase in the variety of intermediate inputs available to the X sector, which is skilled-labor intensive, and a corresponding increase in the wage rate of skilled locals. Therefore, although V and skilled labor are partial equilibrium substitutes, they turn out to be general equilibrium complements. Of course this result is driven by the assumption that intermediate inputs are only used by producers of the skilled-labor final good, but this seems reasonable in the case of business services. If the price of V is further reduced, welfare gains are magnified, and at some stage there is a trade-pattern reversal, the country becoming an exporter of the skilled-intensive good.

Although the general equilibrium complementarity result is crucial, the authors fail to mention another important dimension of their contribution, namely that it brings new light on the FDI-spillovers debate. According to this literature, the very presence of MNCs leads to an increase in the productivity of local firms through various types of externalities, including labor turnover, copying, or increased foreign market access. It is based on a large body of empirical evidence, but which is still controversial in terms of the spillovers' magnitude and usually fails to explain the precise channels through which these externalities take place (for a survey see Blomström and Kokko, 1998). Moreover, even if some theoretical models take the cost of copying into account, it remains unclear why MNCs should let these externalities undermine their relative advantage. In the present paper, the benefits come from a "pure variety effect", not from an exogenous technological leakage. And even if labor turnover is allowed, the MNC keeps its knowledge-based advantage, through the exclusive use of the V input. This reflects the "technological enclave" effect mentioned above but again, this does not preclude host country benefits from the foreign presence.

Still, it is true that these are static results. So the second part of the paper is devoted to dynamics. It is based on an exogenous growth of new vintage labor, with diminishing returns in the "production" of skilled workers at each period. As FDI increases, there is a wage differential in favor of "FDI jobs" which may not vanish immediately because skilled-labor mobility is limited. If this constraint is binding, during the first years of the transition period, all new skilled workers are hired by MNCs (a result made possible by the complementarity format used here). Eventually, the domestic sector contracts sufficiently so that skilled wages are equalized again. The critical factor in this process is the share of mobile skilled individuals: the smaller it is, the larger the length of (and the costs associated with) the transition period.

These results are promising and call for applications with real data. This should help to clarify a number of questions left unanswered by this stylized version to the model. For example, how realistic are the successive decreases in the price of V considered in the simulations? The subsequent increases in welfare are not really surprising as this corresponds to an improvement of the terms of trade. However, at some stage, there would be no other way to further decrease the price of V than to introduce a subsidy, and possibly an optimal one along the analysis of figure 2. Besides, taking the transition period into account, it will also be particularly interesting to estimate how the dynamic welfare impact of FDI openness is sensitive to the degree of intersectoral factor mobility.

Finally, even at this stage, it could be useful to address at least two variants of the model, which may lead to lower welfare gains of the host country. First is the possible existence of entry barriers in the differentiated sector, which would lead to economic profits and introduce the rent-shifting argument for protection in the analysis. Second, but not necessarily exclusively, it could be that the MNC, precisely in order to prevent local firms from benefiting from his presence, integrates vertically, absorbing part of the firms of the X sector. This could again mitigate the case for total liberalization. Of course it can be argued that this is an entirely different question, which is why the paper focuses on the "market for expertise". True in theory, but when turning to real data, where vertical integration is frequent, it will be awkward to handle a framework which rules out this possibility.

REFERENCES

Blomström, M. and A. Kokko (1998), Multinational Corporations and Spillovers, Journal of Economic Surveys, 12, p. 247-277.

RICHARD E. BALDWIN
RIKARD FORSLID
JAN I. HAALAND
KAREN HELENE MIDELFART KNARVIK

EU INTEGRATION AND OUTSIDERS A SIMULATION STUDY OF INDUSTRIAL LOCATION

This paper focuses on the location effects of preferential trade areas (PTA) on non-members. More specifically, using a CGE model calibrated to real data, it focuses on the impact of tighter European integration on outsider regions. We argue that because theoretical models analysing PTAs have very few contact points with reality, further research is needed to evaluate whether the effects highlighted by these models – catastrophic agglomeration and non-monotonic relocation, for example – are theoretical aberrations of highly specific models, or important effects that help us explain real world events. In our 14-sector, 10-region model, we find broad confirmation for the theoretical PTA models, and in particular for the Puga-Venables effects. We find that tighter European integration has a significant impact on Central and Eastern European countries, but the the impact on the other regions of the world is rather small. Our findings do however, suggest that the simple models of economic geography analysing PTAs miss important elements. The most important of these are comparative advantage and real trade costs.

1. INTRODUCTION

Europe's political leaders have, since 1957, chosen ever-tighter economic integration as a means of promoting an ever-closer union among the peoples of Europe. This integration has had, and will continue to have, important effects on the location of industry. The location effects of this integration have traditionally played only a minor role in formal economic analysis of European integration. This has recently changed. Economists in Europe and elsewhere have returned to location issues with new 'breakthrough' modelling tools and fresh excitement. This area, sometimes called the new economic geography, enjoys the happy conflux of new data, new theory and pressing policy relevance. Researchers all across Europe are working on this topic. See, for instance, the 1999 special issue of the *European Economic Review* edited by Elhanan Helpman and Jacques Thisse. Much less attention, however, has been devoted to the location effects on those outside the main European integration initiatives such as the Single European Act.

The focus of this paper is on the location effects of preferential trade arrangements on non-members, i.e. outsiders. The main theory piece on this topic is Puga and Venables (1997). Using a very simple two-sector, three-nation model, Puga and Venables predict that agglomeration forces may foster regional disparity within the preferential trading bloc. In particular, production in both members will rise with the margin of preference, but only up to a point. Beyond this point, the so-called break point, industry in the bloc agglomerates mainly or entirely in one of the

R.E. Baldwin and A. Brunetti (eds.), Economic Impact of EU Membership on Entrants, 45–72.

two member nations. This catastrophic agglomeration initially harms the outsiders, but further raising the preference margin actually increases outsider's production before decreasing it again.

Simple theoretical models, such as Krugman and Venables (1995) and Puga and Venables (1997), are useful for illustrating novel theoretical effects in an intellectually uncluttered setting. These models, however, have very few contact points with reality, so further research is needed to evaluate whether the effects highlighted by these models – catastrophic agglomeration and non-monotonic location effect, for example – are theoretical aberrations of highly specific models, or important effects that help us explain real world events. One way forward would be to empirically estimate the impact of agglomeration forces, as in Midelfart Knarvik and Steen (1999) and Amiti (1997). An alternate route, the one pursued in this paper, is to theoretically investigate the main results in a more realistic model, namely a CGE model calibrated to real data. While the former approach checks the empirical validity of the agglomeration forces within certain industries, our approach focuses on how robust the predictions from simple, symmetric two-goods models are in a more realistic, many-goods, many-countries setting.[1]

Our experiment consists of successive lowering or trade costs within the EEA. While this paper focus on the effects on outsiders, the location effects on the inside countries have been analysed by Forslid, Haaland and Midelfart Knarvik (1999). We therefore here only give a shorter presentation of the within EEA impact.

The plan of the paper is to start with a review of the theoretical literature, in section 2 and to introduce our simulation model, which is an exact replica of Forslid, Haaland and Midelfart Knarvik (1999), in section 3. We discuss our simulation results in section 4 and provide a summary of our findings and some concluding remarks in section 5.

2. THEORY

The vast literature on regional integration agreements (RIA) focuses on the integrating countries since the main line of inquiry revolves around the merits of RIA membership. The main qualitative lesson, i.e. that preferential liberalisation has ambiguous welfare effects on members, has been well known since Viner (1950). However, the impact of RIAs on non-member nations has been subject to much less formal study, as can be seen from a perusal of Pomfret (1997) and Bhagwati, Krishna and Panagariya (1999). The main result here is that an RIA is typically unfavourable for non-member nations. In traditional neoclassical models, the harm to outside nations stems from lower terms of trade and lower export volumes (see Baldwin and Venables, 1995).

---

[1] Several studies using CGE-models, e.g. Haaland and Norman (1992, 1995) and Baldwin, Forslid and Haaland (1996), have also studied effects for outsiders in a European economic integration framework. This study differs from previous work because agglomeration forces and locational effects are more pronounced in the present model, and because the model experiment of succesive lowering of trade costs is explicitly directed towards checking the theoretical predictions of economic geography models.

Krugman (1993) and Puga and Venables (1997). The Krugman paper focuses on the so-called "hub" effect. That is, he considers what happens to industrial production patterns in a three-nation model when one nation has lower trade cost with the other two nations. Puga and Venables also consider this experiment, but more importantly, they study the production shifting effects of the more classical policy experiment, namely customs union formation. For this reason we focus on the Puga-Venables model.

2.1. The Puga-Venables customs union model

The Puga and Venables (1997) paper, which is theoretical, works with an extremely simple economic geography model of the Venables (1996) type. Specifically, the authors assume two sectors in each nation, one representing a Dixit-Stiglitz sector with monopolistic competition, increasing returns, intra-industry linkages and iceberg trade costs. The other sector is a consumer commodity marked by perfect competition, constant returns to scale and zero trade costs. This sector is used as numeraire. There is only one factor of production (labour), and three countries (home, partner and RoW). The representative consumer in each country has Cobb-Douglas preferences over the commodity and a CES aggregate of the industrial goods. The same CES aggregate enters industrial firms' technology. Instead of modelling explicitly an upstream and a downstream sector, firms in the industry sector are both upstream suppliers of intermediates to other firms as well as downstream producers for consumer demand. These are all standard assumptions in the new economic geography literature (see Fujita, Krugman and Venables 1999).

In the Puga-Venables paper, four forces determine the equilibrium location of firms. First there are two dispersion forces stemming from product-market and labour-market competition. That is, all else equal, firms would rather be in a market with few competitors (both for labour and for customers) and this encourages geographical dispersion of industry. Counteracting these there are two agglomeration forces, forward (i.e. cost-related) linkages and backward (i.e. demand-related) linkages. Specifically, industrial firms use output from other industrial firms as intermediate inputs, so a larger number of locally produced varieties imply, everything else being equal, a lower cost of intermediates. This in turn reduces variable and fixed costs of production in the particular region and thus attracts firms. This is the cost-linked agglomeration force. Of course, firms are buyers of intermediates as well as sellers, so a larger number of local firms expands the market size and this also attracts more firms. This is the demand-linked agglomeration force.

Note that a reduction in the level of trade costs weakens both the dispersion and the agglomeration forces. However, in this model the dispersion forces erode more rapidly, so a steady decline in trade costs might for a certain range of parameter values eventually lead to a breakdown in the symmetric distribution of industry. In particular, at least one region will then become fully specialised in industry.

2.2. The thought experiment and results with the simple model

Using this simple set-up, Puga and Venables consider how the location of production is affected by geographically discriminatory trade policies. Their focus is on a couple of key issues related to implications of RIAs for outsiders. Does the RIA formation lead to what Baldwin and Venables (1995) refer to as 'production shifting', as industry is drawn from countries outside the preferential trade area (PTA) to countries inside the PTA? How does the existence of industrial input-output linkages affect the magnitude of production shifting? What are the welfare implications?

The point of departure is a stable symmetric equilibrium with industrial production in all three countries. Ex ante the countries are identical in all respects; however, since this model allows for the possibility of a core-periphery outcome (i.e. all industry is agglomerated in one nation), the initial trade barriers must be assumed to be sufficiently high to ensure that the symmetric outcome is locally stable.

The policy experiment is that of the classic preferential liberalisation: a progressive lowering of trade barriers between two of the countries (home and partner) with no change in the trade barriers between RoW and either home or partner. Assuming for the moment a fixed number of firms in reach region, the model acts very much in a classical fashion. RoW firms face reduced competitiveness in both of their export markets as inside firms get an advantage. Hence, they export less, and there is no offsetting change in competitiveness in their own local market, so output of RoW-firms falls. Since operating profit is proportional to sales under Dixit-Stiglitz monopolistic competition, the preferential liberalisation lowers the profitability of RoW firms. For inside firms, the liberalisation boosts operating profit, although the effects are slightly involved. The two-way preferential barrier reduction exposes them to more competition in their local market, but boosts their competitiveness in the foreign market. These effects tend to offset each other however, so each inside firm gains competitiveness relative to RoW firms in both markets.

Now allowing for free entry and exit, it is clear that firms will relocate from RoW to countries in the RIA, i.e. production shifting occurs, and this process continues until zero profits are restored. The magnitude of the production shifting depends upon the strength of the input-output linkages – the stronger these linkages the larger the production shifting from outsiders to insiders.

These results hold for small margins of preference. When trade costs between home and partner get low enough, a very non-classical event can occur. Lowering home-to-partner trade costs and vice versa weakens the agglomeration and dispersion forces operating in the two markets. That is, as trade costs come down local presence of supplies provides less of an edge and the presence of competitors in the local (as opposed to foreign) market matters less. In the Puga-Venables model – as is the case in all the standard economic geography models – the agglomeration forces erode more slowly. Consequently, at some level of home-partner preferences, the agglomeration forces outstrip the dispersion forces. The result is agglomeration of industry in one of the RIA nations.

This catastrophic agglomeration is not new (indeed it is the hallmark of an economic geography model). What is new is the implications of this for the RoW-based firms. The within-RIA agglomeration increases the degree of competition faced by RoW firms in the RIA-member that receives the extra firms (call this the 'core' for brevity). However, RoW firms now face a sharp drop in competition in the periphery member of the RIA. In other words, the typical RoW-based firm will now see a more fragmented RIA. This fragmentation may raise or lower RoW-profits. An interesting case is when it raises profits because in this case, the internal RIA catastrophic agglomeration actually raises the production in the RoW. That is, as RoW firms get more profitable, more RoW firms enter until profits are restored to zero.

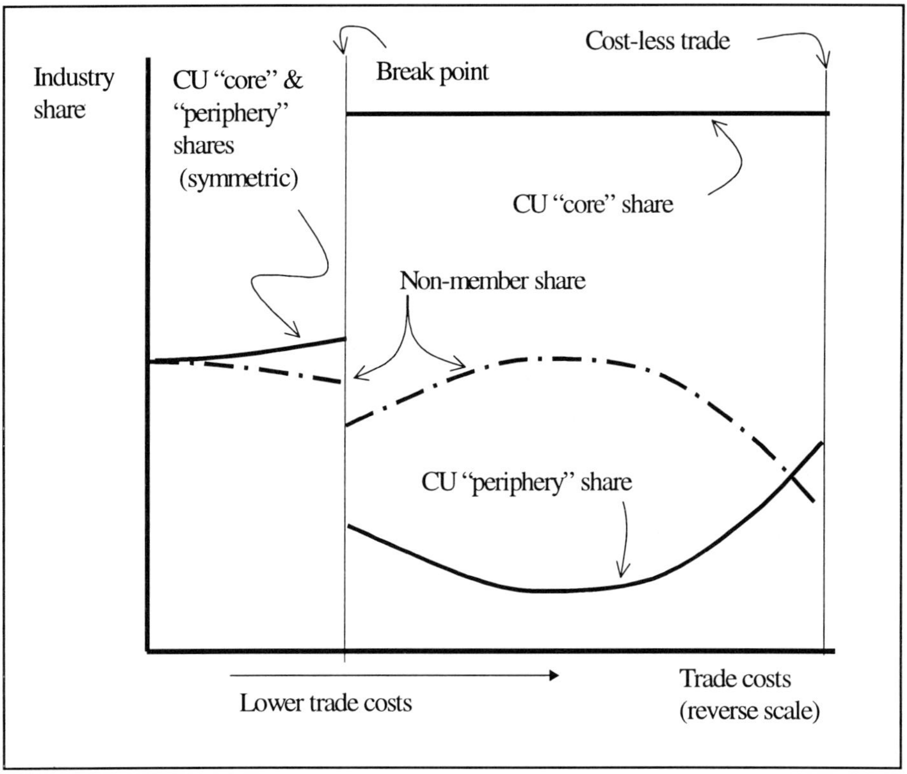

Figure 1. Simulations with the Puga-Venables Model

Figure 1 illustrates the main Puga-Venables results. The first result is that progressive elimination of barriers between two of the three nations produces regional disparities within the RIA. To see this, focus on the solid lines in the diagram. For trade cost reductions between the origin (which represents infinite trade costs) and the "break point", the preferential liberalisation has neoclassical effects. That is, both customs union (CU) members gain industry share at the expense of the RoW. Since the two CU members are initially symmetric, the gain is apportioned equally among them. However, for trade cost reduction greater than this, industry within the RIA tends to agglomerate in one of the two initially symmetric regions. In this model, the concentration within the CU takes the spectacular form of catastrophic agglomeration, as shown by the jump up in the CU "core" share to the flat line and the jump of the CU "periphery" share down to the bowl-shaped curve. The bowl-shaped curve for CU periphery indicates that deeper preferential liberalisation beyond the break point at first exacerbates this intra-CU disparity, but then mitigates it.

As far as the non-member nation is concerned, the catastrophic agglomeration increases the delocation experienced by the non-member nation (as shown by the jump down to the dashed, mound-shaped curve). Further discriminatory liberalisation has a very non-monotonic impact on industry in the non-member nation. At first, the loss of industry is reduced and later it is increased.

We can characterise the Puga and Venables (1997) as making five predictions:

- CU formation might increase regional disparities within the CU.
- The loss of industry for the CU periphery region could be non-monotonically related to the level of trade costs and it could be roughly convex.
- The gain of industry for the CU core could be non-monotonically related to the level of trade costs and it could take the form of a catastrophic agglomeration.
- CU formation should reduce the industry share of non-members.
- The loss of industry for non-members could be non-monotonically related to the level of trade costs and could be roughly concave.

As for welfare effects, these seem to be closely correlated with the location of industry. Hence, the core gains steadily while the inside periphery may lose from integration; the overall effect for the integrating region is, however, a welfare gain. The outside region loses, although the welfare development may be non-monotonous in the same way as it is for industrial production in the outside region.

Before turning to a more realistic model, namely a CGE model of global trade calibrated to a base year, it should be noted that the catastrophic agglomeration is perhaps the most spectacular of the theoretical predictions of this genre of simple theory models. It is also, however, one of the most fragile results. Even quite slight modifications of the model – including allowing for asymmetric regions and/or addition dispersion forces – can rule out catastrophic agglomeration.

2.3. Extending the Puga-Venables framework

The model gives strong results regarding location and welfare effects for both insiders and outsiders. Some of these are "neoclassical" and hence robust in the sense that the results from Puga-Venables model are similar to well-known effects from standard customs-union theory. However, the dispersion and non-monotonicity results are not of this kind; these are new results in the literature on new economic geography and agglomeration. As noted above, the effects for insiders have been studied in some detail in this literature, and while some of the results are fragile –

like the catastrophic agglomerations – others seem to be more robust. Non-monotonic relationships between trade costs and industry location do for example occur under a wider range of assumptions than in the restrictive Puga-Venables model.

In the present paper we focus on the effects for outsiders, to which much less attention has been paid. The fact that outsiders lose from a production shifting effect is well known. However, the possibility of a non-monotonic relationship with a range of preferential trade costs for which the outsider will actually increase its share of manufacturing, is a new and surprising result. An interesting question is then how robust this result is. No formal analysis exists to help us answer this question. However, by considering the importance of the key assumptions behind the result, we may get an impression of the robustness. In the Puga-Venables model countries are assumed to be identical at the outset, and initial trade costs are such that the inside countries are symmetric and experience the same increase in the share of industry for a range of preferential liberalisation. But when the break point is reached, the situation changes dramatically. The core becomes completely specialised and the periphery's industrial production is suddenly less than in any of the other countries, including the RoW. This internal agglomeration thus gives the outsiders (RoW) a market size advantage relative to the inside periphery and this acts as a counterweight to the trade costs disadvantage faced by RoW. As intra-CU trade costs drop further, the trade-off at first favours RoW production and then it disfavours RoW production. The result is a non-monotonic relationship between RoW production and intra-CU trade costs.

How would initial asymmetries affect this? The countries could differ in size or in the pattern of production and trade, and both may be important for the results. Consider first a situation where the outside country's industrial production is small relative to the insiders; in such a case, the outsider may never get a size advantage but will always face a trade costs disadvantage. Hence, we should expect a monotonously decreasing industry sector in the outside country, possibly with a sudden jump down when the break point is reached.

Secondly, let us consider a case with asymmetric inside countries. In such a case, preferential liberalisation would eventually imply a growth in industrial production in the large inside country matched by a decline in the small one. The core country may, however, still be diversified. In this situation, the outsider nation will always be disadvantaged relative to the core and continued intra-CU liberalisation reinforces this disadvantage. Consequently, the decline in periphery production may not boost outsider's production at all.

Thirdly, differences in the pattern of specialisation and trade may yield similar effects to the ones just discussed. If the outsider trades more with one of the insiders than with the other one in a particular industry or in general, then the important thing is what happens to industrial production in the country that is the more important trading partner. If it happens to trade much with the core country, it will definitely lose industrial production due to the preferential liberalisation. If the periphery is the most important partner, then the picture is more complex; the outsider may probably gain industrial production for certain ranges of trade costs in this case.

Finally, the Puga-Venables prediction of non-monotonic effects on outsiders assumes that initial trade costs are high enough to ensure a diversified and symmetric initial equilibrium. When confronted with real data, as in the CGE-model applied below, we should remember that we don't know where we are at the outset in Figure 1. Since there may already be elements of a core-periphery pattern in the initial data, the expected effects of further regional integration should be adjusted accordingly.

To sum up this section, some of the strong results from Puga-Venables model are likely to be modified in more realistic settings. In particular that seems to be true for the predicted non-monotonic relationship between preferential trade costs and industrial production in the outside region. The negative effects for outsiders, on the other hand, seem to be robust results. And it should be clear that the expected negative effects are stronger the more important the core of the regional integration area is as a trading partner for the outsider.

3. SIMULATION MODEL

The Puga-Venables paper is useful to illustrate the basic effects; however, extensions are called for. In particular, it does not tell us what the impact of regional integration is when there are several factors of production, a number of industrial sectors, and not just one outsider country. Which industries will typically be drawn into the integrating countries? What outside countries will be most affected by the RIA – in terms of production, factor prices and welfare? This section uses a medium-size CGE model to analyse the production shifting effects of a RIA in a more realistic framework.

The discussion shall be organised around the five main Puga-Venables predictions. We start, however, with a description of the CGE model employed.

3.1. Features of the CGE model

The model employed is an exact replica of Forslid, Haaland and Midelfart Knarvik (1999). Thus the model is in the line of CGE models introduced by Haaland and Norman (1992) and Gasiorek, Smith and Venables (1991, 1992) and extended by Baldwin, Forslid and Haaland (1996), Allen, Gasiorek and Smith (1998), and Keuschnigg and Kohler (1996). The main modification of the Haaland-Norman structure is that our model adopts large-group rather than small-group monopolistic competition. This change implies that firm scale is invariant to changes in trade barriers (Helpman and Krugman 1985). Furthermore, the model allows for region-specific input-output linkages and highlights the role of non-traded producer services. Finally, the model allows for import duties, export subsidies and real trade costs.

The model has ten regions, of which four are Western European. These together constitute the European Economic Area (EEA) plus Switzerland, which we refer to as the EEA for brevity's sake. The regional split is based on geography rather than economic criteria. The two other European regions are Central and Eastern Europe and the former Soviet Republics. The remaining regions are North America, South East Asia, China & South Asia and the Rest of the World (see Table 1).

Table 1. Regions

Regions	Description
Europe Central (EC)	Austria, Denmark, Germany, Switzerland
Europe North (EN)	Finland, Iceland, Norway, Sweden
Europe South (ES)	Greece, Italy, Portugal, Spain
Europe West (EW)	BeNeLux, Ireland, France, UK
Europe East (EE)	Czech Rep., Slovak Rep., Hungary, Poland, Bulgaria, Romania, Slovenia
"EEA"	EC+EN+ES+EW
Former Soviet Union (FS)	Former Soviet Republics including Estonia, Lithuania, Latvia
USA&Canada (UC)	USA and Canada
South East Asia (SEA)	South East Asia including Japan
China & South Asia (CSA)	China, India, Bangladesh, Bhutan, Maldives, Nepal, Pakistan, Sri Lanka
Rest of World (RoW)	Other nations not elsewhere included

Source: CGE Model Definitions.

Table 2. Industries, Trade Costs and Market Structure

Industry	Description
Public Services, Private Services	Non-traded monopolistically competitive sector linked to all other sectors through the input-output structure
Agriculture, Energy	Traded perfect competitive sectors without trade costs. Each sector has a specific factor, which creates an element of decreasing returns to scale.
Textiles, Leather Products, Wood Products, Metals, Minerals, Chemicals, Food Products, Transport Equipment, Machinery, Other Manufacturing	Traded sectors with monopolistic competition. Transport costs of iceberg type, plus tariffs and export taxes or subsidies. Linked to all other sectors through the input-output structure.

Source: CGE Model Definitions.

The model disaggregates activity into 14 sectors. The key feature of a Venables-style geography model is the input-output linkages among sectors. This is captured in the model via a complete input-output structure, i.e. all linkages across the 14 sectors.

Two of the 14 sectors are perfectly competitive. The others are marked by monopolistic competition of the Dixit-Stiglitz variety. Two of these imperfectly competitive sectors are non-traded services sectors; the others are traded manufacturing sectors. The basic industrial structure of the model is shown in Table 2.

The model allows for 3 intersectorally mobile factors of production, namely unskilled labour, skilled labour and physical capital, in addition to the specific factors in the energy and agriculture sectors. Factor supplies are assumed to be fixed in this version of the model.

3.2. Basic model equations

Representative consumers in each region have Cobb-Douglas preferences across sector aggregates. This implies the standard, upper-tier demand functions:

$$C_{im} = \alpha_{im} \frac{Y_m}{PI_{im}} \tag{1}$$

where C is the sector consumption composite, α is the expenditure share, Y is the income level, and PI_{im} is the usual CES price index for all differentiated goods in sector "i", namely:

$$PI_{im} = \left(\sum_{j=1}^{R} N_{ij} a_{ijm} P_{ijm}^{(1-\sigma_i)} \right)^{\frac{1}{1-\sigma_i}} \tag{2}$$

where P_{ijm} is the consumer price of good "i" made in region "j" and sold in market "m", the parameters σ_i and a_{ijm} are the product-specific demand elasticity and the region-specific and product-specific biases, respectively (for non-traded goods $a_{ijm}=0$ for all m≠j), and N_{ij} is the number of varieties of good i from region j sold in market m (there are 10 regions and thus 10 markets). Note that income and prices indices are region-specific.

The demand function for individual varieties of an imperfectly competitive sector "i" in region "m" is:

$$X_{ijm} = a_{ijm} \left(\frac{P_{ijm}}{PI_{im}} \right)^{\sigma_i} C_{im} \tag{3}$$

Producer prices in the imperfectly competitive sectors are set by the usual mark-up pricing first order conditions, namely:

$$PP_{ij} = \frac{\sigma_i}{\sigma_i - 1} MC_{ij} \tag{4}$$

where PP_{ij} is the producer price of good i produced in region j, and MC_{ij} are region-specific and product-specific marginal costs. Note that the usual mill-pricing behaviour of Dixit-Stiglitz monopolistic competitors means the producer prices are not destination-specific.

For perfectly competitive sectors, firms perceive demand to be perfectly elastic and so set consumer prices equal to marginal cost.

Consumer prices (P_{ijm}) differ from producer prices due to three types of trade costs: export taxes (EXTAX), transport costs (TRANS), and tariff equivalents of import barriers (TAREQ). The transport costs are of the iceberg type, while export taxes and import tariffs are transfers (to the representative consumer). Thus:

$$PI_{ijm} = PPI_{ij}(1 + EXTAX_{ijm})(1 + TRANS_{ijm})(1 + TAREQ_{ijm}) \tag{5}$$

where the trade costs are region-specific, product-specific and destination-specific. Observe that for locally sold differentiated goods (this includes non-traded differentiated goods), producer and consumer prices are identical since $EXTAX_{ijm}$=$TRANS_{ijm}$=$EXTAX_{ijm}$=0 for j=m.

Marginal cost curves are assumed to be flat (i.e. invariant to firm-level output) with the form of the marginal cost function being a nested CES-function. In particular, primary inputs, differentiated intermediates, and homogenous intermediates are nested in a top-level CES function with "S_{top}" as the top-level elasticity of substitution. Thus, the marginal cost function for industry i in region j is:

$$MC_{ij} = (BV_{ij}PV_{ij}^{\;1-S_{top_i}} + BZ_{ij}Q_{ij}^{\;1-S_{top_i}} + BZPC_{ij}QPC_{ij}^{\;1-S_{top_i}})^{\frac{1}{1-S_{top_i}}} \tag{6}$$

where the B's are region-specific and industry-specific cost parameters, and the Q's are price indices. Namely,

$$Q_{hm} = (\sum_{\forall i \in I} g_{ihm} P_{im}^{(1-sq)})^{\frac{1}{1-sq}} \tag{7}$$

is the price index for differentiated intermediate goods; this is specific to each purchasing region and purchasing sector. Here "sq" is the elasticity of substitution among imperfectly competitive goods used as intermediates; in general each

purchasing sector uses inputs from each of the 12 sectors, although in practice some of the "g" constant terms may be close to zero. Observe that this formulation assumes that firms and consumers in a region face the same price indices, PI_{im}. This implies that industries and consumers have identical expenditure shares, as in the Puga-Venables model.
The price indices for perfectly competitive goods (the set PC) as intermediates are constructed in the same way, i.e.:

$$QPC_{hm} = (\sum_{\forall i \in PC} g_{ihm} PPC_i^{(1-sq)})^{\frac{1}{1-sq}} \tag{8}$$

where PC_i is the world market price of perfectly competitive good i. Lastly, QV_{ij} is a price aggregate for the three primary factors used in the production in sector i in region j, namely

$$PV_{ij} = (\sum_{k=1}^{K} b_{ijk} W_{jk}^{1-s_i})^{\frac{1}{1-s_i}} \tag{9}$$

where s_i is the elasticity of substitution among factors, and the b's are region-specific and industry-specific cost parameters.

In the monopolistically competitive sectors, firms face fixed costs as well as marginal costs. The fixed costs are assumed to require inputs in exactly the same proportion as marginal costs. In other words, the cost functions are homothetic. The number of firms in each sector in each region adjusts to eliminate pure profits. Given the homotheticity of costs, this implies that firm size never varies with trade costs. The use of intermediates from own as well as other industries implies the existence of inter- and intra-industry cost linkages. The presence of these linkages, together with trade costs, means that the number of firms producing in the region affects each firm's costs. This creates cost-linkage agglomeration forces since firms located in a region with a large number of suppliers of important intermediates, will be relatively more competitive and this competitiveness will attract many firms. Agglomeration forces do not directly affect the perfectly competitive sectors, but these sectors are linked to other sectors via factor-market competition with the other sectors. The decreasing returns in these sectors (due to a specific factor) act to dampen the expansion of the other sectors.

3.3. Data

A detailed description of the data and data sources can be found in Forslid, Haaland, Mæstad and Midelfart Knarvik (1999), but the main sources are EUROSTAT (input-output tables for Europe), GTAP and NBER World Trade Flows. Forslid et al (1999) also provides a descriptive analysis of the data material, focusing on the distribution of production across regions, trade flows and trade volume, differences in technology and factor use across industries.

4. SIMULATION RESULTS

Using the model described above, we study the effects of a preferential trade cost reduction on industrial location. More specifically, we study the impact of European integration on the regions outside the EEA area. The idea of this exercise is to judge which aspects of the economic geography based predictions, and in particular of the Puga-Venables predictions, carry through in a more realistic model. The approach therefore follows the lines of Forslid, Haaland and Midelfart Knarvik (1999). The main difference is that we focus primarily on the impact on nations outside of the integrating area.

4.1. The simulation experiment

The simulation experiment consists of step-wise changes (both increases and decreases) in the trade costs among the four Western European regions, i.e. Europe Central (EC), Europe North (EN), Europe West (EW) and Europe South (ES). All other trade costs are unchanged so this is a preferential liberalisation. The changes involve all three types of trade costs (transport costs, tariffs and export taxes) with all costs changed in proportion. The step size is 10% per step and we consider three 10% rises and eight 10% decreases starting from the benchmark 1992-data (this benchmark corresponds to 1.0 in the figures).

Table 3 shows the base case trade costs for sales from the regions listed across the top of the table to the EEA region. The numbers are a straight average over the trade costs into EC, EN, ES and EW region. For example, the sixth column shows that Europe East (EE) textiles producers face a 29.3% trade cost in the EEA markets (the 29.3% figure is an average of the four actual trade costs between EE and the four EEA regions). The first four columns show the intra-EEA regional trade costs. Columns five and twelve show the average of the intra-EEA costs and the extra-EEA costs. The contrast between these two columns shows the deep level that European preferential liberalisation had attained by the base year, 1992. It also indicates that our simulation experiments are a long way from most of the CU exercises like that of Puga-Venables, which take all barriers to be initially identical.

4.2. Intra-CU regional disparity results

The five Puga-Venables results discussed above can be grouped into two categories. Results concerning predictions about intra-CU disparities and results concerning the impact on non-members. The first thing to focus on is intra-CU disparities. Since Forslid, Haaland and Midelfart Knarvik (1999) studies these aspects at length, we provide only a limited discussion of these effects. The three internal Puga-Venables predictions are:

- CU formation might increase regional disparities within the CU.

- The loss of industry for the CU periphery region could be non-monotonically related to the level of trade costs and it could be roughly convex.
- The gain of industry for the CU core could be non-monotonically related to the level of trade costs and it could take the form of a catastrophic agglomeration.

Table 3. Trade Costs into EEA area, by Exporting Region and Sector (% of producer price, averaged over the four EEA regions)

	EC	EN	ES	EW	Avg of 4	EE	FS	CSA	SEA	UC	RoW	Avg of 6
Textiles	3.7	6.5	4.2	4.2	4.7	29.3	27.3	50.2	38.0	12.0	24.9	30.3
Leather	3.4	3.8	3.6	3.9	3.7	10.8	9.6	11.4	10.3	9.5	12.3	10.7
Woodprod	3.2	-8.2	3.7	3.5	0.6	6.5	15.6	7.5	10.5	6.4	11.5	9.7
Metals	3.5	6.6	3.9	4.0	4.5	11.4	8.5	9.1	9.2	6.6	10.8	9.3
Minerals	8.0	6.0	7.6	6.3	7.0	16.7	82.2	9.2	9.4	8.9	13.0	23.2
Chemicals	4.2	11.8	5.0	5.1	6.5	20.6	23.4	25.5	25.7	21.7	23.2	23.4
Foodprod	12.5	23.0	12.5	12.4	15.1	46.7	44.4	22.7	25.3	21.0	37.8	33.0
Transeq	1.9	3.0	2.2	2.2	2.3	9.3	10.5	7.7	19.3	4.7	7.2	9.8
Machines	2.3	2.4	2.9	2.9	2.6	6.1	6.7	7.1	30.4	5.6	8.1	10.7
Other manu	3.1	2.8	3.2	3.3	3.1	6.3	6.2	9.3	12.6	5.5	6.3	7.7
Average	4.6	5.8	4.9	4.8	5.0	16.4	23.4	16.0	19.1	10.2	15.5	16.8

Notes: a. EEA includes Switzerland in the model.
b. See Table 1 for regional abbreviations.
c. For EC, EN, ES and EW, the numbers indicate costs within the EEA area. For other regions, the cost shows the trade cost of selling the specific product to the EEA area (using average cost of selling to EC, EN, ES and EW).

In studying the results of the simulation, we focus on the imperfectly competitive, traded goods sectors since these are the sectors most influenced by the economic geography type agglomeration forces, explicitly considered here. Figures 2 and 3 show the impact on production volumes in the four EEA regions. Each line in each diagram represents the change in one of the relevant region's ten sectors that are traded and imperfectly competitive. The numbers have been converted to indices in order to facilitate comparison across the sectors and regions; 100 equals production at the highest trade costs, namely 1.3 times the base case costs. In all four regions, the figures suggest that preferential trade-cost reductions increase regional specialisation within Western Europe; see Forslid, Haaland and Midelfart Knarvik (1999) for a more detailed discussion.

This finding confirms that the first prediction carries through in a model that is more realistic than the theoretical economic geography models (see e.g. Krugman and Venables, 1995, and Puga and Venables, 1997).

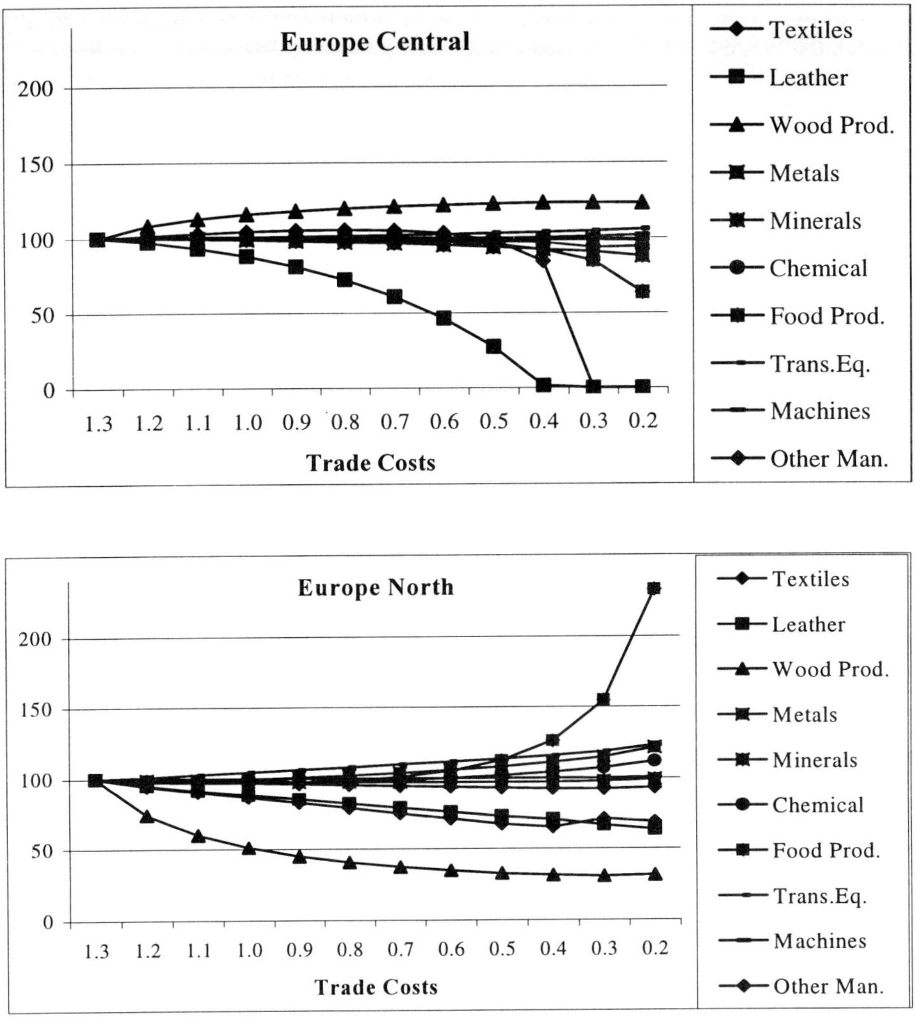

Figure 2. Production volume changes in the EEA regions (Central and North)

Given the range of sectors considered in our model, we can push the prediction further. The core logic of the economic geography finding of heightened regional disparity rests on agglomeration forces. This is easily seen since the two CU nations in the theoretical economic geography models, referred to above, are absolutely symmetric ex ante. Thus there are no endowment-driven or technology-driven comparative advantages to explain the regional disparities that appear. Given this, we can extend well known results from theoretical economic geography analyses to suggest that if agglomeration is the main force driving the regional disparities, we should observe the largest disparities in sectors marked by the strongest agglomeration forces. As discussed above, agglomeration forces in our model and Puga-Venables type models are strengthened by a high share of intermediate usage and strong scale economies. For the 10 sectors, these facts are listed in Table 4. Note that machinery, transport equipment, chemicals and metals have above average scale elasticities. As for intermediate input shares, it is the wood products, metals, chemicals and textile sectors that are above average. Taking these together, we should expect strong agglomeration effects at least in the chemicals and metals sectors.

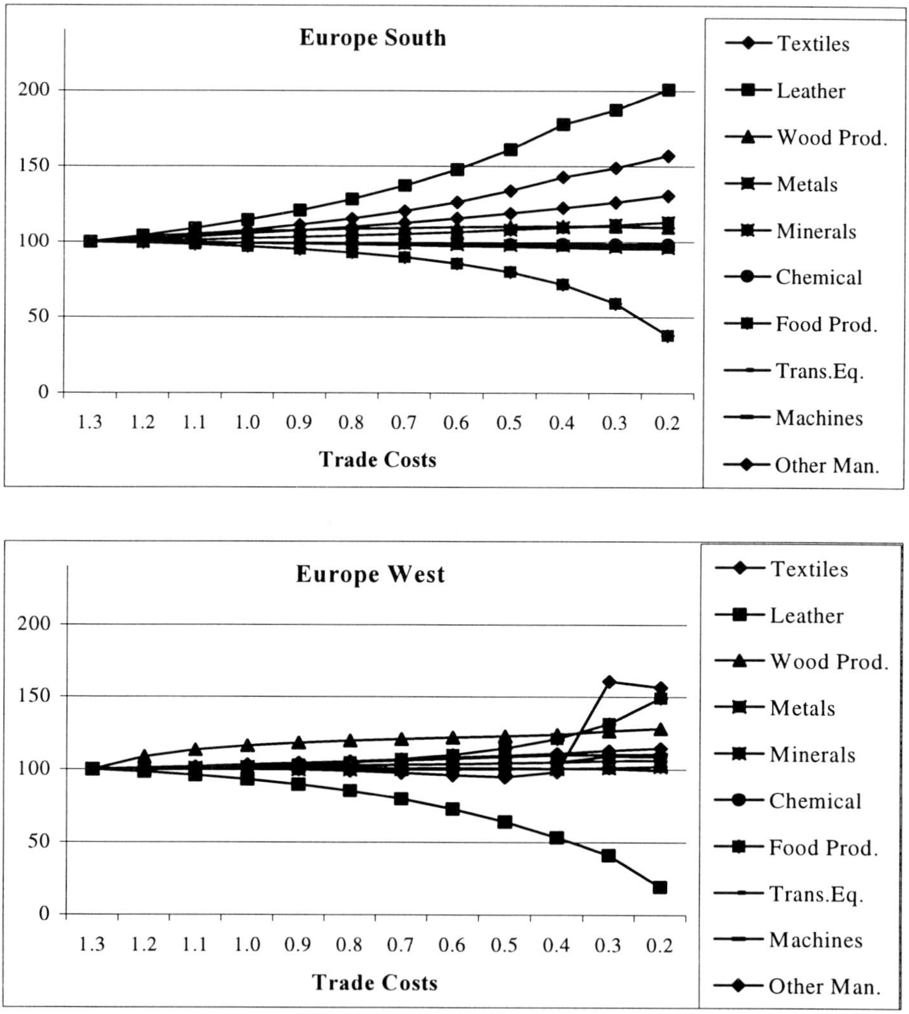

Figure 3. Production volume changes in the EEA regions (South and West)

Figures 2 and 3 also show that various sectors experience quite different effects. In the EEA regions, textiles, leather, wood products and food products experience large shifts, while metals, chemical and machinery experience very small production effects. However, one should note that the latter sectors are relatively concentrated in Europe Central originally – and obviously – remain so as trade is liberalised (see Forslid, Haaland and Midelfart Knarvik 1999 for further analysis on this point). Comparing these findings to Table 4, we see that three of the four sectors that show a very strong tendency towards regional concentration have average or above average intermediate usage. Intermediate usage here refers to use of intermediates from own sector. The food products sector does not have a high intermediate usage cost share, but it does start with very high trade costs so the proportional cuts in our simulations imply massive liberalisation. Further evidence for agglomeration effects can be found in the results for the textile sectors. This sector is marked by something that resembles a catastrophic agglomeration when trade costs are lowered from 40% to 30% of the base-case level. This is a very non-neoclassical result and thus seems to indicate that agglomeration forces are important in this sector. It also confirms the economic geography based predictions on non-monotonicity and catastrophes, at least for one sector.

Table 4. Sectoral Indicators of Agglomeration Forces

	Scale Elasticity*	Intermediates Input Share**	Trade Costs***
Textile	0.06	0.29	4.70
Leather	0.06	0.19	3.70
Wood Products	0.12	0.27	0.60
Metals	0.16	0.37	4.50
Minerals	0.10	0.13	7.00
Chemicals	0.24	0.30	6.50
Food Products	0.08	0.16	15.10
Transport Eq.	0.26	0.15	2.30
Machinery	0.20	0.17	2.60
Oth.Manuf.	0.08	0.03	3.10
Mean	0.14	0.20	5.00

*) Percent reduction in average cost (AC) with a one-percent increase in output.
**) Includes intermediates from own sector only.
***) As a percent of producer prices; unweighted average over all CU regions.

There are, however, some sectors that might seem to defy the economic geography based prediction, namely chemicals and metals. In these sectors we should expect strong agglomeration forces since they have both above average scale economies and above average intermediate use. Yet these sectors experience a small tendency towards regional dispersion. However, as noted above, these are also sectors that originally were relatively concentrated. Hence, we cannot discard the importance of agglomeration forces for the localisation of these industries; but the results indicates that in the interaction with comparative advantage effects, they are losing in significance as the trade liberalisation process proceeds. As demonstrated by Forslid, Haaland and Knarvik (1999), these high scale industries actually display a weak non-monotone localisation pattern with maximal concentration for trade costs around the middle of our range.

Our model includes many more location forces than does Puga and Venables (1997). For instance, we include a sector with diminishing returns to scale, which tends to dampen agglomeration, but we have input-output links with the non-traded service sectors, which should foster agglomeration along the lines of Faini (1984). We turn now to the impact of such forces. For low trade costs, agglomeration forces become weak, so comparative advantage forces will tend to dominate the location of industries. Given that industries have different relative factor intensities, and regions have different relative endowments, we should observe location effects corresponding to comparative advantage. Value added shares and factor intensities ratios are shown in Table 5 (the rankings of different sectors are similar across the EEA, so only the EEA average is shown). Note that chemicals, transport equipment and machinery are skill-intensive sectors, while textiles and leather are relatively unskilled labour intensive. Food products and minerals are relatively capital intensive.

Table 5. Value added shares and factor intensity ratios (European averages).

	Unskilled labour	Skilled labour	Capital	Unskilled /skilled ratio	Labour /capital Ratio
Textiles	0.595	0.175	0.235	3.40	3.28
Leather and Products	0.603	0.175	0.225	3.44	3.46
Wood Products	0.530	0.245	0.228	2.16	3.41
Metals	0.565	0.233	0.203	2.43	3.94
Minerals	0.455	0.195	0.353	2.33	1.84
Chemicals	0.438	0.278	0.285	1.58	2.51
Food Products	0.450	0.185	0.365	2.43	1.74
Transport Equipment	0.540	0.268	0.198	2.02	4.09
Machinery	0.478	0.313	0.210	1.53	3.76
Other Manufacturing	0.553	0.240	0.205	2.30	3.87
MEAN	0.521	0.231	0.251	2.36	3.19

Comparative advantage also depends upon relative factor endowments and these are displayed in Table 6, columns 1 and 2. The table shows that Europe South is relatively abundantly endowed with unskilled labour, while Europe North is relatively abundant in skilled labour. Europe Central and Europe North are relatively more capital abundant than Europe South and Europe West.

Using these facts to interpret the Figure 2 results, we see that comparative advantage does seem to play an important role in explaining the rise in regional disparity. For instance, production of unskilled-labour intensive leather and textile sectors shift to the unskilled-labour abundant Europe South. Food products, which are relatively capital intensive, move sharply to capital-rich Europe North. The big move in wood products is due to the removal of a significant export subsidy initially paid in Europe North (see Table 3).

Table 6. Relative Factor Endowments and relative size

	Unskilled/Skilled labour force	Labour/Capital stock	Share of European GDP *)
Europe Central	4.02	0.019	34.5 %
Europe North	1.69	0.017	5.8 %
Europe South	7.41	0.038	24.3 %
Europe West	2.77	0.037	35.5 %
MEAN	2.99	0.028	

*) Base case (1992) model data.

What all this suggests is that, as Forslid, Haaland and Midelfart Knarvik (1999) point out, regional disparity are related to agglomeration forces as well as neoclassical forces. Which type of forces dominate will depend on industry characteristics. For instance, in the cases of textile, leather and food products, its seems that lowering intra-CU trade costs produces disparities that corresponds to a heightened exploitation of comparative advantages. However, the effects are reinforced by agglomeration forces.

4.3. Impact on outsiders

The second category of Puga-Venables predictions concerns the impact on nations that are not members of the CU. Here there are two Puga-Venables predictions. The first of these comes from both economic geography and neoclassical CU analyses (see Baldwin and Venables , 1995):

- CU formation should reduce the industry share of non-members.
- The loss of industry for non-members could be non-monotonically related to the level of trade costs and could be roughly concave.

Figures 3 and 4 show the production volume indices by region for the four non-Eurasian regions (all graphed to the same scale as in the EEA region figures). From these figures we see that Europe's preferential liberalisation clearly has very little impact on production in South East Asia and RoW (basically Africa, South America, and the Middle East). A glance at Table 7 shows that the Western European markets (EEA) account for only a minor part of Asian and RoW manufacture sales, namely 3.2 % in both cases. Moreover, as Table 3 shows, the initial level of intra-EEA barriers is quite low, so the increase in the margin of preference in our simulations is quite modest. Finally, observe that while all of these production effects on South East Asia and RoW are small, they are all negative as is predicted by the Puga-Venables paper and standard neoclassical analysis.

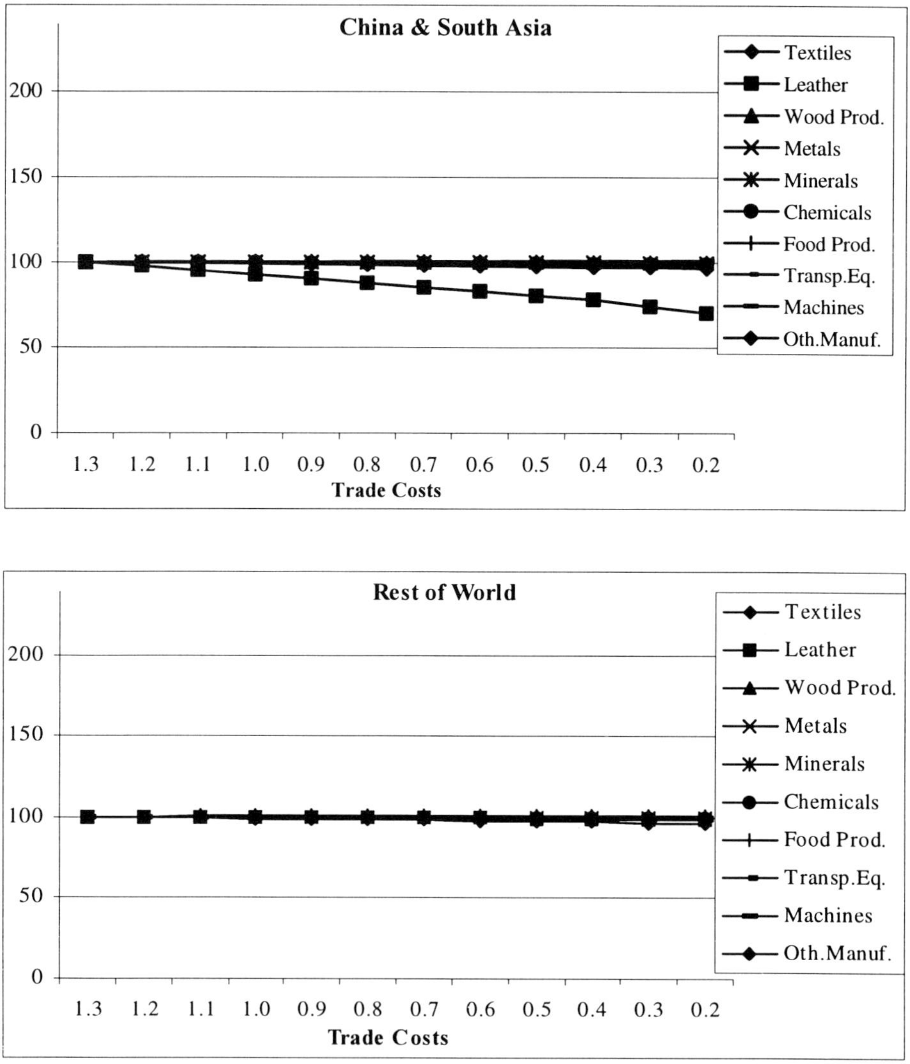

Figure 4. Production volume changes in the non-EEA regions (China and Rest of World)

The figure also shows the production effects on China and South Asia (CSA), and the US and Canada (UC). Putting the leather sector to the side for a moment, the figure shows that CSA and UC production display slightly negative production effects or no effects at all. Again this is in line with the fact that the EEA market accounts for less than 4% of UC sales and less than 3% of CSA sales. It is not, therefore, surprising that changes within the EEA have only a minor impact on UC and CSA industry.

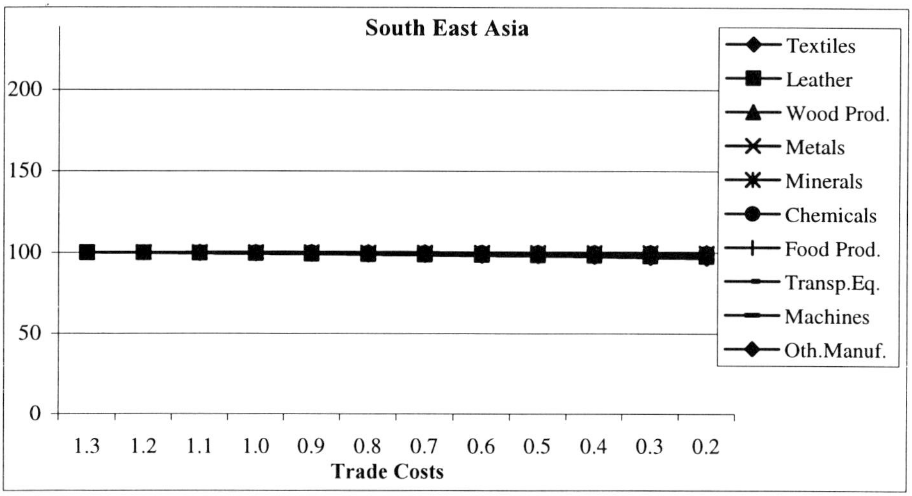

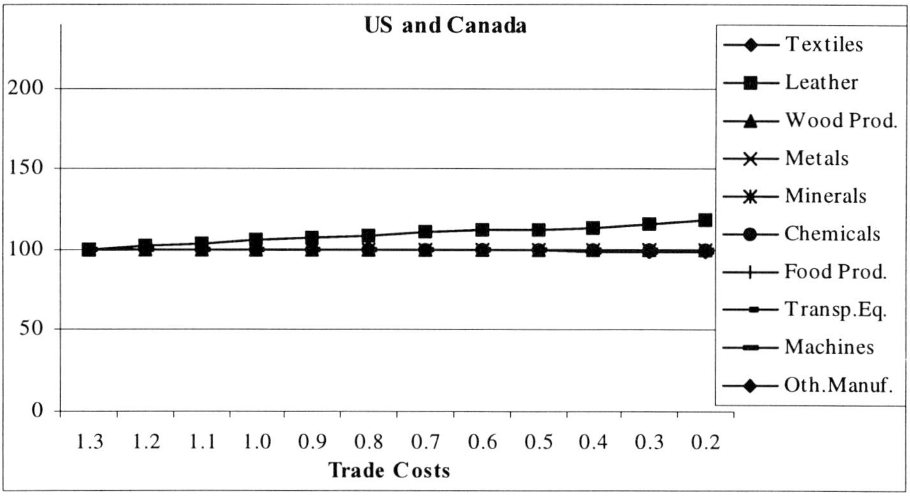

Figure 5. Production volume changes in the non-EEA regions (Southeast Asia & N.America)

The figures also reveal unexpected developments in the leather sector. The dominant impact in this sector is a spectacular rise in Europe South's production and an important drop in the leather output of Europe Central and Europe West. The impacts on the non-member regions are all much milder, including the unexpected rise in North American production. The big shifts in leather production are somewhat curious at first sight, but they follow from the peculiar nature of the sector. Three features act in concert to encourage large production shifts in the leather sector. The sector is quite competitive (since it has close to constant returns to scale) yet trade costs are quite low (a third of those in textiles) and intermediate inputs are quite important. These factors combine to amplify even the small changes in competitiveness caused by the discriminatory trade cost reductions in Europe.

Table 7. Regional distribution of total manufacture sales (percent of total sales from the regions in the left-hand column to the regions across the top row)

	EW	EC	ES	EN	EEA	EE	FS	CSA	SEA	UC	ROW
EW	69.3	11.2	6.9	1.4	88.8	0.5	0.3	0.5	2.5	3.6	3.7
EC	11.9	71.3	5.5	1.9	90.6	1.4	0.6	0.4	2.4	2.5	1.9
ES	8.1	7.0	78.0	0.6	93.7	0.6	0.4	0.2	1.3	1.8	2.1
EN	8.6	7.9	2.7	73.5	92.7	0.5	0.5	0.4	1.8	2.6	1.4
EE	3.6	10.5	3.6	1.0	18.7	74.8	1.2	0.6	0.9	0.8	3.1
FS	0.7	0.9	0.5	0.4	2.5	0.5	94.3	1.3	0.7	0.3	0.5
CSA	1.1	0.9	0.5	0.1	2.6	0.1	0.6	82.0	7.2	4.7	2.9
SEA	1.3	1.2	0.5	0.2	3.2	0.1	0.1	1.6	87.5	5.3	2.3
UC	1.8	0.9	0.5	0.2	3.4	0.1	0.1	0.4	3.1	89.4	3.5
ROW	1.4	0.9	0.8	0.1	3.2	0.2	0.1	0.5	2.2	4.1	89.8

Source: CGE model. See Table 1 for regional abbreviations.

Figure 6 shows the impact of our simulated change in intra-EEA trade costs on the two regions – namely Europe East (EE) and the Former Soviet Republics (FS) – that would be most likely to be affected, given their geographic proximity. What we see from the top panel of the figure is that the impact on the Former Soviet Republics is quite limited, apart from the idiosyncratic leather sector. The reason again follows from the Table 7 sales shares. For the most part FS industry sells in the FS, so the EEA's internal trade cost adjustments have little impact on FS output.

The one region that is significantly affected is Central and Eastern Europe (EE), as the bottom panel of Figure 6 shows. Again, this result follows naturally from the fact that EE industry depends heavily on the West European markets for exports. From Table 7 we see that almost a fifth of EE manufactured goods are sold in the EEA markets, with Europe Central (EC) being a particularly important customer. Plainly, the EE volume of production drops in every sector. Moreover, the drop is largest in transport equipment, a sector marked by both a high intermediate input share and significant scale economies.

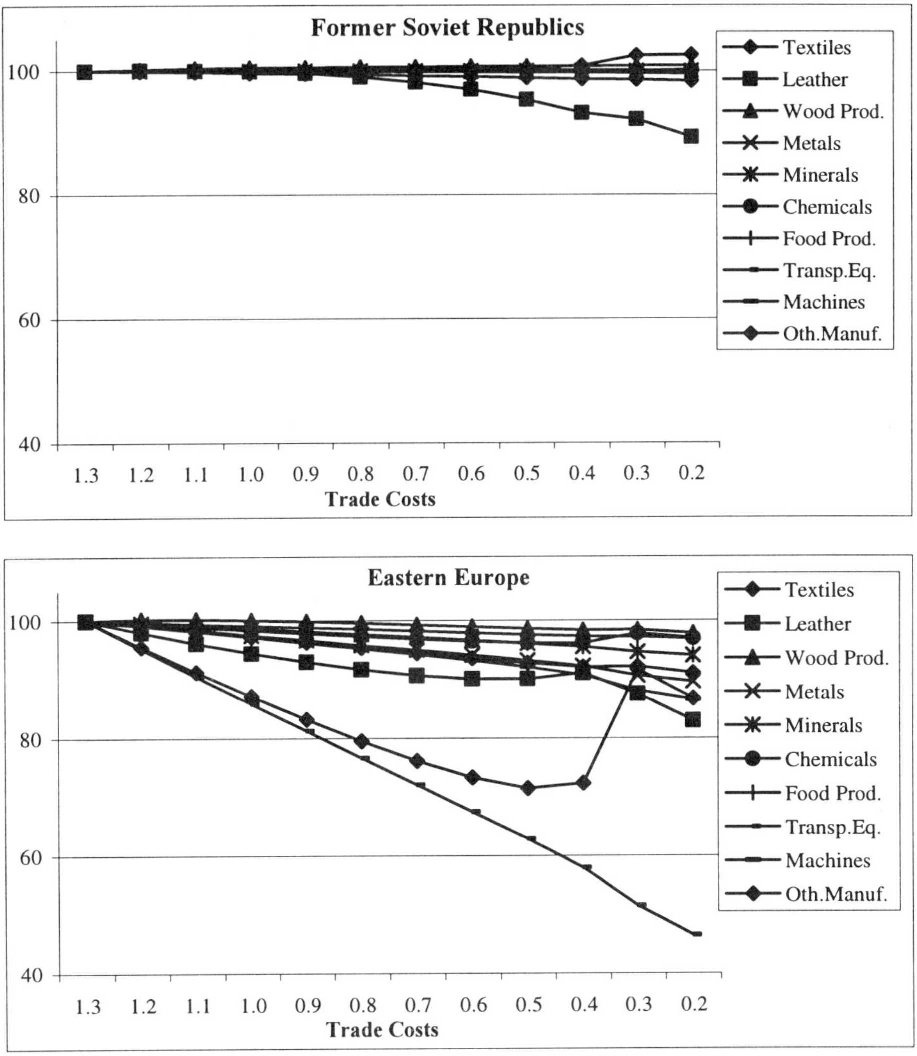

Figure 6. Production volume changes in Eastern Europe and Former USSR

It is also noteworthy that the textile sector displays very non-monotonic behaviour. More precisely, EE textile production generally falls as EEA discriminatory liberalisation proceeds (as expected), however when the trade costs move from 40% of the base case level to 30%, EE experiences a large increase in textile production. This increase can be thought of as the external "echo" of the internal catastrophic collapse of textile production in Europe Central (see Figure 2). As textile production in Europe Central – EE's major Western European trading partner – declines, Europe East producers suddenly find themselves faced with many fewer competitors in the Europe Central market. Since Europe Central accounts for more than a third of the EEA GDP (see Table 6) this significantly benefits production in nearby East European producers. This finding broadly confirms the Puga-Venables emphasis on agglomeration effects. It illustrates how an agglomeration process causing regional disparity and catastrophic agglomeration within a CU, might lead to gains for outsiders.

4.4. Welfare and factor price effects for outsiders

A commonly expressed fear is that closer EU integration will harm outside countries, especially those that are heavily dependent upon EU markets, such as Norway and Switzerland. This is indeed a prediction of neoclassical customs union theory and of the new economic geography theory. The basic story is that outsiders will lose competitiveness relative to insiders, and to compensate for that, factor prices are forced down.

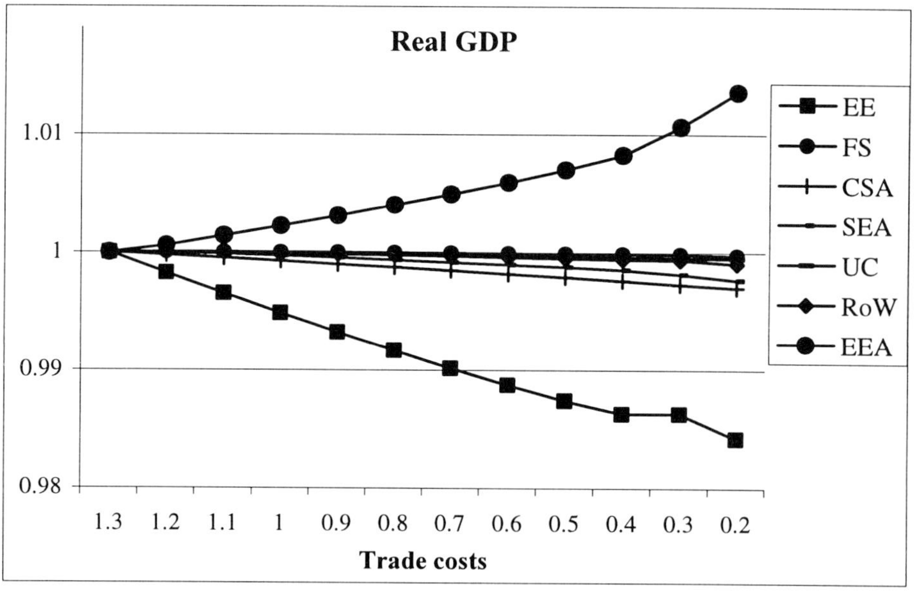

Figure 7. Real GDP effects, winners and losers (change from base case)

Our simulations confirm these predictions. Figure 7 shows the real GDP effects for all the outside regions, as well as the average for the insiders (called EEA). The figure clearly reveals that insiders gain and outsiders lose. However, the loss is only significant for Central and Eastern Europe (EE), as we should expect, based on the analysis above. Indeed, the percentage loss in GDP is approximately of the same magnitude as the gain to the EEA, namely almost 2% in each case.

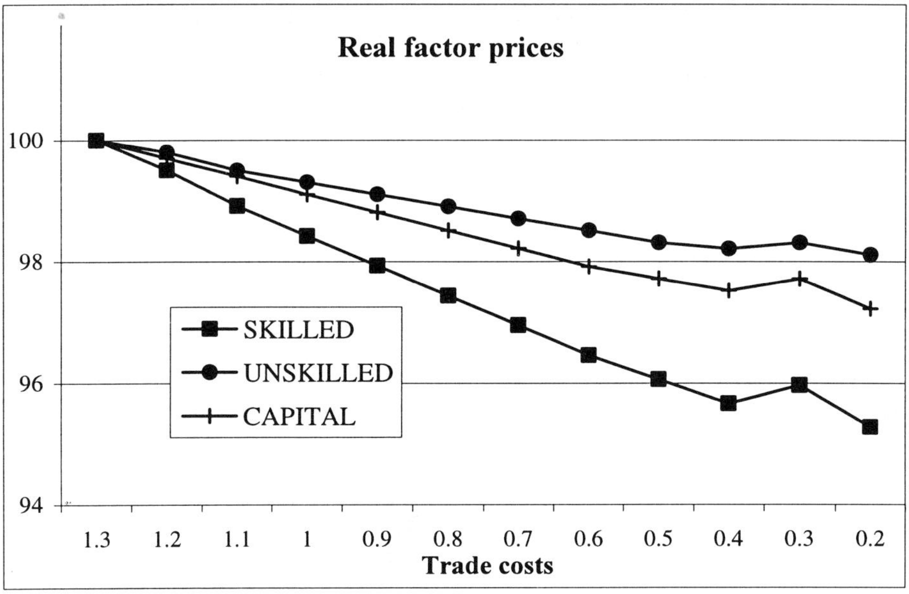

Figure 8. Real factor price effects (% change in real GDP from base case)

Figure 8 shows the real factor price effects for the Europe East region. It is interesting to note that although all real factor prices decline, the loss is less for unskilled labour than for the other factors. There is also an interesting element of non-monotonicity, coinciding with the range of trade costs where the catastrophic agglomeration in the textiles industry inside the EEA – and the accompanying growth in textiles in Eastern Europe – takes place.

5. CONCLUSIONS

The theoretical economic geography literature is useful for illustrating novel theoretical effects in an intellectually uncluttered setting. These models, however, have very few contact points with reality, so further research is needed to evaluate whether the effects highlighted by these model--catastrophic agglomeration and non-monotonic location effect, for example--are theoretical aberrations of highly specific models, or important effects that help us explain real world events. One way forward would be to empirically estimate the impact of agglomeration forces, as in Midelfart Knarvik and Steen (1999) and Amiti (1997). An alternate route, the one pursued in this paper, is to theoretically investigate the main results in a more realistic model, namely a CGE model calibrated to real data.

The focus of this paper is on the location effects of preferential trade arrangements on non-members, i.e. outsiders, and as such it is best seen as a complement to the earlier work by Forslid, Haaland and Midelfart Knarvik (1999). The main theory piece on this topic is Puga and Venables (1997). Using a very simple two-sector, three-nation model, Puga and Venables is one of the economic geography models that predict that agglomeration forces might foster regional disparity within the preferential trading bloc. In particular, production in both members will rise with the margin of preference, but only up to a point. Beyond this point, the so-called break point, industry in the bloc agglomerates mainly or entirely in one of the two member nations. This catastrophic agglomeration initially harms the outsiders, but further raising the preference margin actually increases outsider's production before decreasing it again.

In our 14-sector, 10-region model, we do find broad confirmation for the Puga-Venables effects when we simulate changes in the degree of preferential liberalisation among EEA members. For instance, three of the four sectors that are marked by very strong region agglomeration also have average or above average usage of intermediate inputs. We also find a catastrophic collapse in one sector (textiles) that is marked by strong input-output linkages. Moreover, this collapse within the bloc has important ramifications for production in one outside region, namely the Central and Eastern European countries (EE). Interestingly, we find that the collapse within the EEA is good for EE textile production. The reason is that our model has a more realistic trade cost structure and the collapse moves EEA textile production out of Europe Central and to Europe South. Since the EEs are very close to Europe Central (Austria, Denmark, Germany, and Switzerland) and this market is very large, the collapse actually boosts the competitiveness of EE textile firms.

Overall our findings suggest that the simple models of the economic geography literature miss important elements. The most important of these is comparative advantage and real trade costs differences. In the simplest economic geography models, regions are ex ante symmetric so comparative advantage never appears. In the real world nations and sectors are marked by important differences in factor intensity and factor endowments. As trade costs come down, these neoclassical forces take over.

REFERENCES

Allen, C., M. Gasiorek and A. Smith (1998), The Competition Effects of the Single Market in Europe, Economic Policy, 27, p. 439 – 486.

Amiti, M. (1997), Specialisation Patterns in Europe, CEP Discussion Paper No. 363, London School of Economics.

Baldwin, R. E., J. F. Francois and R. Portes (1997), The Costs and Benefits of Eastern Enlargement: the Impact on the EU and Central Europe, Economic Policy, 24, p. 125-176.

Baldwin, R. E., R. Forslid and J. I. Haaland (1996), Investment Creation and Investment Diversion in Europe, The World Economy, 19, p. 635-659.

Baldwin, R. E. (1994), Towards an Integrated Europe, Centre for Economic Policy Research, London

Baldwin, R. E. and A. J. Venables (1995), Regional Economic Integration, in Grossmank, G. and K. Rogoff (eds.), Handbook of International Economics, Vol. III, Amsterdam: Elsevier.

Bhagwati, J., P. Krishna, and A. Panagariya (1999), Trading Blocs: Alternative Approaches to Analysing Preferential Trade Arrangements, MIT Press.

Cawley, R. and M. Davenport (1988), Partial Equilibrium Calculations of the Impact of Internal Market Barriers in the European Community, in Commission of the European Communities, Research on the cost of non-Europe, Vol. 2, Studies on the Economics of Integration, Luxembourg.

Davis, D. R. (1998), The Home Market, Trade and Industrial Structure, American Economic Review, 88, p. 1264-1276.

EFTA (1994), European Economic Integration. Effects of “1992” on the Services Sectors of the EFTA Countries, EFTA occasional papers, no 49.

Feenstra, R. C. (1997), World Trade Flows, 1970-1992, with Production and Tariff Data, NBER Working Paper no. 5910.

Forslid, R. and I. Wooton (1999), Comparative Advantage and the Location of Production, CEPR Discussion Paper no. 2118.

Forslid, R., J. I. Haaland and K. Midelfart-Knarvik (1999), A U-shaped Europe: A Simulation Study of Industrial Location, CEPR Discussion paper no. 2247.

Forslid, R., J. I. Haaland, O. Mæstad and K. H. Midelfart Knarvik (1999), Integration and Transition: Scenarios for Location of Production and Trade in Europe, NHH Discussion Paper no. 13/99.

Fujita, M., P. R. Krugman and A. J. Venables (1999), The Spatial Economy: Cities, Regions and International Trade, MIT Press.

Gasiorek, M., A. Smith and A. J. Venables (1991), Competing the Internal Market in the EC: Factor Demands and Comparative Advantage, in Venables and Winters (eds.), European Integration: Trade and Industry, Cambridge University Press.

Gasiorek, M., A. Smith and A. J. Venables (1992), '1992': Trade and Welfare - a General Equilibrium Analysis, in Winters, A. (ed.), Trade Flows and Trade Policy after '1992', CEPR and Cambridge University Press.

Haaland, J. I. and V. D. Norman (1992), Global Production Effects of European Integration, in Winters, A. (ed.), Trade Flows and Trade Policy after '1992', CEPR and Cambridge University Press.

Haaland, J. I., H. J. Kind, K. H. Midelfart Knarvik and J. Torstensson (1999), What Determines the Economic Geography of Europe? CEPR Discussion paper no. 2072.

Helpman, E. (1995), The Size of Regions, Working Paper no. 14-95, The Foerder Institute of Economic Research.

Keuschnigg, C. and W. Kohler (1996), Austria in the European Union: Dynamic Gains from Integration and Distributional Implications, Economic Policy, 22, p. 155 – 212.

Krugman, P. R. (1980), Scale Economies, Product Differentiation, and the Pattern of Trade, American Economic Review, 70, p. 950-959.

Krugman, P. R. (1991), Increasing Returns and Economic Geography, Journal of Political Economy, 99, p. 483-499.

Krugman, P. R. and A. J. Venables (1995), Globalization and the Inequality of Nations, Quarterly Journal of Economics, 110, p. 857-879.

Maskus, K. E. and M. Penubarti (1995), How Trade Related are Intellectual Property Rights? Journal of International Economics, 39, p. 227-248.

Midelfart Knarvik, K. H., H. Overman, S. Redding and A. J. Venables (1999), The Location of Production in the EU, Unpublished manuscript.

Midelfart Knarvik, K. H. and F. Steen (1999), Self-Reinforcing Agglomerations? An Empirical Industry Study, Scandinavian Journal of Economics.

Pomfret, R. (1997), The Economics of Regional Trading Arrangements, Clarendon Press, Oxford.

Pratten, C. (1988), A Survey of Economies of Scale, in Commission of the European Communities, Research on the Cost of non-Europe, Vol. 2, Studies on the Economics of Integration, Luxembourg.

Puga, D. and A. J. Venables (1996), The Spread of Industry: Spatial Agglomeration in Economic Development, Journal of the Japanese and International Economies, 10, p. 440-464.

Puga, D. and A. J. Venables (1997), Preferential Trading Arrangements and Industrial Location, Journal of International Economics, 43, p. 347-368.

Venables, A. J. (1996), Equilibrium Locations of Vertically Linked Industries, International Economic Review, 37, p. 341-359.

JOSEPH FRANCOIS

FACTOR MOBILITY, ECONOMIC INTEGRATION, AND THE LOCATION OF INDUSTRY*

This paper examines the importance of factor mobility within countries for the manifestation of agglomeration and location effects emphasized in the new economic geography literature. Working with a model of trade under monopolistic competition, the relationship of factor mobility (in particular labor) to industry adjustment and relocation is developed analytically, and then illustrated with a computational example. The computational exercise involves a notional reduction in trading costs within the European Union.

1. INTRODUCTION

Division of labor models are now a standard analytical tool, along with competitive general equilibrium models like the Ricardian, Heckscher-Ohlin-Samuelson, and Ricardo-Viner models, in public finance, trade, growth, development, and macroeconomics. Unlike competitive general equilibrium models, division of labor models are characterized by multiple equilibria, instability, and emergent structural properties under parameter transformation. An important area of research with this class of models involves the implications of trading costs. This includes Venables (1996a,b) and Krugman and Venables (1995, 1996). Trading costs are used, alternatively, to represent actual trading costs (transport, paperwork, etc.) and government imposed costs, like tariffs and non-tariff barriers. Trading costs have been shown to have important implications for the geographic dispersion of economic activity. In contrast to the recent emphasis on trading costs, this paper focuses instead on the relevance of the mobility of labor between sectors (or generically the ease with which production can be shifted between sectors) for the re-location of industry and adjustment costs associated with economic integration.

Division of labor models play a central role in international trade theory, public economics, regional/urban economics, and macroeconomics (both growth theory and business cycle theory). In international trade theory the model has been used to study both trade patterns (Ethier 1979, 1982; Markusen 1988, 1989; van Marrewikj et al. 1997) and trade policy (Markusen 1990; Francois 1992, 1994; Lovely 1997). One of the most interesting recent applications uses the multiple equilibrium property of these models to derive north-south trade structures endogenously (Markusen 1991; Krugman and Venables, 1995; Krugman, 1995; Venables 1996; Puga and Venables, 1996; Matsuyama 1996).

This class of models (characterized by firm level product differentiation) has also been replacing national product differentiation models (known as Armington

* Thanks are due to Richard Baldwin, James Markusen and Douglas Nelson for helpful comments.

R.E. Baldwin and A. Brunetti (eds.), Economic Impact of EU Membership on Entrants, 73–87.

models) in computational modeling of regional and multilateral liberalization. (See Francois and Roland-Holst 1997). Arguments for following this approach have been offered by Norman (1990) and Brown (1987). Some of the properties of this type of model have been explored computationally by Brown (1994). Generic properties (including multiple equilibria and non-convexities) have been examined in Francois and Nelson (1998).

This paper examines the importance of factor mobility within countries for the manifestation of agglomeration and location effects emphasized in the new economic geography literature and the older literature on trade with scale economies. The result is the integration of issues covered in the older literature on factor mobility (see for example Casas 1984) with the more recent literature on agglomeration. An analytical model is first developed in Section 2. This involves a reformulation of the standard monopolistic competition model that greatly simplifies the analytical properties of the model, wherein we work with "variety scaled" rather than physical products. Working with this model, stability and adjustment properties are explored in Section 3. The relationship of factor mobility (in particular labor) to industry adjustment and relocation is then developed analytically in Section 4. A more complex computational model (involving multiple regions and sectors and intermediate linkages) is employed in Section 5. The computational exercise in section 5 involves a notional reduction in trading costs within the European Union. Conclusions are offered in Section 6.

2. VARIETY SCALING

We start with a representation of trade under monopolistic competition that involves "variety-scaled" rather than physical output. This approach buys us a great deal of analytical simplicity when we turn to stability properties and the scope for inter-sectoral adjustment. Differentiated goods may be differentiated consumer goods, or producer goods that are assembled before the final good is sold locally. In either interpretation, there will be variety-related benefits to location. These benefits are further magnified in the computational section of the paper, where we also add intermediate linkages, reinforcing the advantages of location.

We first assume that individual firms producing variety x_j of good X are monopolists working under a homothetic cost function defined over an input price vector ω and subject to a fixed cost ad constant marginal cost. Free entry forces the standard average cost pricing solution, alongside the monopoly markup rule. The elasticity of is derived from standard S-D-S preferences, and hence is a constant value σ (which also equals the elastiticity of substitution. Formally, in the X sector, we have the following cost and price relationships:

$$C(x) = [\alpha + \beta \cdot x] \cdot f(\omega) \tag{1}$$

$$P \cdot \left[1 - \frac{1}{\sigma}\right] = \beta \cdot f(\omega) \tag{2}$$

$$P = \left[\frac{\alpha}{x} + \beta\right] \cdot f(\omega) \tag{3}$$

In equations (1)-(3), P denotes price, C(.) denotes total cost for the firm producing x, and f(ω) is the linear homothetic cost function for a bundle of inputs (designated Z below). Taken together, equations (2) and (3) mean that firms are of an identical size (we have a symmetric equilibrium), and that change in industry scale will be proportionate to change in the number of varieties in the industry. In particular, we will have:

$$x = \frac{\alpha \cdot (\sigma - 1)}{\beta} \tag{4}$$

$$P = \frac{\beta \cdot f(\omega) \cdot \sigma}{(\sigma - 1)} \tag{5}$$

The scale of individual firms will be fixed, while the equilibrium price for each individual variety will be a linear function of the cost of input bundle Z. The demand for individual varieties follows from the standard S-D-S aggregation function:

$$q = \left[\sum_{i=1}^{n} g \cdot x_i^{\rho}\right]^{1/\rho} \tag{6}$$

In equation (6), the term g denotes a constant applied to each variety. The elasticity of substitution of substitution will be $\sigma = 1/(1-\rho)$, where $0<\rho<1$. For the moment, assume that we have two sources of varieties, designated 1 and 2. These sets of varieties originate in different countries. We will maintain the large group assumption throughout (i.e. demand elasticities remain unchanged), but now we subdivide equation (6) to reflect the split sourcing of varieties. Note that, as long as we maintain the assumption of symmetry across firms from source 1 and 2, then we will consume identical quantities over all source r varieties.

$$q = \left[n_1 \cdot g_1 \cdot x_1^{\rho} + n_2 \cdot g_2 \cdot x_2^{\rho}\right]^{1/\rho} \tag{7}$$

In equation (7), the subscript now designates (identical) varieties from a given national source, and n_r denotes the number of varieties associated with that source. Note that we have a CES weight that applies identical across varieties from a given source. We next modify equation (7) so that it is defined over aggregate physical quantities (i.e. X=nx).

$$q = \left[n_1^{1-\rho} \cdot g_1 \cdot X_1^{\rho} + n_2^{1-\rho} \cdot g_2 \cdot X_2^{1-\rho}\right]^{1/\rho} \tag{8}$$

If we hold variety constant, then equation (8) is operationally identical to an Armington aggregation function. We will next write equation (8) purely in terms of variety-scaled quantities V, so that we can simplify the demand side of the model by specifying it in terms of variety-scaled output. This involves one last rearrangement of equation (8).

$$q = \left[g_1 \cdot V_1^{\rho} + g_2 \cdot V_2^{\rho}\right]^{1/\rho} \tag{9}$$

$$V_i = n_i^{1-\rho} \cdot X_i \tag{10}$$

On the demand side, we will work directly with equation (9). Variety effects are embodied in the variety-scaled quantity defined by equation (10), which we will treat as a supply-side phenomenon. Written in this way, variety works like a regional quality or scale effect that is realized at the industry level.

We turn next to the supply side of the model. We focus on sectoral output to start, but will later embed this structure into a multi-sector framework. On the supply side, assume that in country i bundles Z_i are available for production of varieties x_i of good X. From equation (4), we then have the following:

$$n_i = \frac{Z_i}{2 \cdot \alpha_i \cdot (\sigma - 1)} \tag{11}$$

$$X_{iT} = \frac{Z_i}{\alpha_i \cdot \beta_i} \tag{12}$$

where X_{iT} represents total physical production of X in country i. Because expansion of the X sector involves entry of identically sized firms, both physical output and variety are linear in input of bundles Z. Putting these two terms together with equation (10), we can derive the implicit sectoral production function for variety-scaled output V.

$$V_{iT} = \frac{2 \cdot \alpha_i \cdot (\sigma - 1)^{\frac{\rho-1}{\rho}}}{\alpha_i \cdot \beta_i} \cdot Z_i^{1/\rho} \tag{13}$$

or to simplify

$$V_{iT} = A \cdot Z_i^{1/\rho} = \Theta(Z_i) \tag{14}$$

Taken together, equations (9) and (14) let us simplify (in a useful way) the mathematics of production and trade with specialization-based returns to scale. Basically, sectoral demand is CES and defined over variety-scaled quantities from all sources, while sectoral supply of variety-scaled varieties exhibits a form of external scale economies common in the literature. Our representation of the model works, in reduced form, like a standard Armington model with external scale economies. Working with Armington-type quantities helps in isolating the stability properties of this class of models, and their sensitivity to factor mobility issues.

3. THE SUPPLY SIDE: STABILITY AND THE SCALE OF LOCAL ADJUSTMENT

We now want to embed the production side of the model into a general equilibrium framework. This will allow us to explore, analytically, the relationship between local agglomeration effects (due to variety) and the adjustment of output to price shocks. To do this, we assume a transformation technology between bundles Z and a homogeneous good Y. Factor markets are assumed competitive, so that the price of Z will correspond to the marginal rate of transformation between Z and Y. Furthermore, because we have average cost pricing vis-à-vis equation (14), we can also map the supply-side price of V directly to the price of Z, and hence to the supply response in V and Z as we move along the production possibility frontier.

Our transformation technology, in reduced form, is represented as follows:

$$Y_i = \gamma_i(Z_i) \qquad \gamma' < 0, \gamma'' < 0 \tag{15}$$

The price of bundles will be the following:

$$\frac{P_{Zi}}{P_{Yi}} = \frac{f(\omega)_i}{P_{Yi}} = -\gamma' \tag{16}$$

Average cost pricing means that we will also have

$$P_{Vi} = Z_i^{1-1/\rho} \cdot P_{Zi} = -\gamma' \cdot Z_i^{1-1/\rho} \cdot P_{Yi} \tag{17}$$

Making a substitution of (17) into (16) and solving for percent changes, we can derive the following.

$$\hat{P}_{Vi} - \hat{P}_{Yi} = Z_i \cdot \left[\frac{\gamma''}{\gamma'} - \frac{\Theta''}{\Theta'} \right] \cdot \hat{Z}_i \tag{18}$$

Equation (18) relates changes in equilibrium supply of Z to changes in the relative prices of V and Y. The first term captures the relative curvature of the production possibility frontier (defined over bundles and Y), while the second term captures the relative curvature of the Θ function, which depends on variety effects. In a constant returns to scale model, the second term vanishes, and we simply have a variation of the classic Jones-type equation relating changes in supply to changes in relative prices. In the present setting, however, the presence of variety-specialization effects complicates the analytical mix.

Consider the case where we have local stability (in the sense that the sign of equation (18) is positive). For a policy shock ultimately manifested, at least to producers, as a shift in producer prices, the corresponding magnitude of the shift in output will depend on how strong the scale effect is, as transmitted through the Θ function. The stronger it is, the greater the output response associated with a given price change, if equation (17) is to hold. In other words, even for local adjustment from one stable equilibrium to another, how local such adjustment to a price shock will actually be will depend on the magnitude of scale effects. The larger the scale effects, the greater the corresponding shift in resources associated with an observed shift in relative prices. Of course, if the sign of equation (18) is negative, then the local equilibrium is unstable, with a well-known potential for corner solutions (Francois and Nelson 1998).

The basic properties of the general equilibrium system are illustrated in Figure 1. In the lower left quadrant, the γ function maps the transformation between Y and Z. The upper left quadrant provides a mapping from Z to V through the Θ function. Using the Θ function, combined with a mapping of Y to the horizontal axis, we then have the product transformation frontier, in terms of Z and V, mapped in the upper right quadrant. For a given Θ function, the properties of the Y and V frontier will depend critically on the properties of the γ function. This is the focus of the next section.

4. FACTOR MOBILITY AND OUTPUT ADJUSTMENT

We now turn to the issue of local adjustment, and the role of factor mobility. By factor mobility, we are not referring to cross-country movement of factors. While this is an important theme in the recent geography literature and older scale economy literature (Krugman and Venables 1995; Markusen 1988; Rivera-batiz and Rivera-batiz 1991), our concern instead is the ability of factors (and in particular labor) to move between sectors within a country as employment opportunities shift.

In terms of equation (18), the inter-sectoral mobility of labor can be examined through its impact on the curvature of the γ function.

To develop this issue further, we will impose more structure on the γ function. In particular, we follow the older literature on inter-sectoral factor mobility (see for example Casas 1984; Hertel and Tsigas 1996) and assume that a constant elasticity of transformation will characterize our ability to shift resources between the Z and Y sector. In generic terms, this may follow from underlying differences in technology across sectors, as well as from factor mobility. However, for the moment, we focus on factor mobility.

Formally, the γ function that can be derived from a CET is represented as follows:

$$Y = \gamma(Z) = \left[\frac{Q^{\phi}}{a} - \frac{b}{a} \cdot Z^{\phi} \right]^{1/\phi} \tag{19}$$

In equation (19), the term $\varphi>1$, and we will have an elasticity of substitution along the ZY frontier that is concave to the origin, and characterized by a constant elasticity or transformation $\Omega=1/(\phi-1)$, where $1<\Omega\leq\infty$. With an infinite transformation elasticity, the transformation frontier is linear.

Given equations (14) and (19), equation (18) then can be written as follows:

$$\hat{P}_{Vi} - \hat{P}_{Yi} = Z_i \cdot \left[\left\{ (\phi - 1) \cdot (1 + Z^{\phi} \cdot (b/a) \right\} + \left\{ 1 - 1/\rho \right\} \right] \cdot \hat{Z}_i \tag{20}$$

The first term in brackets {} captures the curvature of the CET, through the parameter ϕ and our location on the transformation frontier, while the second term captures variety scaling effects.

Note that in the large group case, with homothetic cost functions, the variety-scaling term is actually a constant, so that local stability ends up depending entirely on variations in the curvature of the transformation frontier. This actually characterizes much of the recent literature, which employs Ricardian single factor models (i.e. linear transformation surfaces). In effect, this approach assumes, in reduced form, that corner solutions will be highly likely, along the lines of Kemp's (1964) work on Ricardian models with external scale economies.

In the next section of the paper, we will employ equation (19), in a multi-sector general equilibrium model including intermediate linkages and monopolistic competition (aka a computational geography model) to examine the sensitivity of output adjustment to factor mobility. Before doing this, however, we turn in this section to a simpler example.

Assume we have one factor (call it labor), and assume further that the intersectoral mobility of labor is as defined in equation (19). The product transformation surface, for a range of values for ϕ (and assuming $\sigma=2$) is presented in Figure 2. In the Figure, the first "slice" of the surface is the pure Ricardian case, with a linear transform technology between Z and Y. We can see that the scale effects yield a purely convex transformation surface in variety-scaled space. Viewed in variety-scaled space, this class of model can be seen to be a variant of the models studied by Chipman (1970), Jones (1968), Ethier (1982b) and Gomory (1994). Labor is the only productive factor, and as a result the resource constraint in the lower left quadrant of Figure 1 takes the simple form of a straight line. As a result, the convex nature of the VY mapping follows strictly from the curvature of the Θ function. As the transformation elasticity falls below infinity, the increasing curvature of the underlying γ function dominates an increasingly large share of the surface, so that slices of the surface in Figure 2 associated with lower degrees of inter-sectoral factor mobility are characterized by largely concave (and stable) shapes. As will become evident in the next section, the impact of price and policy shocks on the location of activity (i.e. the shifts that occur in various countries across their transformation surface) will depend critically on the curvature of the γ function.

5. A COMPUTATIONAL EXAMPLE

We now turn to a computational example. This involves a large multi-region CGE model. The model includes monopolistic competition in industrial and service sectors as developed above. It also includes sluggish mobility of labor, through a CET as described in equation (19). The experiment involves a reduction in trading costs for intra-EU trade. However, in contrast to the recent literature on location, which focuses on trading cost ranges, our interest is instead in the implications of a range of parameter values characterizing labor mobility.

5.1. The Model

The model is a multi-sector general equilibrium model, characterized by intermediate linkages and monopolistic competition. It is a version of the GTAP model (Hertel 1996), modified to include imperfect competition exactly as developed in Sections 2 and 3 of this paper. (See Francois 1998). This means that Armington trade in industrial and service sectors, a feature of the standard GTAP model, is replaced with monopolistic competition. The Hertel and Francois papers provide full documentation on the theory and implementation of the model.[1]

Like most CGE models, this one is characterized by an input-output structure that explicitly links industries in a value added chain from primary goods, over continuously higher stages of intermediate processing, to the final assembling of goods and services for consumption. Inter-sectoral linkages are direct, like the input of steel in the production of transport equipment, and indirect, via intermediate use in other sectors. CGE models capture these linkages by modeling firms' use of

---

[1] The papers can be downloaded from www.agecon.purdue.edu/gtap, while the model files will be made available for the final version of this paper at www.intereconomics.com.francois. Note that there is a long history of including monopolistic competition in CGE models. Hence, under a different name, some CGE modellers have been working with "new geography" models since the early 1980s. See Francois and Roland-Holst (1997).

factors and intermediate inputs. The most important aspects of the model used here are the following: (i) it covers all world trade and production; and (ii) it allows for scale economies and imperfect competition. Consumer demand is generated from a representative regional household with Cobb-Douglas preferences over sectoral composites. This is a departure from the standard GTAP specification of demand.

The multi-region model used here divides the world into eight regions (Germany, Sweden, Denmark, Finland, the United Kingdom, the rest of the EU, EFTA, and the rest of world) each with 11 sectors (primary goods, food, textiles, clothing, wood, chemicals, metal products, autos, electronic goods, manufactures, and services.) Each sector consists of differentiated products, and consumer and firm demand for these are generated by CES preferences. Government services are produced through a Cobb-Douglas technology, which means that government expenditure shares over product categories are fixed. Consumption is defined as a Cobb-Douglas composite of private and government consumption.

Scale economies and monopolistic competition are modeled in manufacturing and services, exactly as developed in Section 2. In particular, based on evidence of scale economies (OECD 1997), we model sectors as being characterized by Chamberlinian large-group monopolistic competition for traded intermediate and final goods. Other sectors (primary products and food) are characterized by constant returns and perfect competition, ith output differentiated by regions (the Armington assumption). Formally, factors are combined according to a CES function, while intermediates are used in fixed proportions. Both approaches (Armington and monopolistic competition) have two significant ramifications: (i) intermediate input prices enters firms' cost functions, so price-raising trade barriers directly affect firms' costs, and (ii) firms' demands for each variety of intermediates, whether differentiated by region (Armington assumption) or firm (monopolistic competition) follows standard CES derived demand functions. With product differentiation in all sectors, the model supports two-way trade in all traded sectors. Trade and scale elasticities are reported in Table 1.

The cost of trade is modeled explicitly as consisting of a combination of trade and transport services. Revenue from non-frictional trade barriers are returned to the representative consumer in each region. This includes quota rents, which are generally modeled as accruing to exporters. Regional labor and capital supplies are assumed to be fixed. (Capital is held fixed so that we can focus on resource shifts, without the additional complication of resource accumulation.)

With the exception of substitution and scale elasticities, which are drawn from the literature (see Table 1), model parameters are calibrated to social accounting data from the 1999 revision of the Global Trade Analysis Project (GTAP) version 4 data base. The GTAP dataset includes information on national and regional input-output structure, bilateral trade flows, final demand patterns, and government intervention, and is benchmarked to 1995. Bilateral tariff data are based on World Bank and WTO data on pre- and post-Uruguay Round protection, and reflect differential bilateral weighting of detailed trade data within model sectors.

5.2. *The experiment*

The experiment involves a reduction in frictional trading costs within the European Union, corresponding to 2 percent of the value of trade. Sensitivity analysis is conducted vis-à-vis the elasticity of transformation for labor (both skilled and unskilled), which is ranged from infinity (i.e. perfect labor mobility) to 1 (i.e. very limited mobility.)

The basic results for this experiment are summarized in Tables 2 through 4. Table 2 reports national income effects. Table 3 reports an estimate of adjustment costs, and is calculated by taking the mean squared deviation in sectoral output within each country. Table 4 then reports for Denmark (a case of relatively large variations in output), the deviations in output by sector.

The general pattern of national income effects is almost completely unaffected by the value of the transformation elasticity (designated s in the tables). This is not the case, however, as we move to the sectoral reallocation of resources. For the smaller economies in the model, the mobility of labor makes a tremendous difference in terms of sector output. For example, the mean squared deviation in output is far larger in the full mobility case for Denmark, Sweden, Finland, and Germany. As we move to partial mobility, this measure of adjustment costs falls dramatically. Significantly, the impact on EFTA also depends critically on our measure of mobility. EFTA is a region (primarily Norway and Switzerland) that does not benefit from the reduction in trading costs with the European Union. Even so, because it trade is highly focused on the European Union, it experiences effects similar to those of smaller European Union members (like Denmark).

Finally, Table 4 reports changes in output by sector for Denmark across our range of transformation elasticities. What is striking is the pattern of sign reversals across a number of sectors. This reflects the strength of agglomeration effect, and the moderating effect of limitations on factor mobility. For example, the electronic goods sector shrinks dramatically, as production is drawn to other regions, under the full mobility scenario. However, as we limit mobility, the sector instead contracts. The chemicals sector, on the other hand, finds its ability to expand limited, so that the expansion in output falls as we limit factor mobility.

6. SUMMARY AND CONCLUSIONS

This paper has been concerned with the importance of labor mobility (or generally for the ease with which resources are shifted between sectors) for the re-location of industry and adjustment costs associated with economic integration. The problem has been examined analytically through a two-sector model with monopolistic competition, trade in intermediates, and an explicit transformation technology parameterized by a transformation elasticity that measures the ease with which resources can be shifted between sectors. A computational example is then developed, in which the theoretical structure developed here is imposed onto a standard computational general equilibrium model.

The recent literature has emphasized the importance of trading costs for industry re-location. It has been shown here, both through the analytical treatment of the issue and the computation example, that the flexibility with which resources can be shifted between sectors is also critical to realization of both the costs and benefits of economic integration. This means that labor mobility within countries has immediate relevance for assessment of likely agglomeration and scale-related benefits of economic integration.

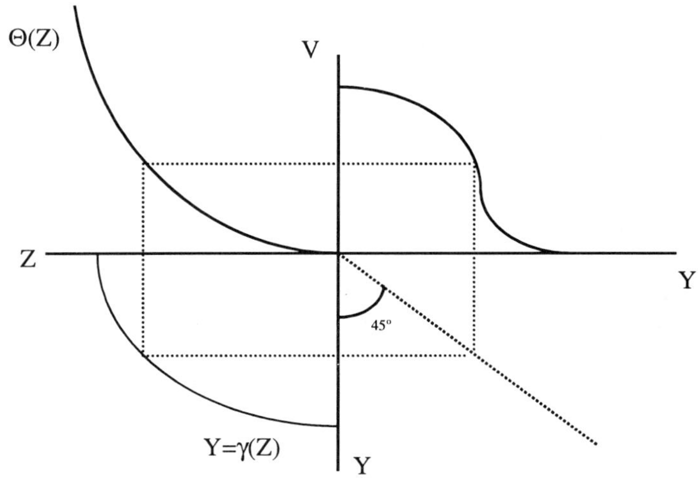

Figure 1. The general equilibrium system

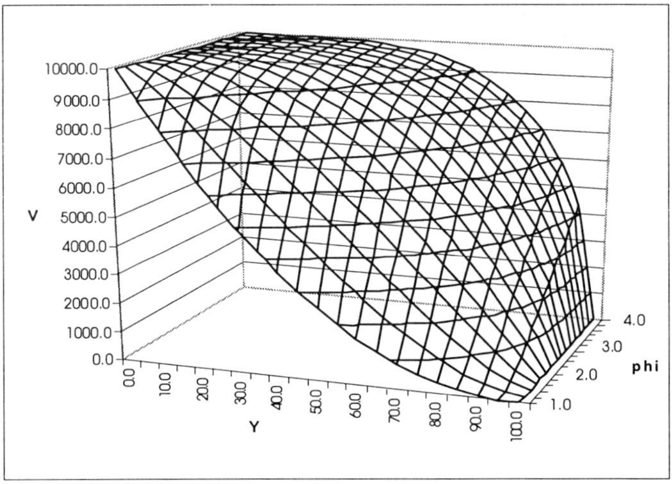

Figure 2. The CET transformation elasticity and the product transformation surface

Table 1. CGE model elasticities

	demand substitution (trade) elasticities	CDR	capital/labor substitution in value added
primary goods	5.60	0.00	0.20
food products	4.60	0.00	0.61
Textiles	8.31	0.12	1.26
Clothing	9.60	0.10	1.26
wood products	6.18	0.16	1.26
Chemicals	6.29	0.16	1.26
metal products	6.39	0.16	1.26
Autos	8.94	0.11	1.26
electronic goods	3.11	0.32	1.26
other manufactures	6.88	0.15	1.26
Services	4.76	0.21	1.40

note: demand elasticities for Armington sectors (where CRD=0) come from the GTAP database. Other substitution elasciticites are determined, under monopolistic competition, by the identity elasticity=1/CDR. The CDR is defined as (Average Cost-Marginal Cost)/Average Cost. CDRs are derived from recent OECD work (and firm level data) on markups, as detailed in Anderson et al 1999.

Table 2. National income effects (percent of GDP)

	s=inf	s=10	s=5	s=2	s=1
United Kingdom	0.30	0.28	0.28	0.27	0.27
Germany	0.24	0.25	0.25	0.25	0.25
Denmark	0.46	0.45	0.44	0.44	0.43
Finland	0.47	0.47	0.46	0.46	0.45
Sweden	0.38	0.51	0.50	0.50	0.50
Rest of EU	0.41	0.40	0.40	0.40	0.40
Total EU	0.35	0.35	0.35	0.34	0.34
EFTA	0.07	-0.03	-0.01	0.00	0.00
Rest of world	-0.01	-0.01	-0.01	-0.01	-0.01

Source: CGE model estimates.
Note: s denotes the CET transformation elasticity for labor movement between sectors.

Table 3. Adjustment cost index (mean squared deviation in sectoral output)

	s=inf	s=10	s=5	s=2	s=1
United Kingdom	2.84	1.53	1.21	0.90	0.74
Germany	8.12	0.91	0.73	0.52	0.42
Denmark	20.28	5.27	3.05	1.79	1.33
Finland	8.13	3.92	2.44	1.39	1.02
Sweden	14.24	3.74	2.13	1.12	0.80
Rest of EU	1.32	1.30	1.08	0.84	0.71
EU average	9.15	2.78	1.77	1.09	0.84
EFTA	34.61	2.02	1.10	0.56	0.36
Rest of world	8.12	0.91	0.73	0.52	0.42

Source: CGE model estimates.
Note: s denotes the CET transformation elasticity for labor movement between sectors.

Table 4. Output changes (percent) for Denmark

	s=inf	s=10	s=5	s=2	s=1	Factor income shares
primary	0.11	0.31	0.36	0.40	0.41	1.58
food	0.40	0.39	0.49	0.55	0.55	8.06
textiles	-35.93	4.18	1.67	0.87	0.71	0.48
clothing	-40.33	14.08	7.65	4.16	2.93	0.48
wood	3.94	3.32	2.88	2.07	1.61	1.07
chemicals	30.37	2.50	1.83	1.26	1.05	2.88
metals	-1.23	-0.35	0.02	0.20	0.24	2.20
autos	-0.92	2.95	3.00	2.26	1.82	0.22
electronics	-25.69	7.90	4.41	2.36	1.67	0.54
mnfc	-2.54	-1.10	-0.45	0.03	0.21	8.37
serv	-0.08	-0.05	-0.04	-0.02	-0.01	74.11

Source: CGE model estimates.
Note: s denotes the CET transformation elasticity for labor movement between sectors.

REFERENCES

Brown, D.K. (1994), Properties of Applied General Equilibrium Trade Models with Monopolistic Competition and Foreign Direct Investment, in Francois, J.F and C.R. Shiells (eds.), Modelling Trade Policy: AGE Models of North American Free Trade, New York: Cambridge University Press.

Brown, D.K. (1987), Tariffs, the Terms of Trade and National Product Differentiation, Journal of Policy Modelling, 9, p. 503-526.

Casas, F.R. (1984), Imperfect Factor Mobility: A Generalization and Synthesis of Two-Sector Models of International Trade, Canadian Journal of Economics, 17.

Chipman, J. (1970), External Economies of Scale and Competitive Equilibrium, Quarterly Journal of Economics, 84, p. 347-385.

Ethier, W. (1979), Internationally Decreasing Costs and World Trade. Journal of International Economics, 9, p. 1-24.

Ethier, W. (1982a), National and International Returns to Scale in the Modern Theory of International Trade, American Economic Review, 72, p. 388-405.

Ethier, W. (1982b), Decreasing Costs in International Trade and Frank Graham's Argument for Protection, Econometrica, 50, p. 1243-1268.

Francois, J. (1992), Optimal Commercial Policy with International Returns to Scale, Canadian Journal of Economics, 25, p. 184-195.

Francois, J. (1994), Global Production and Trade: Factor Migration and Commercial Policy with International Scale Economies, International Economic Review, 35, p. 565-581.

Francois, J. (1998), Scale Economies and Imperfect Competition in the GTAP Model, Global Trade Analysis Project Consortium Technical Paper.

Francois, J. and D.W. Roland-Holst (1997), Scale Economies and Imperfect Competition, in Francois, J.F. and K.A. Reinert (eds.), Applied Methods for Trade Policy Analysis: A Handbook, Cambridge: Cambridge University Press.

Francois, J. and D. Nelson (1998), A Geometry of Specilization, Centre for Economic Policy Research Discussion Paper.

Gomory, R. (1994), A Ricardo Model with Economies of Scale, Journal of Economic Theory, 62, p. 394-419.

Hertel, T, and M. Tsigas (1996), The Structure of the GTAP Model, in Hertel, T. (ed.), Global Trade Analysis, New York: Cambridge University Press.

Jones, R. (1968), Variable Returns to Scale in General Equilibrium Theory, International Economic Review, 9, p. 261-272.

Kemp, M.C. (1964), The Pure Theory of International Trade, Englewood Cliffs, N.J.: Prentice-Hall.

Krugman, P. (1995), Complexity and Emergent Structure in the International Economy, in Levinsohn, J., A. Deardorff, and R. Stern (eds.), New Directions in Trade Theory, Ann Arbor: University of Michigan Press.

Krugman, P. and A. Venables (1995), Globalisation and the Inequality of Nations, Quarterly Journal of Economics, 110, p. 857-880.

Lopes-de-Silanes, F., J. Markusen and T. Rutherford (1994), Complementarity and Increasing Returns in Intermediate Inputs, Journal of Development Economics, 45, p. 101-119.

Lovely, M. (1997), Playing by the New Subsidy Rules: Capital Subsidies as Substitutes for Sectoral Subsidies, Journal of International Economics, 43, p. 463-482.

Markusen, J. (1988), Production, Trade, and Migration with Differentiated, Skilled Workers, Canadian Journal of Economics, 21, p. 492-506.

Markusen, J. (1989), Trade in Producer Services and in Other Specialized Inputs, American Economic Review; 79, p. 85-95.

Markusen, J. (1990), Micro-Foundations of External Economies, Canadian Journal of Economics, 23, p. 495-508.

Markusen, J. (1991), First Mover Advantages, Blockaded Entry, and the Economics of Uneven Development, in Helpman E. and A. Razin (eds.), International Trade and Trade Policy, Cambridge: MIT Press.

Matsuyama, K. (1996), Why are There Rich and Poor Countries? Symmetry-Breaking in the World Economy, Journal of the Japanese and International Economies, 10, p. 419-439.

Norman, V.D. (1990), Assessing Trade and Welfare Effects of Trade Liberalization: A Comparison of Alternative Approaches to CGE Modelling with Imperfect Competition, European Economic Review, 34, p. 725-745.

Puga, D. and A. Venables (1996), The Spread of Industry: Spatial Agglomeration in Economic Development, Journal of the Japanese and International Economies, 10, p. 440-464.

Rivera-Batiz, F. and L. Rivera-Batiz (1991), The Effects of Direct Foreign Investment in the Presence of Increasing Returns Due to Specialization, Journal of Development Economics, 34, p. 287-307.

van Marrewikj, C., J. Stibora, A. de Vaal, and J.M. Viaene (1997), Producer Services, Comparative Advantage, and International Trade Patterns, Journal of International Economics, 42, p. 195-220.

Venables, A. (1996a), Trade Policy, Cumulative Causation, and Industrial Development, Journal of Development Economics, Vol. 49(1), p. 179-197.

Venables, A. (1996b), Equilibrium Location of Vertically Linked Industries, International Economic Review, 37, p. 341-358.

Venables, A. and P. Krugman (1996), Integration, Specialization, and Adjustment, European Economic Review, 40, p. 959-967.

JAMES R. MARKUSEN

FACTOR MOBILITY, ECONOMIC INTEGRATION, AND THE LOCATION OF INDUSTRY

A Comment

Francois's paper makes two separate contributions, and my first task is to try and distinguish between them. First, there is an analytical contribution in showing how the standard monopolistic-competition model can be manipulated into a more tractable form that resembles the older external-economies model. The second contribution is to discuss how the degree of internal mobility of factors (intersectoral factor mobility) within a country affects the responsiveness of the economy to changes in trade costs.

The first contribution is quite useful in that it can aid researchers in simplifying both theoretical and computational investigations by converting a seemingly more complicated problem into a simpler one. I am particularly pleased to see this personally, since I have made a similar point in some of my own work. The "new trade theory" and especially the so-called "new economic geography" is not nearly as novel as some researchers have claimed. Both literatures bear a closer relationship to older literatures which are rarely referenced.

Analytically, the "conversion" used by Francois changes a general-equilibrium problem with imperfect competition into essentially a competitive general-equilibrium problem with a positive production externality in one sector. The latter is often simpler to analyze and to compute, and it is easier to analyze the properties of the aggregate production set in particular. In the simple two-good case, the local and even global convexity of the production set can be determined, which is in turn an important determinant of the degree of specialization and the existence of multiple equilibria.

Now I will turn to the second contribution, and offer some microfoundations for the "reduced form" of the production frontier that Francois uses in his paper. Consider the simple two-good, three-factor model popular in trade theory, where each sector has a specific factor and the third factor, "labor" is mobile between sectors. The goods are X and Y, and the specific factors are referred to as "capital" and denoted K_x and K_y, which are fixed throughout the analysis. Labor is in fixed supply but freely mobile between sectors.

$$X = L_x^{\alpha} K_x^{1-\alpha}, \quad Y = L_y^{\alpha} K_y^{1-\alpha}; \quad L = L_x + L_y, \quad 0 \leq \alpha \leq 1 \qquad (1)$$

Invert the production functions to get labor demand as a function of outputs.

R.E. Baldwin and A. Brunetti (eds.), Economic Impact of EU Membership on Entrants, 89–91.

$$L_x = K_x^{\frac{\alpha-1}{\alpha}} X^{\frac{1}{\alpha}} \qquad L_y = K_y^{\frac{\alpha-1}{\alpha}} Y^{\frac{1}{\alpha}} \tag{2}$$

$$L_x = \left[K_x^{\frac{\alpha-1}{\alpha}} \right]^{\frac{1}{\alpha}} X^{\frac{1}{\alpha}} \qquad L_y = \left[K_x^{\frac{\alpha-1}{\alpha}} \right]^{\frac{1}{\alpha}} Y^{\frac{1}{\alpha}} \tag{3}$$

Summing these labor demands together, we have (fixed) total labor supply.

$$L^{\alpha} = \left[aX^{\frac{1}{\alpha}} + bY^{\frac{1}{\alpha}} \right]^{\alpha} \qquad a \equiv K_x^{\frac{\alpha-1}{\alpha}} \qquad b \equiv K_y^{\frac{\alpha-1}{\alpha}} \tag{4}$$

Equation (4) is recognized by all modelers as a constant elasticity of transformation (CET) function. This elasticity of transformation is given by $\sigma = \alpha/(1-\alpha)$, and approaches infinity as α approaches 1. The latter is of course the case of the linear production frontier of the Ricardian model in which labor is the only (meaningful) factor of production. A value of $\alpha = 1/2$ gives an elasticity of transformation equal to one.

Equations (1) and (4) are useful for providing microfoundations for Francois' suggestion that internal factor mobility determines the flatness of the production frontier and hence the responsiveness of the economy to changes in trade costs. Instead of interpreting the K's as a different factor, simply interpret them as the amount of labor and other factors that, for whatever reason, is stuck in a sector and cannot move in response to price changes. What the above analysis tells us is that it is not the quantities of the factors that are stuck that matters for the transformation elasticity and frontier flatness, but rather the share parameter α in the production function between the mobile and the stuck factors. The higher is α, the less "stickiness" matters for the responsiveness of of production to price changes.

To interpret it another way, recall that for Cobb-Douglas production functions α is the share of factor payments going to labor and $(1 - \alpha)$ is the share going to the fixed factor. The analysis shows that it is the value share of the fixed factor that matters, not the physical quantity. But that is fine, since the value share is much more easily measured in any case. The conclusion is then that the smaller the value share of the fixed factor (the larger is α), the more responsive production will be to price changes.

We can now complete the analogy by converting (4) into an explicit function as done in Francois' paper.

$$Y = \left[\left(\frac{L}{K_y^{1-1/\alpha}} \right) - \left(\frac{K_x}{K_y} \right)^{\frac{\alpha-1}{\alpha}} X^{\frac{1}{\alpha}} \right]^{\alpha} \tag{5}$$

Continuing, Francois uses V to denote actual output and what I call X above is essentially what he calls factor bundles (Z). Replace my X in (5) with Z and we have Francois' equation (19). Converting Z (or my X) to V, we have:

$$V = cX^{1/\rho} \qquad 0 < \rho \le 1 \tag{6}$$

$$Y = \left[\left(\frac{L}{K_y^{\,1-1/\alpha}} \right) - \left(\frac{K_x}{K_y} \right)^{\frac{\alpha-1}{\alpha}} c^{\rho} V^{\frac{\rho}{\alpha}} \right]^{\alpha} \tag{7}$$

where my α is equivalent to Francois' 1/ρ. We can note two special cases in which the global curvature is determined. If there are not variety/scale effects, ρ = 1, then the production frontier is globally concave provided α < 1 (the production set is globally convex). If the value share of the fixed factor is zero (α = 1) and there are scale/variety effects (0 < ρ < 1), the production frontier is globally convex.

I have only one final comment, which is a question and confusion. Francois' focuses on the supply output/price relationship in discussing specialization and stability, and seems to suggest that a negative price/output relationship (negatively-sloped supply curve) indicates instability. But we need to remember that the goods of each country are imperfect substitutes for the goods of the other country, and hence the demand function always has a negative slope as well. As the goods become poorer substitutes, the supply function is more likely to have a negative slope, but this same change makes the demand curve more negatively sloped as well. Thus the question of stability cannot be analyzed by examining the supply side alone.

To summarize, I think that the paper makes two worthwhile contributions which will be of interest to both analytical and numerical modelers. Adding my parable about fixed factors may help tighten the link between internal factor mobility and the elasticity of transformation.

RENGER VAN NIEUWKOOP
ANDRÉ MÜLLER

THE ECONOMIC EFFECTS OF THE BILATERAL SECTORAL AGREEMENTS AND THE SWISS EU MEMBERSHIP*

This paper investigates the economic effects of a possible Swiss EU-Membership as well as the completed Bilateral Sectoral Agreements between the EU and Switzerland using MULTISWISS, a multi-county computable general equilibrium model. The simulations show that the welfare gains for Switzerland (and the EU) in both scenarios will be small but positive in the long run. They also indicate that Switzerland, from an economic point of view, should pursue the EU membership.

1. INTRODUCTION

Several studies dealing with the macroeconomic implications of the European Union (EU) single market programme (SMP) show positive static and steady state growth welfare effects for the EU countries.[1] Studies on the economic effects of the Eastern Expansion of the EU predict welfare gains for the Central and Eastern European Countries.[2] Does this mean that a Swiss EU membership will also have a positive economic effect in Switzerland and the EU countries or should Switzerland, one of the richest countries in the world[3]just reconcile the Bilateral Sectoral Agreements (BA) with the EU and refrain from the EU membership? These questions will continue to raise controversial discussions in Switzerland.

Switzerland has had a free trade agreement with the EC since 1972, as well as more than one hundred bilateral agreements with the EC. It negotiated, but did not ratify, the European Economic Area (EEA) Treaty extending the European Single Market to the EFTA countries. This treaty was rejected by 50.3% of the Swiss population and 16 (of 26) cantons in 1992. In order to reduce the negative impacts of non-

* This paper is based on a project commissioned and financed by the Swiss Federal Office for Economic Development and Labour. The views expressed here are those of the authors and do not represent the opinions of the commissioning agency. The authors may be contacted at renger@ecoplan.ch.

1 For example: Harrison, Rutherford and Tarr [1996], European Commission [1998a], Cecchini [1988], European Commission [1998b].

2 Cf. for example Francois (1998), Baldwin, Francois and Portes (1997).

3 According to the Worldbank's World Development Indicators for 1999 Switzerland is ranked number two in the world.

R.E. Baldwin and A. Brunetti (eds.), Economic Impact of EU Membership on Entrants, 93–114.

participation, Switzerland and the EU negotiated on bilateral agreements in the following areas: elimination of technical barriers to trade, public procurement, research and development, free movement of people, agricultural products, transport and civil aviation. In 1998 the bilateral negotiations with the EU have been concluded and now the Swiss Parliament has to them. The possibility of having a referendum on the BA is not excluded.

However, full membership of the EU is the long-term political goal of the Swiss Government. In the next two years the Swiss Federal Council will assess, based on the domestic and European political and economic conditions, whether it should pursue in the short run the bilateral sectoral approach, or whether it should reactivate the membership application submitted in May 1992 and request the commencement of negotiations with the EU.

In this paper we will have a look at the possible economic effects of the BA as well as the full EU membership in Switzerland. In order to get a better insight in the forces leading to the overall welfare gains we do a complete welfare decomposition by scenario step (e.g. reduction of tariffs, ntb's or agriculture subsidies).

We will show that the overall welfare gains from giving up its isolation will be small but positive for Switzerland as well as for the EU countries. The results of this study indicate that Switzerland, from an economic point of view, should go a step farther than just reconciling the BA and should pursue the EU membership.

The paper starts with an overview of MULTISWISS, the multi regional general equilibrium model and the data used for the simulations. In section 3 we report on the main policy simulations. In section 4 we will discuss the results, while the concluding comments are provided in section 5.

2. BRIEF DESCRIPTION OF THE MODEL AND DATA

In this section we give a brief description of the model and data used.[4] The starting point for the model was the basic model developed by the researchers of the Global Trade Analysis Project (GTAP).[5] MULTISWISS is an applied general equilibrium model involving 11 regions and countries (cf. Table 1). These regions are linked through trade of goods and services.

---

[4] A detailed description can be found in ECOPLAN [1999].

[5] For a detailed description of the GTAP model and data cf. Hertel [1997] and McDougall et al [1998]. The model was implemented in the GAMS modelling language using the GTAPinGAMS software for integrating the GTAP data base in GAMS models. GTAPinGAMS was developed by T. Rutherford of the University of Colorado. and can be downloaded from http://robles.colorado.edu/~tomruth/.

Table 1. Countries and regions

	Country/Region	Description
1	Switzerland	
2	Germany	EU-country, EMU-member
3	Finland	EU-country, EMU-member
4	Rest of Europe	Belgium, France, Greece, Italy, Ireland, Luxembourg, Netherlands, Austria, Portugal, Spain: EU-countries and EMU-members
5	Great Britain	EU-country
6	Denmark	EU-country
7	Sweden	EU-country
8	Eastern Europe	Former Soviet Union, Bulgaria, Czech Republic, Slovenia, Poland, Rumania,
9	North America	USA, Canada
10	Asia	Among others: Japan, China, India, Hong Kong, Indonesia, Korea, Malaysia, Philippines, Singapore, Taiwan, Thailand
11	Rest of World	Among others: Africa, Australia, New Zealand, Middle East, South America, Norway

Every region is characterized by 18 sectors (cf. Table 2). Every sector produces one single commodity for the home as well as the foreign market. Producers are assumed to maximize profits by a nested constant-elasticity of substitution (CES) function. We assume that some sectors operate under an imperfect competition market regime and exhibit increasing returns to scale (IRTS)[6]. We use estimates from Oliveira Martins et al[7] on mark-ups.

6 A good introduction on scale economies and imperfect competition can be found in Francois and Roland-Holst [1997].

7 Cf. Oliveira Martins, Scarpetta and Pilat [1996]. This study contains estimates on mark-ups based on data from 1970 to 1990 and does not rely on the often used estimates surveyed by Pratten [1988], of which many date from the 1950s, 1960s and early 1970s.

Table 2. Sectoral disaggregation

	Sector	Description
1	Agriculture	Agriculture, forestry, fishery
2	Energy, water	Manufacture and distribution of gas and electricity, water
3	Food	Meat products, vegetable oils and fats, dairy products, processed rice, sugar
4	Beverages and tobacco products	
5	Textiles	Manufacture of textiles
6	Clothes, Leather	Wearing apparel, leather products
7	Wood	Wood products
8	Paper	Paper products, publishing
9	Chemistry	Chemical, rubber, plastic products
10	Non-metals	Mineral products, coal, oil, gas
11	Metals	(Ferrous) metals
12	Electronics	Electronic equipment, metal products, manufactures
13	Motor vehicles, machines	Motor vehicles and parts, transport equipment, machinery
14	Construction	Construction
15	Trade, transport, catering	Trade, transport and catering trade
16	Financial business	Financial business, recreational services
17	Dwellings	Dwellings
18	Administration	Public administration, defense, education

Every regional household is characterized by a CES utility function, including demand for consumer goods and leisure. Governmental expenditures are assumed to be fixed.

An equation relating the cost of capital and the return to capital determines the steady-state capital stock. Tobin's Q is calibrated to unity in the base year and remains fixed at that value in the counterfactual. We assume following values for the steady state parameters:

- Growth rate: 2%
- Depreciation rate: 7%
- Interest rate: 3%

We calibrated the social accounting data for the model using the Global Trade Analysis Project Version 4 data set for the year 1995 (GTAP 4)[8]. GTAP 4 does not contain separate data on the Swiss economy, so we worked out a Swiss set of social accounting data in collaboration with the University of Geneva. The data were merged with GTAP 4 using software developed by T. Rutherford of the University of Colorado[9]. For those not acquainted with the Swiss economy we summarize some statistics in Table 3[10].

Table 3. Some statistics for Switzerland and the EU (1995)

	Switzerland	EUR 15
Population (in million)	7.1	372.7
Employment (in million)	3.8	150
GDP (billion ECU)	230	6'765
Exports to EU (% of total exports)	60.7%	62.9%
Imports from EU (% of total imports)	79.0%	63.6%

3. SCENARIOS

We will have a look at the economic effects of changes in policy parameters due to the Bilateral Sectoral Agreements (BA) or a Swiss EU membership (e.g. removal of tariffs, harmonization of compliance to EU standards, market integration, shift in consumer preferences). The implemented changes in market parameters can be grouped in three broad categories:

- Swiss Access to the European Common Market
- Tax harmonization in Switzerland and Swiss net transfers to the EU
- Swiss membership of the European Monetary System (EMS)

Table 4 gives an overview of the implemented changes, which we will comment briefly.[11]

3.1. *Access to the European Single Market*

- **Tariffs**: In the case of the BA Switzerland will only have to reduce the tariffs on agricultural and food products slightly. According to trade theory this will lead to positive welfare effects. In the case of an EU membership Switzerland will abol-

[8] Centre for Global Trade Analysis [1998].

[9] The Swiss data will be made available this year to GTAP for the release of GTAP 5.

[10] Europäische Kommision [1997], Bundesamt für Statistik [1998].

[11] A detailed description can be found in ECOPLAN (1999), chapters 3, 4 and 5.

ish tariffs on trade with the EU and adopt the common EU tariff structure for imports from non-EU countries (passing the revenue to the EU)[12]. These EU tariffs are in most cases higher than the original Swiss tariffs. The changes in the tariff structure will probably lead to trade diversion and creation or reduction. All the changes are modeled as changes in the ad-valorem values of the tariffs.

Table 4. Overview of the changes in policy parameters

	Description: Changes relative to the Base-case scenario «Status Quo»
Swiss Access to the European Common Market	
Tariff structure	*EU-Membership:* reduction of tariffs on agricultural products; raising tariffs on imports from non-EU countries, revenue accrues to the EU.
	BA: moderate reduction of tariffs on agricultural products
Border formalities	*EU Membership:* removal of border controls, reduction of border formalities
Transportation costs	*EU Membership:* reduction of delays at the border, increasing maximum weight for heavy goods vehicles from 28 tons to 40 tons
	Bilateral: increasing maximum weight for heavy goods vehicles to 40 tons
Compliance costs	*EU Membership:* reduction of compliance costs, principle of Cassis-de-Dijon
	Bilateral: reduction of compliance costs
Factor productivity	*EU Membership:* slightly increased pressure on innovations because of intensified competition
	Bilateral: slightly increased pressure on innovations
Labor mobility	*Both scenarios*: 115'000 persons immigrate, of whom 55'000 working people
Market integration	*EU Membership:* no market segmentation, higher product diversity, intensified competition because of demand side pressure, scale effects
	Bilateral: same effects (but smaller) as in the case of an EU Membership

[12] We adjusted the EU tariffs for imports from non-EU countries in the GTAP data base to the level of the tariffs according to the Uruguay Round.

Tax harmonization and fiscal policy	
Further fiscal policy measures	*EU Membership:* additional costs for unemployment insurance, reduction of subsidies and cost reductions in agricultural sectors *Bilateral:* additional costs for unemployment insurance
Net transfers	*EU Membership:* net transfers to the EU of 3 billion Swiss francs, VAT financed
Fiscal measures	*EU Membership:* Raising VAT from 7.5% to 15%, reduction of wage taxes
European Monetary Union	
Transaction costs	*EU Membership:* cost reductions trade transactions, inter banking, lower currency volatility risk
Interest rate	*EU Membership:* raise in interest rate, higher costs of public debt, higher capital price, increased foreign investment
Price transparency	*EU Membership:* Swiss and EU goods become closer substitutes, intensified competition

- **Border formalities**: Abolishing border control (only in case of an EU membership) will lead to a reduction of administrative costs of transacting over international boundaries. These changes are modeled as a reduction of the transport costs and range from 0.5% to 1.4%.[13]
- **Transportation costs**: Abolishing border controls will also lead to a reduction of the transportation costs (e.g. less delays at the border) of 0.04% to 1%. Furthermore, dropping the Swiss 28 tons limit for heavy goods vehicles and adopting the European weight limit of 40 tons will lead to a reduction of transportation costs (ca. 30%[14] in both scenarios).
- **Compliance costs**: In the case of the BA and an EU membership, Switzerland will adopt (part of) the EU standards (e.g. as an EU member, Switzerland has to adjust their regulations according to the Cassis-de-Dijon principle). In the Single Market Review the savings were estimated at 0.5% of the value of traded goods. We adjusted this figure downwards because of the harmonization measures already undertaken (BA: 0.08%, EU Membership 0.18% reduction).
- **Technological progress**: Factor productivity gains due to the SMP are estimated in the order of 0.1% on average and for all sectors.[15] We used this figure for the

---

[13] Transport costs are modeled as a complementary input for every traded good. Estimates were taken from the Single Market Review (European Commission [1998]) and adjusted for Switzerland.

[14] Cf. ECOPLAN [1997].

[15] Cf. European Commission [1998a].

EU membership scenario. For the BA scenario we assumed half of the technological progress.

- **Labor mobility**: Both scenarios do not differ regarding the assumptions on labor mobility. We assume that 115'000 persons, of which 55'000 working people, will immigrate to Switzerland in the next 15 years.[16] This change in the population is modeled exogenously.
- **Market integration**: We assume that consumers have preferences for products depending on region of origin. Accessing the European Market Swiss consumers will more easily substitute between European and Swiss products (one reason could be that because of uniform standards, products of different origin do not differ that much anymore). This is modeled using two different preference structures („market segmentation" and „market integration"; cf. Figure 1).

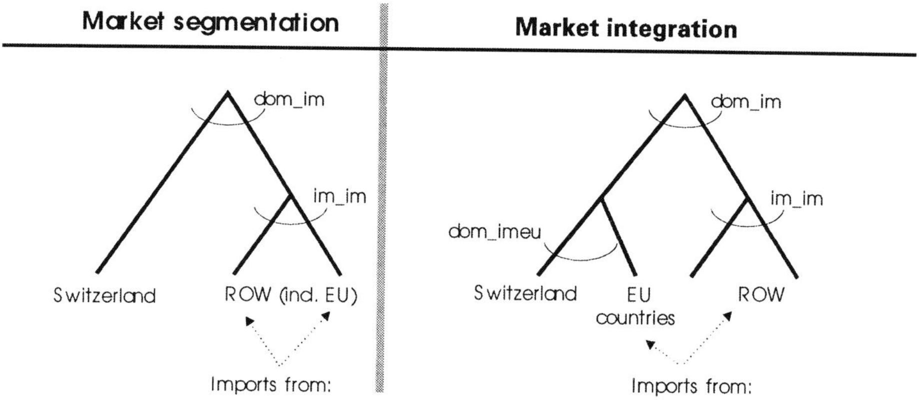

Figure 1. Market segmentation and integration

3.2. *Tax harmonization and transfers*

- **Net transfers to the EU**: In the case of an EU membership Switzerland has to contribute to the EU budget (agricultural levies and sugar levies, customs duties, VAT resource and GNP resource). Switzerland will also receive money from the EU funds (agricultural and social spending as well as research funds). The net transfer to the EU amounts to ca. 3 billion Swiss francs.
- **Fiscal policy**: Switzerland has to raise its VAT of 7.5% to the EU level of 15%. A part of the additional revenue (ca. 14 billion Swiss francs) will be used to finance the transfers to the EU. The use of the remaining VAT revenue is still a point of discussion. In the main scenario we assume that the remaining VAT

---

16 Cf. Straubhaar [1999].

revenue will be used for lowering the marginal income tax rate. We also examine the impact of a per capita refund.

- **Further fiscal policy measures**: Becoming a EU member, Switzerland has to adopt the EU agriculture policy. This will lead to a reduction of the Swiss agriculture subsidies of ca. 1 billion Swiss francs. Adopting the regulations concerning unemployment benefits will lead to additional costs of 0.5 billion Swiss francs. We assume that these additional costs will be financed by raising the unemployment insurance rate.

3.3. *European Monetary Union*

Estimating the effects of accessing the European Monetary Union (EMU) is not easy because:

- a CGE model is not the appropriate tool for studying monetary policies
- there is no common accepted economic opinion or theory on the effects of the EMU: Will the Euro become a strong or weak currency, will it boost or depress the economy?

Based on a study for the European Single Market[17] and own estimates we assume that if Switzerland joins the EMU this will have the following effects:

- a reduction of the **transaction costs** (trade transactions, inter banking) because of the reduced currency volatility and one European common currency (trade transaction costs are reduced by 0.5%, savings of 0.4 billion Swiss francs in interbanking services, and 1.6 billion Swiss francs in bank-related customer services).
- increased **price transparency**: We suppose that Swiss consumers will more easily substitute between domestic products and products imported from EMU-member countries (the Armington substitution elasticity „dom_imeu" in Figure 1 is multiplied by 1.25).
- **loss of interest rate advantage**: The interest rate in Switzerland will adjust to the European interest level resulting in higher capital costs for Swiss residents (1%), a higher public debt burden (1.5 billion Swiss francs, VAT financed) and higher interest payments to foreign owners of Swiss capital.

4. RESULTS

In the following sections we will have a look at the results of the scenarios. We will look at the relative deviations of the two main scenarios «Bilateral Sectoral Agreements» and «EU membership» from the benchmark scenario («Status Quo») and decompose these effects according to the changes in the policy parameters as defined in the preceding section.

---

[17] Cf. European Commission [1998a].

These deviations can be interpreted as deviations from the Status-quo steady state growth path in the long run (cf. Figure 2). Because of the steady-state nature of the model, it is not possible to say something about the adjustment costs. A positive result in the long run could mean low or high adjustment costs.

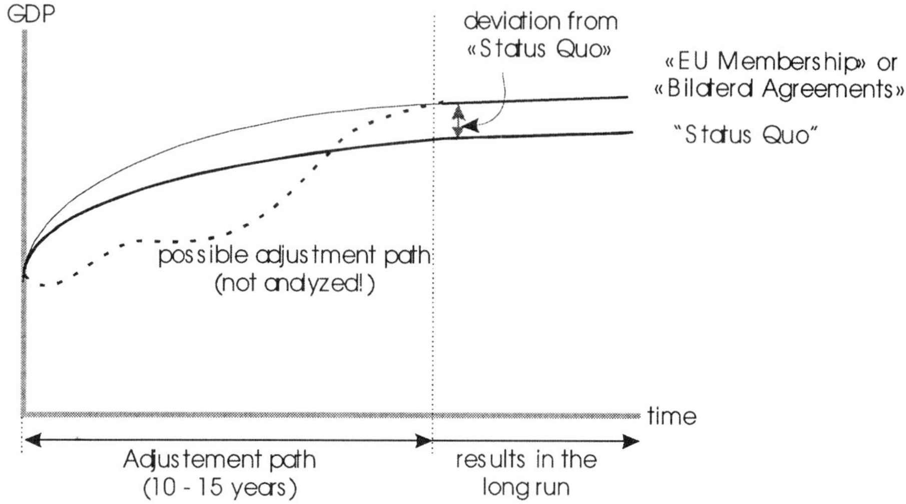

Figure 2. Results in the long run

4.1. Welfare effects and GDP

Figure *3* shows the decomposition of the welfare effects as a percentage of GDP (equivalent variations) for the two main scenarios «Bilateral Sectoral Agreements» and «EU Membership». The effects on gross domestic product (GDP) are in the same order and direction.

A quick look shows that the welfare effects for the scenario «Bilateral Sectoral Agreements» are mostly positive and smaller than the welfare effects for the Scenario «EU Membership». We will concentrate in the following on the scenario «EU Membership».

4.1.1. Access to the European Single Market

- The negative effects of the changes in the tariff regime („tariffs") in the Scenario «EU Membership» may amaze at first glance. According to trade theory abolishing Swiss tariffs on EU imports should at least lead to a non-negative welfare improvement. However, Switzerland has to adopt the common EU tariff structure for imports from non-EU countries and has to pass on the revenue to the EU. These tariffs are much higher than the original Swiss tariffs. The negative welfare effects from the higher tariffs and transferring the revenue to the EU more than cancel out the positive welfare effects from abolishing the tariffs on EU imports.

– Technological progress, reductions in the border formalities, transportation and compliance costs as well as opening up the EU markets („market integration“) have small positive welfare effects (between 0.1% and 0.4%).

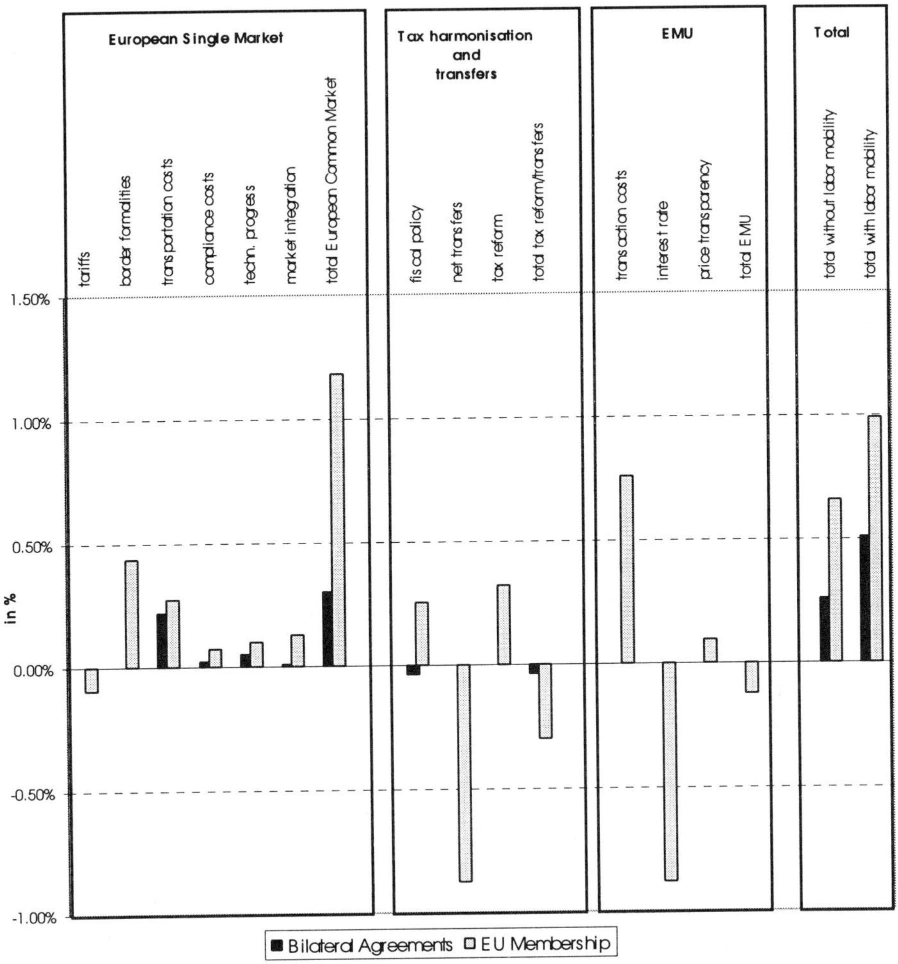

Figure 3. Welfare Effects in GDP% (per capita)

If we compare these results with the long-run results of the Single Market Review (cf. Table 5)[18] we see that if Switzerland joins the EU would not gain as much as the other European countries did in the case of the Single Market Programme. This is due to the fact that Switzerland already benefits from the European Market and reduced the NTBs on its own in the last few years.

Table 5. Comparison of Swiss welfare effects with SMP results

Country	GDP-change
EU	2.1%
- Belgium	4.7%
- Denmark	2.9%
- France	1.8%
- Germany	1.8%
- Greece	1.3%
- Ireland	3.5%
- Italy	2.3%
- The Netherlands	2.5%
- Portugal	2.8%
- Spain	3.0%
- Great Britain	1.3%
Switzerland	1.3%

4.1.2. Tax harmonization and transfers

Raising the Swiss VAT (7.5%) to the European level (15%) and the net transfers to the EU of ca. 3 billion Swiss francs will have negative welfare effects. The higher VAT will have distortionary effects and the transfers will reduce the income of the Swiss consumers. Adopting the Common Agricultural Policy (CAP) will have positive welfare effects as distortionary subsidies will be reduced. If raising the VAT is accompanied by a (small) tax reform in which the marginal taxes are reduced, the negative effects of the distortions and the transfers can be countered and a welfare gain of 0.8% will be the result.[19]

---

[18] Cf. European Commission [1998a]. For this comparison we had to leave out the adoption of the European weight limit and the tariff reduction.

[19] Although the marginal labour tax is rather high (ca. 30%), the combination of raising the VAT and reducing the marginal labour tax does not lead to higher welfare effects. This is due to the fact that the Swiss VAT is not an uniform tax and the VAT is raised proportionally, so the distortion will be high.

4.1.3. *European Monetary Union*

The decomposition of the EMU effects (Figure 3) shows that negative and positive welfare effects almost cancel out. The higher price transparency has only a small positive effect. The main positive effect can be expected from the reduction of the transaction costs. The loss of the interest rate advantage is a highly debated topic in Switzerland. Some studies, for example Peytrignet, Jordan and Kleinewefers Lehner [1999] show extreme negative effects, other studies come to the opposite conclusion (for example, Müller and Grether [1999]). We conclude that the effect will be negative (ca. 0.9% welfare loss).

4.1.4. *Total effects*

Both the Bilateral Sectoral Agreements and the EU Membership will have positive welfare effects. In the case of the EU Membership the welfare gains of the Swiss access to the European common market will be 0.7% of GDP. If one adds the welfare effects of the expected inflow of about 110'000 EU citizens, this will lead to an additional 0.3% per capita welfare gain (total 1.0%). In the case of the Bilateral Sectoral Agreements the welfare gains are much smaller but also positive.

4.2. *Trade effects*

A reduction of tariffs or technological barriers often leads to lower prices and/or diminished costs. Foreign products become cheaper for consumers and producers. These changes in prices and cost structures can cause following gains or losses from:

- trade creating and trade diversion
- increased competitiveness and scale effects.

Increased competitiveness and scale effects will be the subject of the next section on sectoral effects. We will first look at the trade creation and diversion effects.

The phasing out of the internal tariffs in case of an EU-Membership will cause the Swiss home market prices to fall. This will lead to an increase in the total volume of imports and a fall in domestic production. The overall effect will be positive. The trade-diverting effect (replacing inexpensive imports from non-EU countries by more expensive products from EU-countries) will be negative. The sum of the effects depends on the elasticities and price differences.

4.2.1. *European Single Market*

As already discussed in the preceding section on welfare effects, negative effects are due to the fact that Switzerland has to adopt the EU tariff structure for imports from non-EU countries, that lie above the original Swiss tariffs. This will lead to a reduction of the total import volume. The reduction of border formalities, delay times at the border, increasing the maximum weight for heavy goods vehicles to 40 tons as well as the reduction of the compliance costs have a positive influence on the import volume.

4.2.2. Tax harmonization and transfers
As imports are subject to the VAT the increase of the Swiss VAT will have a negative effect on the imports. Another reason for the fall in imports is the reduction of GDP resulting in a loss in income.

4.2.3. European Monetary Union
The EMU will have a positive effect on imports in spite of the higher interest rate that leads to a smaller GDP. The positive effect is due to the reduction of the transaction costs in trade and the higher price transparency.

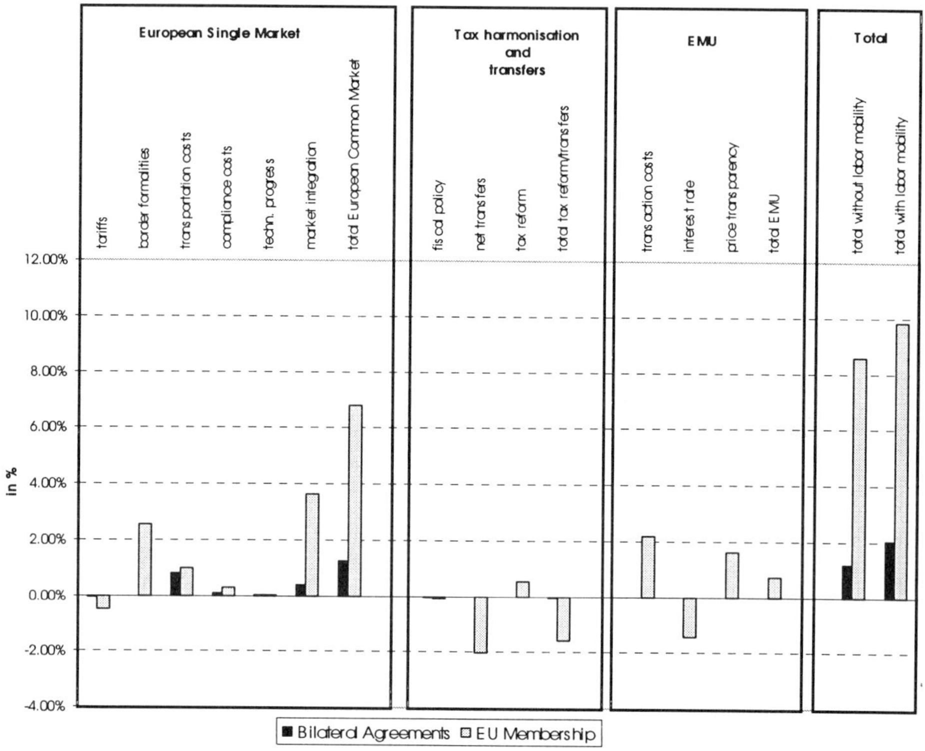

Figure 4. Change in import volume

Figure 5 shows that especially in the case of an EU membership a trade diversion will occur. Switzerland will import more from the EU countries at the cost of non-EU countries. Although the Swiss imports from non-EU countries increase, they fall relatively to the increase in GDP.

The changes in total export volume are comparable to the changes in imports.

4.3. Sectoral effects

The following figures (6 and 7) show the sectoral effects (sales, imports and exports) for both scenarios «Bilateral Sectoral Agreements»" and «EU Membership». Only in the case of an EU Membership there are some obvious winners and losers: The sectors „Agriculture", „Food", and „Beverages and Tobacco" loose up to 18% of their sales. The sectors „Chemicals", Textiles", „Electronic Equipment and Machines" and „Motor Vehicles" gain up to 20%.

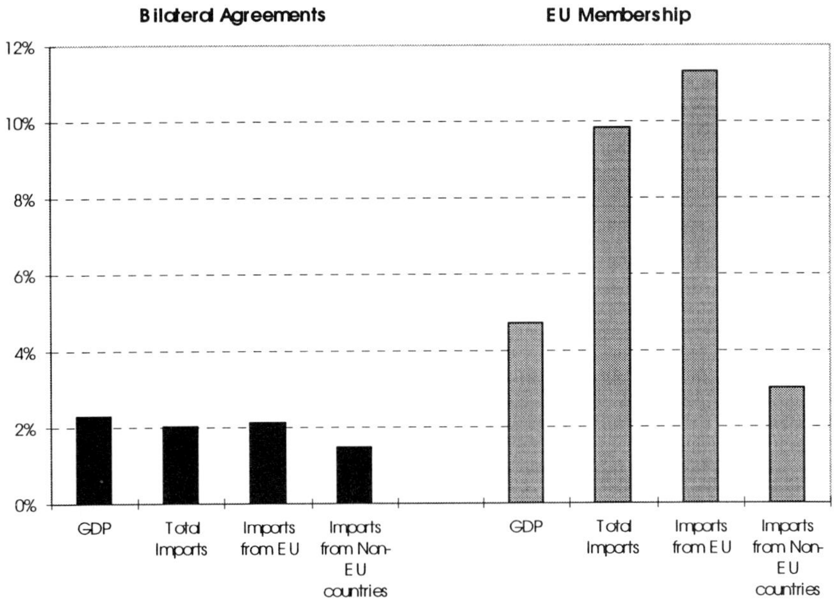

Figure 5. Trade creation and diversion (GDP and Imports)

These effects are easily explained looking at the characteristic features of the loosing and gaining sectors:

The „looser" sectors

- are either sectors that sell a high percentage of their production on the domestic market or rely heavily on imports,
- face, due to the phasing out of tariffs, the reduction of ntb's, etc., an intensified competition on the European and Swiss market,
- loose part of their competition advantage as agricultural subsidies are reduced,
- are characterized by small scale effects.

A quick glance at Table 6 with some indicators concerning competition shows that the number of firms in the loosing sectors is reduced (which is accompanied by a raise in scale effects and markup). An EU membership will lead to a concentration process in these sectors and a decline of X-inefficencies.

The „gaining" sectors

- are highly specialized sectors,
- rely heavily on exports and gain from the improved access to the European market,
- are sectors characterized by a high potential of scale effects,
- are only partly affected by the reduction or rise of the tariffs.

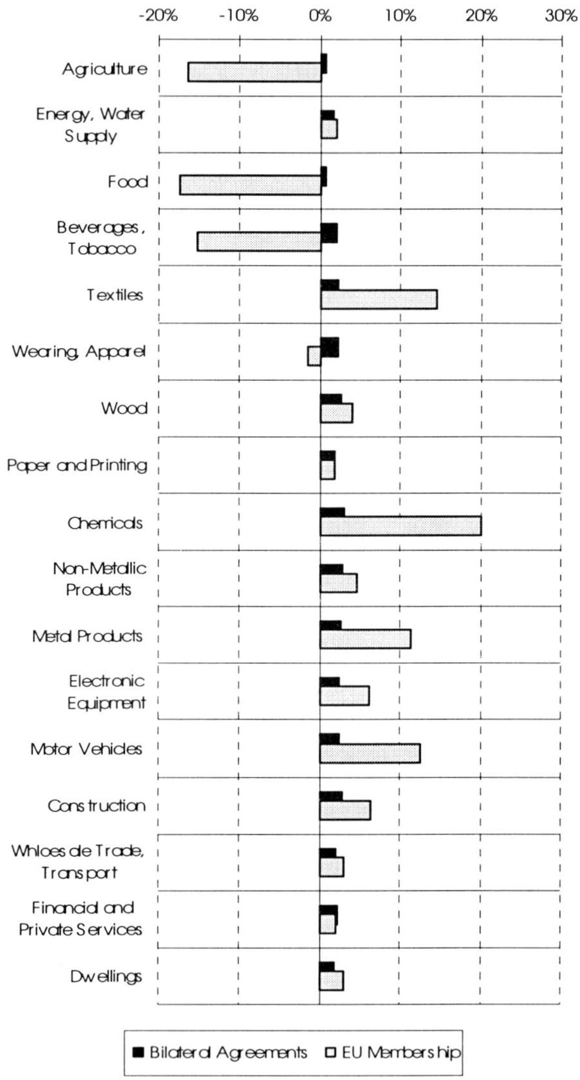

Figure 6. Sectoral effects: sales (changes in %)

Table 6. Changes in number of firms, scale effects and mark-up (Scenario «EU Membership»)

	Number of Firms	Skale effects	Mark-up
Agriculture	--	++	++
Energy, Water supply	+		
Food	--	++	++
Beverages, Tobacco	--	++	+
Textiles	++	-	-
Wearing Apparel, Leather Products	-	++	+
Wood	+		
Paper and Printing			
Chemicals	++	--	--
Non-Metallic Products	+	+	
Metal Products	++	-	-
Electronic Equipment, Machinery	+		
Motor Vehicles	+	++	
Construction		+	
Trade, Transport			
Financial and private business			
Dwellings			
Public Administration			

++: Increase more than 5%; +: Increase between 1% and 5%
--: Reduction more than 5%; -: Reduction between 1% and 5%

Table 6 shows that an EU Membership will lead to an intensified competition on the sectoral markets (the number of firms increases; scale effects and markups are smaller).

Figure 7 shows the sectoral trade effects. Exports will rise in almost every sector and once again, the gaining sectors mentioned above will gain relatively more. The changes in sectoral imports show that the Swiss consumers will gain especially from the lower prices for products from the agricultural and food sectors.

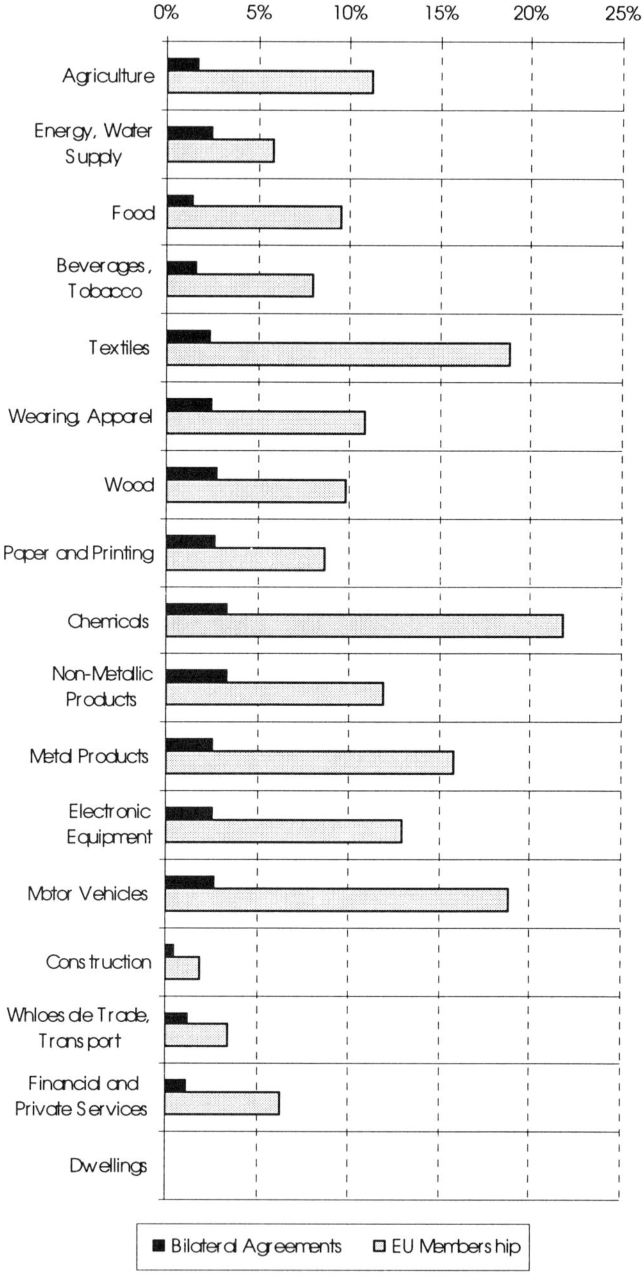

Figure 7a. Sectoral effects: exports (changes in %)

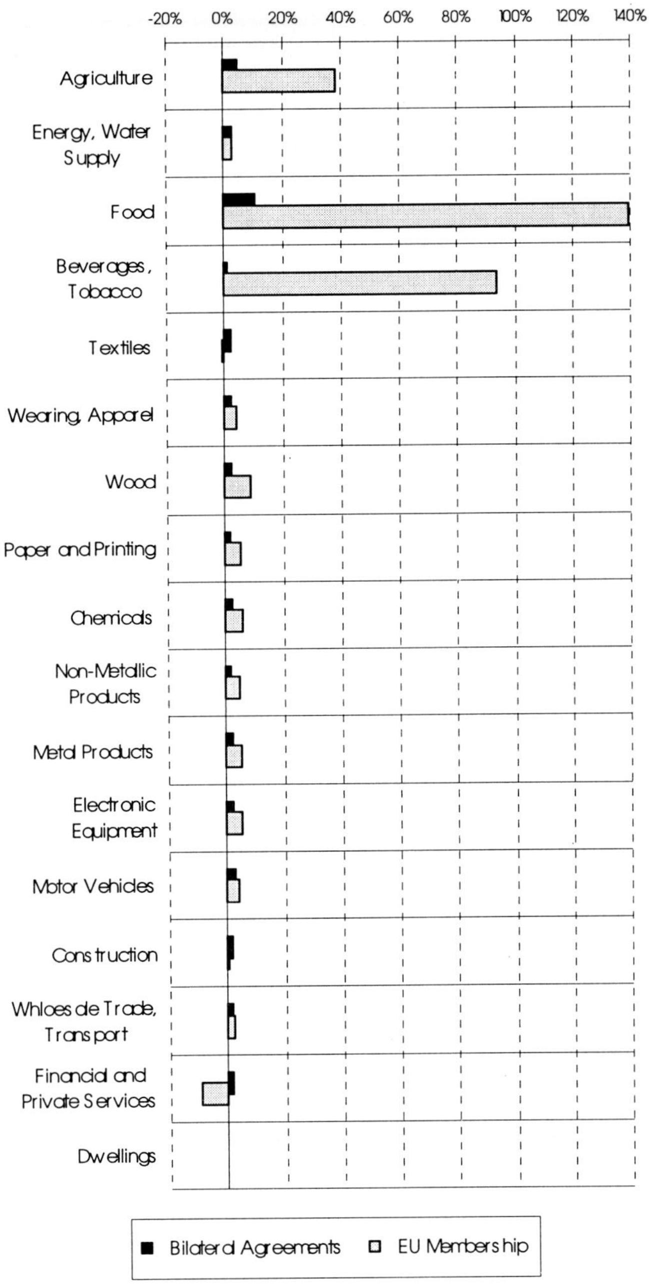

Figure 7b. Sectoral effects: imports (changes in %)

4.4. *Regional welfare effects*

Although the analysis of the effects on the Swiss economy is the main subject of our study, we will take a quick glance at the welfare effects for the EU. If Switzerland pursues the EU Membership burdensome negotiations with the EU will follow. If most of the EU countries would gain from the Swiss EU-membership, this would facilitate the negotiations with the EU for Switzerland.

Figure 8 shows the per capita welfare gains for Switzerland and the EU. As Switzerland is only a small country concerning population or GDP, the positive welfare effects of 1% per capita (or 4 billion Swiss francs) will hardly result in an equivalent welfare gain or loss for the EU. Figure indicates that there are no losses for the EU countries if Switzerland joins the EU. On the other hand, these gains will be very small (less than 0.2% of GDP or 9 billion Swiss Franc yearly).

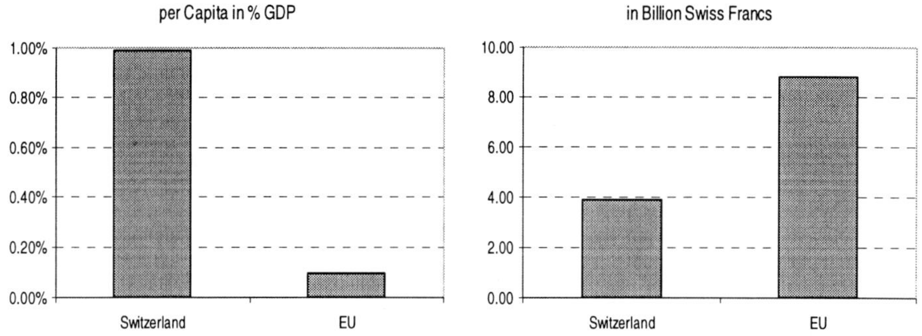

Figure 8. Welfare effects (Scenario «EU Membership»)

5. SENSITIVITY ANALYSIS

We conducted a sensitivity analysis regarding the policy scenarios and the model parameter. The main results can be summarized as follows:

- Government expenditure: In the base case we assumed that the immigration of 110'000 EU citizens does not lead to an increase in governmental expenditures. In the sensitivity analysis we assumed a proportional increase of the governmental expenditures (1.5%). This leads to a small reduction of the welfare effects of 0.2%. The overall effect however will stay positive.
- VAT revenue: If the extra revenue of the VAT (after paying the transfers to the EU) will not be used for a reduction of the marginal income tax but will be returned to the Swiss population on a per capita base, the welfare effects are reduced by 0.8%. The use of the extra revenue of the VAT should therefore be intensively discussed in case of an EU-membership.

- The welfare effects for a static version of the model are almost 0.2% lower as for the dynamic model. This shows, that the dynamic effects play a very important role and the incorporation of dynamics is a must.
- If we assume full capital mobility, the welfare effects increase by almost 0.4%.
- Assuming perfect instead of imperfect competition reduces the welfare effects by almost 0.4%. Under perfect competition the effects of increased competition on the markets will be neglected.

6. CONCLUSIONS

Our study shows that:

- the Bilateral Sectoral Agreements lead to welfare gains in the order of 0.5%. These gains are mainly due to the increased immigration of EU citizens and the productivity gains in overland transport due to the higher maximum weight limit for heavy goods vehicles
- a Swiss EU membership will lead to higher welfare gains compared with the Bilateral Sectoral Agreements. This in spite of Switzerland becoming a net payer of transfers to the EU in case of an EU membership. The relative small gains are due to the fact that Switzerland already reaps some of the profits of the European Single Market.
- The advantages of an EU membership compared to the Bilateral Sectoral Agreements are the abolition of border formalities, more competition, reduced transaction costs, and the opening up of the agriculture market. The disadvantages for Switzerland are the higher interest rate and the net transfers to the EU.
- If Switzerland joins the EU and raises its VAT, it could use part of the revenue for a reduction of the high Swiss income tax, thereby improving Switzerland's international competitiveness.
- The Bilateral Sectoral Agreements do not lead to structural changes. A Swiss EU Membership by contrast will produce sectors that gain and loose. The sectors „Agriculture", „Food" and „Beverages and Tobacco" belong to the group of loosing sectors. The sectors „Chemicals", Textiles", „Electronic Equipment and Machines" and „Motor Vehicles" notch up gains in sales.
- In the case of a Swiss EU Membership Switzerland will increase trade with the EU and (relatively to GDP) reduce trade with non-EU countries.

Switzerland and the EU countries will gain from a Swiss access to the EU.
The results of this study indicate that Switzerland should go a step farther than just reconciling the BA and should, from a long-run economic point of view, pursue the EU membership.

REFERENCES

Baldwin, R.E., J. F. Francois and R. Portes (1997), The Cost and Benefits of EU Enlargement to the East, Economic Policy.

Bundesamt für Statistik (1998), Statistisches Jahrbuch der Schweiz, Zürich.

Cecchini, P. (1988), Europa '92, Der Vorteil des Binnenmarkts, Nomos-Verlagsgesellschaft, Baden-Baden.

ECOPLAN (1999), EU-Integration der Schweiz, wirtschaftliche Auswirkungen, Bundesamt für Wirtschaft und Arbeit, Bern.

European Commission (1988a), Aggregate Results of the Single Market Programme, The Single Market Review, Subseries VI: Aggregate and Regional Impact, Vol. 5, Luxembourg.

European Commission (1988b), The Economics of 1992, European Economy, No. 35, Luxembourg.

EUROSTAT (1997), EUROSTAT Jahrbuch '97, Europa im Blick der Statistik 1986-1996, Luxembourg.

Francois, J.F. (1998), Scale Economies, Imperfect Competition, and the Eastern Expansion of the EU, in Brockmeier, M. et al (eds.), The Eastern Enlargement of the EU, Justus Leibig University Giessen.

Harrison, G., T. Rutherford and D. Tarr (1994), Product Standards, Imperfect Competition, and Completion of the Market in the European Union, Policy Research Working Paper, The World Bank, April 1994.

McDougall, R. A., A. Elbhehri and T. P. Truong (1998), Global Trade, Assistance, and Protection: The GTAP 4 Data Base, Center for Global Trade Analysis, Purdue University.

Müller, T. and J.-M. Grether (1999), Effets à long terme d'une intégration de la Suisse à l'Europe, BWA-Schriftenreihe, Beiträge zur Wirtschaftspolitik, Bern.

Oliveira, Martins J., S. Scarpetta and D. Pilat (1996), Mark-Up Ratios in Manufacturing Industries, Estimates for 14 OECD Countries, OECD, Paris.

Peytrignet, M., Th. Jordan and A. Kleinewefers Lehner (1999), Auswirkungen einer Angleichung der schweizerischen Zinssätze an das europäische Zinsniveau nach einem Beitritt der Schweiz zur EU, Arbeitspapier der SNB.

Pratten C. (1988), A Survey of the Economies of Scale, in: Research on the Cost of Non-Europe, Vol. 2, Commission of the European Communities, Luxembourg.

Straubhaar, T. (1999), Integration und Arbeitsmarkt, Auswirkungen einer Annäherung der Schweiz an die Europäische Union, BWA-Schriftenreihe, Beiträge zur Wirtschaftspolitik, Bern.

CHRISTIAN KEUSCHNIGG

LABOR MARKET AND BUDGETARY EFFECTS OF EASTERN ENLARGEMENT IN GERMANY

A Comment

Switzerland is a small, open country that trades predominantly with the European Union (EU). Since about 80 percent of its imports stem from the EU and 60 percent of its exports are shipped to the EU, full membership will hold important benefits from participating fully in the single market. On the negative side, the expected *net* contributions to the EU budget and the expected loss of the current interest rate advantage from participation in EMU may undo much of the benefits and, conceivably, may turn EU membership to a net burden for Switzerland. With benefits and costs largely offsetting, a quantitative analysis is called for to arrive at a conclusion. The authors apply a theoretically sound and by now standard computable general equilibrium (CGE) model with 11 regions and 18 interrelated production sectors. Based on this model, they calculate that participation in the single market program (SMP) should give a welfare gain equivalent to 1.3 percent of GDP while full membership, depending on the immigration scenario, would be worth between .7 to 1 percent of GDP. Comparing to other studies, these estimates appear reasonable.

It is somewhat difficult to discuss and evaluate the study because the authors fail to give sufficient insight into the structure of their model. The main transmission channels for policy effects, thus, largely remain in the dark. What is the savings and investment theory? How is the interest rate determined and how is it related to the interest rate in other countries? What, if at all, is the role of international capital flows? Which economic decisions are most directly affected by which parts of the accession scenario? While the trade creation and diversion effects are reasonably clear, the reader hardly develops much intuition how EU membership impacts on the incentives for labour supply, savings and consumption as well as investment within the authors' framework. How the results depend on the particular transmission mechanisms is certainly important for thinking about an appropriate policy response that might help to mitigate some of the negative consequences of membership.

The reported welfare gain of 1 percent of GDP is certainly not a very precisely calculated number since CGE analysis – like other methods as well - is always fraught with uncertainties. Model structure and choice of parameters is one source of errors. In a separate report, the authors provide a sensitivity analysis. These calculations show that the magnitude of welfare effects importantly hinges on the power of scale and pro-competitive effects. Induced capital accumulation is even more important. The induced accumulation effect boosts the welfare gain from .2 to 1 percent of GDP! This large difference is a puzzle, however. If capital accumulation

R.E. Baldwin and A. Brunetti (eds.), Economic Impact of EU Membership on Entrants, 115–117.

were optimal in the outset, as it would be in an undistorted, competitive market economy, the welfare effect from induced capital accumulation should be zero! Some of the gains may be due to the fact that capital goods are priced higher than their marginal cost because of imperfect competition. In this case, investment is too low initially whence induced accumulation will yield first order welfare gains. However, the largest part of the reported welfare gains from capital accumulation is probably due to the fact that the authors calculate only a long-run, steady state solution of the model that ignores the welfare cost of postponed consumption during the transition. For this reason, the overall welfare result is probably biased upward.

The authors' base case solution does not allow for international capital mobility. For this reason, the reported welfare gains are probably biased downwards. Given the long-run, steady state nature of the analysis, I would have preferred the main scenario to allow for full capital mobility, and consider the case of capital immobility as part of the sensitivity analysis. Finally, the sensitivity analysis should include the Armington elasticity that determines the substitution between home and foreign goods. The econometrics literature estimates this elasticity with quite some error margin. The Armington elasticities control the terms of trade effects which importantly determine the welfare implications of integration. A final remark on welfare analysis concerns the modelling of market integration and segmentation by means of a change in preferences that should capture better substitutability between EU and Swiss goods after membership. Strictly speaking, this approach invalidates the welfare results on the market integration scenario since welfare analysis is consistent only if preferences remain invariant to the policy shock.

The results of the study also are subject to some uncertainties with respect to the policy scenario. The fiscal gains from membership contain some respectable savings in agricultural subsidies. The Swiss farm sector is even more protected than under the common agricultural policy (CAP) of the EU. With the agricultural sector being the main looser of Swiss EU membership, farmers are expected to press vigorously for compensation. Accession negotiations in Austria resulted in quite generous transitional arrangements that are partly financed by the EU and partly by the Austrian government. One could, thus, argue that the fiscal gains may not be that large after all. The fiscal scenario holds another aspect which makes the welfare gains appear very large. When Switzerland raises its low VAT rate of 7.5 percent to the minimum EU rate of 15 percent, the additional public revenues are more than enough to pay for the transfers to the EU budget. The main scenario assumes that the excess revenues are used to lower the income tax rate. This amounts to reducing some important savings, investment and labour supply distortions. Other uses of the excess revenue, however, would probably give less favourable results. If the excess revenue were rebated in lump-sum form, instead, the overall welfare gain of 1 percent of GDP would melt down to a mere .2 percent. Finally, the expected immigration of 115.000 persons to Switzerland on account of higher labour mobility boosts welfare by an amount equivalent to .3 percent of GDP. The model, however, assumes frictionless labour markets and simply treats immigration as a resource gain. The general public, however, is rather afraid that immigration might contribute to higher unemployment and, thereby, impose a considerable cost on Switzerland.

Furthermore, immigration may hold adverse distributional consequences since it should squeeze wages of domestic workers. These more negative aspects are not captured by the analysis.

The discussion of the benefits and costs of Swiss EU membership would surely gain by drawing on the experience of other recent accession countries such as Austria. Notwithstanding some important differences, Austria and the Nordic countries faced quite similar problems in joining the single market program, subjecting an overly subsidised agricultural sector to the rules of the CAP, and financing considerable net contributions. By now, these countries allow to study some ex post evidence which should be informative for the Swiss case as well.

Overall, the study includes a comprehensive policy scenario and yields important insights into the principal benefits and costs of Swiss EU membership as well as their quantitative significance. Given that costs and benefits are largely offsetting each other, a quantitative approach is called for. The study concludes that EU membership clearly holds *net* welfare gains for Switzerland. It identified pro-competitive effects from participation in the single market program, induced capital accumulation effects (with some qualification), and the shifting from direct to indirect taxation as major sources of welfare gains. The study also helps to identify where possible uncertainties with respect to the magnitude of the gains and costs of EU membership are located. It is a valuable contribution to inform the policy debate on this important issue.

HANS GENBERG
ARJAN KADAREJA

THE SWISS FRANC AND THE EURO

INTRODUCTION

This paper investigates two aspects of the relationship between the Swiss Franc and the Euro: the likely long-term trend in the bilateral exchange rate, on the one hand, and the role of nominal exchange rate smoothing for short-run macroeconomic stability, on the other.

Using past behavior as a guide, we argue that the Swiss National Bank will either have to tolerate an (implicit) exchange rate of the Swiss Franc relative to the German Mark of less than .80 SFr/DM, or a somewhat higher rate of inflation in Switzerland compared to the Euro region.

With the help of simulations with a multi-country macroeconometric model incorporating Switzerland as well as countries from the EU, Japan and the United States, we show that a monetary policy incorporating some exchange-rate smoothing improves economic performance. This appears to support the procedure for setting interest rates that the Swiss National Bank has been using recently.

The paper is divided into four sections. The next one presents some stylized facts about the behavior of the Swiss Franc during the past twenty-five years, and outlines the questions that will be studies in the remainder of the paper. Section II deals with the implication of the arrival of the Euro for the long-run behavior of the Swiss Franc/Euro exchange rate, while Section III presents the results of the simulation results relating to short-run macroeconomic stability. Section IV concludes.

1. FACTS AND ISSUES

1.1. Some facts

1.1.1. Since 'the great appreciation' of 1978 there has been no trend in the value of the Swiss franc relative to the German mark

The CHF appreciated sharply with respect to both the USD and the DEM during 1978. It went from 1.98 to a low of 1.47 with respect to the dollar and from .94 to a low of .80 with respect to the mark. It is well known that the Swiss National Bank at the time deviated from its monetary target in order to put a stop to the appreciation and prevent serious difficulties for the Swiss export sector. Germany being the most important competitor, the temporary exchange rate 'target' was expressed as a floor to the mark exchange rate of .80 CHF/DEM. Since that episode the exchange rate

R.E. Baldwin and A. Brunetti (eds.), Economic Impact of EU Membership on Entrants, 119–148.

has stayed above that rate, and it has most of the time fluctuated within the .8 - .9 range. It almost looks as if the SNB has operated with a 'target zone' for the DEM rate even after 1978. This is not the official view of the Bank itself, which explains that its policy has been to steer monetary aggregates in such a way as to maintain a low rate of inflation.

Note, however, that a policy reaction function where the monetary policy instrument reacts to the deviation of the exchange rate from a target level can be perfectly consistent with an objective of the central bank that only includes inflation. Camen, Genberg and Salemi (1990) used a VAR framework to estimate both a policy reaction function of the SNB and a transmission mechanism of monetary policy to inflation in the Swiss economy. The policy reaction equation showed that the SNB seemed to react systematically to the exchange rate vis-a-vis the German mark. Nevertheless, the estimated transmission mechanism implied that this monetary policy was consistent with the SNB caring only about inflation and not about the exchange rate itself.

Another possible explanation of the behavior of CHF/DEM exchange rate is that traders in the foreign exchange market believe that official policy will keep the rate within the .80-.90 range. Their trading strategies will then keep it in that range as long as SNB policy is not significantly at odds with the traders' underlying belief.

Visual inspection of Figure I.1 and formal econometric tests suggest that there has been no trend in the monthly Swiss Franc value of the DEM after the 1978 appreciation.[1] It is possible that this absence of a trend in the nominal exchange rate will be the automatic outcome if the objectives of the SNB and the Bundesbank are the same. In fact, both central banks stated repeatedly that their primary objective was price stability during the period we are discussing. The purchasing power parity proposition then implies that over the long term the bilateral exchange rate will be constant provided the inflation targets are the same.

1.1.2. The Swiss franc has appreciated persistently in real terms against the German mark

Using consumer prices to calculate a real exchange rate results in an index that has a clear downward long-term trend. Figure I.2 provides a visual illustration. Log-linear regressions against time give estimates of an annual rate of real appreciation of about six tenth of one percent since 1979 and about nine tenth since 1975.[2]

---

[1] For the sample period 1979:1-1999:4 augmented Dickey-Fuller tests reject the presence of a unit root (stochastic trend) in the monthly series at the 90% level. Likewise there is no evidence of the presence of a deterministic trend in autoregressive models of the exchange rate during this period.

[2] If the sample is extended back to the beginning of the floating rate period, the rate of appreciation is over one percent per year. It is not possible to reject the hypothesis of a unit root in the real exchange rate using conventional significance levels for any of these samples. However, even if a stochastic trend does characterize the data series, the presence of a negative <u>deterministic</u> trend can not be rejected either.

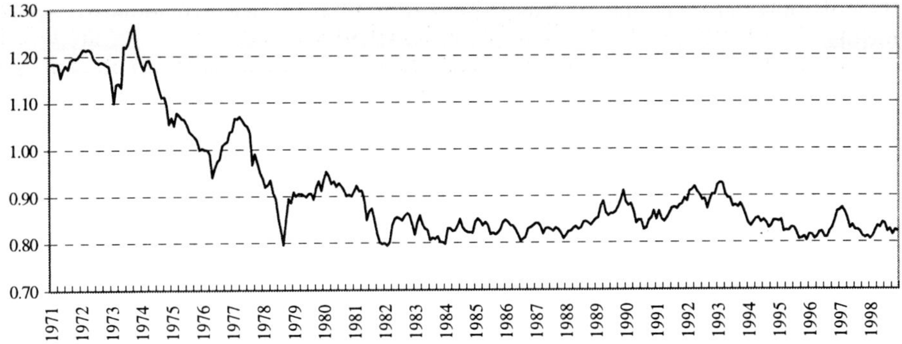

Figure I.1. The Swiss Franc/German Mark exchange rate

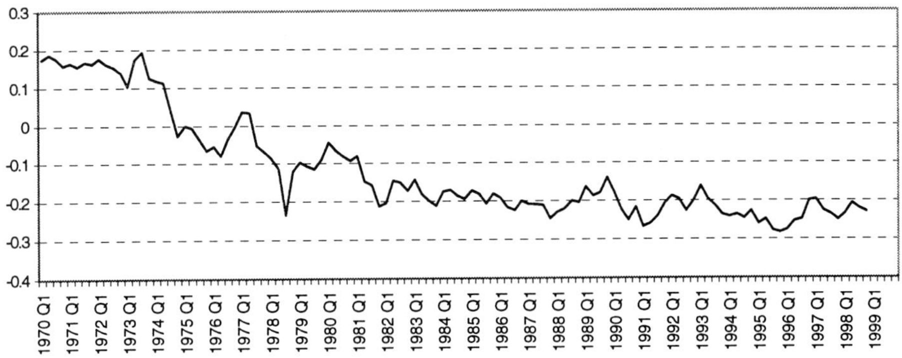

Figure I.2. Index of the real exchange rate relative to Germany

The usual explanation for such long-term trends in the real exchange rate relies on the so-called Balassa-Samuelson effect, which emphasizes productivity differentials between the sectors producing traded and non-traded goods. If labor productivity increases faster in the traded goods sector, and if wage increases are equalized across sectors, then the relative price of non-traded goods will increase over time. This tends to push up the exchange-rate adjusted price level at home relative to that abroad, provided the price of traded goods evolve according to the purchasing power parity principle. Using data on labor productivity at the sectoral level in Germany and Switzerland, Aebersold and Brunetti (1998) find evidence supporting the Balassa-Samuelson hypothesis in the case of the Swiss Franc/German Mark real exchange rate. In fact, they show that the entire real appreciation during the 1970-94 period can be explained in this way.

The fact that Switzerland's current account position has been quite strong also suggests that the real currency appreciation has not lead to a loss of international competitiveness, and that the explanation based on productivity differentials is quite plausible.

A nominal rate against the DEM that has had no trend since 1979 and an appreciating real exchange rate implies that the Swiss inflation rate has on average been slightly over one-half percentage point higher than the German rate. This can be seen either as a conscious choice on the part of the SNB or the result of a policy that has been reluctant to allow the Swiss franc appreciate beyond 80 centimes to the mark.

1.1.3. The volatility of the CHF/DEM exchange rate is relatively small and declining

Volatility of asset prices is often measured by the standard deviation of percentage changes over a given period. Table I.1 shows this measure for the Swiss Franc relative to the German mark and the US dollar and for different time periods. Although volatility is determined by many factors including the shocks that affect the foreign exchange market, a central bank can have a certain influence as well, if its monetary policy is at least partly determined by exchange-rate developments.

Table I.1. Volatility of monthly CHF exchange rates (percent)

1	2	3	4
Sample	CHF/DEM	CHF/USD	Col. 3/Col. 2
1973:06 - 1998:12	1.66	3.70	2.23
1973:06 - 1977:12	2.11	3.05	1.46
1980:01 - 1998:12	1.39	3.67	2.64
1980:01 - 1989:12	1.48	3.88	2.62
1990:01 - 1998:12	1.29	3.45	2.67

Note: Volatility is measured by the standard deviation of the percentage change of the exchange rate.

The numbers in the Table show that volatility of the CHF/DEM rate is generally less than half of that of the CHF/USD rate. In addition the following two points are important to emphasize:

- The volatility of the DEM rate during 1973:06 - 1977:12 was fifty percent higher than the volatility since 1980:01.
- The volatility or both exchange rates has been declining over time since 1980. However, the ratio of the two has been roughly constant.

1.1.4. The CHF/Euro exchange rate volatility has been exceptionally low since the first of January 1999 compared to the volatility of the CHF/DEM rate before.

A fourth interesting fact, which is reported in the Tables I.2m and I.2d, is that the CHF/Euro exchange rate volatility has been exceptionally low since the first of

January 1999 compared to the volatility of the CHF/DEM rate before. From the Tables I.2 can be seen that the monthly volatilities for the same exchange rate calculated on the basis of different frequency data are close to each other. From the Tables I.1 and I.2d can be seen that while CHF/USD volatility reported in the column 3 of I.2d is in the range of the volatilities reported in column 3 of I.1, the CHF/Euro volatility of I.2d represents only 60% of the lowest volatility entry of I.1 corresponding to CHF/DEM.

Table 1.2m Volatility of monthly CHF exchange rates

1	2	3	4
Sample 99:01-00:01	CHF/Euro 0.66	CHF/USD 2.6	Col.3/Col.2 3.96
Calculating is done using monthly data points			

Table 1.2d Volatility of monthly CHF exchange rates

1	2	3	4
Sample 1.01.99-31.12.99	CHF/Euro 0.79	CHF/USD 3.2	Col.3/Col.2 4.00
Calculating is done using 261 daily data points			

Data source: Datastream

1.1.5. The exchange rate seems to play a role in SNB interest rate policy.

The policy strategy of the Swiss National Bank since 1973 has focused on target growth rates for monetary aggregates, M_1 in the seventies and M_0 thereafter.[3] These were until 1990 expressed as pre-announced annual growth rates, and since that as five-year target growth paths. Adherence to the announced target paths were never meant to be exact, and deviations have often been substantial, especially in the 1990s. Attempts have been made to explain the short-run policy stance of the SNB with empirical policy reaction function that take into account the evolution of inflation, output, the exchange rate, and external interest rates. In a recent study, Hviding (1999) argued that variations in Swiss short-term interest rates can be explained by a so-called Taylor rule [Taylor (1993)] according which the central bank sets a money-market interest rate with reference to deviations of inflation and output from their respective target paths. Camen, Genberg and Salemi (1990) and Dueker and Fischer (1996) show that the exchange rate vis-a-vis the German mark also plays a role in the short-run evolution of the SNB's policy instrument.

[3] See Rich and Béguelin (1985), Rich (1997) and Genberg and Kohli (1997) for general overviews.

1.2. Questions raised by these facts as we enter the euro era.

Like all empirical facts, those reported in the previous section refer to the past. Now that we have entered into a new monetary era in Europe, it is of interest to ask whether these developments will continue but with the euro replacing the mark as the reference currency. A number of specific questions come to mind and they will be stated and explained briefly here. Sections II and III of the paper will discuss possible answers.

1.2.1. Will the trend in the real exchange rate with respect to the euro be the same as it has been with respect to the mark in the past?

At issue is (i) the behavior of the CHF with respect to the average of the EMU countries on the one hand, and (ii) the influence of EMU on productivity differentials on the other.

1.2.2. Will the Swiss franc remain stable in nominal terms with respect to the euro as it has with respect to the German mark since 1979.

SNB officials have stated that during the initial period of the EMU, the franc will not be allowed to appreciate significantly with respect to the euro. (Reference to be provided) Fact 4 above bears this out. What remains to be seen is how long this policy will be in effect.

1.2.3. What will be the consequences for long run evolution of the price level and the nominal exchange rate with respect to the euro of the answer to question 2.2?

The evolution of the real exchange rate constrains either the evolution of the inflation differential or the nominal exchange rate with respect to the euro countries.

1.2.4 If the reduced volatility of the euro is due to an explicit policy of the SNB, and if this policy continues, what will be the consequence for short-run output and price stability?

How does more or less exchange-rate stabilization influence the business cycle and the short-run evolution of the domestic inflation rate? An estimated macroeconomic model will be used to give some possible answers.

2. LONG RUN TRENDS OF INFLATION AND THE EXCHANGE RATE

Let

B_{CH} = the Swiss inflation rate

B_{EU} = the inflation rate in the eleven euro countries

K(i,CH) = the rate of change of the nominal exchange rate of the Swiss Franc relative to currency i
Λ(i,CH) = the rate of change of the real exchange rate of the Swiss Franc relative to currency i

Then it is by definition true that

$$K(EU,CH) = B_{CH} - B_{EU} + \Lambda(EU,CH)$$

If the SNB adopts a medium-term inflation target that will be the same as that of the ECB, then the nominal exchange rate with respect to the euro will evolve is the same way as the real rate. On the other hand, if the medium-term trend of the nominal rate is as flat as it has been with respect to the German mark, then the domestic inflation rate will be higher or lower that the euro inflation rate depending again on the evolution of the real exchange rate.

2.1. *Will the Swiss Franc continue to appreciate with respect to the Euro?*

The rate of change of the real exchange rate of the Swiss Franc relative to the Euro can be written

$$\Lambda(EU,CH) = \Gamma\, s_i\, \Lambda(i,CH)$$

or

$$\Lambda(EU,CH) = s_{GE}\, \Lambda(GE,CH) + (1 - s_{GE})\, \Lambda(REU,CH)$$

where

s_i (s_{GE}) = the share of member country i (Germany) in the Euro price index
Λ(REU,CH) = rate of change of the real exchange rate of the Swiss Franc relative to the rest of EU.

We have documented the persistent real appreciation of the Swiss Franc relative to the German mark during the past three two and a half decades. While it is true that the mark has depreciated in real terms with respect to the other EMU members, this effect has been quantitatively very small. This implies that the Swiss Franc has appreciated persistently also with the EMU member currencies as a group.[4] Is this likely to continue?

The Balassa-Samuelson argument points to productivity differences as the explanation for the long-term movements in real exchange rates.

---

[4] The deterministic trends from 1975:1 until 1998:4 are 0.88 % per year with respect to the mark and 0.72% per year with respect to the EMU members. The difference between these is not significant at the 95% level.

If

$\Delta_i =$ the difference between the rate of productivity growth in the traded and non-traded sectors in country i

then the movement of the real exchange rate between Switzerland and the Euro group will depend (positively) on

$\Delta_i - \Delta_{ch}$ for all eleven countries i

or, equivalently, on

$\Delta_{GE} - \Delta_{ch}$ and $\Delta_{REU} - \Delta_{GE}$.

According to this explanation, the real appreciation of the Swiss Franc has been due to high relative productivity growth in the Swiss traded goods sector. How the introduction of the Euro will influence this is ambiguous. The question is whether the expected productivity gains from the Euro will be biased towards the traded or the non-traded sectors. At first sight, it might be argued that the traded goods sectors should benefit most from the reduction in exchange rate risk and transactions costs in Euroland. This would tend to slow the real appreciation of the Franc. On the other hand, the generally increased integration among the EMU members that is expected to result from the single currency could put increased pressure to restructure and increase productivity also in the traditional non-traded sectors. Further theoretical and empirical evidence is needed to have a clear indication which of these effects will dominate.

If past trends continue, the Franc will appreciate in real terms relative to the euro by somewhere between .7 and 1.2% per year. As we have already noted this will either imply a correspondingly higher inflation rate in Switzerland or a gradual nominal appreciation of the Swiss Franc. Although the numbers may not seem large, a one percent annual rate of appreciation will bring the implicit CHF/DEM rate to .78 by the end of 2002. This is 2.5% below the all-time low of the Franc!

3. EXCHANGE-RATE POLICY FOR SHORT-RUN STABILITY.

In this section we investigate of the role of the exchange rate in short-run stabilization policy. Specifically we attempt to assess the performance of alternative monetary policy strategies that differ mainly with respect to the importance they give to exchange rate changes in the determination of monetary policy. The different strategies are judged by the short- to medium-run stability of the Swiss economy that they deliver in response to exogenous shocks.

To carry out the comparisons of policy strategies, we make use of a multi-country econometric model originally developed by John Taylor in the early 1990s. That model covered seven countries - Canada, France, Germany, Italy, Japan, the United Kingdom, and the United States - and was estimated with quarterly data from 1970 to 1986. In order to study monetary policy options for Switzerland without increasing the number of countries, we added a Swiss module to Taylor's group and removed Canada. We also re-estimated the entire model with data from 1980 to 1996.[5]

3.1. *The multi-country Taylor model*

Taylor's model can perhaps most easily be described as a sophisticated Mundell-Fleming model with two important additions: a set of wage-price relationships on the one hand, and rational expectations that are important notably in interest parity relationships, wage setting, and the determination of long-term interest rates.

The model, which is nonlinear, contains equations for the standard expenditure items (consumption, investment, exports and imports) that together with exogenous government spending determine aggregate demand. The supply side is modeled with a set of wage and price equations. Actual wages are determined by contract wages that are set on the basis of expected future wages and a measure of aggregate demand. Prices of domestic output are determined by labor costs and import prices.

Monetary policy and the exchange rate influence the real side of the model through the usual channels, long-term interest rates in consumption and investment and relative prices (which depend on the exchange rate) in exports and imports. Long-term interest rates depend on future expected short-term rates through a term structure relationship. Exchange rates and short-term interest rates are linked in an ex ante open interest parity relationship, where the future exchange rate is the rationally expected one. The model is closed with an equation for the short-term interest rate, which is determined either directly by the Central Bank in a policy reaction function (a type of Taylor rule), or indirectly through a money market equilibrium condition with an exogenous money supply.

The model that is used in this paper contains blocks for the United States and Japan, a EMU group represented by Germany, Italy and France, the United Kingdom representing a non-EMU EU country, and Switzerland. All in all there are 112 equations, including identities. The parameters in the model were estimated with quarterly data from 1980 to 1996. The estimation results and the properties of the model will be reported in Kadareja (2000). Here we simply note that for the countries that were also in Taylor's sample, the re-estimated model behaves quite similarly to the original, and for Switzerland the in-sample one-step ahead forecasts are generally quite close to the actual values of the endogenous variables.

3.2. *The simulation strategy*

3.2.1. *Does the existence of the EMU make any difference for Switzerland?*

To assess the implications of the creation EMU for Switzerland we simulated the model under two scenarios, one mimicking a large EMU and one a counterfactual

[5] The most comprehensive reference to the specification and performance of Taylor's model is Taylor (1993a). The re-estimation of the entire model and the specification/estimation of the Swiss module will be described in detail in the PhD dissertation of one of us. See Kadareja (2000).

Europe with freely floating exchange rates. In the EMU scenario all four EU countries had identical short- and long-term interest rates and a completely fixed exchange rate between them.[6] In the counter-factual scenario, on the other hand, each country pursued a monetary policy defined by a Taylor rule for the domestic short-term interest. In both cases, the simulations were stochastic, and the random shocks to the system were assumed to have properties similar to those of the estimated shocks.

3.2.2. *What role should the exchange rate play in Swiss monetary policy?*

The consequences of different types of monetary/exchange-rate policies by the Swiss National Bank in the presence of the EMU were investigated with two types of simulations. In the first, deterministic simulations of the effects of specific exogenous shocks were carried out, and in the second stochastic simulations were conducted with shocks that were meant to replicate those that occurred during the estimation period. In each case, three different environments for the Swiss exchange rate and monetary policy were examined:

a. Switzerland is a member of the EMU (Referred to as EMU5 in the tables and figures containing the results).

b. The Swiss Franc is floating but the short-term interest rate is set in part with the objective to limit fluctuations in the exchange rate vis-B-vis the euro. The other variables in the reaction function are the expected inflation rate, and deviations of the price level and output from their respective base-line paths as in the usual Taylor rule. (EXTENDED TAYLOR)

   The policy reaction function for the short-term rate was:

$$RS(t) - RS^B(t) = [LP^{exp}(t+4) - LP(t) - LP^B(t+4) + LP^B(t)] + \alpha * [LP(t) - LP^B(t)] + \beta * [LY(t) - LY^B(t)] + (\gamma * [LE(t) - LE^B(t)]$$

   where
   RS = the short-term nominal interest rate
   P = the price level(gdp deflator)
   Y = real income
   E = the exchange relative to the Euro
   and where L represents the natural logarithm and B refers to the baseline path.

c. Swiss Franc is floating and the short-term interest rate is set as in b. except there is no exchange-rate stabilization (γ=0). (TAYLOR)

---

[6] The United Kingdom was included in the EMU group in the first scenario on the assumption that the UK will in fact be a member when Swiss membership becomes a possibility.

To solve this nonlinear model we used a numerical method, the so-called Fair and Taylor extended path algorithm. (See Fair and Taylor (1983) for details.) In the stochastic simulations, the shocks were drawn from a multivariate normal distribution with a covariance matrix calculated on the basis of the estimated shocks. In all cases the simulated outcomes were compared, variable-by-variable, with a baseline simulation of the model assuming no shocks. When comparisons between different rules were made, the metric was the root mean square percentage deviation from the baseline path, RMSD.

3.3. *Results*

3.3.1. *Comparison of the effects of fixed vs. floating rates in the EU*

In a first set of simulations we look at the difference between a situation where the four EU countries in the model (UK, Germany, France, and Italy) have joined together to form a monetary union, and a case where the exchange rates between them are floating. The three other countries have floating exchange rates in both cases. Monetary policy in countries with floating exchange rates (and in the EMU) is determined by identical Taylor rules of the following type:

$$RS(t) - RS^{B}(t) = [LP^{exp}(t+4) - LP(t) - LP^{B}(t+4) + LP^{B}(t)]$$
$$+ 2.0 * [LP(t) - LP^{B}(t)] + 0.3 * [LY(t) - LY^{B}(t)]$$

Table II.1 contains a summary of the results, which point to the following three conclusions:

- For the GDP deflator and for wages, flexible exchange rates are better than the EMU solution for the EU countries. For almost all other variables, the opposite is the case for France, Italy, and the United Kingdom
- EMU is better for stability of the CPI for France, Germany, and Italy but not for the United Kingdom.[7]
- For Switzerland it generally makes little difference if the EU countries have fixed or floating exchange rates except for the CPI and export prices, where it would be better if the European currencies were floating vis-a-vis each other.

To understand these results in terms of the usual arguments surrounding monetary integration, it is important to keep in mind first of all that the criterion for

---

[7] The CPI:s do not appear explicitly in the estimated the model. However, assuming that they can be expressed as log-linear functions of the GDP deflator and import prices, it is possible to simulate also the effect on them. To this end we estimated equations of the following form for each of the countries in the model: $\Delta \ln CPI = a + b\ \Delta \ln\ PGDP + c\ \Delta \ln\ PIM$. Using two-stage-least-squares and quarterly date from 1980 to 1997 we obtained the following estimates (b and c were constrained to sum to 1): France (b=0.83, c=0.17), Germany (b= 0.62, c=0.38), Italy (b=0.86, c= 0.14), Switzerland (b= 0.66, c= 0.34), and the UK (b=0.71, c=0.29).

deciding between the regimes only takes into account macroeconomic stability. The efficiency gains from a single currency are not considered. Related to this is the fact that the model assigns no special importance to the variance of exchange rates in any behavioral equation. Secondly, countries are assumed to follow identical policy rules in the floating exchange rate environment. In the floating rate simulations, this eliminates one of the potential sources of instability that proponents of EMU have emphasized, namely policy-induced asymmetric shocks. Nevertheless, the results are interesting is so far as they suggest that the EMU is most stabilizing for France and Italy and least for Germany, suggesting that other considerations must have induced Germany to favor its creation.

Table II.1. Comparisons of fixed versus floating exchange rates among EU countries

	EMU COUNTRIES			SWITZERLAND
	FLEXIBLE	EMU	EQUAL	
Output	**G**	**I,UK**	**F**	**EQUAL**
Consumption	G	UK,I	F	EQUAL
Investment	G	UK,I,F	0	EQUAL
Net Exports (% of GDP)	**0**	**UK,I,F**	**G**	**EQUAL**
Exports	0	G,F,I	UK	EQUAL
Imports	G	I	F,UK	EQUAL
Exchange Rate	**0**	**UK,F,G**	**I**	**EQUAL**
Interest Rates	**G**	**I,UK**	**F**	**EQUAL**
Real Interest Rates	G	I,UK,F	0	EQUAL
Long-Term Interest Rates	G	I,UK,F	0	EQUAL
CPI	**UK**	**G**	**F,I**	**FLEXIBLE**
GDP Deflator	UK,F,I,G	0	0	EQUAL
Export Prices	0	G,I,UK F	0	FLEXIBLE
Import Prices	0	I,UK,F G	0	EQUAL
Wages	UK,F,I,G	0	0	EQUAL

Note: Results are averages over 100 stochastic simulations. Shocks are based on the estimated covariance matrix. In the flexible exchange rate case all countries have floating exchange rates and short-term interest rates are set according to identical Taylor rules. In the EMU case, the four EU countries have a fixed exchange rate and the monetary policy is set by a single Taylor rule. All other countries behave as in the floating case. The entries in the first two columns of the table refer to the countries (G = Germany, F = France, UK = United Kingdom, I = Italy) for which the system in the corresponding column has a lower RMSD, i.e. the countries for which it results in more stability. When there are more than one country in a cell then the list is done in decreasing order from the country which benefits more in stability to the country (or countries) which benefits (benefit) less. The RMSD are judged to be equal if they differ by less than 5% and this case is shown in column three. The column under the heading "Switzerland" shows the EMU effects on the Swiss economy.

3.3.2. The effects of specific foreign shocks under alternative domestic policy regimes.[8]

In order to gain intuition about the functioning of the model and about the role of exchange rate smoothing in the conduct of monetary policy, we performed deterministic simulations of the following external shocks:

1. 5% one-period negative shock to the interest parity condition US$/Euro.
2. 5% one-period negative shock to the interest parity condition US$/SF.
3. 3% permanent monetary expansion in the USA.
4. 3% permanent monetary expansion in the EMU countries.
5. 1% of GDP permanent fiscal expansion in the USA.
6. 1% of GDP permanent fiscal expansion in the EMU countries.

In each case we compared the outcome of the three domestic policy regimes defined in the previous section. The results that are summarized in Figures III.1 - III.6 confirm the conventional analysis, which emphasizes that the optimal exchange policy depends crucially on the type of disturbance that is considered.

As Figures III.1 - III.2 show when there are *asset market shocks* the EMU5 regime dominates all other policy regimes with regard to the stability of GDP and prices, and some degree of exchange-rate smoothing is preferred to pure floating. Since Switzerland trades predominantly with the EMU countries, limiting the fluctuation of the SF/Euro rate is desirable in such cases.

When *nominal disturbances* (such as money expansion in USA and EMU) occur, on the other hand, exchange rate flexibility tends to reduce fluctuations in GDP and prices as compared with other policy regimes (see Figures III.3 - III.4). Note also the overshooting of USD/CHF rate, in the third graph of III.3 .

When *real disturbances* (such as fiscal expansion in USA and EMU) occur, the results are mixed, so a fully flexible regime ('Taylor') dominates the others in the case of USA fiscal expansion, though the effects on the Swiss economy are small and so the stability differences are small (Figure III.5). On the other hand 'Extended Taylor' dominates clearly in terms of prices stability as does 'Taylor' in terms of GDP, in case of EMU fiscal expansion (Figure III.6).

[8] The performance of the economy in response to domestic disturbances will be analyzed in a separate paper.

Figure III.1: 5% One-period, unexpected negative shock to interest parityUS$/Euro

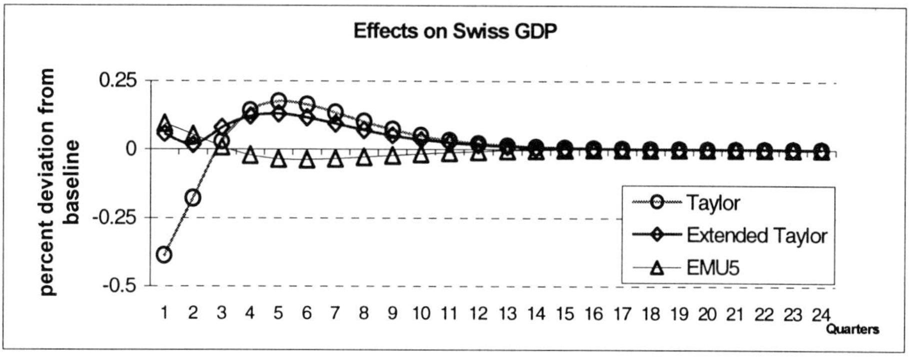

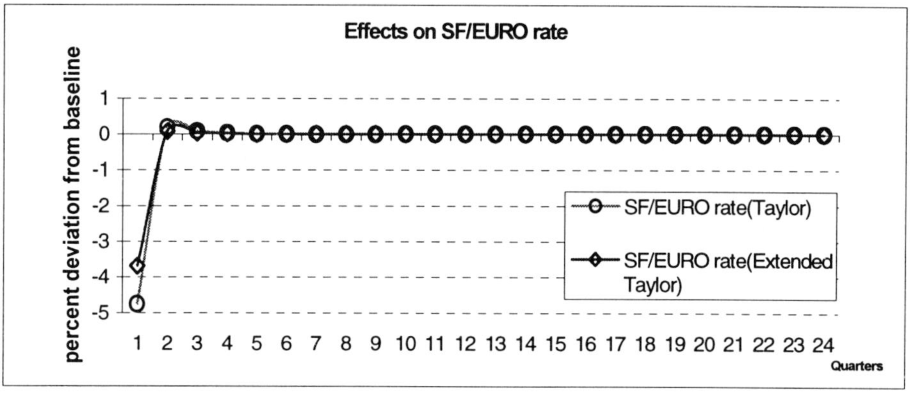

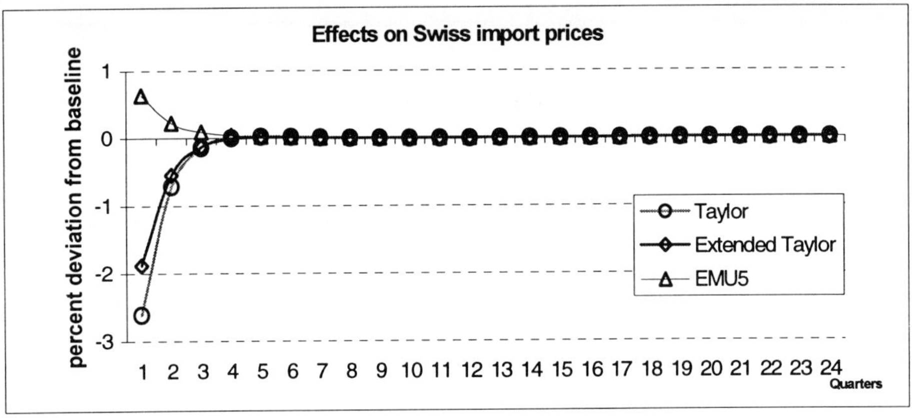
Effects on Swiss import prices
percent deviation from baseline
1
0
-1
-2
-3
1 2 3 4 5 6 7 8 9 10 11 12 13 14 15 16 17 18 19 20 21 22 23 24
Quarters
Taylor
Extended Taylor
EMU5

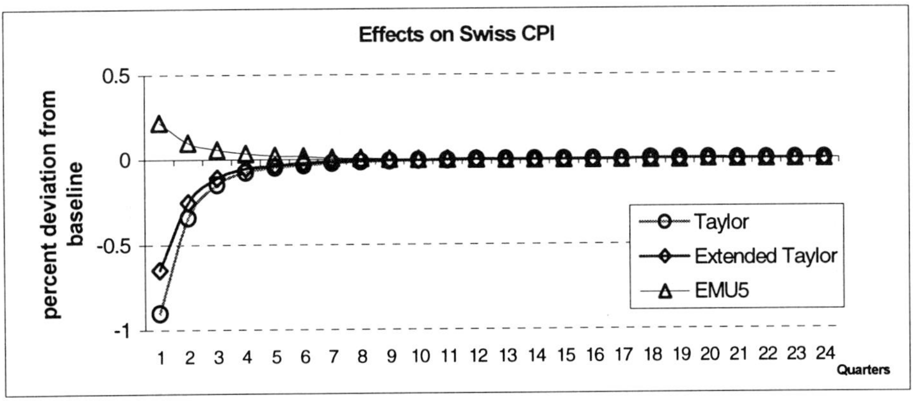
Effects on Swiss CPI
percent deviation from baseline
0.5
0
-0.5
-1
1 2 3 4 5 6 7 8 9 10 11 12 13 14 15 16 17 18 19 20 21 22 23 24
Quarters
Taylor
Extended Taylor
EMU5

Figure III.2: 5% One-period, unexpected negative shock to interest parityUS$/CHF

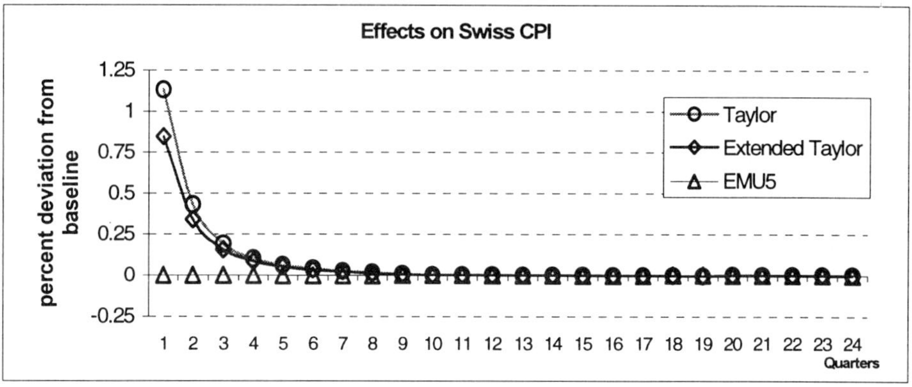

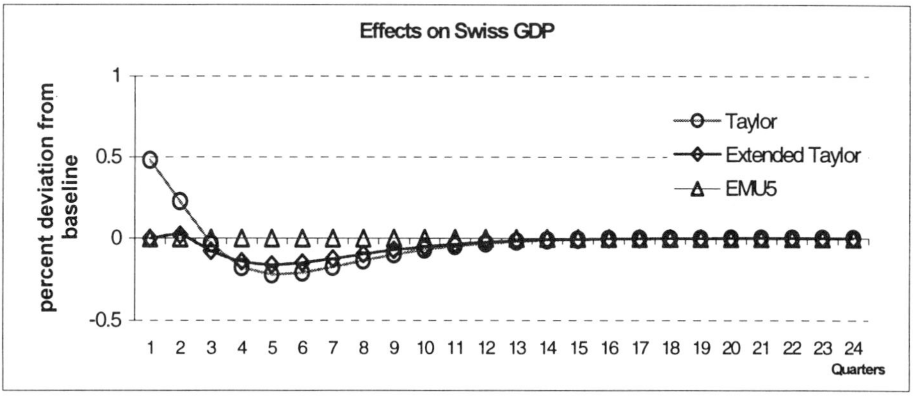

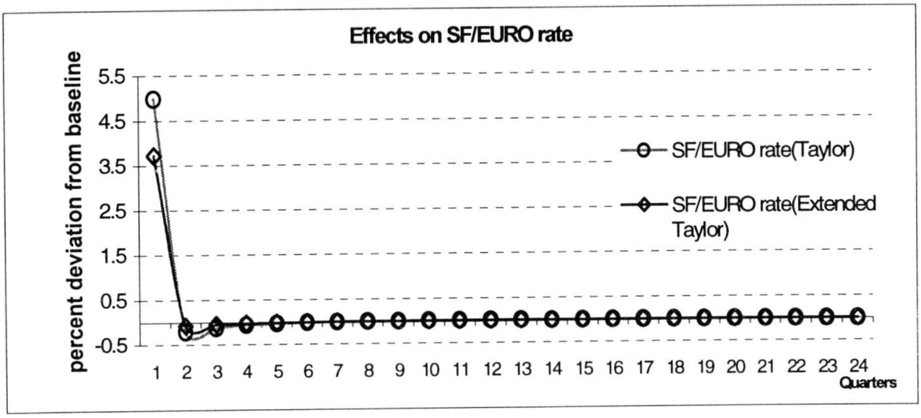
Effects on SF/EURO rate
percent deviation from baseline
5.5
4.5
3.5
2.5
1.5
0.5
-0.5
SF/EURO rate(Taylor)
SF/EURO rate(Extended Taylor)
1 2 3 4 5 6 7 8 9 10 11 12 13 14 15 16 17 18 19 20 21 22 23 24
Quarters

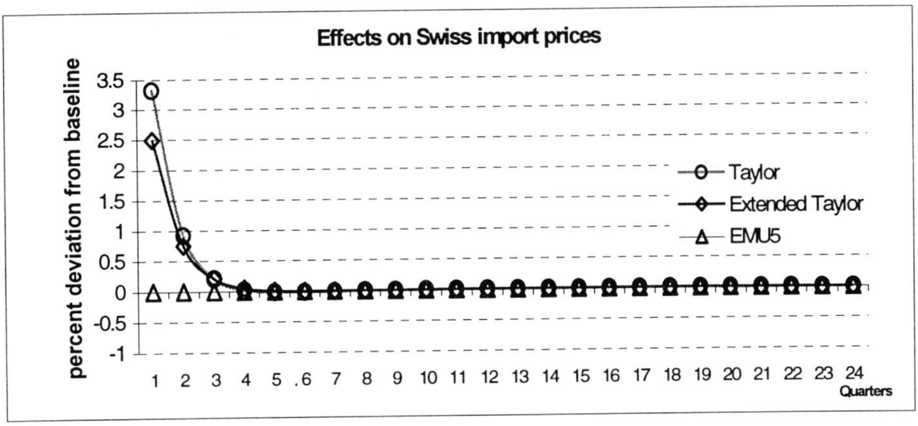
Effects on Swiss import prices
percent deviation from baseline
3.5
3
2.5
2
1.5
1
0.5
0
-0.5
-1
Taylor
Extended Taylor
EMU5
1 2 3 4 5 .6 7 8 9 10 11 12 13 14 15 16 17 18 19 20 21 22 23 24
Quarters

Figure III.3: 3% Permanent and unexpected monetary expansion in USA

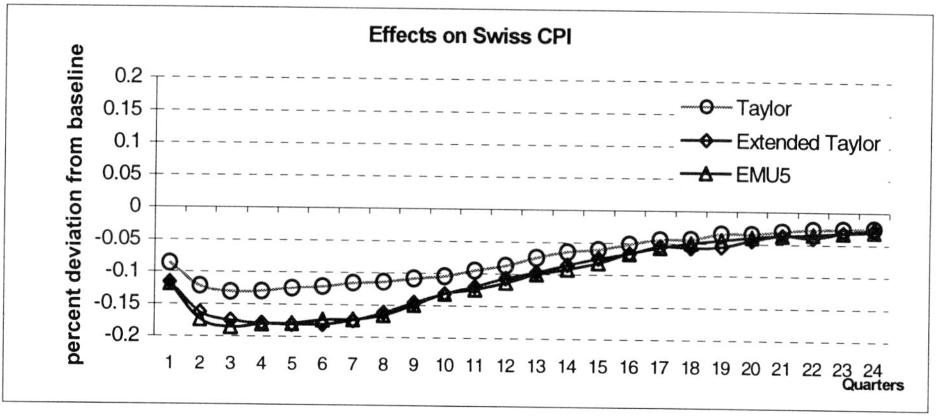

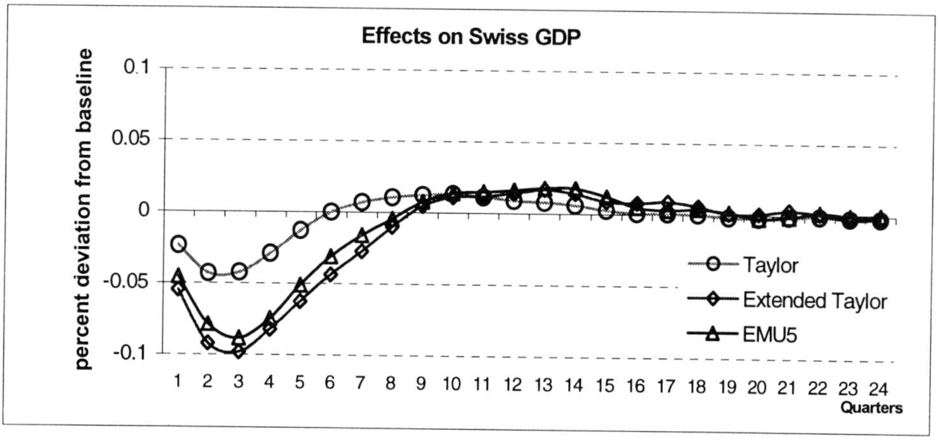

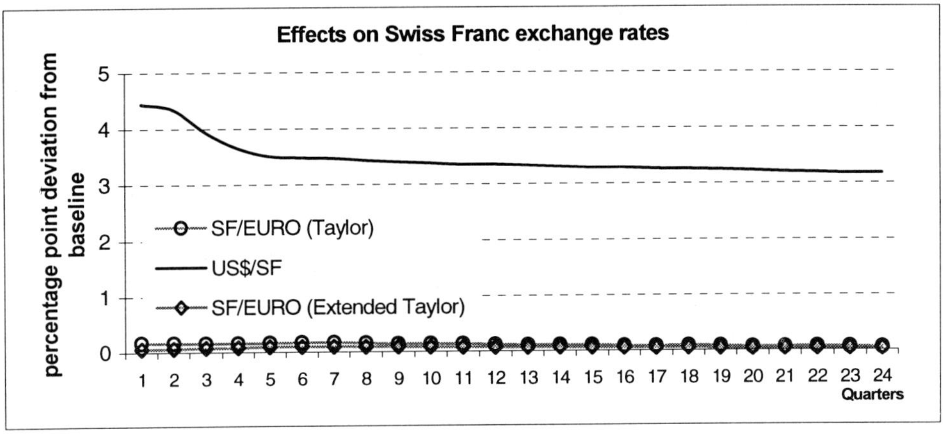
Effects on Swiss Franc exchange rates
percentage point deviation from baseline
5
4
3
2
1
0
SF/EURO (Taylor)
US$/SF
SF/EURO (Extended Taylor)
1 2 3 4 5 6 7 8 9 10 11 12 13 14 15 16 17 18 19 20 21 22 23 24
Quarters

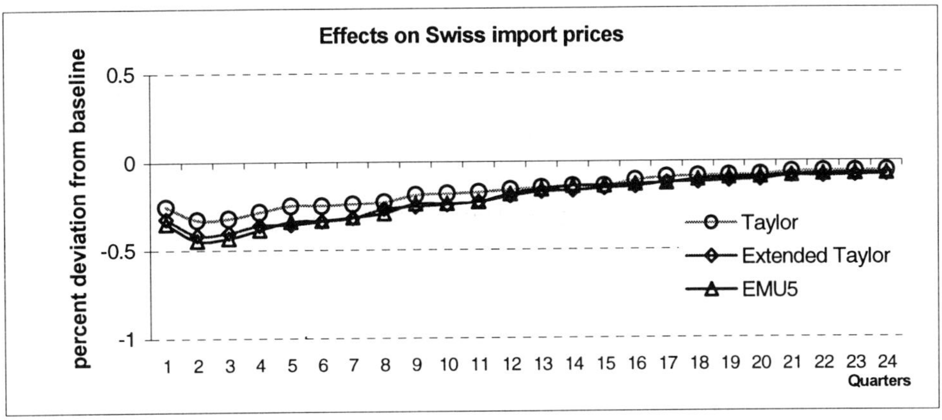
Effects on Swiss import prices
percent deviation from baseline
0.5
0
-0.5
-1
Taylor
Extended Taylor
EMU5
1 2 3 4 5 6 7 8 9 10 11 12 13 14 15 16 17 18 19 20 21 22 23 24
Quarters

Figure III.4: 3% Permanent and unexpected monetary expansion in EMU

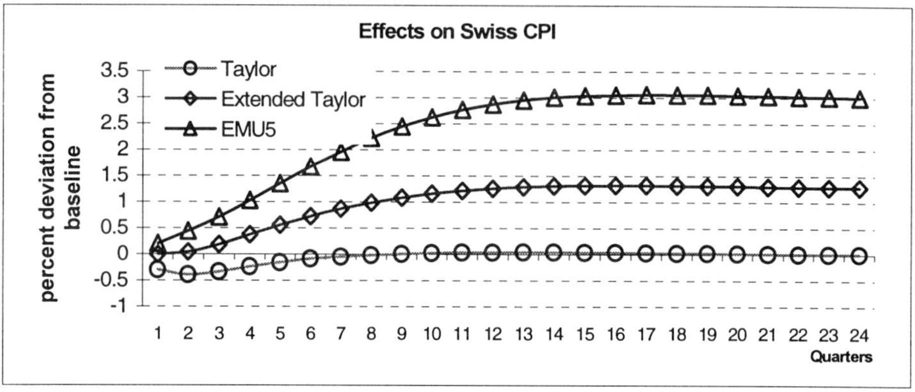

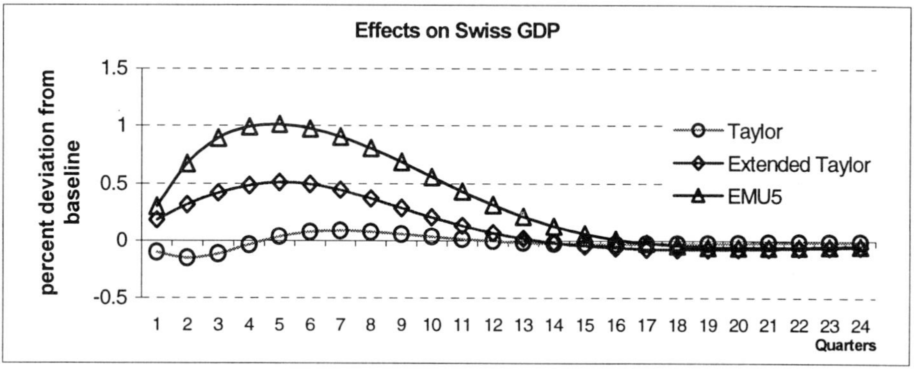

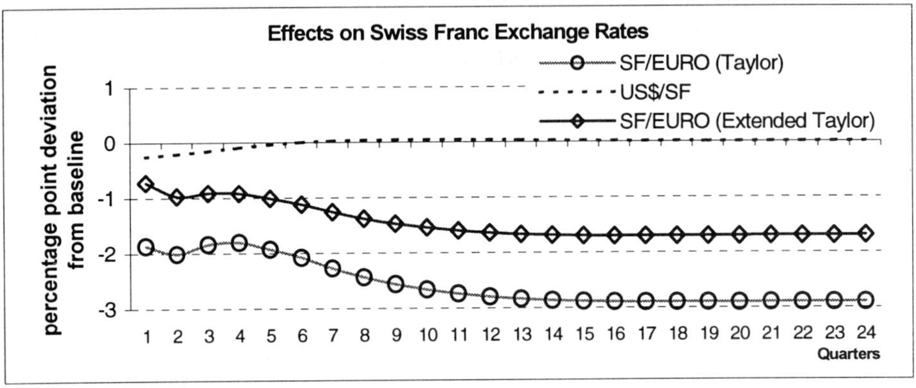
Effects on Swiss Franc Exchange Rates
SF/EURO (Taylor)
US$/SF
SF/EURO (Extended Taylor)
percentage point deviation from baseline
1
0
-1
-2
-3
1 2 3 4 5 6 7 8 9 10 11 12 13 14 15 16 17 18 19 20 21 22 23 24
Quarters

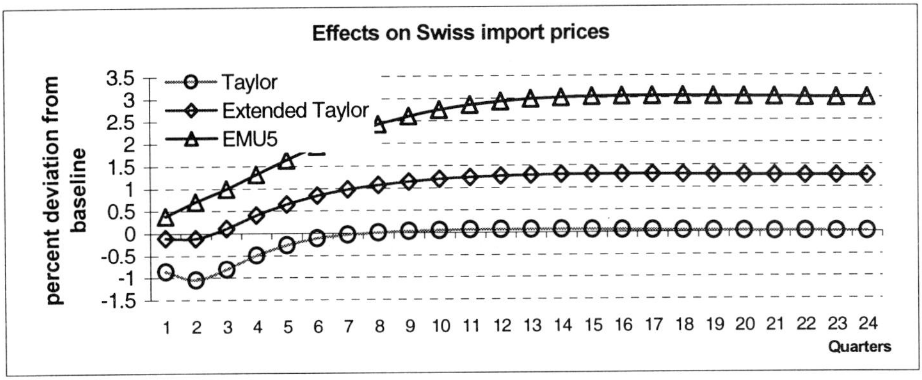
Effects on Swiss import prices
Taylor
Extended Taylor
EMU5
percent deviation from baseline
3.5
3
2.5
2
1.5
1
0.5
0
-0.5
-1
-1.5
1 2 3 4 5 6 7 8 9 10 11 12 13 14 15 16 17 18 19 20 21 22 23 24
Quarters

Figure III.5: 1% of GDP, Permanent and unexpected fiscal expansion in USA

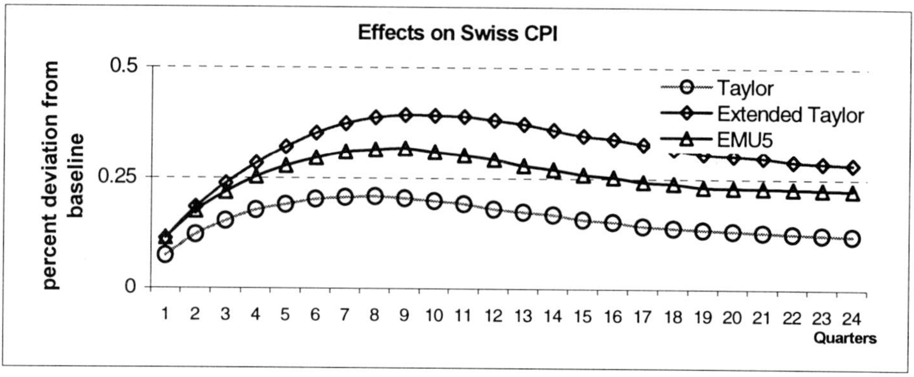

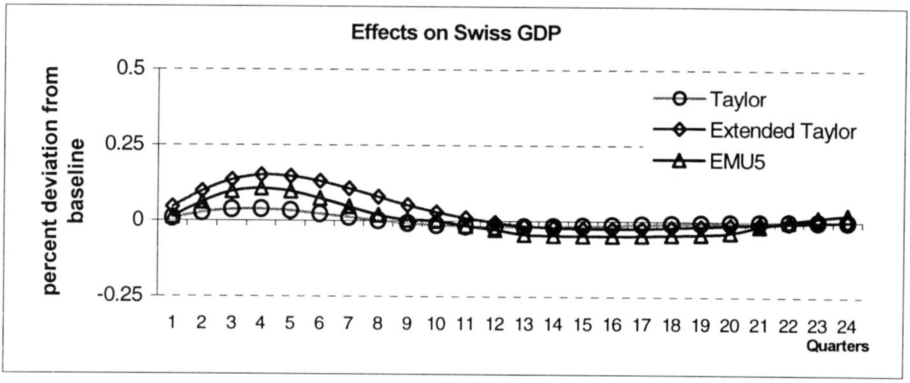

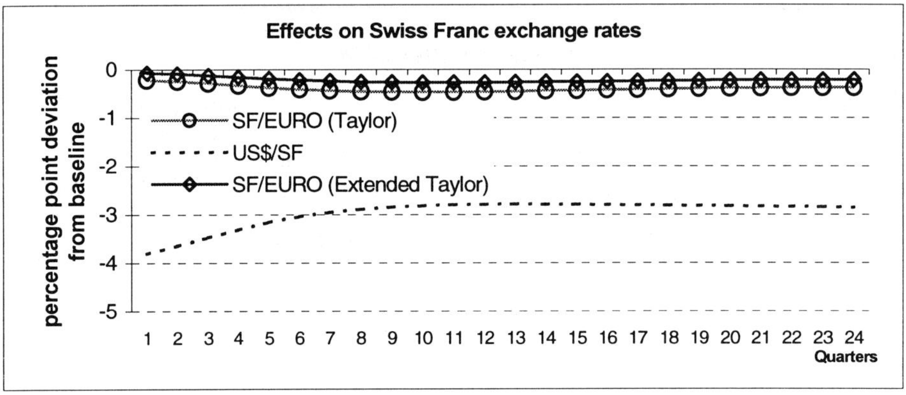
Effects on Swiss Franc exchange rates
percentage point deviation from baseline
0
-1
-2
-3
-4
-5
SF/EURO (Taylor)
US$/SF
SF/EURO (Extended Taylor)
1 2 3 4 5 6 7 8 9 10 11 12 13 14 15 16 17 18 19 20 21 22 23 24
Quarters

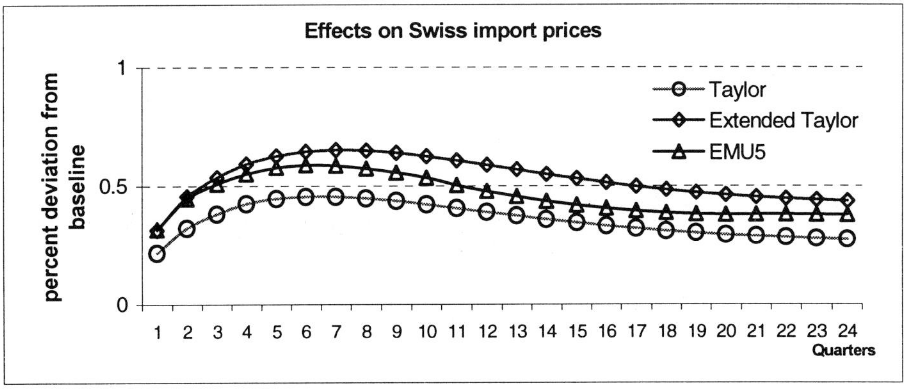
Effects on Swiss import prices
percent deviation from baseline
1
0.5
0
Taylor
Extended Taylor
EMU5
1 2 3 4 5 6 7 8 9 10 11 12 13 14 15 16 17 18 19 20 21 22 23 24
Quarters

Figure III.6. 1% of GDP, Permanent and unexpected fiscal expansion in EMU

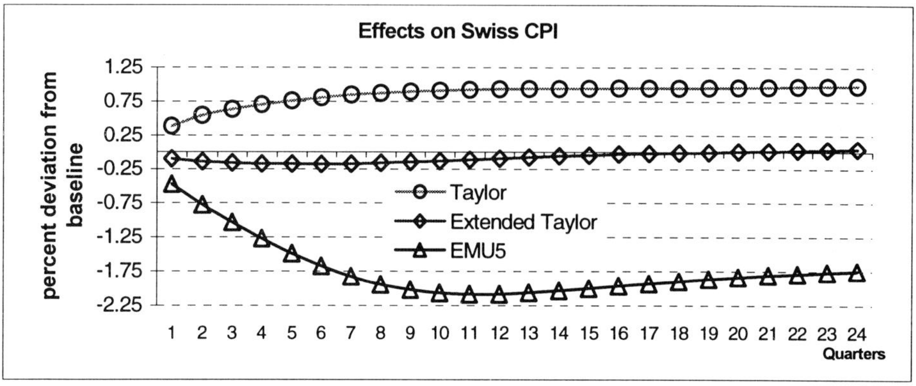

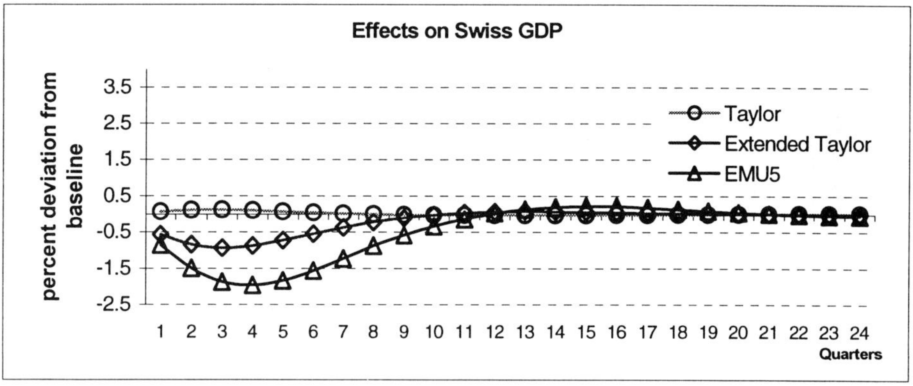

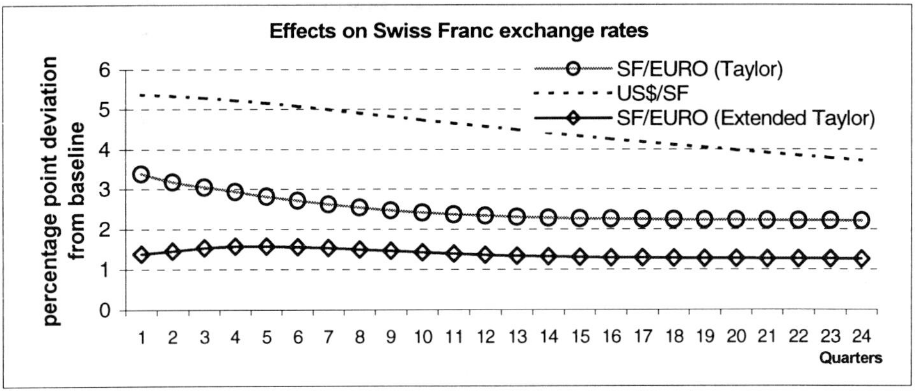
Effects on Swiss Franc exchange rates
SF/EURO (Taylor)
US$/SF
SF/EURO (Extended Taylor)
percentage point deviation from baseline
Quarters

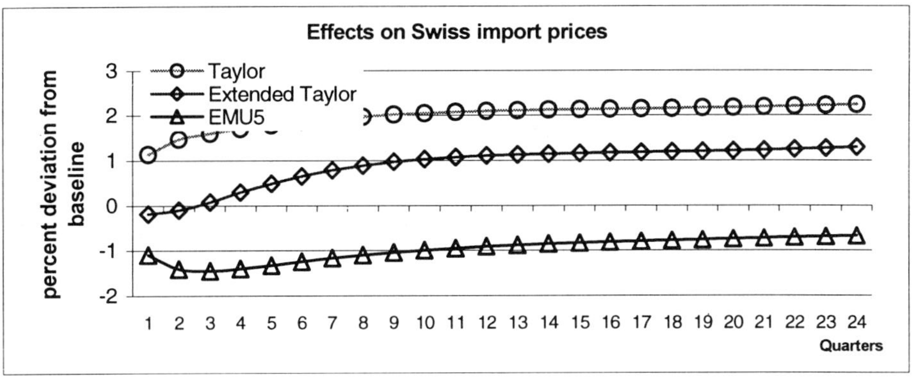
Effects on Swiss import prices
Taylor
Extended Taylor
EMU5
percent deviation from baseline
Quarters

If shocks could be observed, an appropriate monetary policy response could in principle be designed. With the exchange rate (and asset prices in general) serving as a rapid source of information, the optimal degree of exchange-rate smoothing could be decided on a case-by-case basis. Unfortunately, when there are more shocks than sources of information this strategy is inadequate. Instead it will be necessary to rely on policy rules that perform well on average given the typical shocks that characterize the economic environment of the country. In the next section we attempt to determine what role the exchange rate would play in such a rule for the Swiss National Bank.

3.3.3. Alternative policy rules for Switzerland.

Assuming that all four EU countries represented in the model have joined the EMU, the next set of simulations investigates the consequences of alternative policy regimes followed by the Swiss National Bank. Three regimes are considered, two with a floating exchange rate with respect to the Euro, and one supposing Switzerland has joined the EMU. The two floating exchange rate scenarios differ with respect to the assumed behavior of the Swiss National Bank. In the case called "Taylor" the SNB is assumed to set the Swiss short-term real interest rate in response to deviations of prices and output from the baseline path. This results in a volatility of the Swiss Franc/Euro rate that is 110 percent larger than the observed volatility with respect to the mark during the sample period used for estimation. In order to attempt to mimic the lower observed volatility an 'extended Taylor' rule is defined in which the short-term interest rate also responds to the deviation of the CHF/EUR rate from the baseline. To this end, the value of the reaction coefficient (() was chosen so as to produce a volatility of the Euro exchange rate that is equal to the observed (⇕ resulted close to 1.5).

The results are reported in Table III.2. As before, the policy rules are ranked according to the average over 100 simulations of the root mean square deviation from the baseline path. The shocks are drawn from a multivariate normal distribution with a covariance matrix equal to the estimated one. Not surprisingly, the relative performance of the policy rules depends on which variable we consider.

For example, stability of net exports as % of GDP, output, investments and consumption is fostered with completely fixed exchange rate (i.e. EMU5), and some degree of exchange rate smoothing is preferred to pure floating.

On the other hand the pure Taylor rule does a good job of stabilizing the GDP deflator. This is to be expected since this rule contains a strong feedback from price deviations to the short-term interest rate. However, the stability of domestic prices comes at the cost of greater exchange rate variability, and therefore greater variability of import prices, compared to both the other policy rules. In fact, the large amount of trade with the EU countries implies that a completely fixed exchange rate with respect to the euro minimizes import price fluctuations. Combining these two results leads to the conclusion that our synthetic CPI[9] will be

---

[9] Recall that the CPI is defined as the geometrically weighted average of the GDP deflator and the import price index, with weights equal to .66 and .34 respectively.

most stable with an interest rate rule that contains some degree of exchange rate smoothing.

Table III.2. The consequences of different monetary and exchange rate policies in Switzerland

	Floating		Fixed
	Taylor	Extended Taylor	EMU5
	↦ =2, ↕ =.3,⇕ =0	↦ =2, ↕ =.3,⇕ = 1.5	
Output	5.2 %	Equal	BEST
Consumption	5.0 %	Equal	BEST
Investment	8.9 %	6.6 %	BEST
Exports	Equal	Equal	BEST
Imports	BEST	Equal	Equal
Net Exports (% of GDP)	23.0 %	22.1 %	BEST
Short-term Interest Rates	26.4 %	84.8 %	BEST
Real Bond Interest Rates	Equal	Equal	BEST
GDP Deflator	BEST	10.9 %	39.4 %
CPI	7.5 %	BEST	12.4 %
Export Prices	Equal	BEST	12.4 %
Import Prices	91.3 %	52.8 %	BEST
Exchange Rate (SF / US$)	5 %	BEST	Equal
Wages	BEST	5.8 %	19.1 %

Note: The four EU countries are jointly floating with respect to both Japan and the USA. The Yen/dollar exchange rate is also flexible. Europe, Japan and the USA are following identical Taylor rules with ∀= 2.0 and ∃= 0.3. The table identifies the best policy rule for Switzerland in the sense of the rule with the lowest RMSD. The percentages refer to the difference of the RMSD relative to the best rule. The RMSD are judged to be equal with the BEST rule if they differ by less than 5%. Results are averages over 100 stochastic simulations. Shocks are based on the estimated covariance matrix.

This confirms the intuition from small analytical models that some degree of exchange rate management is superior (in terms of prices stability) to both a purely floating and a completely fixed exchange rate. Figure III.7 represents an attempt to define an "optimal" degree of exchange rate smoothing. It shows in an index form the weighted average of the RMSDs of the CPI and real GDP.[10] The lines in the graph represent different weights associated with the two components. The indices

[10] The formula is $(RMSD_{CPI})^{w} (RMSD_{GDP})^{1-w}$.

have been normalized to equal 1 when the exchange rate is completely fixed. The horizontal axis measures the volatility of the Swiss Franc/Euro exchange rate, calculated as the standard deviation of quarterly changes. This index is normalized so that a value of 1 is equal to the measured volatility during the 1980-97. The maximum volatility occurs when there policy of the SNB is represented by the pure Taylor rule without exchange-rate smoothing. A fixed exchange rate relative to the Euro obviously corresponds to zero volatility. To complete the graph with points between the two volatility limits, we simulated five 'Extended Taylor' rules which differ from each other only with respect to the exchange rate smoothing (i.e. for different ⇕-s).

From the figure we see that an objective function that only contains real GDP is minimized for a completely fixed exchange rate (i.e. for Switzerland being an EMU member). If only CPI stability is considered important, there should be about 20% less exchange rate smoothing than the one likely to have been used in the period 1980-1996. If the weights in the objective function are the same 0.5 then the instability index for 'EMU5' and 'Taylor' cases equals one, whereas equals 0.95 for three 'Extended Taylor' rules which imply the CHF/Euro volatility index in the range from 1 to 1.2. "Optimal" exchange rate smoothing in the intermediate cases can be determined from the figure.

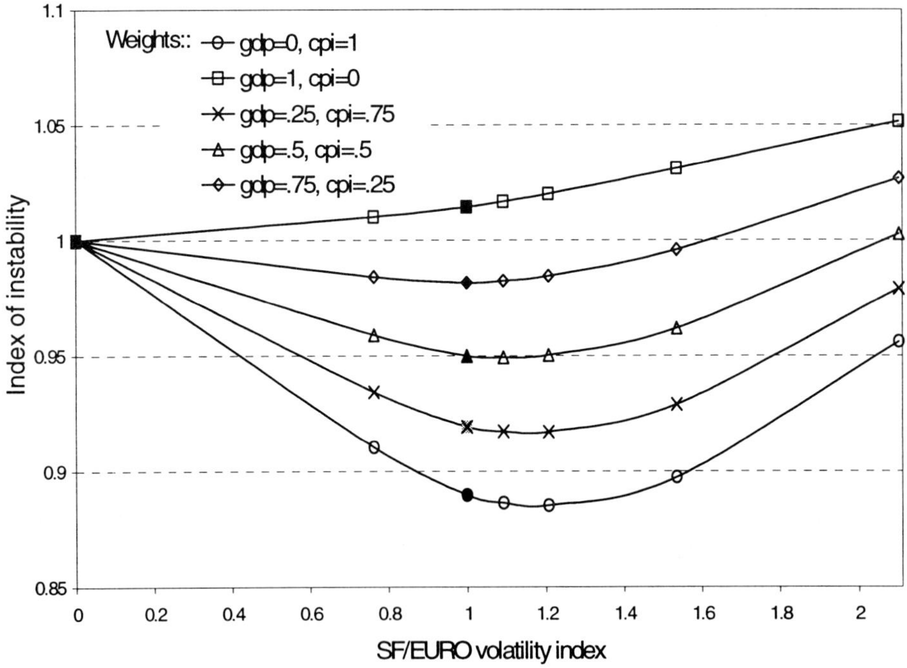

Figure III.7. The "optimal degree of exchange rate smoothing

The results from these simulations suggest that the apparent policy of the SNB to smooth fluctuations of the Swiss Franc/DEM rate can be justified by a desire to limit fluctuations not only of the consumer price index but also of real GDP. It is of course possible that exchange-rate stability is desirable for other reasons than stabilization. For example, a smoother path of the exchange rate might be associated with less exchange rate uncertainty, which may have a value of its own that is not captured by the model used here. Alternatively, the absence of large exchange rate fluctuations may be thought of as a way to avoid drawing attention to the currency and thereby avoid having it be considered as a refuge of speculative funds. Be that as it may, the simulation results presented here point to the importance for a small open economy to limit the free fluctuations of the exchange even if the policy objectives can be expressed exclusively in terms of output and price stability.

3.4. Caveats

A number of caveats should be kept in mind when the above results are interpreted. Even though expectations in the model are rational, and therefore incorporate changes in the policy rules, the Lucas' critique will apply to other aspects of the model especially when we consider as substantial a change in the policy environment as joining the EMU. Wage contracts may change character when the mobility of labor increases, trade patterns may change when exchange risk is eliminated completely, the nature and correlation of shocks may be altered, etc. Such changes are very difficult to model, let alone estimate, given the very limited experience with the formation of monetary unions.

In the deterministic simulations it is assumed that economic agents learn with only a one-quarter lag about the true nature of the shock impinging on the economy. If some learning process has to take place with respect not only to the type of shock but also with respect to its persistence, then the dynamic adjustment of the economy is likely to be different, and the appropriate policy response may change as well.

Lags in the availability of data constitute a practical difficulty in the implementation of policy rules of the Taylor type. Lagged values of output and inflation gaps may be more appropriate as conditioning variables for the policy rules. Alternatively, as done partly here and as implemented by several Central Banks, the policy reaction function can be specified in terms of expectations of inflation and output gaps.[11] This raises the question of what information the authorities has available when they form their expectations, and what model they use to evaluate the effect of this information on the future inflation rate. The possibility that the model used by the authorities and that used by the private sector are different could lead to potential problems of credibility and conflict.

---

[11] The Central Bank of Sweden explains its strategy as targeting the expected inflation rate. See Berg (1999).

4. CONCLUSIONS

Based on our simulations results, movements in the exchange rate appears to contain useful information in addition to expected inflation and the output gap for the conduct of monetary policy. Some degree of short-run exchange-rate smoothing is desirable even when the authorities objectives can be expressed only in terms of inflation and output stability. The optimal degree of smoothing increases with the importance of output fluctuations in the objective function. If exchange-rate stability, *per se*, is desirable, perhaps because it would reduce exchange risk, then the degree of smoothing would of course increase further.

The relationship between long-term trends in the nominal exchange rate and inflation is determined by the behavior of the real exchange rate. If past experience can serve as a guide, the Swiss Franc will appreciate relative to the Euro if monetary policy by the Swiss National Bank adopts the same target rate of inflation as the European Central Bank. The recent close relationship between the Swiss Franc and the Euro will therefore have to be abandoned eventually.

REFERENCES

Aebersold, C. and A. Brunetti (1998), Die langfristige reale Aufwerkung des Schweizer Frankens gegenüber der D-Mark, Aussenwirtschaft, 53, p. 365-86.

Camen, U., H. Genberg and M. Salemi (1990), Optimal Monetary Policy and the Revealed Preference Function of the Swiss National Bank, in Artus, P., and Y. Barroux (eds.), Monetary Policy: a Theoretical and Econometric Approach, Kluwer Academic Publishers.

Dueker, M. and A. M. Fischer (1997), Inflation Targeting in a Small Open Economy: Empirical Results for Switzerland, Journal of Monetary Economics, 37, p. 89-103.

Fair, R. C., and J. B. Taylor (1983), Solution and Maximum Likelihood Estimation of Dynamic Nonlinear Rational Expectations Models, Econometrica, 51, p. 1169-85.

Genberg, H. (1990), In the Shadow of the Mark: Exchange Rate and Monetary Policy in Austria and Switzerland., in Argy, V. and P. de Grauwe (eds.), Choosing an Exchange Rate Regime: the Challenge for Smaller Industrial Countries, p. 197-219.

Genberg, H. and U. Kohli (1997), Recent Developments in Swiss Monetary Policy, in Bacchetta, Ph. and W. Wasserfallen (eds.), Economic Policy in Switzerland, London: Macmillan Press Ltd.

Hviding, K. (1999), Switzerland's Monetary Policy Framework, in Switzerland - Selected Issues and Statistical Appendix. Washington, D.C., International Monetary Fund.

Kadareja, A. (2000).

Lucas, R. E. Jr. (1976), Econometric Policy Evaluation: A Critique, Carnegie Rochester Conference Series on Public Policy 1, Amsterdam.

Pesaran, H. M. (1989), The Limits to Rational Expectations, London: Basil Blackwell Ltd.

Rich, G. (1997), Monetary Targets as a Policy Rule: Lessons from the Swiss Experience, Journal of Monetary Economics, 39, p. 113-41.

Rich, G. and J.-P. Béguelin (1985), Swiss Monetary Policy in the 1970's and 1980's, in K. Brunner and others, Monetary Policy and Monetary Regimes, Center Symposium Series, No. CS-17. Center for Research in Government Policy and Business, University of Rochester.

Roth, J.-P. (1997), Politique monétaire et reprise - où en sommes nous ? Centre International d'etudes monétaires et bancaires.

Taylor, J. B. (1993a), Macroeconomic Policy in a World Economy: From Econometric Design to Practical Operation. New York: W.W.Norton.

Taylor, J. B. (1993b), Discretion versus Policy Rules in Practice, Carnegie-Rochester Conference on Public Policy, 39, p. 195-214.

UMBERTO SCHWARZ

THE SWISS FRANC AND THE EURO

A Comment

Genberg and Kadareja consider four facts to have characterized the exchange rate of the Swiss franc vis-à-vis the Deutsche mark since 1979: nominal exchange rate stability, real appreciation of the Swiss franc, small and declining volatility, and that "the exchange rate seems to play a significant role in SNB interest rate policy." This last point is, however, more an interpretation than a fact. Based on these observations the authors raise two questions concerning the relation of the Swiss franc to the euro. First, how will price stability be affected in the long run, taking past trends of the real and nominal exchange rates as given? They answer that if past trends continue, Switzerland will either experience a higher inflation rate than in the euro area or will have to give up nominal exchange rate stability. Second, what is the best monetary regime for short-run price and output stability? They answer that in the short run price stability, as measured by the GDP deflator, is best served by a floating exchange rate. However, the stability of the consumer price index, as defined by a weighted average of the GDP deflator and the import price index, is best achieved by a monetary regime which takes the exchange rate into account.

Before going into the specifics of the two questions discussed by Genberg and Kadareja, I would like to offer some comments on the volatility of the Swiss franc vis-à-vis the euro during the first nine months of 1999 and on the role of the exchange rate in our current monetary policy framework.

Low volatility

The volatility of the Swiss franc was very low during the first nine months of 1999. This was not due to a significant or frequent presence of the Swiss National Bank in the foreign exchange market or in the money market. In my view, this was rather due to repeated announcements by bank officials – already before the launch of the euro – that no undue appreciation of the Swiss franc against the euro would be tolerated. Words were followed by deeds. In 1998, two episodes of resolute expansionary monetary stance occurred in response to exchange rate pressure. In 1999, the SNB reduced its discount rate the same day the European Central Bank lowered its interest rates. Taking into account the fact that the economic situations in the euro area and in Switzerland were to a large extent similar, nobody in the market dared to bet against the prevailing exchange rate. Any deviation would not be considered as being a first step towards a new equilibrium exchange rate, but as an opportunity for

R.E. Baldwin and A. Brunetti (eds.), Economic Impact of EU Membership on Entrants, 149–152.

profit taking by restoring the initial exchange rate. The interaction of words and deeds led to a situation of stabilizing speculation.

Role of the exchange rate in Swiss monetary policy

Ever since the abandonment of a fixed exchange rate, the Swiss National Bank has kept an eye on the exchange rate. This seems unavoidable because Switzerland is a small and open economy. Actually the exchange rate plays two different roles in our framework. It is important to consider them separately because their possible consequences are different. The exchange rate plays a role, first, as an indicator of future inflation. The other indicators are the cyclical development of economic activity and the course of monetary aggregates, be it the monetary base or a broader aggregate such as M3. As long as the evolution of the monetary aggregates does not signal any possible future inflationary occurrence, the business cycle and the exchange rate are used as indicators of more proximate inflationary or deflationary tension. This was, for example, the case during the first nine months of 1999. The exchange rate plays a role, second, as an "escape clause". When strong pressures appear on the foreign exchange market, a change in the monetary policy stance may be considered necessary even if that means endangering future price stability. The clearest example occurred in 1978, when M1 monetary growth of 16% exceeded its target by about 11 percentage points. The fact that the exchange rate plays a role does not mean that the Swiss National Bank has a systematic policy in this regard. In particular, there is no shadow exchange rate target.

Long-run price stability

I shall now turn to the first of the two topics discussed by Genberg and Kadareja. They essentially say that nominal exchange rate stability vis-à-vis the euro might be a problem in the future if the trend for the real exchange rate continues as in the past thirty years. In that case Switzerland would have to bear a higher inflation rate than in the euro area. The only way of avoiding higher inflation would be to give up nominal exchange rate stability.

I would question whether their assumption regarding the trend of the real exchange rate is appropriate. The authors consider the past thirty years as one, and only one, period. However, visual inspection of the evolution of the real exchange rate of the Swiss franc vis-à-vis the deutsche mark during these last thirty years (figure I.2) reveals that there have been at least two periods. The 70's and 80's were characterized by a clear trend of real appreciation. This was not the case in the 90's. What then has changed in this last decade? According to the Balassa-Samuelson model, real appreciation might have come to a halt in the 90's because productivity growth in the sector that produces tradables in Switzerland has slowed down relative to Germany. Reunification may have widened the path of productivity growth in the tradable goods sector in Germany relative to Switzerland. It is also possible that real appreciation has been arrested because of the relative evolutions in the sectors producing non-tradables. In these sectors, this would have been due to an increase in relative productivity growth in Switzerland compared to Germany. Actually, during the 90's, Switzerland implemented various measures aimed at overcoming some of the structural weaknesses which mainly afflicted its non-tradables producing sector.

I have, moreover, a second, more fundamental, remark which, incidentally, also applies to what I have just said. The real exchange rate, as displayed in figure I.2, is obtained by multiplying the nominal exchange rate with the ratio of the two price levels. These variables are all monetary variables. In that case, the only way to get real appreciation while having nominal stability is through a higher price level which, in turn, results from an increased money supply. Nevertheless, we interpret the evolution of the real exchange rate with the aid of the Balassa-Samuelson model, which is not a monetary model. We do that even if we do not know how higher relative productivity growth in the tradables sector or lower productivity growth in the non-tradables sector translates into an increased money supply. We should be more prudent when attempting to draw any conclusions from productivity-growth evolutions on the inflation rate in the long run as long as we do not have a theory on how these evolutions impact on monetary policy.

Short-run price stability

The second topic Genberg and Kadareja discuss is the choice of the best monetary strategy for short-run price and output stability. They compare three monetary policy strategies. The first is represented by a Taylor rule, in which the interest rate is a function of the deviations of prices and output from a baseline path. The second strategy is represented by an extended Taylor rule, in which the interest rate is also a function of deviations of the exchange rate from the baseline path. Let me immediately add that these rules are not a description of the behavior of the monetary authorities, but a useful device to capture the result of this behavior. In the same vein, Rich (1999) wrote that "monetary policies of central banks successful in meeting the ultimate objective of price stability are likely to trigger interest rate movements broadly consistent with the benchmark of the Taylor rule." The third regime is one of perfectly fixed exchange rates without any probability of parity change. This would be the result of Switzerland joining EMU.

In my view, the measure of success of the various monetary policy alternatives should be close to what the central bank has as its primary objective, that is CPI stability. This is, first, preferable to GDP deflator stability or import price stability taken separately. And, second, output stability should not be considered as an objective as such. This does not mean that output considerations should be neglected. Output *in*stability should be considered as a cost factor in achieving CPI stability. Thus, the best regime would be one which conduces to CPI stability with lower output costs.

The results shown by Genberg and Kadareja support the attitude of the SNB towards the exchange rate. They show, first, that CPI stability is best achieved by an extended Taylor rule. I consider this to be in support of our taking the exchange rate as a further indicator for inflation. They show, second, that in the event of serious disturbances appearing in the foreign exchange market, which in their model translates into a deterministic shock affecting the interest rate parity relationship, "more fixity with respect to the euro is desirable". I interpret this as giving support to our attitude of allowing the exchange rate to play the role of an "escape clause" in our monetary policy framework.

REFERENCES

Rich, G. (1999), Inflation and Money Stock Targets: Is There Really a Difference ? mimeo, March 1999.

PETER STALDER

MACROECONOMIC CONSEQUENCES OF SWISS EU-ACCESSION: THE EFFECTS OF ENTERING THE MONETARY UNION

1. INTRODUCTION

Although skepticism about an EU-membership is still widespread in Switzerland, particularly in rural areas of the German speaking part of the country, the public opinion seems to have gradually changed in favor of a stronger European integration of Switzerland since the referendum of December 1992, in which the ratification of the Treaty on the European Economic Area (EEA) has been rejected. Today, the Federal Council (central government of Switzerland) and at least one of the big parties, the Social Democrats, strongly support a speedy move towards a full EU-membership of Switzerland, whereas other major parties seem to favor weaker forms of integration, at least for the time being, like the ratification of the recently signed bilateral agreements between Switzerland and the EU.

Economically, a full EU-membership differs from the weaker forms of integration in two main respects. First, as a member state with a relatively high per capita income, Switzerland would have to make a sizable *contribution to the EU budget*, presumably amounting to about 1% of Swiss GDP and to be financed by raising the VAT rate. Second, Switzerland would have to *join the EMU*, i.e. to replace the Swiss franc by the Euro. This paper deals only with the prospective repercussions on the Swiss economy resulting from joining the EMU. It has to be seen as part of a larger study which considers the effects of moving from the status quo to the bilateral agreements and to an EU-membership (Bärlocher, Schips, Stalder 1999).

As is well known, the Swiss economy had repeatedly to cope with strong upward pressures on the Swiss franc in recent years in connection with its role as a "safe haven" in times of international financial turmoil. Moreover, there was also a trend appreciation in the real exchange rate over the last three decades. On the other hand, Swiss interest rates – even when adjusted for the exchange rate appreciation – have been notably lower than in other industrialized economies, including Germany as the main trading partner and competitor on third markets. This deviation from the standard interest rate parity condition can be interpreted as an exchange rate risk

R.E. Baldwin and A. Brunetti (eds.), Economic Impact of EU Membership on Entrants, 153–175.

premium, reflecting the willingness of international investors to hold assets in Swiss francs even though the rate of return is lower than for assets denominated in other currencies. Hence, by joining the EMU, Switzerland could benefit from *a stable exchange rate* at the cost of *loosing the historical advantage of comparatively low real interest rates*.

The consequences of such a change in the monetary environment of the Swiss economy are analyzed by means of the KOF/ETH-Macromodel. The equations of the monetary block (short and long-term interest rates, foreign exchange rate) involve the assumption of rational (model-consistent) expectations. The real sector of the model analyzes the resulting adjustments in prices, wages, consumption, investment, exports, imports, total GDP and employment. These effects are determined by comparing a baseline simulation with an EMU-scenario over a period of 12 years (1999-2010).

In the *baseline simulation*, the Swiss *short-term interest rate* is determined by a historically estimated monetary reaction function, which can be seen as kind of a *Taylor rule*. The *long-term interest rate* is set equal to the expected return from holding a comparable sequence of short-term assets corrected for a liquidity premium (term structure condition). The *exchange rate path* is derived from the open interest rate parity condition in which the historically estimated mean residual (risk premium) is carried over to the forecast period.

In the EMU-scenario, the introduction of the Euro implies a *regime switch*: The nominal exchange rate is fixed and the short-term interest rate is no longer determined by the monetary reaction function but equated via the interest rate parity condition with the higher Euro short-term rate. Through the term-structure equation this also affects Swiss long-term interest rates.

This regime switch is the main part, but not the beginning of the story. Whereas one may doubt the general applicability of the concept of *rational expectations*, it is certainly an appropriate device for modeling a political change with economic consequences that are far-reaching, obvious in several respects (fixing of the exchange rate, convergence of interest rates to the higher Euro level) and moreover widely discussed in public. Hence adjustments in the monetary sector will set in as soon as economic agents begin to anticipate the EMU move of Switzerland. In view of the extensive and complex democratic process in Switzerland (negotiations with the EU, discussion of the agreement in parliament, ratification in a mandatory public referendum), one should realistically think that the conviction of economic agents that Switzerland will join the EU grows gradually during this process. In the model, however, things are simplified by assuming a *sudden swing in opinion* from not expecting an EU-membership to expecting it with certainty three years in advance. At that point, low-yield Swiss assets at once appear unattractive. The resulting portfolio shift towards assets in other currencies weakens the Swiss franc and pushes Swiss interest rates up. This process must quickly proceed to the point where the narrowed short-term interest rate differential is justified – within the interest rate parity condition - by the expectation of a revaluation of the Swiss franc until the actual entry of Switzerland into EMU. During this phase, the expected or preannounced rate by which the Swiss franc will enter the EMU plays an important role. Furthermore, Swiss monetary policy may influence the speed by which Swiss interest rates converge to the higher Euro interest rates and thus the extent of the temporary weakness of the Swiss franc.

2. THE MONETARY BLOCK OF THE KOF/ETH-MACROMODEL

2.1. *Equations used for short-term forecasting*

The monetary block of the KOF/ETH-Macromodel, as used in the regular short-term forecasts for the Swiss economy, determines *short-term interest rates* (3-month Euro francs), *long-term interest rates* (government bond rate) and the *exchange rate of the Swiss franc*, defined as trade-weighted external value. The specification of this part of the model is based on the following assumptions:

A) The *stance of monetary policy* depends on real *GDP growth*, the *inflation rate* and the course of the *exchange rate*. The Swiss National Bank (SNB) tightens money supply in response to high GDP growth and high inflation, whereas an increase in the external value of the Swiss franc entails a relative loosening of monetary reins.

B) The stance of monetary policy is reflected in the development of *short-term interest rates*.

C) Swiss *long-term interest rates* depend on Swiss short-term interest rates and foreign long-term interest rates.

D) The *exchange rate of the Swiss franc* reacts to interest rate and inflation differentials and the balance on current account.

Institutional changes like the introduction of the Swiss Interbank Clearing System and new reserve requirements in 1988, the increasing importance of cashless payments and other financial innovations caused *instabilities* in the money supply process (relationship between base money and monetary aggregates like M1 or M3) as well as the money demand function. Given these instabilities, it seems rather problematical to measure the stance of monetary policy in terms of money growth rates. A more satisfactory approach is to *shortcut* the relationships postulated in A and B, i.e. to directly model the response of short-term interest rates to *target variables* like GDP growth, inflation and exchange rate in the spirit of a *Taylor rule.*

Furthermore, taking into account the orientation of Swiss exports (in terms of regions, products and competitors) as well as the origin of Swiss imports, it seems likely that the SNB pays special attention to the exchange rate of the Swiss franc against the DM or the DM-block (the Euro in the forecast period) and the policy of the Bundesbank (the ECB in the forecast period). Therefore, the model is focused on the Swiss franc/DM (Euro) exchange rate and the corresponding interest rate and inflation differentials. The overall trade-weighted external value is determined then by the endogenous Swiss franc/DM (Euro) exchange rate and the exogenous external value of the DM (Euro) against other currencies.

Based on these considerations, Swiss monetary policy is assumed to be conducted in such a way that Swiss *short-term interest rates* (*srate*) go up if real GDP growth ($\dot{y}$) and inflation ($\dot{p}$) rise, whereas an appreciation of the Swiss franc ($\dot{e}$) and an increasing unemployment rate (*urate*) are counteracted by lowering short-term interest rates. These reactions of *srate* take place in relation to the German (Euro) short-term interest rate (*srate**) as a point of reference:[1]

$$srate_t = f_1(\underset{+}{srate_t^*},\ \underset{+}{\dot{y}_t},\ \underset{+}{\dot{p}_t},\ \underset{-}{\dot{e}_t},\ \underset{-}{urate_t}) \tag{1}$$

The exchange rate e is defined as DM (Euro) per Swiss franc (external value, 1990 = 1), so that $\dot{e} > 0$ means that the Swiss franc appreciates. Empirically, the impact of the inflation rate in (1) turns out to be insignificant. This result is not really surprising: On the one hand, in case of a cost-induced inflation, the appropriate policy response is rather to accommodate higher money demand than to tighten monetary reins. On the other hand, in case of a demand-pull inflation, high GDP growth precedes high inflation, so that tightening of monetary policy is advisable already when GDP growth rises. Moreover, *urate* is the driving force in the wage-price block of the model. Hence low values of *urate* can be viewed as a leading indicator of rising inflation as well.

The *long-term interest rate* ($lrate$) depends on the German long-term interest rate ($lrate^*$) and the differential of short-term interest rates ($srate - srate^*$):

$$lrate_t = f_2(\underset{+}{lrate_t^*},\ \underset{+}{srate_t - srate_t^*}) \tag{2}$$

The *external value of the Swiss franc* moves in response to the spreads of Swiss and foreign interest rates and the trade balance including commodities, tourism and other services (*bal*).[2] In addition, the lagged level of the real external value (*er*) works in the sense of an error correction mechanism towards PPP in the long run:

$$\dot{e}_t = f_3(\underset{+}{srate_t - lrate_t},\ \underset{-}{srate_t^* - lrate_t^*},\ \underset{+}{bal_t},\ \underset{-}{er_{t-1}}) \tag{3}$$

$$er_t = e_t \frac{p_t}{p_t^*} \tag{4}$$

---

[1] A dot above a variable indicates a rate of change, i.e. $\dot{x}_t = \Delta \log(x_t) = \log(x_t / x_{t-1})$.

[2] We use the trade balance instead of the overall balance on current account since foreign assets and the corresponding flows of capital incomes are not included in the current version of the KOF/ETH-Macromodel.

The *overall external value* of the Swiss franc is defined as $etot_t = e_t^{1-r} erest_t^r$, where $erest$ denotes the external value of the Swiss franc against currencies outside the DM-block (the Euro area in the forecast period) and *r* is the corresponding trade share. As $erest$ can be approximately expressed as $erest_t = eeuro_t e_t$, where $eeuro$ is the external value of the DM (Euro), one obtains:

$$etot_t = e_t eeuro_t^r \qquad (5)$$

Equations (1)-(5) determine the variables *srate, lrate, e, er* and *etot* in dependence of *y, p, srate*, lrate*, p*, bal* and *eeuro*. In the complete model, *y, p* and *bal* become endogenous whereas the world variables *srate*, lrate*, p** and *eeuro* remain exogenous.

Obviously, this specification has a strong *ad hoc* flavor. Theoretical considerations like the *uncovered interest rate parity* condition and the *term structure of interest rates* are not taken into account explicitly, although the concrete dynamic *econometric formulation* of the equations, which is described elsewhere (Stalder, 1999), involves some rough approximation to these concepts. Empirically, however, the specification works better than everything else that has been tried out in terms of historical fit, parameter stability and accuracy of ex post forecasts. Figure 1 shows the historical tracking performance of the monetary block in a dynamic simulation when *y, p, srate*, lrate*, p*, bal* and *eeuro* are treated as exogenous. Short-term and long-term interest rates are tracked quite well, whereas the course of the exchange rate is reproduced with some less accuracy. In particular, the strong appreciation of the Swiss franc from 1993 to 1995 is underestimated by the model, i.e. it can only partly be explained by the fundamental factors included in the model but has to be viewed to some extent as a speculative bubble.

2.2. *Modifications: interest rate parity and term structure*

Despite the satisfactory performance of the monetary block, only equation (1) (monetary reaction function) and of course the definitions (4) and (5) are retained for analyzing the effects of an EMU entry of Switzerland, while equations (2) and (3) are replaced by the *term structure of interest rates* and the *uncovered interest rate parity condition* respectively. The general motivation for using these concepts has been given in the introduction. Once economic agents anticipate EU-membership of Switzerland, there is no room for expecting exchange rate movements beyond the EMU entry date. As a consequence, interest rate differentials in favor of Swiss francs can only survive to the extent that the going external value of the Swiss franc is lower than the external value at which the Swiss franc is expected to enter EMU. Put differently, given the certain prospect of a definite fixing of the exchange rate in the near future, interest rate parity considerations cannot be neglected by *rational investors*. Hence, interest and exchange rate movements in the pre-EMU phase must conform to the interest rate parity condition, although equation (3) is better suited to track exchange rate movements historically under conditions of uncertainty. Similar considerations apply to equation (2). The econometric version of this equation represents the reaction of *lrate* to *srate* in the form of a partial adjustment scheme, showing a rather weak short-run impact of *srate* on *lrate*. This empirical result is plausible since it is mostly unclear for economic agents for how long a change in *srate* will last. In case of an anticipated EU-membership, however, it is plainly clear that Swiss short-term interest rates must permanently adjust to the higher Euro rates. It is straightforward then to figure out the increase in *lrate* needed to fulfill the term structure requirement (*lrate* = expected return from holding a comparable sequence of short-term assets). Hence *lrate* must reflect the higher expected values of *srate* immediately rather than responding to the current *srate* according to a partial adjustment mechanism, as equation (2) implies.

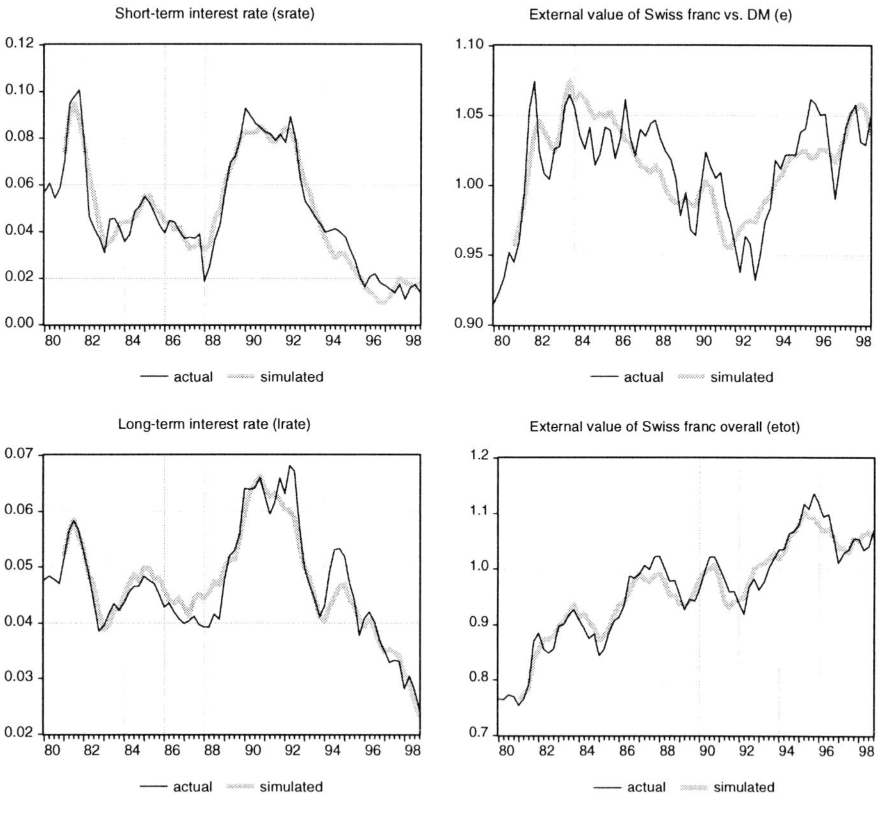

Figure 1. Historical tracking performance

Estimation results for the retained *short-term interest rate equation*, extended into a *partial adjustment* form, are as follows (estimation period: 1981q1 to 1998q1):

$$srate = S_0 + (1-S_\rho)\, srate(-1) + S_\rho\, srate^* + S_e \log(e/e(-4)) + 4\, S_y \log(y/y(-1)) + S_U\, urate + S_t{*}t \qquad (1')$$

	Estimate	*Standard error*	*t-value*
S_0	-0.00550	0.00208	-2.645
S_ρ	0.49764	0.06046	8.231
S_e	-0.07262	0.02004	-3.624
S_y	0.16856	0.03621	4.655
S_U	-0.16224	0.05307	-3.057
S_t	0.00012	0.00006	2.169

$R^2 = 0.945$ $\quad SER = 0.00588 \quad DW = 1.419$

The equation involves the data-admissible parameter constraint that changes in *srate** are fully reflected in *srate* in the long run, while the immediate response of *srate* is about half of that size (S_ρ). A 1% appreciation of the Swiss franc (over the same quarter one year before) leads to a reduction in *srate* of 0.073 percentage points (S_e). An increase in the annualized quarterly GDP growth rate of 1 percentage point entails a increase in *srate* of 0.17 percentage points (S_y). If the unemployment rate rises by 1 percentage point, *srate* falls by 0.16 percentage point (S_U). All these are short-run (immediate) effects, the long-run effects being about twice as large ($1/S_\rho$). In addition, the equation contains a weak but statistically significant positive time trend (S_t), implying that *srate* increases slightly if all explanatory variables are unchanged.

The *uncovered interest rate parity condition* can be written as

$$E_t \log(e_{t+1}) - \log(e_t) = \log(1 + srate_t^* / 4) - \log(1 + srate_t / 4) \qquad (6)$$

where *e* is the nominal external value of the Swiss franc vis-à-vis the DM (the Euro in the forecast period) and *srate* and *srate** are annualized Swiss and foreign nominal interest rates on 3-month deposits. According to (6), *srate* can only be lower than *srate** to the extent that the Swiss franc is expected to appreciate. Using the approximation $\log(1+x) \approx x$ for small *x* and replacing the expected value of $\log(e_{t+1})$ by the actual realization, one may restate (6) as

$$\log(e_{t+1}) - \log(e_t) = srate_t^* / 4 - srate_t / 4 + \theta + \varepsilon_t \qquad (7)$$

where θ should be zero and the residual ε_t can be interpreted as an *expectation error*. However, running a regression on (7) for the Swiss Franc/DM-relationship over the period 1980q1 to 1998q4, one obtains $\theta = -0.0017$. Hence the actual appreciation of the Swiss franc was not sufficient to fully compensate for lower Swiss interest rates on average. This can be interpreted as an *exchange rate risk premium* or a *interest rate bonus*, reflecting the willingness of international investors to hold assets in Swiss francs even though the rate of return is lower than for assets denominated in DM. Expressed with respect to *srate*, the interest rate bonus is -0.0068 (-0.0017*4) for the period under consideration, i.e. short-term Swiss interest rates were 0.68 percentage points "too low" in comparison with German short-term interest rates after correcting for the actual appreciation of the Swiss franc.

The *term structure condition of interest rates* can be written as[3]

$$lrate_t = \frac{1}{k}\sum_{i=0}^{k-1} srate_{t+i} + \lambda + \eta_t \ , \qquad (8)$$

where $\lambda > 0$ has the interpretation of *a liquidity premium* and η_t is the expectation error with respect to the future values of *srate*. We set k = 20 (quarters) and run a regression on (8) over the period 1990q1 to 1998q4 with an AR(1)-process substituted for η_t. This produces an estimate for λ of 0.0166, implying that long-term interest rates have on average been 1.66 percentage points higher than the 5-year sequence of future short-term interest rates.

The simulation study carried out in the sequel, addressing the prospective repercussions on the Swiss economy resulting from joining the EMU, will be based on equations (1'), (7) and (8) on the assumption of *model-consistent expectations* with respect to the external value of the Swiss franc and short-term interest rates. Before turning to these simulations, a short description of the *real sector* of the KOF/ETH-Macromodel is provided (IS-part, production function, labor market, wage/price-dynamics).

3. THE REAL SECTOR OF THE KOF/ETH-MACROMODEL

The KOF/ETH-Macromodel is a quarterly structural model for the Swiss economy. With 36 stochastic equations it is relatively small in size. Originally developed in 1993/94, the model was subject to several revisions and extensions in recent years. Since 1994 it forms the basis of the regular KOF/ETH forecasts and is also used to carry out policy simulations. Judged from recent experience, the model *forecasts* turn out to be *too optimistic* with respect to economic growth in Switzerland (which was practically zero on average in the years 1991-96). The prediction errors can however to a large part be traced back to *two factors*. First, the forecasts were based on too optimistic assumptions as to *GDP growth in Western Europe*, which is the

---

[3] This holds only in an approximative sense. See e.g. Walsh (1998, p. 449 ff).

dominant component in the exogenous world activity indicator of the model. Second, the increase in the *foreign exchange rate* of the Swiss franc was underestimated. In an *ex post* forecast based on the actual developments of these two variables the prediction errors are notably reduced but they do not disappear completely. This suggests that some of the factors hampering growth in Switzerland in recent years are not captured by the model.

Although the model is rather conventional in most respects, two *distinguishing features* should be pointed out. *First*, firms' decisions on investment, production capacity, the choice of optimal factor intensities and the determination of labor demand and prices are derived from a *vintage production function* and the assumption of *monopolistic competition in the product market* (firms face a downward sloping demand curve with a constant price elasticity). On the other hand, it is assumed that the decision of firms on factor inputs does not affect factor prices, i.e. the *wage and the price of capital goods* can be *treated as given* in the theoretical model of the firm (although they are of course endogenous variables of the macromodel). On these assumptions, the problem of the firm is to choose on each investment vintage the cost-minimizing factor mix, to pursue an optimal policy of replacing old investment vintages by new equipment and to adjust capacity, output, prices and employment in response to changes in goods demand and factor costs (Ando et al. 1974, Stalder 1994a+b, 1995). In this framework, the development of the factor input ratios and production capacity over time is specifically connected to the process of replacing old by new equipment.

Second, transposing a model of this kind to the empirical level entails the problem that several theoretically relevant variables are *not directly observable*. In the goods market, we observe *actual output Y* (real GDP) but not *capacity output YC* and *goods demand YD* since these variables will in general differ from *Y* due to delays in the adjustment of production capacity and possibly price inertia. In the labor market, we observe *actual employment L* but not *labor demand LD* and *labor supply LS* since wages adjust too slowly to ensure permanent market clearing. Moreover, if actual output is smaller than capacity output, *effective labor demand LD* will fall short of *capacity labor demand LC*. In order to link these latent demand and supply variables with observed output and employment, the model exploits - as a *second novelty* - the information of business surveys (firms' assessments of available capacity and labor bottlenecks) in a "smoothing by aggregation" procedure (Drèze, Bean 1990, Kooiman 1984, Lambert 1988, Sneessens 1990, Stalder 1989,1991a+b,1995). Consider for instance a single firm that assesses capacities as being "too small" and at the same time reports "no labor bottlenecks". In this case, one has $y = yc < yd$ and $l = ld = lc < ls$. Other firms will however be in different regimes. Generally, one may write at the micro or firm level $y = min(yc, yd)$ and $l = \min(ls, ld)$, where $ld = lc*(y/yc)^{\gamma}$. On the assumption of continuous distributions of the demand/supply ratios across firms, one obtains at the aggregate level smooth mappings from (YC,YD) on Y and from (LS,LD) on L. Denoting the proportion of firms reporting capacities as being "too small" by π_G and the proportion of firms facing "labor bottlenecks" by π_L, the aggregate relationships in the model take the form:

$$Y(1-\pi_G)^{-\kappa} = YD$$

$$Y\pi_G{}^{-\kappa} = YC \qquad L(1-\pi_L)^{-\upsilon} = LD = LC\pi_G{}^{\kappa} \tag{9}$$

$$L\pi_L{}^{-\upsilon} = LS \qquad \kappa,\ \upsilon > 0$$

These four equations define a one-to-one mapping from the latent variables *YD, YC, LC, LS* (to be explained by econometric equations) to the observable variables *Y, L,* π_G, π_L. The specific situation of the individual firm referred to above obtains at the aggregate level as a limiting case for sufficiently large values of *YD* and *LS*: More precisely, if *YD* increases in relation to *YC,* π_G tends to 1, implying that *Y* converges from below to *YC* and *LD* converges from below to *LC*. If at the same time *LS* is sufficiently large in relation to *LD,* π_L tends to zero, implying that *L* converges from below to *LD* = LC. The variables π_G and π_L can be regarded as regime indicators or tension measures and parameters κ and υ reflect the dispersion or *mismatch* of the demand/supply ratios in the cross-section of firms. The higher these mismatch measures, the lower are *Y* and *L* for given values of *YD, YC, LC* and *LS*. The *unemployment rate implied by the model* is

$$URATE = 1 - L/LS = 1 - \pi_L{}^{\upsilon} \tag{10}$$

The model-implied unemployment rate turns out to be about twice as large as the *official unemployment rate* in recent years, but the movements are largely parallel. The tension measures π_G and π_L are the driving force in the *wage-price block* of the model.

The rest of the model, consisting of the equations for the various components of aggregate demand and income determination, is rather conventional and therefore not described here.

4. DESIGN OF THE SCENARIOS

The effects on the development of the Swiss economy of joining EMU will be determined in the sequel of this paper in comparison with a baseline simulation in which monetary conditions remain unchanged. As noted in the introduction, in a more comprehensive study (Bärlocher, Schips, Stalder 1999) we consider three scenarios, namely the development of the Swiss economy under the conditions of the *status quo*, the *bilateral agreements* and a full *EU-membership*. This paper uses as baseline simulation the scenario of the bilateral agreements, which differs from the status quo in two main respects: (1) *efficiency gains* resulting from the mutual recognition of product standards and certificates and other administrative facilitations; (2) the assumption of *free movement of labor between* the EU and Switzerland. A full EU-membership differs from the bilateral agreements also in two main respects: (1) Switzerland would have to make a sizable *contribution to the EU budget*, to be financed by raising the VAT rate; (2) the *Swiss franc would enter EMU*. This paper does not present the full EU scenario but concentrates on the effects resulting from EMU.

The EMU scenario assumes that the Swiss franc/Euro exchange rate gets fixed at the beginning of the year 2002 and that this event is perfectly anticipated by economic agents three years in advance. This set-up is *not realistic* for two reasons. *First,* preceding to EMU, the Swiss franc would have to enter the EMS regime, under which fluctuations of the Swiss franc/Euro exchange rate are still possible. However, as they are confined to a narrow band, the difference to EMU entry with respect to interest rate and real effects is minor and in any case much smaller than the difference in comparison with the current state of affairs. *Second,* EU-membership of Switzerland as soon as in 2002 is politically out of question. The motivation for simulating the EU entrance in 2002 is methodological: It allows us to compare (in the more comprehensive study) the scenario of the *bilateral agreements,* for which ratification seems realistic in 2002, and the *EU-membership* under conditions that are otherwise identical. Moreover, the exact entry date does not matter much since the economy in the baseline simulation is on a fairly smooth growth path anyway.

Routinely, the KOF/ETH-Macromodel is used for short-term forecasts with a horizon of about two years. In this study, however, we want to analyze the repercussions on the Swiss economy resulting from joining EMU in a medium-term perspective. Therefore the simulation period is extended to the year 2010. In what follows, we briefly describe the main characteristics of the baseline simulation.

5. BASELINE SIMULATION

5.1. Exogenous variables, risk and liquidity premiums

To simulate the Swiss economy until the year 2010, we need series for the exogenous variables of the model of according length. Up to the 4th quarter of the year 2000, the values of the exogenous variables can be taken from a recent KOF/ETH forecast (fall 1998). From 2001q1 on, the exogenous variables are determined as follows:

- Several variables that are usually treated as exogenous in the forecasting process (public construction, government consumption, direct taxes, health insurance premiums and social security contributions) are endogenized in a schematic manner by assuming a strict proportionality to macroeconomic aggregates like GDP, total household income or wage income.

- The VAT rate is assumed to be raised between 2002 to 2005 stepwise from 7.5% to 10% in view of the otherwise looming deficit of social security.
- For the population variables (number of permanent residents and potential labor force, i.e. permanent residents in the age group 20 to 64) we refer to the demographic scenario "Trend" of the Federal Statistical Office (BFS).[4]
- The (truly exogenous) *world economy variables* (interest rates, prices, GDP in the EU, the USA and Japan) are forecast on basis of auxiliary univariate time series models. Hence, depending on the appropriate time series representation (stationarity, trend-stationarity, difference-stationarity), these variables converge - after the 4th quarter of 2000 - either to their historical averages or to their historical growth trends.

As a remaining issue that has to be settled for the baseline simulation, we turn to the residuals of the interest rate parity equation (7) and the term structure equation (8). As noted above, historically the *interest rate parity condition* vis-à-vis the DM shows a negative constant term θ (-0.0017). This can be interpreted as exchange rate risk premium or as interest rate bonus for Switzerland (corresponding to a 0.68 percentage points differential). At the end of the observation period (1998q4) the residual ε_t is negative ($\theta + \varepsilon_t$ = -0.0055). In the baseline simulation, we assume that the term $\theta + \varepsilon_t$ continuously goes back from –0.0055 to –0.0022 during the simulation period. In other words, the Swiss interest rate bonus in relation to the Euro approaches the interest rate bonus that has been observed on average against the DM, although not completely (-0.0022 vs. –0.0017). On this assumption, the currently large short-term interest rate differential (about 2 percentage) could only persist if investors were to anticipate a strong appreciation of the Swiss franc in the simulation period. The external value e would have to go substantially beyond historical peak values. Turning the argument around, if such a strong appreciation is considered unlikely by investors, the interest rate differential must narrow. Somewhat arbitrarily, we assume that the Swiss franc – currently (1998q4) at 1.605 SFr/Euro – cannot become stronger than 1.55 SFr/Euro (0.7925 SFr/DM) in the simulation period. In terms of the external value e (index 1990 = 1) this corresponds to a value of 1.085 (1998q4 = 1.046). Technically, this constraint is introduced into the model in the form of a *terminal condition* for e.[5]

In the *term structure condition* (8) it seem natural to let η_t decay according to the estimated AR(1)-process. As η_t is negative at the end of the observation period, this implies that $\lambda + \eta_t$ converges from below to λ = 0.0166 (liquidity premium) during the simulation period. However, the estimate of λ is larger than the liquidity premium implicit in the exogenous foreign interest rates in the simulation period (λ*

---

4 The number of seasonal and frontier workers and the additional immigration under the bilateral agreements are endogenous variables of the model.

5 In contrast to the usual approach of econometric rational expectations model, the terminal condition is not set on a date that far in the future that the variables in the period under consideration are practically unaffected. Rather, the terminal condition is introduced in order to impose an upper bound on the external value of the Swiss franc in the simulation period. The algorithm used (stacked-time) is described in Hollinger (1996).

= 0.0096). This would imply that Swiss long-term interest rates (*lrate*) tend to exceed foreign long-term interest rates (*lrate**) in a situation where *srate* converges to *srate** (which will happen in the EMU-scenario). Such a constellation (*lrate* > *lrate**, *srate* = *srate**) seems very unlikely. In fact, one would rather suppose the opposite, i.e. that Swiss long-term interest rates may preserve a small bonus (due to solvency considerations and a high Swiss savings ratio in combination with imperfect capital mobility) even if Swiss and foreign short-term interest rates equalize. Therefore, the liquidity premium is constrained in such a way that it cannot become larger than the liquidity premium present in foreign interest rates during the simulation period.

5.2. Results

On these conditions, the baseline simulation (1999q1 to 2010q4) shows a fairly smooth course of the Swiss economy (figure 2). The external value of the Swiss franc first increases and then, as the short-term interest rate differential continuously narrows, levels off. GDP growth is dampened from 1999 to 2003 by the rather strong increase in Swiss interest rates (due to foreign interest rates tending to their historical averages and a reduced differential between Swiss and foreign interest rates). Thereafter, annual GDP growth rates lie between 2% and 2.5% and employment slightly increases. Accordingly, the output gap, which is defined as $(Y-YC)/YC = \pi_G{}^{\kappa} - 1$ on basis of (9), is reduced in two steps. The unemployment rate, computed from the model on basis of equation (10), first falls (1998-2000), then slightly increases (2001-2003) and eventually falls again (2004-2010). Hence on both the goods and labor market tension increases towards the end of the simulation period. However, markets to not become that tight as to set in motion an inflation spiral. To the contrary, consumer price inflation goes back to 1.5% after being pushed to about 2% by the VAT increase in the period 2002-2005.

The outcome of this baseline simulation looks quite reasonable. To be sure, this is not really crucial in the context of our study since eventually we are not interested in the baseline scenario or the EMU scenario by themselves but in the *differences* between the two, showing us the impact of an EMU entry. Nevertheless, the baseline simulation is not completely irrelevant because - due to the nonlinearity of the model - the effects resulting from EMU to some extent depend on the baseline course. For instance, the decomposition of changing aggregate demand into a price effect and a real output effect would differ according to prevailing market tension. What would be disturbing thus is a baseline simulation that moves to extreme cyclical situations. Obviously, this is not the case. The EMU shock hits the Swiss economy in a situation that can be considered *average* from the perspective of the historical business cycle.

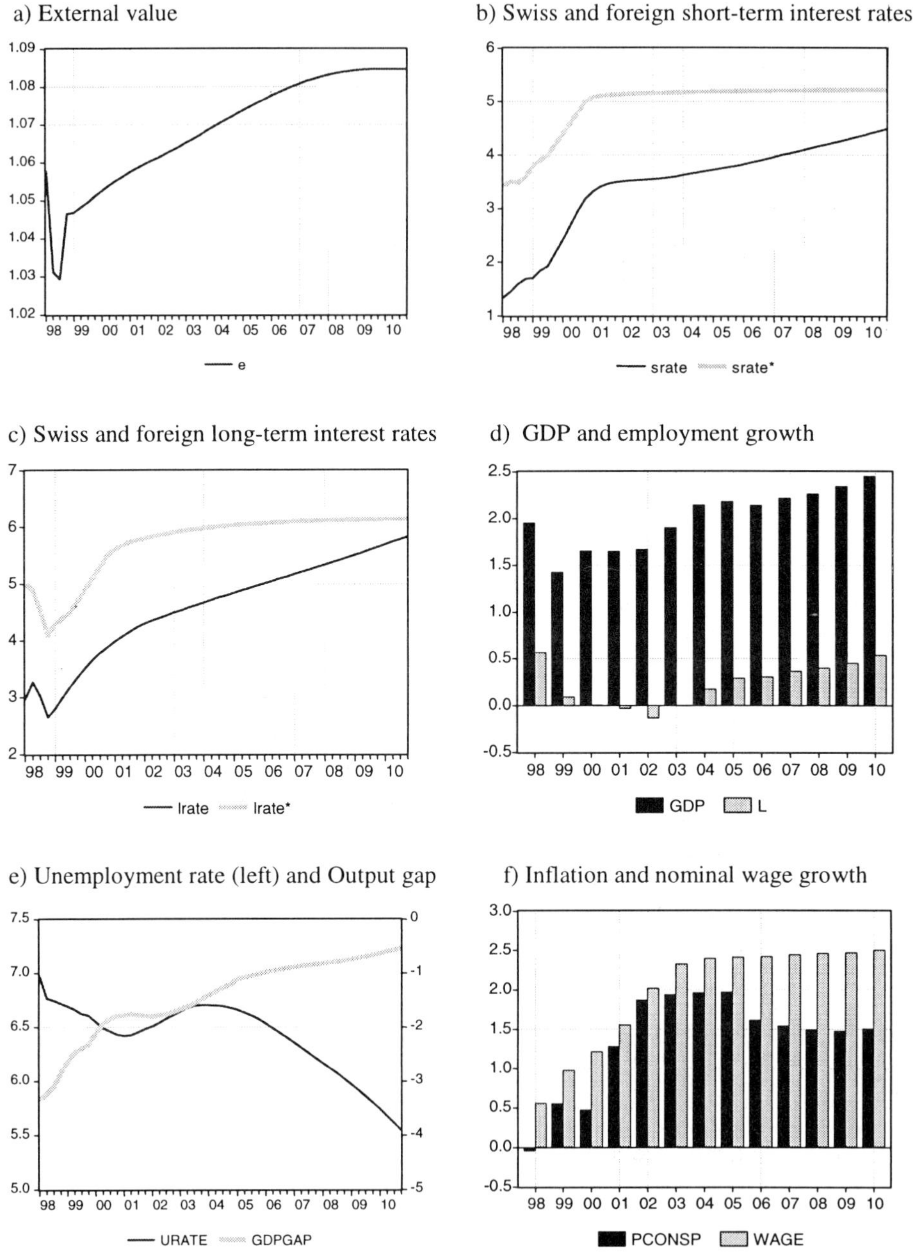

Figure 2. Baseline Simulation (1999q1 to 2010q4)

6. EMU SCENARIO

6.1. *Monetary reactions*

After all these preliminaries, it is straightforward to simulate the EMU entrance of the Swiss franc. All what is needed in the model is a modification of the interest parity condition (7),

$$\log(e_{t+1}) - \log(e_t) = srate_t^* / 4 - srate_t / 4 + \theta + \varepsilon_t \qquad (7)$$

with respect to the exchange rate risk premium and the terminal condition for the external value *e*. In the baseline scenario it was assumed that interest parity holds for the Swiss franc/Euro relationship with an exchange rate risk premium ($\theta + \varepsilon_t$) that slowly approaches the average value estimated for the Swiss franc/DM relationship (θ). The terminal condition for *e* was set in a way that left some room for the Swiss franc to appreciate in the simulation period. In contrast, the EMU scenario now assumes that the Swiss Franc/Euro exchange rate gets fixed in 2002q1 so that there is no more exchange rate uncertainty as of that date. This is taken into account in the model by two modifications. First, we draw the *terminal condition* forward to 2002q1 such that *e* remains constant thereafter. Second, we let the *exchange rate risk premium* quickly go to zero from 1998q4 to 2002q1, as shown in figure 3. Hence, from 2002q1 onwards we have $e_{t+1} = e_t = const$ *and* $\theta + \varepsilon_t = 0$. This amounts to a *regime switch*: The short-term interest rate is no longer determined by the monetary reaction function (1') – which is skipped over in the model - but given by equation (7) as

$$srate_t = srate_t^* .$$

The corresponding jump of *srate* to the higher Euro level (*srate**) affects Swiss long-term interest rates through the term-structure condition (8).

As already noted in the introduction, effects on interest rates and the exchange rate will set in as soon as economic agents begin to *anticipate* the EMU move of Switzerland. The pre-EMU phase is assumed to start in 1999q1, i.e. three years in advance of the Swiss EMU entry. During this phase, the monetary reaction function is still effective. The terminal condition for *e* in 2002q1 is to be interpreted as the exchange rate by which the Swiss franc is expected to enter EMU. The reactions in the pre-EMU phase are determined by the properties of the complete model. The role of the interest rate parity condition (7) is solely to define the admissible combinations of exchange rate paths and short-term interest rate developments. The monetary reaction function (1'), together with the big rest of the model, chooses one of these combinations.

Actual values ($\theta+\varepsilon_t$) and historical mean (θ)
(Swiss franc/DM-relationship)

BASELINE and EMU scenario (1999q1 to 2010q4)
(Swiss franc/Euro-relationship)

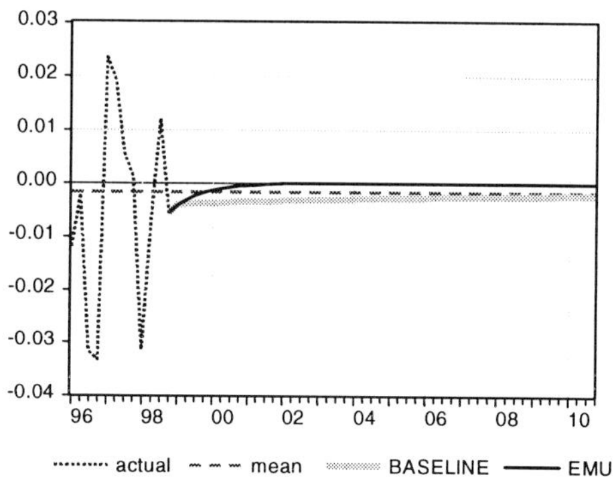

Figure 3. Exchange Rate Risk Premium

DM/Swiss franc (Index 1990 = 1) and
mean value (1990q1 to 1998q4)

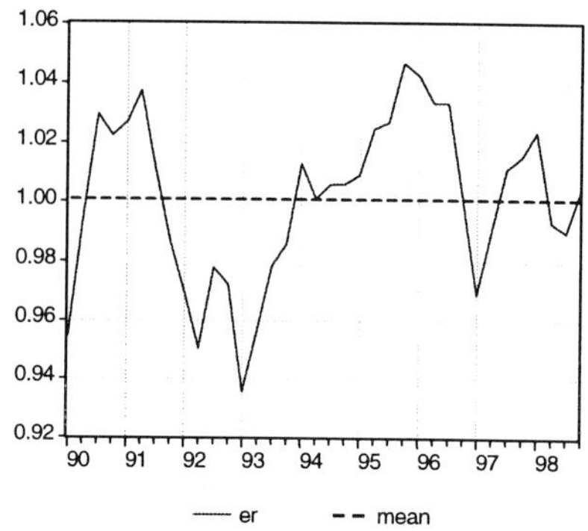

Figure 4. Real external value

The terminal condition for e is critical to the outcome. In the main version of the EMU scenario, we assume that economic agents expect the Swiss franc to enter EMU in 2002q1 at the current exchange rate, i.e. $e_{2002q1} = e_{1998q4}$. To judge the adequacy of this assumption, one should consider the development of the external value in *real terms* as a measure of international competitiveness. In 1998q4, the real external value was 2.5% above its long-run mean value (1980q1 to 1998q4) and practically equal to the mean value recorded over the period 1990q1 to 1998q4 (figure 4). One may further note that complaints about an overvalued Swiss franc have largely disappeared in recent times. Against this background, the assumption that economic agents expect the Swiss franc to enter EMU in 2002q1 at the exchange rate of 1998q4 seems plausible, although the concrete value imposed on e in 2002q1 remains of course a matter of conjecture.

Given the terminal condition for e, it is instructive to consider two extreme cases in the pre-EMU phase (1999q1 to 2001q4). If *srate* were to jump to the higher *srate** at once, the interest rate parity condition (with $\theta+\varepsilon_t = 0$) would imply a constant external value e already as of 1999q1. The other extreme is an unchanged interest rate differential. In this case, the external value would have to drop in 1999q1 to a level sufficiently low in relation to the anticipated entry rate so that the expected revaluation from 1999q1 to 2002q1 would just compensate for the interest rate differential. What actually happens in the model is something between these two extremes. Once investors begin to anticipate EMU, low-yield Swiss assets appear unattractive. The resulting portfolio shift towards assets in other currencies weakens the Swiss franc and at the same time pushes Swiss interest rates up. This process must go exactly to the point where the narrowed short-term interest rate differential is justified – within the interest rate parity condition - by the expectation of a revaluation of the Swiss franc until the actual EMU entry date. Swiss monetary policy may influence the speed by which Swiss interest rates converge to the higher Euro interest rates and thus the extent to which the Swiss franc temporarily weakens. Figure 5 illustrates this last point by comparing *three alternative monetary reactions* (EMU1, EMU2, EMU3).

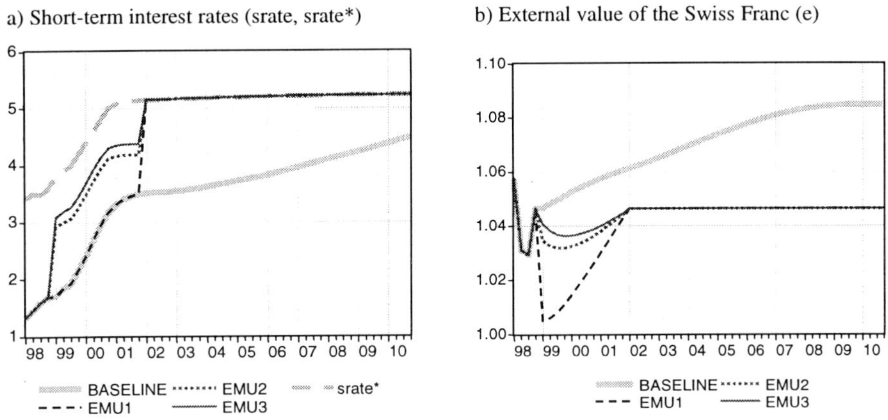

Figure 5: Alternative Monetary Reactions in the pre-EMU phase

EMU1: Monetary policy is conducted in such a way that *srate* is kept at the baseline path from 1999q1 to 2001q4. This requires that the effect of the portfolio shift on *srate* is neutralized by monetary policy so that its full burden falls on the exchange rate. In this case, the short-term interest rate differential remains practically unchanged in the pre-EMU phase and disappears with one bang in 2002q1.

EMU2: Parameter S_0 in the monetary reaction function (1') is set to a value that is a bit lower than the historical estimate (by 0.001). This means that monetary policy is assumed to be relatively loose in the pre-EMU phase as compared to historical standards. Nevertheless, the interest differential is roughly cut in half in 1999q1 on this assumption and the decline in the external value *e* is much less pronounced than in EMU1. The rest of the interest rate differential vanishes in 2002q1.

EMU3: Parameter S_0 in equation (1') is set to a value that is a bit higher than the historical estimate (also by 0.001). This amounts to the assumption that monetary policy is relatively tight in the pre-EMU phase as compared to historical standards. Accordingly, the interest differential contracts by more in 1999q1 than in EMU2 and the external value falls by less. Again, the rest of the interest rate differential is eliminated in 2002q1.

The *terminal condition* for the external value affects the pre-EMU phase in an obvious way. If *e* is set to a higher value in 2002q1, a larger interest rate differential can persist and the temporary decline in *e* is mitigated of even prevented. If *e* is set to a lower value in 2002q1, the interest rate differential must contract more and the fall in *e* becomes more pronounced. In the following, we concentrate on the scenario EMU2 (referred to as EMU) and turn to the adjustments in the real economy.

6.2. *Adjustments in the real economy*

Figure 6 first restates the effects of an EMU entry of the Swiss franc in 2002q1 on short-term interest rates and the external value, as discussed above (panel a and c). Panel b presents the adjustment in the long-term interest rate (*lrate*). According to the term structure condition and the assumption of model-consistent expectations, *lrate* anticipates the higher future values of *srate* and thus shows a big upward jump three years ahead of the actual EMU entry. GDP and employment are adversely affected in the pre-EMU phase, and negative deviations from the baseline path persist for several years (panel d). The maximum GDP loss (in levels) is recorded with -1.5% seven quarters after EMU entry. Annual GDP growth falls to 1% in 2001 (panel e). From 2004 onwards, GDP growth in the EMU scenario however begins to surmount GDP growth in the baseline simulation, so that GDP moves back to the baseline path and eventually exceeds it. At the end of the simulation period (2010q4), the EMU scenario shows a GDP gain of 1.3% over the baseline scenario. The effects on employment are similar. The unemployment rate exceeds the baseline values by a maximum of 0.46 percentage points in 2003, but falls by the same amount below the baseline path towards the end of the simulation period (panel f). This is mirrored in the deviations of the output gap, although the reactions are somewhat more pronounced and quicker. The output gap is widened by a maximum of 0.7 percentage points. This is less than the maximum GDP loss, reflecting that capacity output is also negatively affected through lower investment.

What are the mechanisms in the model behind these results. A first thing to notice is that private consumption (CONSP) and - even more so - housing investment (IHOUSE) remain below the baseline values throughout the simulation period (panel g) - although GDP and employment move beyond the baseline path after 2008. In case of housing investment, the unfavorable development in the EMU scenario is mainly due to higher long-term interest rates and the associated deterioration of profitability of housing investment. Private consumption is also directly hampered by higher long-term interest rates to some extent, in particular at the beginning of the simulation period. More important is however an indirect effect (panel k): Housing rents (PHR) increase strongly in response to higher interest rates[6], and this – together with the lower external value of the Swiss franc and increasing import prices (panel m) - pushes overall consumer prices (PCONSP) notably in excess of the baseline path (maximum deviation: 2%). The nominal wage (WAGE) on the other hand shows only a weak reaction. This result is due to the fact that wages depend in the model more on the GDP-deflator (PGDP) than on consumer prices. From a policy perspective, this has the advantage that increasing

---

[6] The estimated PHR-equation of the model reflects the Swiss legislation on rent control which stipulates a link between mortgage rates and housing rents.

import prices to not entail a wage-price spiral and a higher NAIRU. The drawback for private households is that they suffer a real income loss. As shown in panel h, the responses of private consumption and real disposable household incomes almost coincide (maximum deviation from baseline: –3%), except at the beginning of the simulation, where the direct interest rate effect plays some role.

The main stimulus on GDP and employment in the EMU scenario comes from foreign trade in connection with the fixed exchange rate (panel i). Total exports (EXTOT) benefit with a maximum deviation from the baseline path of 1.3 % in 2009/2010. This can be confronted with an exchange rate advantage against the baseline scenario of -3.6% in terms of the external value *e* at the end of the simulation period (panel c). What matters in the export equations[7] is however not the nominal external value *e* but the real external value computed on basis of export prices. This relative export price is only 2.4% lower in the EMU scenario than in the baseline simulation (due to the higher domestic price level). Thus the price elasticity of total exports is slightly larger than 0.5. The fact that the external value is fixed in the EMU scenario (instead of showing an increase) also affects imports. The decline of total imports (IMTOT) (maximum deviation from baseline: -3.6%) is however only partly the result of reduced import competition. More important is the dependence of imports on domestic demand and production. Nevertheless, as a comparison of panels i and d reveals, imports also decrease in relation to GDP (reduced absorption). In particular, at the end of the simulation period, where GDP exceeds the baseline path by 1.3%, total imports are practically on the baseline path. This can be attributed to the relative price effect.

---

[7] There are three export equations in the model (commodities, tourism, services).

Figure 6: EMU-Effects and the Real Economy

Graph types: (1) BASELINE and EMU-scenario, quarterly levels
(2) BASELINE and EMU-scenario, annual growth rates in %
(3) Deviation of EMU from BASELINE in % , quarterly levels

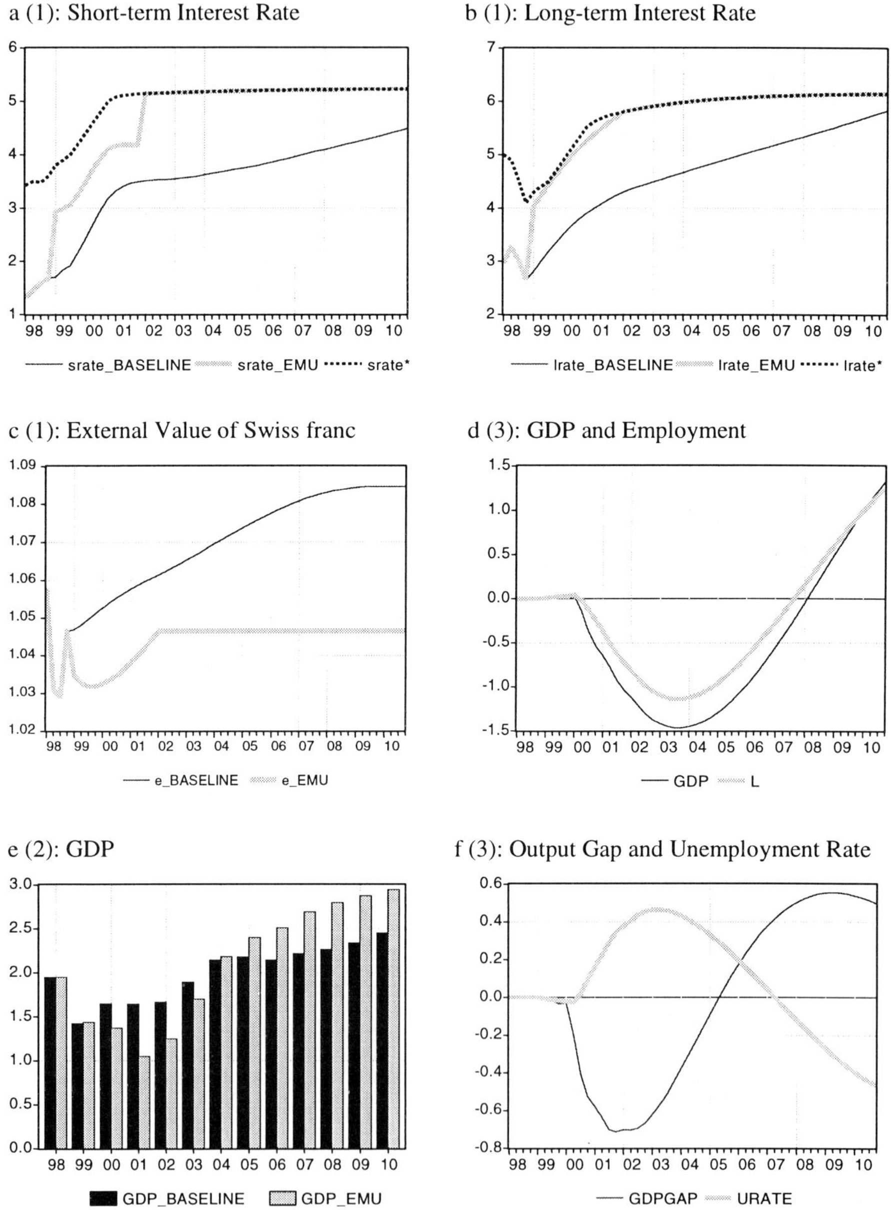

(Figure 6, continued)

g (3): Consumption, Business Investment, Housing Investment

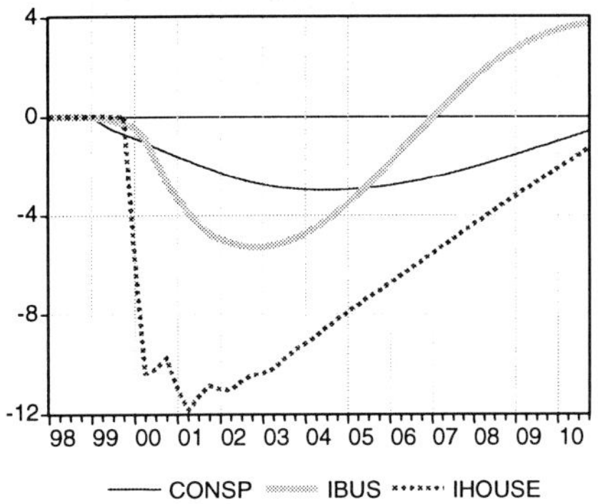

h (3): Consumption and Disposable Household Income

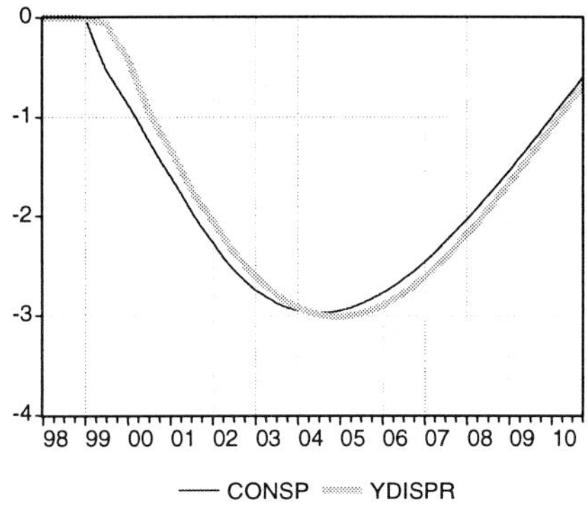

i (3): Exports and Imports

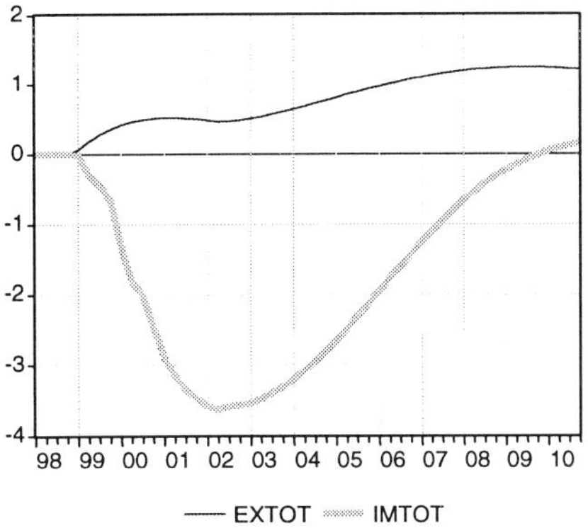

k (3): Nominal Wage and various Prices (consumption, GDP, housing rents, construction)

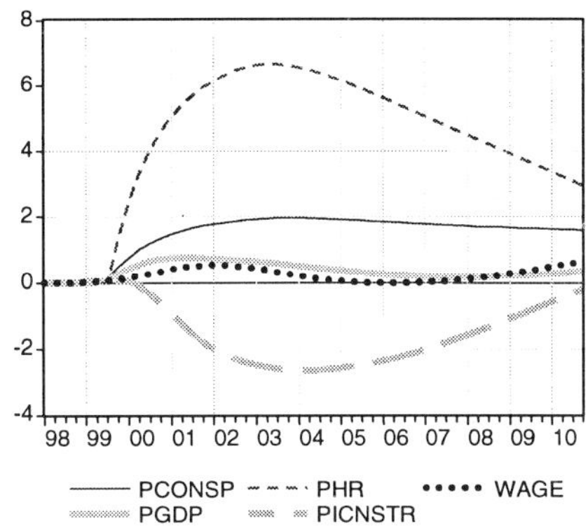

l (2): Consumption Prices

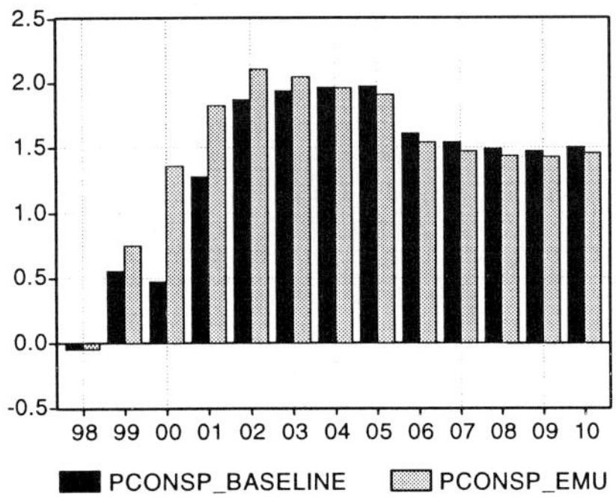

m (3): Prices of Exports and Imports

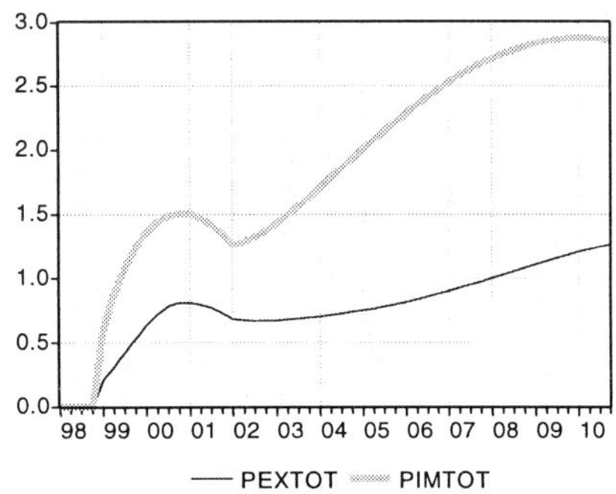

7. CONCLUSION

The results of this simulation study can be summarized in terms of an *interest rate effect* and an *exchange rate effect*. In the short run, by joining EMU, Switzerland would suffer quite strongly from loosing its historical interest rate advantage. The shock of higher interest rates in particular hampers housing investment and – via the "mortgage rate–housing rent" channel – also disposable household income and private consumption. In the longer run (about 6 years after EMU entry) the advantage of the stable exchange rate and the corresponding stimulus on exports begin to overcompensate the negative impact of higher interest rates, at least as far as total GDP and employment are concerned. For disposable household income, private consumption and housing investment, the adverse effects last notably longer, the more so as the nominal wage adjusts only partly to the higher level of consumer prices (brought about by the fixed exchange and the increase in housing rents), entailing a decline of real wages. Hence, EMU entry also changes the *distribution of income* and the *composition of GDP* for quite some time. These distributional effects make it difficult to draw a clear conclusion. While EMU entry may appear as rather favorable in a long-term perspective, the adjustment problems in the short and medium run are considerable. Private households are better off in the baseline scenario until the end of the simulation period.

Moreover, when comparing the two scenarios, one might suspect that the baseline simulation involves *two elements* that work in favor of EMU. First, there is an ongoing appreciation of the Swiss franc. Second, the interest rate differential narrows, despite non-entry into EMU. As a consequence, in comparison with the baseline scenario, the advantage of a fixed exchange rate in the EMU scenario increases towards the end of the simulation period whereas the disadvantage of higher interest rates dwindles. One should note though that the two elements are not independent of each other under the assumption of rational expectations. More precisely, manipulating the baseline simulation in a way that produces a weaker appreciation would automatically give rise to a stronger contraction of the interest rate differential. The only way to mitigate the appreciation of the Swiss franc against the Euro without reducing the interest rate differential is to augment the exchange rate risk premium. However, this parameter is set to the value that was observed for the Swiss franc/DM relationship historically, and a much higher risk premium for the Swiss franc/Euro relationship does not seem realistic. Hence, the model offers little room for changing the results in favor of the baseline scenario. In other words, the result of a GDP gain in the EMU scenario towards the end of the simulation period seems well-founded and cannot be attributed to "deliberately" unfavorable conditions in the baseline scenario.

Nevertheless, the simulation results are rather mixed and do not lend themselves to a clear and balanced conclusion about whether Switzerland should join EMU. Of course, EMU entry is not a policy option by itself but has to be seen in the broader context of an EU-membership. A more comprehensive assessment of the effects of an EU move of Switzerland is given in Bärlocher, Schips, Stalder (1999) and beyond the scope of the partial analysis.

REFERENCES

Ando, A.K., F. Modigliani, R. Rasche and S.J. Turnovsky (1974), On the Role of Expectations and Technological Change in an Investment Function, International Economic Review, 15, p. 384-414.

Bärlocher J., B. Schips, P. Stalder (1999), Makroökonomische Auswirkungen eines EU-Beitritts der Schweiz, BWA-Schriftenreihe, Beiträge zur Wirtschaftspolitik, Bern.

Drèze, J.H., Ch. Bean (1990), Europe's Unemployment Problem, MIT Press, Cambridge.

Hollinger, P. (1996), The Stacked-Time Simulator in TROLL: A Robust Algorithm for Solving Forward-Looking Models, Second International Conference on Computing in Economics and Finance, Geneva (Intex Solutions, Inc., Needham MA).

Kooiman, P. (1984), Smoothing the Aggregate Fix-Price Model and the Use of Business Survey Data, The Economic Journal, 94, p. 899-913.

Lambert, J.P. (1988), Disequilibrium Macro Models, Theory and Estimation for Rationing Models Using Business Survey Data, Cambridge University Press, Cambridge MA.

Sneessens, H.R. (1990), Structural Problems in Macroeconomic Models, Structural Change and Economic Dynamics 1, p. 27-40.

Stalder, P. (1989), A Disequilibrium Model with Smooth Regime Transitions and a Keynesian Spillover for Switzerland's Labor Market, European Economic Review, 33, p. 863-893.

Stalder, P. (1991a), A Macro Disequilibrium Model for Switzerland, Recherches Economiques de Louvain, 57, p. 125-158.

Stalder, P. (1991b), Regime Transitions, Spillovers and Buffer Stocks - Analysing the Swiss Economy by Means of a Disequilibrium Model, Lecture Notes in Economics and Mathematical Systems, 360, Berlin: Springer-Verlag.

Stalder, P. (1993), Disequilibrium Models and the Use of Business Survey Data, in Karmann, A. et al., Operations Research '92, Physica-Verlag, Heidelberg.

Stalder, P. (1994a), Excess Demand, Capacity Adjustments and Price Setting - An Econometric Model for Swiss Manufacturing Based on Survey Data, KOF-Arbeitspapier, Konjunkturforschungsstelle der ETH, Zürich.

Stalder, P. (1994b), Ungleichgewichte auf dem schweizerischen Arbeitsmarkt - Eine ökonometrische Modellschätzung, Schweiz. Zeitschrift für Volkswirtschaft und Statistik, 130, p. 445-463.

Stalder, P. (1995), Wage-Price Dynamics and Unemployment Persistence in Switzerland - The Case of a Small Economy with a Large Share of Foreign Labor, CEPR-Workshop on Nominal Wage-Price Sluggishness, Centre for Economic Policy Research, University of Aarhus.

Stalder, P. (1999), The Monetary Block of the KOF/ETH-Macromodel, mimeo, Konjunkturforschungsstelle der ETH, Zürich.

Walsh, C.E. (1998), Monetary Theory and Policy, Cambridge: MIT Press.

JÜRG BÄRLOCHER

MACROECONOMIC CONSEQUENCES OF SWISS EU ACCESSION: EFFECTS OF FISCAL MEASURES

1. INTRODUCTION

The desirable degree of integration into the European Union is still hotly debated in Switzerland. A study commissioned by the "Staatssekretariat für Wirtschaft" (seco) in 1998 intended to add scientific evidence on the likely effects of different degrees of integration on the Swiss economy. As part of this study, KOF/ETH (Swiss Institute for Business Cycle Research) analyzed the macroeconomic effects with emphasis on the short- to medium-run. The investigation method are simulations within a suitably modified version of the KOF/ETH-Macromodel, the institute's model used for forecasting and policy analysis since 1994.

Scenarios ranging from "Status quo" without implementation of the bilateral agreements between Switzerland and the EU to full EU-membership including EMU are discussed in Bärlocher, Schips and Stalder (1999). In Stalder (1999) details and refined simulation results regarding the effects of EMU are added. The subject of this paper are the effects of fiscal measures associated with Swiss EU accession. Simulation results are basically as in the first mentioned report, but some scenarios are added and a few technical aspects of the simulations clarified. In section 2 the properties of the model most relevant for the effects of fiscal policy are presented. Design and results of the simulations are the subject of section 3. In the final section some conclusions are drawn.

2. MODEL STRUCTURE

The KOF/ETH-Macromodel is a quarterly structural model for the Swiss economy. With less than forty stochastic equations it is relatively small in size. Originally developed in 1993/94, the model was subject to several revisions and extensions since. It forms the basis of the regular KOF/ETH forecasts and is also used to carry out policy simulations. For a general description see Stalder (1997a). This model was considered to be a suitable basis for the EU accession simulations (project EUmacro). However, some adjustments in the model structure were necessary. Moreover, since the simulation period in project EUmacro exceeds the forecasting horizon of the regular KOF/ETH forecasts (two years), extra restrictions of parameters were imposed to achieve a sensible medium- to long-run solution of the

R.E. Baldwin and A. Brunetti (eds.), Economic Impact of EU Membership on Entrants, 177–191.

model (at the cost of some loss of historical tracking performance). Modifications in the monetary block are discussed in Stalder (1999). The adjustments most relevant to simulating the effects of fiscal policy are described in the following two subsections.

2.1. The government and social security sector

In the autumn 1998 version of the KOF/ETH-Macromodel, the starting point for the EUmacro project, modeling of government actions (central, cantonal and local level aggregated; including the social security sector) concentrated on those activities, which most heavily influenced aggregate demand. Income of private households (and therefore private consumption) is influenced in two ways (figure 1). First, disposable income (YDISP) is less than the sum of labor income and income from business and property (YPRIM) by an amount NETTAX which stands for the net amount of direct taxes, social security contributions (health insurance / others), social security benefits (unemployment benefits / others) and net transfers to private households. Second, the influence of VAT on prices affects real disposable income of private households (YDISPR). The other government actions considered in the original model were consumption (CGOV) and investment (IGOV).

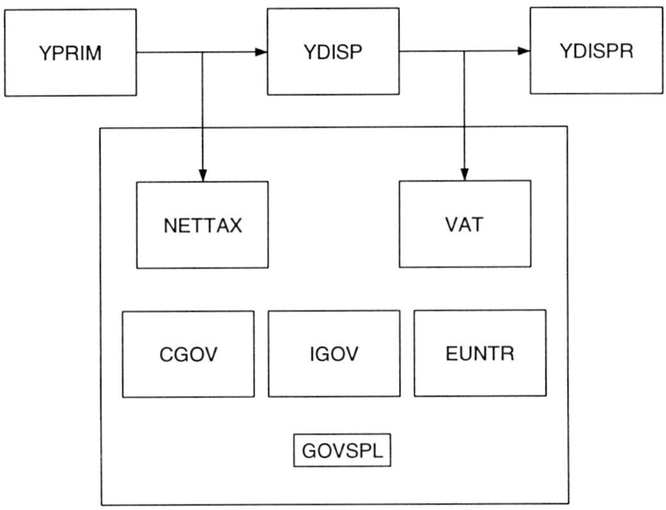

Figure 1. The government and income of private households in the KOF/ETH-Macromodel

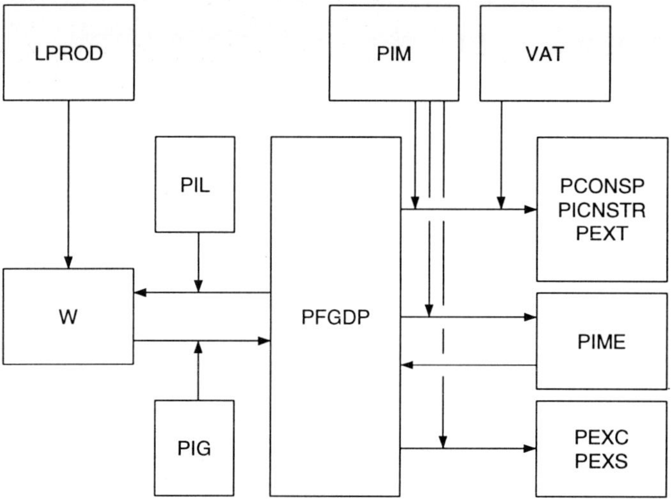

Figure 2. Wage price dynamics and prices of components of aggregate demand in the KOF/ETH-Macromodel

In the EUmacro version of the model, three (related) modifications were made. First, in the EU accession scenarios the effects of large changes in VAT compared to the changes up to 1998 (or up to 2000, the horizon of the KOF/ETH forecast in autumn 1998) were to be simulated. For this reason, more sophisticated modeling of the relation between VAT and prices, explained in the next subsection, was implemented. Second, originally VAT receipts were not (explicitly) modeled. An augmentation in this respect was necessary, because the EU accession scenarios involve a substantial shift from direct taxes to VAT. Third, as the shift between direct and indirect taxes has to occur under the constraint of an unchanged position of the government budget position, an indicator for the latter was needed. For that aim, a variable GOVSPL was constructed by adding NETTAX and the receipts from VAT (and other indirect taxes which are of minor importance in the present context) and subtracting CGOV and IGOV. In addition, depending on the scenario, a net transfer to the EU (EUNTR) may be included in GOVSPL. Because accounting rules and definition of sectors in the accounts compiled by government authorities differ from the concept employed here, GOVSPL is not directly related to official statements of the government budget position. However, GOVSPL corresponds with net lending of the government and social security sector according to the national accounts, except for direct taxes of firms (2% of GDP; for comparison: direct taxes of private households, VAT and other indirect taxes 20% of GDP), net interest income (4% of GDP) and some current transfers. Given the magnitude and likely variation of the omitted variables in the simulation context, GOVSPL seems to be a reasonable proxy for the government budget position.

2.2. *Wage price dynamics and prices of components of aggregate demand*

In the KOF/ETH-Macromodel a single price variable links wages with prices of consumer goods, investment goods and exports (figure 2). In various simulations this rather unusual feature turns out to be very convenient, since it allows the imposition of some useful constraints to the long-run solution of the model in a straightforward manner.

As indicated in the left part of figure 2, wages (W) depend in the EUmacro Version of the KOF/ETH-Macromodel on the "price" of value added (GDP-deflator), labor productivity (LPROD), and the proportion of micro labor markets in excess demand (PIL, historically measured by the proportion of firms reporting "labor bottlenecks"). In the main scenarios it is assumed, that price changes caused by changes in VAT have no direct effect on wages. In a sensitivity analysis this assumption is relaxed. Technically, the assumption of no direct VAT effect is implemented by using the deflator of GDP at factor costs (PFGDP), not market prices. In the general specification of the KOF/ETH-Macromodel, PFGDP as well as consumer prices enter the wage equation as explanatory variables, the sum of the long-run elasticities of W with respect to the two prices constrained to be one. In Stalder (1997b), based on data from 1975 to 1994 and W measured by the BFS wage index, it is found that wages respond stronger on movements in consumer prices than on movements in the GDP-deflator. But measuring W by labor income per employee, the concept used in the KOF/ETH-Macromodel since 1998, and switching to a estimation period from the early 1980's to 1997, empirical results support a specification with PFGDP alone. Consistent with the outcome of a t-test, the long-run elasticity of W with respect to LPROD is set to one. With unit elasticities of W with respect to PFOHG and LPROD the wage equation implies a constant share of labor income in GDP at factor costs in the long-run, except for variation in PIL.

PFGDP is determined by W, the price of machinery and equipment (PIME), and the share of capacity constrained firms (PIG). A micro foundation for the aggregate price equation under the conditions of monopolistic competition in the goods market, perfect competition in the factor markets, and a vintage technology is given in Stalder (1997a). The prices of consumer goods, investment goods and exports are modeled as functions of PFGDP, the price of imports (PIM), VAT as discussed below, and some sector specific variables such as the vacancy rate in the rent component of consumer prices (right part of figure 2). Consistency between the equation for PFGDP, real GDP and nominal GDP is achieved by treating inventory investment at current prices as a residual in the breakup of GDP according to terms of expenditure.

In the case of the price of consumption of domestic private households (PCONSP), the price of exports of tourism (PEXT), and the price of investment in construction (PICNSTR), a mark-up for covering the full amount of non-deductable VAT is taken into account. Reduced rates and exemption from VAT of some consumer goods are considered. The dependence of PICNSTR on VAT reflects the fact, that in the Swiss system VAT on housing is not deductable. No VAT adjustment is necessary for the price of machinery and equipment, exports of commodities, and exports of services other than tourism (PIME, PEXC and PEXS).

3. SIMULATING THE EFFECTS OF EU ACCESSION

3.1. Reference scenario

In the more comprehensive study Bärlocher, Schips and Stalder (1999), scenarios ranging from "Status quo", without implementation of the bilateral agreements, to EU-membership including EMU are considered. For the assessment of the effects of fiscal measures associated with EU accession, a natural starting point is a scenario in which the bilateral agreements are already implemented. In this paper simulation results will usually be stated with reference to a scenario termed BIL. This reference scenario corresponds to BILeff in Bärlocher, Schips and Stalder (1999), where "eff" refers to the inclusion of efficiency gains, an assumption not significant in the present context.

3.2. Design of EU accession scenarios

The following two fiscal measures are required by the rules of the EU. First, Swiss membership entails a significant net transfer to the EU. In the simulations, a transfer of 0.9% of GDP is assumed. This estimate is based on current rules. It ignores that rules may change in favor of net contributors to the EU budget and that some (net) contributions are negotiable. The assumption concerning the amount of the transfer may therefore be seen as "worst case". Second, the (normal) rate of VAT has to be increased to at least 15%. A transition period of five years is allowed for this measure. As suggested by the mandator, the constraint of no deterioration in the government budget position was imposed in most simulations.

Five scenarios are considered. An overview of assumptions is shown in table 1. The effects of the net transfer to the EU and the increase in VAT are analyzed in two steps. In scenarios Fis1a, Fis1b, and Fis1c VAT is only increased in order to finance the net transfer to the EU (VAT rate increase of 2 percentage points). Fis1a and Fis1b differ in the modeling of government consumption and investment. In Fis1a government consumption and investment is proportional to GDP, in Fis1b it is exogenous (taken from the reference scenario BIL). Fis1c is the only scenario in which a temporary deterioration of the government budget deficit (compared to the reference scenario BIL) is allowed. More technically, in the KOF/ETH-Macromodel the ratio of direct taxes to income of private households may be defined as exogenous and the ratio of GOVSPL to GDP as endogenous or vice versa. Only in Fis1c is the rate of direct taxes the exogenous variable, in all other scenarios the rate of direct taxes is endogenously determined to maintain the exogenously given government budget position. In Fis2a the (normal) VAT rate is immediately increased to 15% with a compensation in direct taxes of private households. The other assumptions in Fis2a correspond to those in Fis1a. To make the effects of a shift from income tax to VAT more clear, in Fis2b the VAT rate is raised to 15%, as in Fis2a, but now the transfer to the EU is assumed to be zero. With GOVSPL exogenous, this implies a bigger reduction in income tax than in Fis2a.

Table 1. Scenarios and assumptions

Scenario	Net transfer to EU	VAT rate 15%	Government consumption and investment	Deterioration of government budget deficit
Fis1a	yes	no	endogenous	no
Fis1b	yes	no	exogenous	no
Fis1c	yes	no	exogenous	yes
Fis2a	yes	yes	endogenous	no
Fis2b	no	yes	endogenous	no

Simulation results will be shown over a ten year period, with T standing for the year in the beginning of which Swiss EU accession supposedly occurs. Short- to medium-run effects are emphasized, because this is the time range in which the data supported dynamics of the simulation model are important, while the long-run solution may be influenced by some debatable ad hoc constraints. At least in theory, CGE-models, as employed in the present context by Müller and Grether (1999) and Müller and van Nieuwkoop (1999), are superior instruments to assess the long-run effects of EU accession.

In the simulations in Stalder (1999) with a focus on the monetary sector, the anticipation of Swiss EU accession affects the economy well in advance of the accession date. In the simulation context here, no announcement effects occur, since interest rates and exchange rates are treated as exogenous variables and the current version of the KOF/ETH-Macromodel has no forward-looking features outside the monetary block.

3.3. Net transfer to EU financed by an increase in VAT

As mentioned in the last subsection, in a scenario Fis1a a VAT financed net transfer to the EU is introduced. The effect of this fiscal measures on GDP is illustrated in figure 3. The line in the figure shows deviations of the GDP level from the reference scenario BIL in percent (quarterly data). The bars are differences in growth rates in percentage points (annual data).

The net transfer to the EU (0.9% of GDP) and the corresponding increase in VAT (rate increase of 2 percentage points) is introduced in the first quarter of year T. Aggregate demand is reduced by a fall in consumer spending due to VAT-induced price increases. With multiplier effects, GDP-growth is hampered until four years after the introduction of the fiscal measure. In T+4 a GDP-deviation of -0.7% is reached. The corresponding rise in the unemployment rate is shown in figure 4.

From T+5 onward, as the economy returns to full-employment (as defined by actual employment in the reference scenario), the gap between GDP in Fis1a and in the reference scenario diminishes. Eventually the gap is expected to vanish almost completely. This reflects the fact that in the long-run GDP is not determined by demand but by the size of the labor force and technical progress.

The effect of the VAT-financed transfer to the EU on GDP and employment, while clearly negative, is temporary and moderate compared to, e.g., the short- to medium-run effects of entering the monetary union as simulated in Stalder (1999). More significant is the effect on real disposable income of private households (figure 5). The initial drop in the first quarter of T, in comparison to the reference scenario, is almost entirely due to the VAT-induced price increases (figure 6). Subsequently, real disposable income diminishes further, first due to the rise in unemployment, later intensified by a decrease in real wages (also shown in figure 6) caused by the worsening of the labor market conditions. Due to the lags in the wage formation process, the gap between GDP in Fis1a and in the reference scenario widens until six years after the introduction of the fiscal measure, significantly longer than in the case of GDP and unemployment. The maximum of the simulated gap of real disposable income is 2%. Later on some convergence occurs. However, in contrast to GDP, due to the specific design of the fiscal package, which implies that private households bear the burden of the net transfer to the EU, a significant gap is permanent.

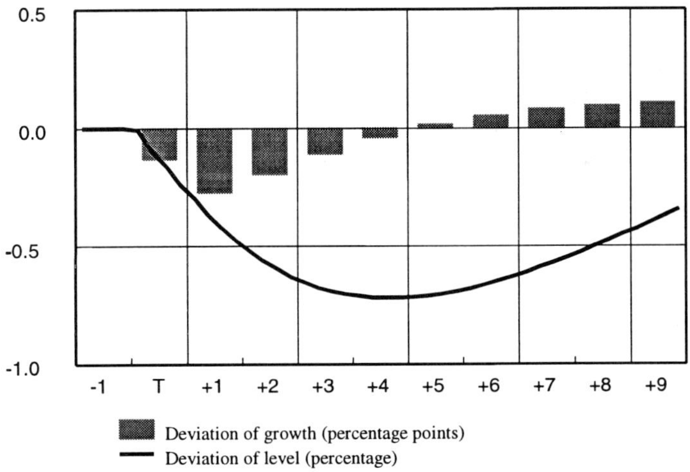

Figure 3. Fis 1a, GDP (Reference scenario is BIL)

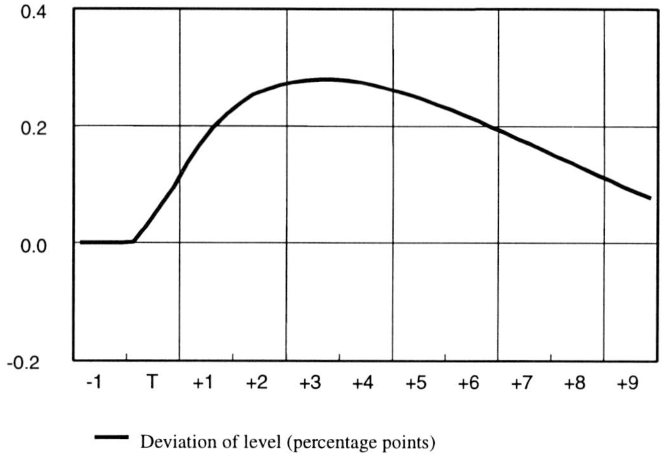

Figure 4. Fis 1a, unemployment rate (Reference scenario is BIL)

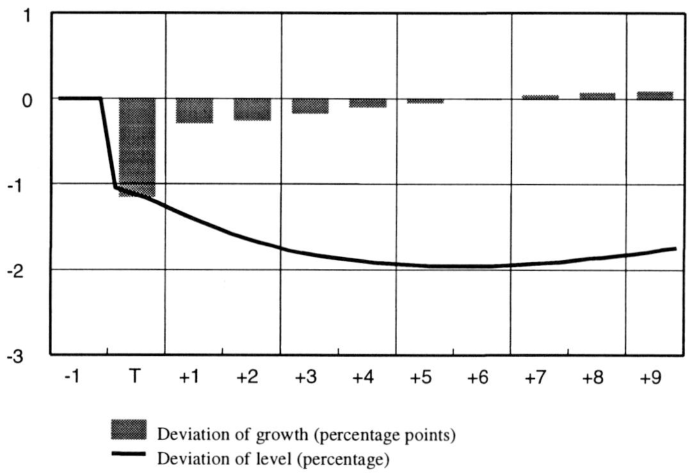

Figure 5. Fis 1a, disposable income (Reference scenario is BIL)

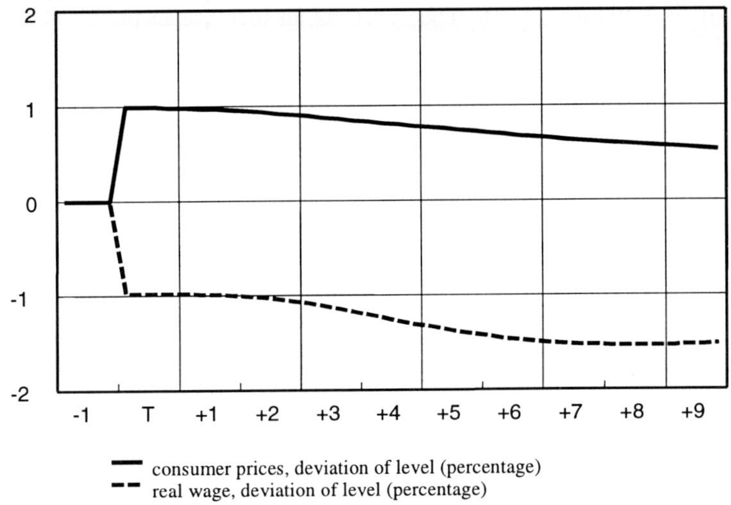

Figure 6. Fis 1a, consumer prices and real wage (Reference scenario is BIL)

Scenario Fis1a may be seen an extreme case. With deteriorating GDP (with respect to BIL), the budget position is maintained in Fis1a by adjusting expenditures as well as taxes. Government consumption and investment varies with GDP. The remaining adjustment necessary to prevent the government budget deficit from worsening is achieved by shifting the rate of income tax. Various alternatives to this fiscal policy are conceivable. To give an idea of the significance of the specific assumptions, two variants are considered in the remainder of this subsection.

In scenarios Fis1b and Fis1c government consumption and investment is exogenous, their respective values corresponding to scenario BIL. With respect to Fis1a, this implies higher government expenditures. In Fis1b these extra expenditures are financed by rising direct income tax (flexibly) to maintain the government budget of the reference scenario in the entire simulation period. In scenario Fis1c income tax rates are predetermined such that the government budget deficit coincides with the reference scenario once GDP has reached the reference level. In the short- to medium-run, however, a higher budget deficit than in the reference scenario is allowed.

GDP is almost identical in Fis1b and Fis1c (figure 7). In both scenarios, the maximum deviation from BIL is roughly 0.5%, compared to 0.7% in Fis1a. This highlights the crucial role of government expenditures to stabilize GDP-growth in the first years after EU accession. With respect to GDP, differences in income tax appear to be of minor importance. Stronger effects of taxation occur in real disposable income of private households (figure 8). Despite the more favorable GDP, in terms of income, private households in Fis1b are hardly any better off than in Fis1a. This is because in Fis1b they are taxed for the extra government expenditures. In Fis1c, the shortfall in real disposable income with respect to scenario BIL is limited to 1.7%. The "cost" is an increase in public debt of about 0.5% of GDP.

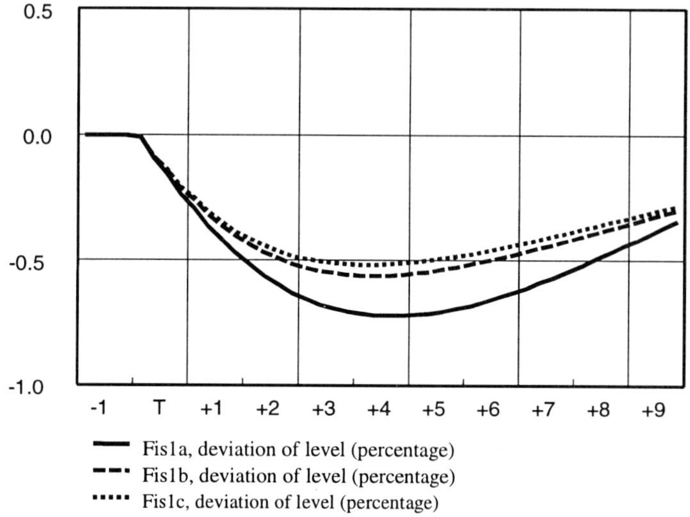

Figure 7. Fis 1a/b/c, GDP (Reference scenario is BIL)

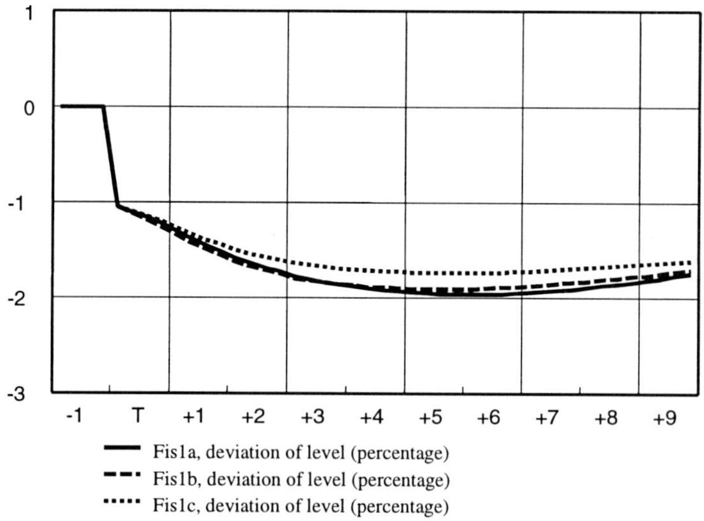

Figure 8. Fis 1a/b/c, disposable income (Reference scenario is BIL)

3.4. Shift from income tax to VAT

In the scenarios discussed so far, VAT was raised only by the amount needed to finance the net transfer to the EU. In scenario Fis2a, the (normal) VAT-rate is immediately raised to 15%. The government budget deficit is held at the level of the reference scenario BIL, leaving some VAT-receipts to reduce income tax. In period T, the VAT-rate in the reference scenario is 8%. It rises to 10% over a period of three years because it is supposed, that a larger fraction of VAT-receipts is needed for social security. In Fis2a 2 percentage points of VAT are used to finance the net transfer to the EU. This leaves initially 5 percentage points of VAT to reduce income tax of private households. In subsequent years, this tax rebate diminishes in accordance with the mentioned increase in funds for social security

GDP and real disposable income of private households in Fis2a are shown in figures 9 and 10. There is little difference in GDP compared to scenario Fis1a. But in terms of real disposable income, domestic private households in Fis2a are clearly better off. This occurs, because some of the additional VAT is paid by foreigners, while the reduction in direct taxes benefits residents only.

The more favorable disposable income in Fis2a means, that the depressing effect on GDP stemming from a fall in private consumption is smaller than in Fis1a. On the other hand, in Fis2a the bigger change in relative price of consumption at home and abroad - implied by the VAT-increase - causes a larger shift of consumption from Switzerland to the rest of the world (see net exports of tourism in figure 11). In addition, the increase in VAT negatively affects housing investment, which, as mentioned in section 2, is not exempt from VAT in Switzerland.

The comparison of Fis2a and Fis1a shows, that not the rise in VAT but the transfer to the EU is the root of the depressive effects on the economy. This fact becomes even more clear from scenario Fis2b. In Fis2b the VAT-rate is 15%, but the transfer to the EU is assumed to be zero, leaving the entire VAT-increase to reduce income tax. GDP is almost identical with the reference scenario, but real disposable income is about 1% above the reference level (figures 9 and 10).

According to scenario Fis2a, an immediate increase in VAT may be seen as a measure to alleviate the burden of private households following EU accession. However, a limitation of the model should be noted. The increase in VAT implies a shift in the composition of aggregate demand. A corresponding shift of resources between sectors is necessary. In reality this entails costs. In the KOF/ETH-Macromodel these adjustment costs are ignored, since the supply side is modeled as a single sector. Therefore, the simulation results offer no final answer to the question about the optimal timing of the VAT-increase.

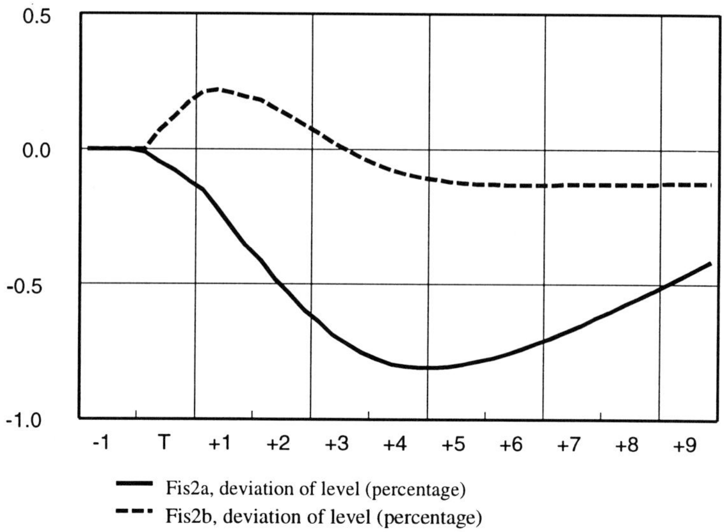

Figure 9. Fis 2a/b, GDP (Reference scenario is BIL)

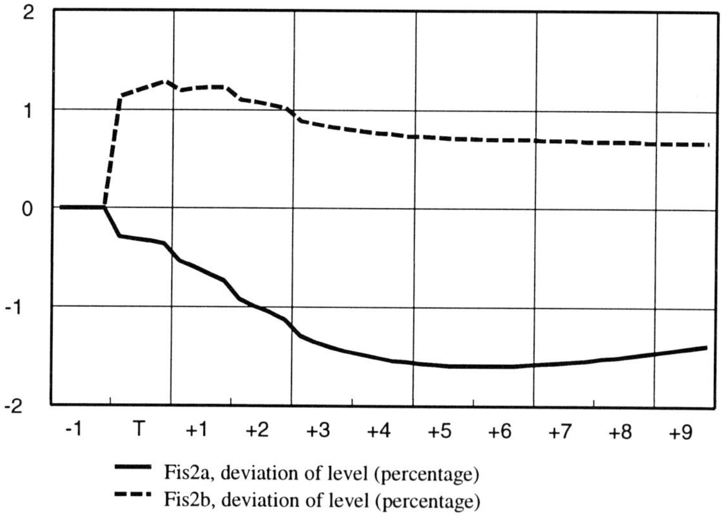

Figure 10. Fis 2a/b, disposable income (Reference scenario is BIL)

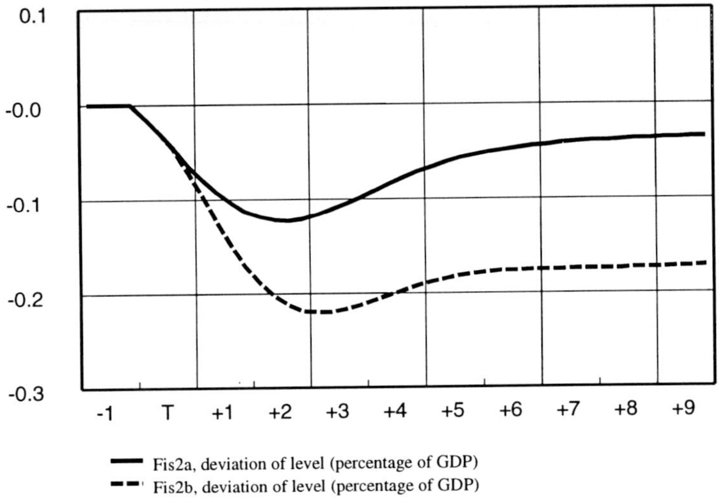

Figure 11. Fis 2a/b, net exports of tourism (Reference scenario is BIL)

3.5. *Compensation of VAT increase in wages*

In discussions of preliminary results it was suggested, that the assumption of no compensation of VAT in wages could be crucial for the initially depressing effects following EU accession in our simulations. The idea seems to be, that the drop in consumption is smaller if wages rise in response to a VAT increase and this would alleviate the negative effect on GDP. A subsequent analysis made clear, that in the KOF/ETH-Macromodel the consequences of a compensation of VAT in wages are more complicated. It is true, that real disposable income of private households initially falls less than without VAT-effect in wages, but a conflict in the income distribution occurs. By increasing VAT, the government secures for itself a rising share of income. In the scenarios described so far, with wages (directly) unaffected by changes in VAT, workers accept "voluntarily" a corresponding reduction in real income. With wages responding to a VAT-increase and price setting behavior of firms unchanged, wage determination and price setting become initially inconsistent in the sense that labor and firms together claim more of GDP than is left after the augmented share of the government is subtracted. The consequence is a wage price spiral which hampers growth. This leads to rising unemployment which weakens the position of employees in the wage bargaining process (in figure 2 above a decrease of PIL). A drop in capacity utilization reduces inflation (in figure 2 a decrease of PIG). This process continues until wage claims by workers and price setting of firms are compatible regarding the functional income distribution.

In a sensitivity analysis in Bärlocher, Schips and Stalder (1999), one quarter of the VAT-induced price increases were compensated in wages. In the short- to medium-run the consequences of this modification are higher inflation, lower GDP and lower employment. Regarding the components of aggregate demand, higher real wages stimulate consumption while exports are hampered. Private households are better off in terms of real disposable income. It follows, that compensating wages for the VAT-increase does not alleviate the initially negative effects on GDP following EU accession, but it may prevent some of the deterioration of income of private households. The problem is higher unemployment.

4. CONCLUSIONS

The simulations using the KOF/ETH-Macromodel show, that fiscal measures associated with EU accession are likely to depress GDP temporarily. This may be desirable, if the economy would otherwise show signs of overheating. However, the chances for the latter are dimmed, since in the period following EU accession macro economic activity is hampered by adjustments in the monetary sector due to the (eventual) entry into EMU. Therefore, a careful analysis of the effects of fiscal policy is necessary.

In the simulations, the root of the depressing effect on macro economic activity appears to be the net transfer to the EU. If this transfer has to be made and fiscal policy is designed to avoid a deterioration of the government budget position, the government sector claims a rising share of total income, without a corresponding adjustment of its demand. This implies lower aggregate demand, which in turn has temporarily a negative effect on GDP.

In contrast to the transfer to the EU, the requirement of a VAT-rate of at least 15% does not pose a problem at the macro level. As long as extra VAT-receipts are compensated by lower income tax, the composition of demand is affected, but the aggregate is almost unchanged. Consequently, only minor effects on GDP occur.

While the effect of the transfer to the EU on GDP is temporary, the influence on disposable income is permanent. The standard assumption in the simulations is, that the transfer is financed by rising VAT and wages are not compensated for VAT-induced price changes. In this setting, workers accept a reduction of real income corresponding to the transfer to the EU. Adjusting wages for VAT-induced price changes has an effect on the functional income distribution. It does not, however, alleviate the negative effect on GDP.

REFERENCES

Bärlocher, J., B. Schips, and P. Stalder (1999), Makroökonomische Auswirkungen eines EU-Beitrittes der Schweiz, BWA-Schriftenreihe, Beiträge zur Wirtschaftspolitik Nr. 6, Bern.

Müller, A. and R. van Nieuwkoop (1999), EU-Integration der Schweiz: Wirtschaftliche Auswirkungen, BWA-Schriftenreihe, Beiträge zur Wirtschaftspolitik Nr. 8, Bern.

Müller, T. and J.-M. Grether (1999), Effets à long terme d'une integration de la Suisse à l'Europe, BWA-Schriftenreihe, Beiträge zur Wirtschaftspolitik Nr. 4, Bern..

Stalder, P. (1997a), The KOF/ETH-Macromodel for Switzerland – Simulating the Swiss Economy in a European Context, Paper presented at the TROLL Conference, Brussels.

Stalder, P. (1997b), Unemployment in Switzerland: Lost Paradise of Better Coverage? – Wage-Price Dynamics and Cyclical Flexibility of Labor Supply, Paper Presented at the International Symposium on Economic Modeling, London.

BANU SIMMONS-SÜER
MARGIT HIMMEL

THE COSTS OF THE EU INTEGRATION FOR SWITZERLAND: ALTERNATIVE SCENARIOS

PREFACE

This paper is based on a more comprehensive study by Vaterlaus, Himmel, Koellreuter and Simmons (1999)[1] which was commissioned by the Secretariat for Economic Affairs (SECO) in an attempt to evaluate the economic effects of a Swiss entry into the European Union (EU) from the year 2002. Given the *ex-ante* nature of the study, our analysis using a macro-model framework relies heavily on introducing various shocks in an exogenous manner, and using our judgement in a pragmatic way in forming assumptions, where the nature of the current model is inadequate to address certain issues. Although our approach can be criticised for containing some *ad-hoc* elements, various sensitivity tests reveal that the main conclusions of the study are not challenged a great deal by different formulation of the shocks in question.

1. INTRODUCTION

The purpose of this study is to investigate the macroeconomic effects of a possible Swiss entry into the European Union via a structural model of the Swiss economy. Several scenarios have been conducted to analyse these effects with variations in the timing and the magnitude of the shocks to be carried out. The focus of the paper is on the costs rather than the benefits of European integration, primarily because benefits are rather difficult to quantify *ex-ante* especially within a macro model framework. The date of Swiss entry is expected to be 1st of January 2002 . The shocks were introduced either from the year 2002 as once and for all shocks or allowing a transitional period between 2002 and 2007. We label the former scenario "Cold Turkey" and the latter "Transition".

Swiss entry into the EU has several implications for fiscal and monetary policy in Switzerland. In the case of the entry, Switzerland is to be faced with a net transfer of 3.7 billion SFr to EU which amounts to 0.84% of the forecast nominal GDP in the year 2002. Net transfers from Switzerland is expected to be financed through introduction of subsequent increases in the rate of value-added tax (VAT). VAT receipts in excess of financing EU transfers, will be matched by an equivalent reduction in the income tax rate of cantons so that the final effect on the government's budget is neutralised.

Entry to the European Monetary Union implies that the Swiss National Bank will

[1] We thank the other project participants C. Koellreuter and S. Vaterlaus for their valuable comments on the paper.

R.E. Baldwin and A. Brunetti (eds.), Economic Impact of EU Membership on Entrants, 193–212.

no longer be able to follow an autonomous monetary policy. Swiss interest rates have had the long tradition of being lower than their European counterparts. With the announcement of the entry, long-term interest rates in Switzerland are expected to converge fairly quickly from the year 2000 to the European levels with any discrepancy being attributable to differences in the level of government debts. Short term interest rates are expected to adjust more slowly, gradually reaching the European level, whilst the value of the Swiss franc vis-à-vis Euro will be permanently fixed. Table 1 below summarises the simulation assumptions for "Cold Turkey" and "Transition" scenarios.

Table 1. Simulation Assumptions

	EU entry "Cold Turkey"	EU entry "Transition"
	Net transfers to EU	
• Amount	0.84% per annum of nominal GDP	0.84% per annum of nominal GDP
• Timing	from 2002	from 2002
	VAT increase	
• Tax change	from 8.13% to15%	from 8.13% to 15% gradual increases
• Timing	from 2002	between 2003 and 2007
	Reduction in income tax rate	
• Amount	VAT-Net transfers	VAT- Net transfers
• Timing	from 2002	from 2005
	Short-term interest rates	
• Level	EU Level	EU Level
• Timing	Fixed from 2002	Fixed from 2007
	Long-term interest rates	
• Level	EU Level – Margin due to differences in fiscal solvency	EU Level- Margin due to differences in fiscal solvency
• Timing	from 2000	from 2000
	Exchange rate SFr/Euro in the EU	
• Level	1.62	1.62
• Timing	Fixed from 2002	Fixed from 2007

2. MODEL OUTLINE

The BAK Swiss Macro-model is a quarterly structural model which is based on the income-expenditure accounting framework wherein the level of output and employment is determined principally by the level of demand. Countries in the model are inter-linked via trade variables, exchange rates and interest rates. As there is no published description of the BAK model available to cite as a reference, we allocate this section to a review of the core equations of the model so that simulation reactions of the model can be judged better by the reader[2].

Core demand variables of the Swiss macro model are the components of the aggregate expenditure at constant and current prices. Among these demand variables, consumption is inarguably the most important contributor to GDP with a share around 55% of the Swiss GDP. The general form of the consumption equation can be expressed as follows[3]

$$\Delta(c)=\alpha_1\Delta(y) - .25*(c(-1)-.75*y(-1)-.25*w(-1)+\alpha_4 R(-1)), \qquad (1)$$

$$\alpha_1>0, \alpha_4>0$$

where c is the consumption expenditure, y is the real disposable income, w is real wealth and R is the real personal sector interest rate[4]. This equation and many other equations of endogenous variables in the model were estimated according to the Error Correction methodology which was first developed by Engle and Granger (1987). The terms in parenthesis reflect the long-term equilibrium relationship between level of consumption and its explanatory variables. The long-run elasticity of consumption with respect to the sum of real income and wealth is unity. Adjustment to this long-term path is 25 % per quarter.

Investment decisions in the model are based on 'Tobin's q' approach. Tobin's q is defined as the ratio of the market value of an additional unit of capital to its replacement cost . In the model, firms are assumed to invest when the marginal return of capital is greater than the replacement cost (Tobin's q exceeds unity) and reduce investment when the converse occurs. However, in the long-run, capital stock converges to its desired level and marginal return (post-tax marginal product of capital) is equal to the replacement cost (post-depreciation real interest rate). In the private non-residential investment equation defined below, a 10% increase in the q ratio (qr) causes 2% increase in investment (i) with a slow adjustment to the desired level of capital stock (k). Private non-residential Investment in the short-run responds to acceleration effects of GDP as it is shown in the following equation:

$$\Delta(i) = .2*qr - .13*(i(-1) - k(-1)) + \alpha_3\Delta(gdp(-1)) \qquad (2)$$

$$\alpha_3>0$$

Exports (x) in the model respond to changes in world trade (wt) in a homogenous manner both in the short-run and in the long-run and to changes in price competitiveness which is measured by export prices (px) relative to the world prices

---

[2] For a more detailed review of structural macro models, the reader can refer to Whitley (1994).

[3] Letters in lower case mark the variables that are in natural logarithms

[4] We do not report here all the coefficients of the equations but only the important elasticities and the Error Correction coefficients.

(wp), adjusted for the exchange rate (rx). World trade is defined as a weighted average index of other countries' import volumes where the weights come from the world trade matrix. the price effect measured as export price/world price is more potent in the fixed exchange rate system. The export equation is expressed as follows

$$\Delta(x) = \Delta(wt)+\alpha_2\Delta(px/(wp.rx)) -.55*(x(-1)-wt(-1)+.39*(px(-1)/(wp(-1).rx(-1)))+ \alpha_4 Trend) \quad (3)$$

$\alpha_2<0$

As far as the effects of the fiscal policy shocks on trade is concerned, an expansionary policy leads to higher unit wage costs which result in higher export prices. Under the flexible exchange rate system, the price increase is matched by depreciation of the currency (rx), dampening the competitiveness effect. The entry into the European Monetary Union is expected to increase potency of changes in the relative price as the exchange rate will be permanently fixed.

Total final expenditure (tfe) is the main determinant of imports (m) and in the long run has an elasticity of unity. Elasticity of imports to import prices with respect to the tfe deflator is .6 as given in the following equation.

$$\Delta(m) = \alpha_1\Delta(tfe) + \alpha_2\Delta(pm/ptfe)-.11*(m(-1) - tfe(-1) +.6*(pm(-1)/ptfe(-1))) \quad (4)$$

$\alpha_1>0, \ \alpha_2<0$

An implication of the equations (3) and (4) is that an expansionary fiscal shock would be likely to result in deteriorating current-account balance in the short-run, given the sluggish reaction of exports accompanied with the imports rising with the total final expenditure. In the long-term, current-account balance recovers as GDP gets crowded out.

The supply side of the BAK Swiss macro-model is based on a vertical long-run 'Phillips Curve', where the productive capacity is determined by capital stock, potential employment and technological progress, and a Cobb-Douglas production function characterises the production relationship. Potential employment is taken to be the level of labour supply after adjusting for the natural rate of unemployment. Since the employment entering the production function is consistent with the natural rate of unemployment, in the long-run equilibrium, the country has a natural growth rate which is beyond the power of the government to alter through demand-management policies, and output cycles around this trend. Hence, the gap between the potential output and GDP is the capacity utilisation, according to which firms set prices.

In the model, prices are determined as a mark-up on wage and import costs and capacity utilisation explains the price changes caused by the variations in the pressure of demand. Price homogeneity is a restriction imposed in the long-run, i.e. prices are fully flexible in the long-run.

The wage (w) equation in (5) is formulated so that in the long run the share of labour in output is constant, represented as a product of the real wage rate and productivity of labour (prod) and any deviations from this constant share is explained by the ratio of unemployment (up) to the natural rate of unemployment (naru). Existence of wage rigidity in the short-run is depicted by the dynamics of the equation, namely the wage rates and prices expressed in differences. High real wages lead to higher unemployment with respect to the natural rate, which in return exerts downward pressure on wages. By including the wedge between the consumer price index (cpi) and the GDP deflator (p), formulation of the wage equation allows, to an extent, the changes in indirect taxes to be reflected in the wage demands of workers.

$$\Delta(w)=\Delta(p) + \alpha_1\Delta(cpi/p) + \alpha_{2\Delta}(prod)-\alpha_3(w(-1)-p(-1)-prod(-1)) + \alpha_4(up(-1)/naru(-1)))) \quad (5)$$

$\alpha_1>0, \alpha_2>0$

Interest rate determination in the BAK model is based on a 'Money-Targeting' approach which is formulated as follows:

$$\Delta(R) = \alpha_1\Delta(mbg/p)+\alpha_2\Delta(gdp)-.25*(R(-1) -\Delta(p(-1))) \quad (6)$$

$\alpha_1<0, \alpha_2>0$

where R and mbg denote the short-term interest rates and the bank reserves respectively. This equation is basically an inverted partial-adjustment equation for the demand for bank reserves. The long run path of the short-term interest rates is determined by inflation. The deviations from the long-run path is brought about by changes in the real reserve holdings of the Swiss National Bank (SNB), and changes in real output.

Bank reserves are modelled to respond to the extent to which consumer prices deviate from their long term trend, and also to changes in the unemployment ratio and in German interest rates. The estimated mbg equation is the following:

$$\Delta(mbg) = .012 - 1.106 *tdcpi(-1) - .27*\Delta (R, Germany) + .0356 * \Delta(u) \quad (7)$$

where tdcpi is the deviation of the consumer price index (cpi) from its long term trend, given by (7):

$$tdcpi = cpi - 4.29 -.0075*T \quad (8)$$

T is a time-trend starting from 1980. The inclusion of the de-trended price level is justified on the basis of a study by Kugler (1998) who shows that the Swiss price level in contrast to other major OECD countries, reverts to a constant deterministic trend during a flexible exchange rate period.

The exchange rate equation in the model is based on the mainstream 'Uncovered Interest Parity' (UIP) paradigm which relates the exchange rate to its expected future level, interest differentials and a risk premium. 'Purchasing Power Parity' (PPP), is maintained in the long-run, but the expected rate of change of the exchange rate is linked to the differences in interest rates between Switzerland and Germany. Historically, the capital gains from appreciation of the Swiss franc has been inadequate to offset fully the differences in interest rates with Germany which indicates an explicitly unidentified risk premium which in the case of Switzerland can be attributed to factors such as secrecy rules of Swiss banks and tax concessions with respect to investment in Switzerland. Given the uncertainty associated with these factors in the pre-EMU period, in our EU integration simulations we choose to exogenise both the exchange rate and the interest rates rather than enforcing an endogenous path for the latter, which is strictly consistent with a disappearing risk premium.

3. THE FISCAL POLICY IN THE MODEL

Any shocks with respect to the exogenous components of demand clearly have implications for prices, wages, interest rates and exchange rates. For example, an increase in real government spending initially leads to higher GDP, but the positive effect is gradually eroded as "crowding-out" sets in . The transmission mechanism in the model operates as follows: The increase in aggregate demand in the short run leads to higher capacity utilisation as the gap between GDP and potential output narrows, and subsequently, prices and wages increase. The reaction function in the model is such that, as the price level prevails above its long-run underlying trend, and as unemployment falls, bank reserves contract. Interest rates are required to rise as a response to the reduced real bank reserves. This increases the replacement cost of capital with respect to its marginal product (q ratio), leading to lower investment. In other words, private investment is crowded-out. The rise in real interest rates also crowds-out, to a certain extent, consumption since the interest rate has a negative coefficient in the consumption function. Consequently, the initial increase in GDP starts to fade out, and the favourable effects on unemployment, likewise, cease to exist confirming that the long-run aggregate supply is vertical.

An interesting aspect of fiscal policy is the distribution implications of the various policy instruments. A direct tax shock is borne by either private households or companies depending on whether the shock is introduced by changing the rate of direct income tax of households or the rate of corporate tax. An indirect tax shock, however has more complicated distribution effects. Increasing the indirect tax rate by 1 percent leads to higher consumer prices in the short-term as the consumer price index equation quickly adjusts to the change in the tax rate. Wage rigidity in the model dictates that the reaction of wages to the price increases is not immediate, resulting in reduced real disposable income and negative second-round effects on consumption. National income is also affected as the wedge between gross national product and national income grows due to higher indirect taxes. Reduced national income implies lower undistributed business income as the latter is derived from the former by subtracting the incomes of the households and the government. In our macro-model, business profits are hit hard following an indirect tax increase. Consumers on the other hand do not suffer the full effect while nominal wages are linked not only to the GDP deflator but also to the wedge between the consumer price index and the GDP deflator.

Changes in foreign transfers have an immediate effect on the balance of payments. Since transfers abroad are to be financed via additional taxes and/or cuts in government spending, the real economy will be influenced depending on the chosen means of finance. In the model, an increase in net foreign transfers, in other words a deterioration in transfer balance implies lower disposable income for the whole economy and reduced welfare. Since we disregard the labour migration effects of the European integration in this paper, our population scenario is not different than the reference scenario, and the changes in the income variables can be viewed as per-capita changes.

4. MONETARY POLICY IN THE MODEL

For the purpose of this study, in the context of monetary policy we consider the exogenous shocks to the nominal short term and long term interest rates and their impact on the Swiss economy.

Increasing the nominal interest rates through a contraction in bank reserves translates in the model to a rise in real interest rates and in the cost of capital with respect to the marginal product of capital, hence reducing the q ratio. Both investment and consumption expenditures contract, and the falling demand with respect to the potential output causes excess capacity to emerge which consequently exerts downward pressure on prices. When the interest rates are free to respond to the price changes, the initial shock in the interest rates gradually disappears. Thus, monetary policy only alters the price level in the long-run, leaving real output unchanged. If the interest rates are fixed permanently, however, falling prices would lead to higher real interest rates and thereby curtailing investment and consumption even further. Therefore, the effect of an exogenous monetary shock on real output can last long in contrast with an endogenous change in interest rates.

5. TOTAL COSTS OF THE EUROPEAN INTEGRATION: "COLD TURKEY" CASE

In this scenario, we evaluate the macro-economic impact of the fiscal and monetary shocks associated with a possible entry into the European Union by Switzerland in 2002 assuming that all the costs are administered without allowing a transitional period.

In our reference scenario, the rate of value-added tax is 7.5% between 1999 and 2001, and with annual increases of 0.625%, gradually rising to 10% in 2005. In order to finance the increase in net transfers, the rate of value-added tax is required to be raised to 15%. In our "Cold Turkey" scenario, we consider the case where 15%

is levied from 2002. Since the value-added tax rate was not assumed to be a flat rate in the base scenario, importance of the effect of raising VAT to 15% is not uniform, ranging from a 6.875% increase in 2002 to a 5% increase in 2005. In order to relieve the tax incidence of consumers, it is assumed in this simulation that the VAT receipts in excess of financing the increase in net transfers will be matched by equivalent reductions in the direct income tax of households, starting also from 2002.

Monetary simulations involved increasing the Swiss interest rates to the EU level and fixing the value of the Swiss Franc vis-à-vis the Euro. In the reference scenario, Swiss short-term and long-term interest rates are 90 basis points lower than the EU rates until the end of 2010. Observing the recent experience of the EU countries, one expects the adjustment process in the long-term interest rates to begin fairly quickly, possibly from the date of announcement of the prospective Swiss entry. In the BAK Swiss macro-model, long term interest rates adjust slowly to short-term rates with a deviation attributable to government deficit ratio. This formulation is clearly inadequate to predict the behaviour of the long-term rates in the pre-EMU period since forward-looking investors would most likely be reducing the share of Swiss assets in their portfolios and thereby pushing the long-term interest rates up. We attempt to impose rational behaviour on the model through our exogenous treatment of the long-term rates. It is assumed that excepting a 20 basis points margin due to differences in fiscal solvency of Switzerland and Germany[5], the convergence of the long-term interest rates to the EU rates will be already achieved by the end of the year 2000, well before the actual entry date of 2002. Swiss short-term interest rates, however, are assumed to converge to the EU level in 2002. The exchange rate is fixed from 2002 at 1.62 SFr per Euro which corresponds to the five-year average value of the reference scenario preceding the year 2002. Alternative scenarios about the entry exchange rates have been conducted to test the sensitivity of our results.

The simulation results are presented in Table 3 and in Table 4. Negative effects on real GDP can be already observed from the year 2000 due to falling investment and consumption caused by the increase in long-term interest rates. The effect is intensified as short-term rates start adjusting upward in 2001. The cut in the direct income tax rate of cantons provide certain recovery in consumption expenditure in 2002. However, VAT increase soon are passed on as higher consumer prices, thereby, squeezing real disposable incomes. In the year 2003, consumption expenditure falls 0.7% from the previous year. Given the fixed nominal interest rates, investment benefits from rising inflation for a while as the q ratio recovers slightly. However, aggregate demand continues to fall in relation to the productive capacity thereby dampening the price inflation. Fixing of the nominal exchange rate from 2002 leads to lower exports during the period of higher inflation. Owing to falling prices, exports grow stronger after 2006.

Despite the gradual recovery, by the end of our simulation period (2010) we observe that GDP is still 0.9% lower than the reference scenario. Table 5 shows that

---

[5]In the post EMU period, long-term interest rates are given by the following equation: $LR = LR^* + \alpha(GDEBT/GDP - GDEBT^*/GDP^*)$, $\alpha>0$ where (*) denotes Germany and GDEBT/GDP, government debt with respect to nominal GDP .

when the fiscal and monetary shocks of the entry to EU are introduced to the model separately, their respective impact on GDP is of equal magnitude. While the negative impact of the higher interest rates is particularly strong on consumption and investment, exports benefiting from the fixed exchange rate system and the reduction in imports partly alleviates the problem.

Real disposable income of the economy which is defined as net national product plus balance of net transfers serves as useful indicator in order to judge the distribution of costs. Comparison of this measure with the real disposable income of households reveals that most of the cost burden to the economy is borne by the business sector, whilst cuts in the direct income tax rate provided some relief to consumers.

Continuously declining investment in the long-run results in reduction of the capital stock, which on the supply side causes permanent contraction in potential output (1% lower than the reference scenario in 2010).

We test the sensitivity of our results to an alternative entry exchange rate for the Swiss franc. Assuming an exchange rate of 1.68 SFr per Euro, we impose a 3.7% devaluation with respect to the reference scenario. As can be seen in Table 6, the negative effects of the entry shocks are slightly weakened. Although fixing the exchange rate at 1.68 implies higher exports and lower imports in the short- and medium-term, rising prices and wages start to erode the competitive advantage, slowing down the recovery in GDP. Investment seems to suffer less compared to the 1.62 SFr/Euro scenario, as the real interest rates stemming from the stronger price inflation is less of a hindrance.

Table 3. Total Costs in "Cold Turkey" Scenario
% Deviation from the reference scenario (unless otherwise told)

Year	Real Consump-tion Expendi-ture	Real Dispo-sable Income	Real GDP	Unem-ployment (in 1´000)	Employ-ment	Wage rate	Consu-mer Prices	Short term interest rates (%-Points)	Exchange rate SFr/-EURO
2000	-0.1	0.0	-0.1	1.8	0.0	-0.1	0.0	-0.1	1.62
2001	-0.4	-0.1	-0.3	4.9	-0.1	-0.3	-0.1	0.1	1.62
2002	0.2	2.0	-0.1	3.9	-0.1	-0.1	1.8	0.9	1.62
2003	-0.4	-0.7	-0.6	11.5	-0.3	0.8	4.9	0.9	1.62
2004	-2.0	-1.0	-1.4	28.3	-0.7	0.4	4.3	0.9	1.62
2005	-3.1	-1.0	-1.9	41.6	-1.0	-0.9	2.5	0.9	1.62
2006	-3.4	-0.9	-2.1	47.1	-1.2	-2.3	0.9	0.9	1.62
2007	-3.2	-1.0	-1.9	45.9	-1.2	-3.4	-0.1	0.9	1.62
2008	-2.8	-1.0	-1.6	40.8	-1.1	-4.0	-0.9	0.9	1.62
2009	-2.4	-0.9	-1.2	33.6	-0.9	-4.4	-1.5	0.9	1.62
2010	-2.0	-0.7	-0.9	26.4	-0.7	-4.5	-1.8	0.9	1.62

Table 4. Detailed Results: Total Costs in "Cold Turkey" Case

	1999	2000	2001	2002	2003	2004	2005	2006	2007	2008	2009	2010
Components of GDP and Supply-side: % Deviation from the base												
Consumption expenditure	0.0	-0.1	-0.4	0.3	-0.4	-2.0	-3.1	-3.4	-3.2	-2.8	-2.4	-2.0
Investment	0.0	-0.2	-0.7	-1.4	-1.7	-1.7	-2.9	-4.6	-5.8	-6.4	-6.5	-6.3
Construction investment	0.0	-0.3	-0.9	-1.6	-1.8	-3.1	-4.1	-4.4	-4.0	-3.4	-2.8	-2.4
Investment in equipment	0.0	-0.1	-0.4	-1.2	-1.5	-0.4	-1.8	-4.7	-7.3	-8.8	-9.3	-9.2
Domestic demand	0.0	-0.2	-0.4	-0.3	-0.7	-1.8	-2.8	-3.4	-3.5	-3.4	-3.2	-2.9
Exports	0.0	0.0	0.0	0.0	-0.3	-0.4	-0.2	0.2	0.5	0.8	0.9	1.1
Imports	0.0	-0.1	-0.4	-0.2	-0.6	-1.3	-2.0	-2.4	-2.6	-2.6	-2.7	-2.6
GDP	0.0	-0.1	-0.3	-0.1	-0.6	-1.4	-1.9	-2.1	-1.9	-1.6	-1.2	-0.9
Potential Output	0.0	0.0	0.0	0.0	-0.1	-0.1	-0.2	-0.3	-0.5	-0.7	-0.8	-1.0
Capital stock	0.0	0.0	-0.1	-0.2	-0.3	-0.4	-0.6	-1.0	-1.4	-1.9	-2.4	-2.8
Labour productivity	0.0	-0.1	-0.2	-0.1	-0.4	-1.0	-1.3	-1.3	-1.1	-0.8	-0.5	-0.3
q ratio	-0.1	-0.4	-1.0	-1.6	0.2	-0.8	-3.2	-4.3	-4.1	-3.4	-2.8	-2.3
Welfare indicators (real): % Deviation from the base												
Disposable income *	0.0	-0.1	-0.3	-2.7	-4.9	-5.1	-4.9	-4.7	-4.4	-3.9	-3.2	-2.6
Disposable income of the households	0.0	-0.1	-0.1	2.0	-0.7	-1.0	-1.0	-0.9	-1.0	-1.0	-0.9	-0.7
National income	0.0	-0.1	-0.3	-5.9	-7.7	-7.5	-7.0	-6.8	-6.5	-5.9	-5.2	-4.6
Deflators: % deviation from the base												
Consumption	0.0	0.0	-0.1	1.7	4.9	4.4	2.5	0.9	-0.1	-0.9	-1.5	-1.8
Government consumption	0.0	0.0	-0.1	-0.1	1.0	1.3	0.2	-1.2	-2.4	-3.3	-3.9	-4.2
Investment	0.0	0.0	-0.2	0.0	1.0	1.1	0.1	-1.2	-2.4	-3.2	-3.8	-4.2
Exports	0.0	0.0	-0.1	0.0	0.9	1.0	0.2	-0.9	-1.7	-2.3	-2.7	-2.9
Imports	0.0	0.0	0.0	0.0	0.3	0.2	-0.2	-0.4	-0.5	-0.5	-0.4	-0.4
GDP	0.0	0.0	-0.2	0.0	1.0	1.1	0.1	-1.2	-2.4	-3.2	-3.8	-4.2
Wage rate	0.0	0.0	-0.1	0.0	-0.2	-0.7	-1.0	-1.1	-1.0	-0.8	-0.6	-0.4
Foreign Trade: Deviation from the base in %-points												
Trade balance (% of nominal GDP)	0.0	0.0	0.1	0.1	0.3	0.6	0.8	0.8	0.7	0.6	0.5	0.4
Current Account Balance (in % of nominal GDP)	0.0	0.1	0.2	-0.7	-0.4	0.1	0.5	0.7	0.7	0.7	0.7	0.7
Interest rates and Unemployment ratio: Deviation from the base in %-points												
Mortgage interest rates	0.1	0.2	0.6	0.7	0.7	0.7	0.7	0.7	0.7	0.7	0.7	0.7
Short-term interest rates	0.0	-0.1	0.1	0.9	0.9	0.9	0.9	0.9	0.9	0.9	0.9	0.9
Long-term interest rates	0.1	0.4	0.7	0.7	0.7	0.7	0.7	0.7	0.7	0.7	0.7	0.7
Unemployment ratio	0.0	0.0	0.1	0.1	0.3	0.8	1.1	1.3	1.3	1.1	0.9	0.7

*Net national product at market prices + Net transfer balance

Table 5. The Components of the Real GDP, and Employment in 2010 and the Respective Contributions of the Shocks (% Deviation from the base)

	Total Costs	Fiscal	Monetary
GDP	-0.9	-0.4	-0.4
Consumption	-2.0	-0.2	-1.2
Investment	-6.3	-1.8	-4.4
Exports	+1.1	+0.1	+0.8
Imports	-2.6	-0.4	-2.0
Employment	-0.7	-0.4	-0.3

Table 6. Sensitivity simulation: EMU entry at 1.68 SFr/Euro
% Deviation from the "Cold Turkey" scenario with the exchange rate fixed at 1.62 SFr/Euro (unless otherwise told)

	1999	2000	2001	2002	2003	2004	2005	2006	2007	2008	2009	2010
Consumption	0.0	0.1	0.0	0.0	0.1	0.2	0.1	0.0	-0.1	-0.2	-0.3	-0.4
Investment	0.0	0.1	0.2	0.6	1.0	1.4	1.7	1.8	1.7	1.6	1.4	1.1
Exports	0.4	0.4	0.6	0.6	0.5	0.4	0.3	0.2	0.1	0.1	0.0	0.0
Imports	-0.1	-0.2	-0.3	-0.4	-0.3	-0.2	-0.2	-0.1	-0.1	-0.1	-0.1	-0.1
GDP	0.2	0.4	0.5	0.7	0.8	0.8	0.8	0.7	0.5	0.4	0.2	0.1
Potential Output	0.0	0.0	0.0	0.0	0.0	0.1	0.1	0.2	0.2	0.2	0.3	0.3
q ratio	-0.1	0.0	0.3	0.8	1.0	1.1	1.0	0.9	0.6	0.4	0.2	0.0
Unemployment ratio in %-Points	-0.1	-0.2	-0.3	-0.4	-0.5	-0.5	-0.5	-0.5	-0.4	-0.3	-0.3	-0.2

6. EU ENTRY WITH A TRANSITION PERIOD

In this section we investigate the effects on the Swiss economy of a softer transition to the EU. For this scenario, the increase in value-added tax is introduced gradually from 2003 by means of 1.5% increases per annum, hence extending the transition period for the VAT to 2007. This assumption of incremental increases of VAT was put forward by the project sponsor (SECO). Since the rise of the VAT rate is only gradual, for the years 2003 and 2004 a transient deficit in government budget emerges and thereby, what is left over from the value-added revenue is not enough to justify a cut in the rate of direct income tax prior to 2005. Regarding the monetary adjustments required by the European Monetary Union, upward movement in short term interest rates is assumed to begin from 2006, achieving full convergence to the EU level in the year 2007. Between the actual entry date of 2002 and 2006 lies the period where the Swiss National Bank continues to determine the interest rates via the instrument of bank reserves. Likewise the value of the Swiss franc is assumed to be fixed against the Euro from 2007 at 1.62 SFr /Euro. For the development of the exchange rate prior to 2007, we consider three possibilities. In the first instance, we assume that the exchange rate is managed via foreign exchange market intervention so that it stabilises around 1.62 SFr/Euro parity already in the period preceding 2007. As the interest rates are used to mitigate the effects of the fiscal shock rather than to target the exchange rate, foreign exchange reserves of the SNB is to be used to stabilise the exchange rate. The results presented below are based on this assumption. As far as the EMU entry exchange rate in the year 2007 is concerned we carry out alternative simulations of revaluation and devaluation.

Table 7. The Total Costs in "Transition" Scenario
% deviation from reference scenario (unless otherwise told)

Year	Real Consumption Expenditure	Real Disposable Income	Real GDP	Unemployment (in 1'000)	Employment	Wage rate	Consumer Prices	Short term interest rates (%-Points)	Exchange rate SFr/ EURO
2000	-0.1	0.0	-0.1	1.8	0.0	-0.1	0.0	-0.1	1.62
2001	-0.4	-0.1	-0.3	4.9	-0.1	-0.3	-0.1	-0.2	1.62
2002	-0.5	-0.2	-0.4	7.6	-0.2	-0.5	-0.3	-0.3	1.62
2003	-0.5	-0.3	-0.4	8.0	-0.2	-0.7	-0.4	-0.3	1.62
2004	-0.6	-0.6	-0.4	8.2	-0.2	-0.8	-0.3	-0.2	1.62
2005	-0.8	-0.9	-0.5	10.0	-0.3	-0.9	0.3	0.0	1.62
2006	-0.9	-0.5	-0.5	11.9	-0.3	-0.8	0.9	0.3	1.62
2007	-1.0	-0.2	-0.7	14.9	-0.4	-0.7	1.9	0.9	1.62
2008	-1.6	-0.7	-1.0	21.8	-0.5	-0.8	2.3	0.9	1.62
2009	-2.2	-0.7	-1.3	29.0	-0.7	-1.4	1.7	0.9	1.62
2010	-2.5	-0.7	-1.4	33.2	-0.8	-2.1	1.0	0.9	1.62

Table 8. Detailed Results: The Total Costs in "Transition" Scenario

	1999	2000	2001	2002	2003	2004	2005	2006	2007	2008	2009	2010
Components of GDP and Supply-side: % Deviation from the base												
Consumption expenditure	0.0	-0.1	-0.4	-0.5	-0.5	-0.6	-0.8	-0.9	-1.0	-1.6	-2.2	-2.5
Investment	0.0	-0.2	-0.7	-1.1	-1.4	-1.5	-1.7	-1.8	-2.2	-2.6	-3.3	-4.1
Construction investment	0.0	-0.3	-0.9	-1.5	-1.4	-1.3	-1.5	-1.7	-2.1	-2.7	-3.2	-3.5
Investment in equipment	0.0	-0.1	-0.4	-0.8	-1.3	-1.7	-1.8	-1.9	-2.2	-2.6	-3.3	-4.6
Domestic demand	0.0	-0.2	-0.4	-0.7	-0.7	-0.8	-0.9	-1.0	-1.2	-1.7	-2.3	-2.7
Exports	0.0	0.0	0.0	0.1	0.1	0.2	0.1	0.1	0.1	0.0	0.1	0.3
Imports	0.0	-0.1	-0.4	-0.5	-0.6	-0.7	-0.8	-0.9	-1.0	-1.4	-1.8	-2.1
GDP	0.0	-0.1	-0.3	-0.4	-0.4	-0.4	-0.5	-0.5	-0.7	-1.0	-1.3	-1.4
Potential Output	0.0	0.0	0.0	-0.1	-0.1	-0.1	-0.2	-0.2	-0.2	-0.3	-0.4	-0.5
Capital stock	0.0	0.0	-0.1	-0.1	-0.3	-0.4	-0.5	-0.6	-0.8	-0.9	-1.2	-1.4
Labour productivity	0.0	-0.1	-0.2	-0.2	-0.2	-0.2	-0.3	-0.3	-0.4	-0.6	-0.8	-0.9
q ratio	-0.1	-0.4	-0.7	-0.8	-0.8	-0.8	-0.7	-0.9	-1.2	-1.4	-2.1	-2.8
Welfare indicators (real): % Deviation from the base												
Disposable income*	0.0	-0.1	-0.3	-1.3	-1.3	-1.6	-2.1	-2.7	-3.5	-4.0	-4.1	-4.0
Disposable income of the households	0.0	-0.1	-0.1	-0.2	-0.3	-0.6	-0.9	-0.5	-0.2	-0.7	-0.7	-0.7
National income	0.0	-0.1	-0.3	-0.4	-0.5	-1.3	-2.4	-3.9	-5.5	-6.1	-6.1	-6.0
Deflators: % Deviation from the base												
Consumption	0.0	0.0	-0.1	-0.3	-0.5	-0.3	0.3	0.9	1.9	2.3	1.8	1.0
Government consumption	0.0	0.0	-0.1	-0.3	-0.6	-0.7	-0.7	-0.6	-0.4	-0.3	-0.7	-1.4
Investment	0.0	0.0	-0.2	-0.3	-0.5	-0.7	-0.7	-0.6	-0.4	-0.4	-0.7	-1.4
Exports	0.0	0.0	-0.1	-0.2	-0.4	-0.4	-0.4	-0.3	-0.2	-0.1	-0.4	-0.9
Imports	0.0	0.0	0.0	-0.1	-0.1	-0.1	0.0	0.0	0.0	0.0	-0.1	-0.2
GDP	0.0	0.0	-0.2	-0.3	-0.5	-0.7	-0.7	-0.6	-0.4	-0.4	-0.7	-1.4
Wage rate	0.0	0.0	-0.1	-0.2	-0.2	-0.2	-0.2	-0.3	-0.3	-0.5	-0.7	-0.7
Foreign Trade: Deviation from the base in %-points												
Trade balance (in % of nominal GDP)	0.0	0.0	0.1	0.2	0.2	0.2	0.2	0.3	0.3	0.5	0.6	0.7
Current Account Balance (in % of nominal GDP)	0.0	0.1	0.2	-0.6	-0.6	-0.6	-0.5	-0.4	-0.3	0.0	0.2	0.4
Interest rates and Unemployment ratio: Deviation from the base in %-points												
Mortgage interest rates	0.1	0.2	0.6	0.7	0.7	0.7	0.7	0.7	0.7	0.7	0.7	0.7
Short-term interest rates	0.0	-0.1	-0.2	-0.3	-0.3	-0.2	0.0	0.3	0.9	0.9	0.9	0.9
Long-term interest rates	0.1	0.4	0.7	0.7	0.7	0.7	0.7	0.7	0.7	0.7	0.7	0.7
Unemployment ratio	0.0	0.0	0.1	0.2	0.2	0.2	0.3	0.3	0.4	0.6	0.8	0.9

*Net national product at market prices + Net transfer balance

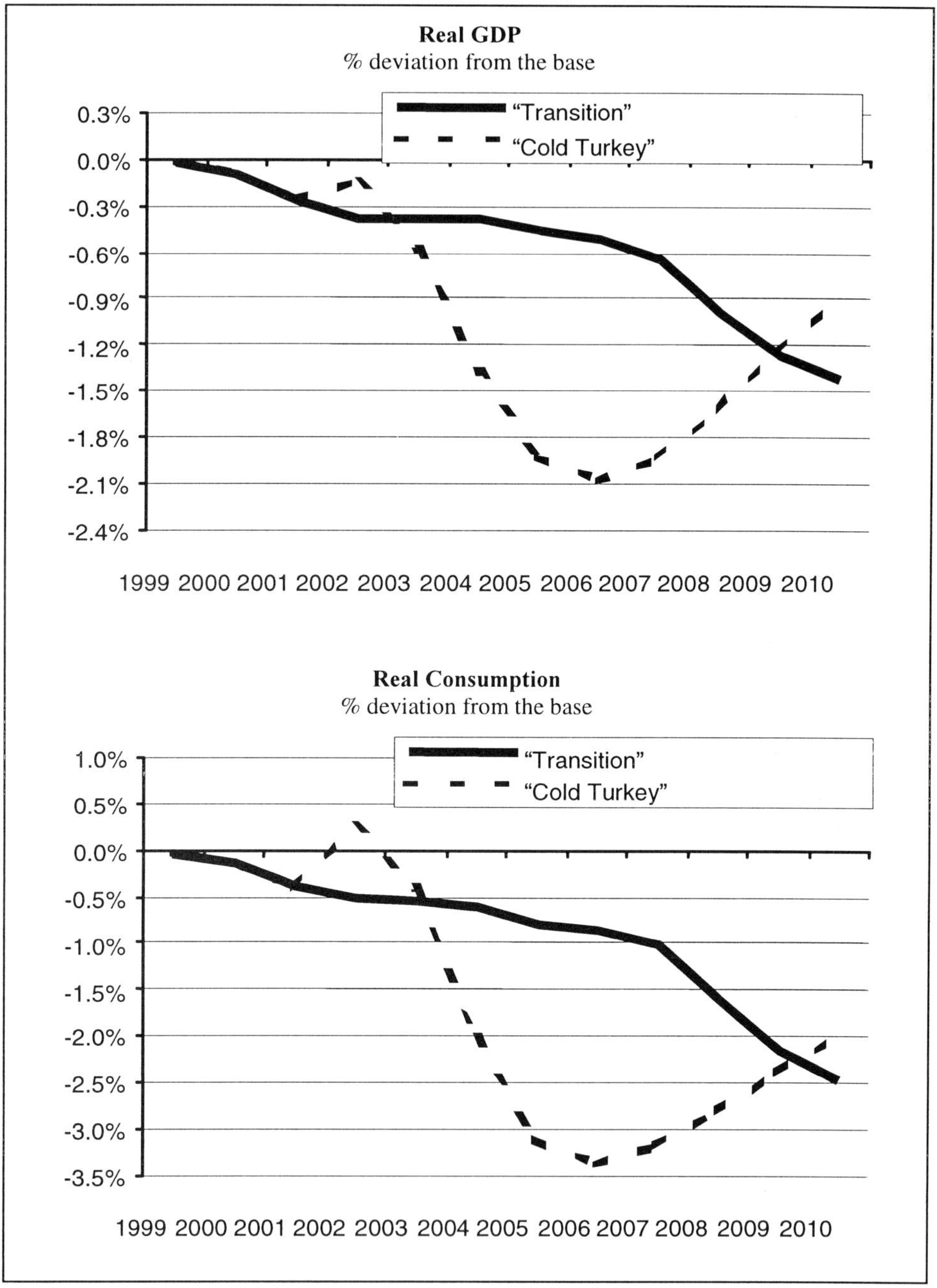

Figure 1. GDP and real consumption

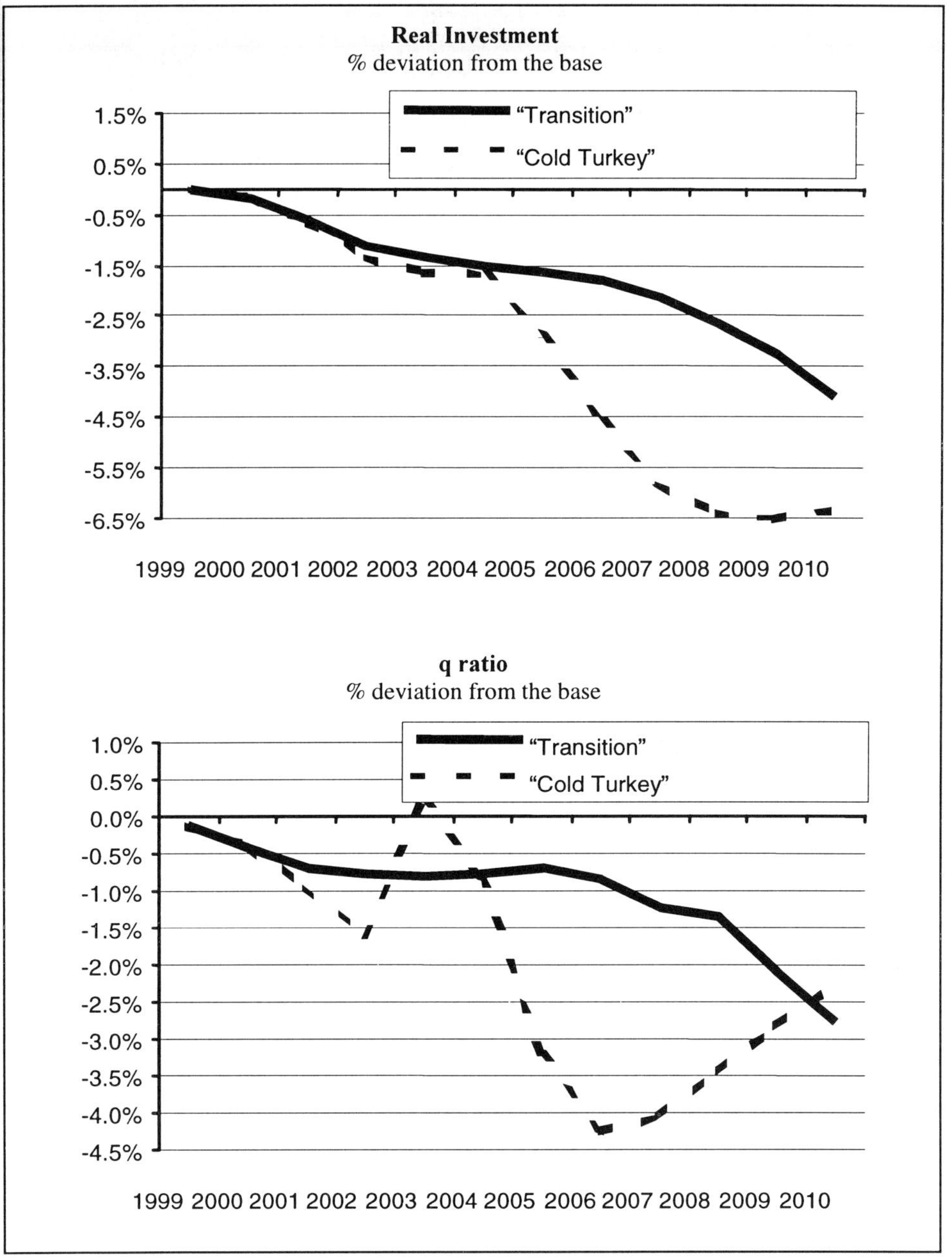

Figure 2. Real investment and the q ratio

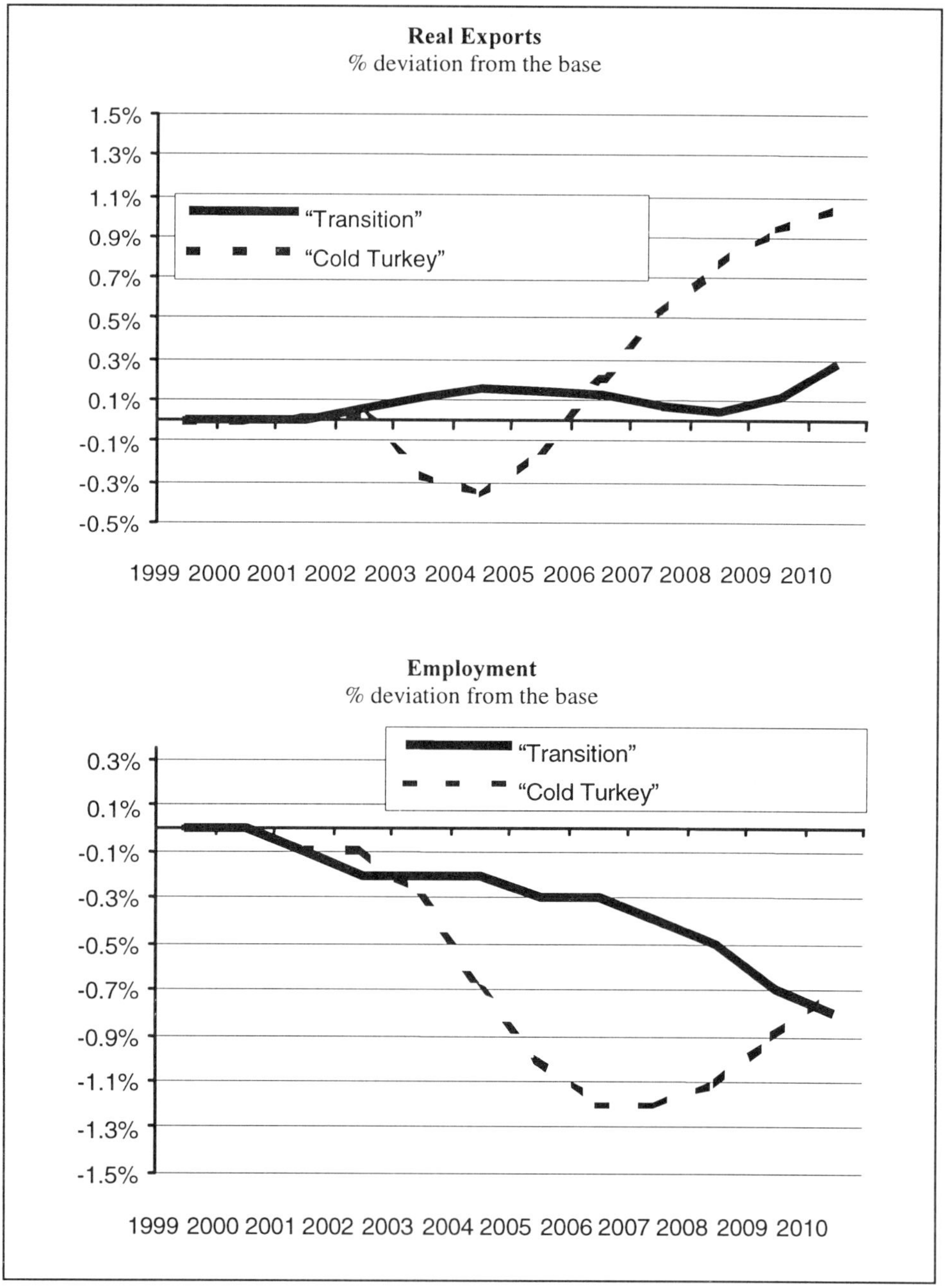

Figure 3. Real exports and employment

The major difference of these results compared with the "Cold Turkey " scenario is that negative effects on the economy linger longer in the simulation horizon, and also turn out to be less severe (Figure 1-3). As can be seen in Table 7, GDP in the year 2010 is 1.4% lower than the base compared with 0.9% in the "Cold Turkey" scenario. In the "Transition" scenario, price increases brought about by the VAT hike spread over a longer time horizon, causing a relatively gentler deterioration in disposable income and consumption. As in the "Cold Turkey" case, both real consumption and investment are negatively influenced by the increase in the real long-term interest rates. Short-term interest rates, however, adjust to accommodate the changes in the price level and the business cycle in the period prior to 2007 during which SNB continues to enjoy some autonomy regarding the execution of monetary policy. Since the economy experiences contraction due to the fiscal and monetary shocks, short-term rates fall below the base rate until 2005. These reductions in the short term interest rates lessen the extent of the recession. By 2005, additional relief is underway through cuts in direct taxes. As the short term interest rates converge to the European levels in 2007, we observe at this point the impact of the second interest rate shock on GDP.

In the "Transition" scenario, postponed price effects are translated into relatively modest export performance in the simulation horizon. In fact, in the long term, the increase in exports relative to the base amounts to less than half the increase in the "Cold Turkey" scenario.

Allowing a transitional period for the monetary and fiscal shocks to come through leads to a visibly less painful adjustment in labour markets. In the simulation period, the unemployment ratio does not record an increase exceeding 1% (See Table 8). In contrast, in the "Cold Turkey " scenario, the unemployment ratio in the four consecutive years are 1% higher than the base.

When we consider an entry exchange rate of 1.60 SFr/Euro from 2007, total costs of the EU entry increase. As can be seen in Table 10, appreciation of the currency through its negative impact on trade results in 0.2% further deterioration of GDP at the end of our simulation horizon. Appreciation of the SFr prior to 2007, is indeed a model consistent result caused by higher interest rates and falling GDP deflator.

As in the "Cold Turkey" case, an entry exchange rate of 1.68 SFr/Euro in 2007 and adjustment toward this parity in the preceding period has a favourable impact on the economy in the simulation horizon (see Table 11). Due to spreading the costs over a longer period, exchange rate benefits are still strongly felt in 2010, although improvement in exports start levelling off as price competitiveness weakens. Investment suffers less under this scenario as higher inflation corrodes real interest rates, and the unemployment ratio is about 0.4% lower than the scenario where the exchange rate was fixed at 1.62 SFr/Euro.

Admittedly, the long-term effects regarding the "Transition" scenario cannot possibly be captured in our simulation horizon which terminates in 2010. However, the choice of the simulation period was decided by the project sponsor. The impact of a delayed entry into the EU can be better assessed perhaps when the effects of the pure fiscal shocks are disentangled from the total effects. Table 12 presents the results of a pure fiscal shock in the "Cold Turkey" and "Transition" scenarios. What is remarkable to observe is that whilst the costs appear to be more or less equally distributed between the fiscal and monetary shocks in the "Cold Turkey" scenario, costs of the fiscal shock is dominant in the "Transition" scenario in the end of the simulation horizon.

Table 10. Sensitivity Simulation: EMU entry at 1.60 SFr/Euro
% Deviation from the "Transition" scenario with the exchange rate fixed at 1.62 SFr/Euro (unless otherwise told)

	1999	2000	2001	2002	2003	2004	2005	2006	2007	2008	2009	2010
Consumption	0.0	0.0	0.0	0.0	0.0	0.0	0.0	0.1	0.1	0.0	0.0	0.0
Investment	0.0	0.0	0.0	0.0	0.0	-0.1	-0.1	-0.1	-0.2	-0.3	-0.4	-0.5
Exports	0.0	0.0	0.0	-0.1	-0.1	-0.1	-0.2	-0.1	-0.2	-0.1	-0.1	-0.1
Imports	0.0	0.0	0.0	0.0	0.0	0.1	0.1	0.2	0.1	0.1	0.1	0.1
GDP	0.0	0.0	0.0	0.0	-0.1	-0.1	-0.2	-0.2	-0.2	-0.2	-0.2	-0.2
Potential Output	0.0	0.0	0.0	0.0	0.0	0.0	0.0	0.0	0.0	0.0	0.0	0.0
q ratio	0.0	0.0	0.0	0.0	0.0	0.0	0.0	-0.1	-0.2	-0.3	-0.3	-0.3
Unemployment ratio in %-Points	0.0	0.0	0.0	0.0	0.0	0.1	0.1	0.1	0.1	0.1	0.2	0.2

Table 11. Sensitivity simulation : EMU Entry at 1.68 SFr/Euro
% Deviation from the "Transition" scenario with the exchange rate fixed at 1.62 SFr/Euro (unless otherwise told)

	1999	2000	2001	2002	2003	2004	2005	2006	2007	2008	2009	2010
Consumption	0.0	0.0	0.0	-0.1	-0.2	-0.2	-0.3	-0.4	-0.3	-0.2	-0.1	-0.1
Investment	0.0	0.1	0.2	0.2	0.2	0.3	0.3	0.3	0.5	0.8	1.1	1.3
Exports	0.3	0.2	0.2	0.3	0.4	0.4	0.5	0.5	0.5	0.4	0.3	0.2
Imports	-0.1	-0.1	-0.2	-0.3	-0.3	-0.4	-0.5	-0.6	-0.6	-0.4	-0.3	-0.2
GDP	0.2	0.3	0.2	0.3	0.3	0.4	0.4	0.4	0.5	0.6	0.6	0.6
Potential Output	0.0	0.0	0.0	0.0	0.0	0.0	0.0	0.0	0.0	0.0	0.0	0.0
q ratio	-0.1	0.1	0.1	0.1	0.0	0.0	0.0	0.2	0.6	0.7	0.7	0.7
Unemployment ratio in %-Points	-0.1	-0.1	-0.1	-0.2	-0.2	-0.2	-0.3	-0.3	-0.4	-0.4	-0.4	-0.4

Table 12. Fiscal Shock without the EMU % Deviation of real GDP from the base scenario

	2000	2001	2002	2003	2004	2005	2006	2007	2008	2009	2010
"Cold Turkey"	0.0	0.0	0.4	-0.1	-1.5	-2.0	-1.3	-0.8	-0.6	-0.5	-0.4
"Transition"	0.0	0.0	0.0	0.0	-0.1	-0.2	-0.4	-0.5	-0.8	-1.1	-1.0

8. CONCLUSIONS

In this paper, we evaluate the effects on the Swiss economy of a possible Swiss entry into the European Union in the near future. Entry into the EU for Switzerland implies losing the advantage of low interest rates and increasing indirect taxes to finance the net transfers amounting to almost 1 % of GDP. The fiscal and monetary costs to the economy have been assessed under "Cold Turkey" and "Transition" scenarios. It is observed that even in a fairly long simulation period, the costs of the EU entry to the Swiss economy seems to be long-lasting. The effects are less severe but even longer lasting in the case when the entry process is allowed to go through a transitional period. On the basis of the costs of the two scenarios, a transitional entry into the EU appears to be a politically less risky alternative for Switzerland. However, consideration of the speed at which efficiency gains will be exploited in a quick or a delayed entry situation makes this conclusion less decisive.

One fair criticism that can be directed at the BAK Swiss-macro model is that expectations are formed in an adaptive manner and inevitably the model assumes that all changes to policy instruments are unanticipated. This imposes limits on the effectiveness of the model in policy analysis as far as the behaviour of economic agents is concerned given the anticipation of a certain EU entry in a future date. We try to remedy this to an extent through our exogenous treatment of the shocks. In principal, the assumption of forward-looking behaviour could somewhat alter findings of our study with respect to the development of consumption and investment expenditure when a shock is fully anticipated. However, as far as the experience of the current members of the EMU is concerned, behaviour of economic agents in the pre-EMU period did not appear to exhibit significant variation due to inter-temporal considerations in decision-making. Italy, for example maintained a fairly stable saving ratio in the pre-EMU period despite the imminent interest rate reductions.

In order to judge the net benefits of a Swiss entry to the EU, one needs to weigh the costs against the alleged efficiency gains. Among the advantages often mentioned are some static efficiency gains as a result of the removal of the trade barriers and more importantly dynamic efficiency gains stemming from intensified competition which are stimulated by transparent prices, the major advantage of a single currency. Although bilateral agreements aim to achieve a similar objective in terms of efficiency gains, it is generally accepted that participating in the European Monetary Union would be more conducive to achieving these efficiency gains. Since the cost scenarios revealed a permanent reduction in potential output brought about by the contracting capital stock, the magnitude of the efficiency gains has to be at least large enough to counterbalance the reduction in capacity output. In a macro-model framework such as ours, it is almost futile to attempt to measure the efficiency gains *ex-ante*, which led us to incorporate some politically determined parameters regarding the magnitude of these effects. Shocking the productive capacity of the economy by a pre-determined amount of efficiency gain , we can induce the model to generate price deflation, the benefits of which are reaped through higher exports while consumption and investment suffer because of higher real interest rates. We will not elaborate further on these exercises given the arbitrary nature of the efficiency assumptions. Nevertheless, within the framework of our study it is interesting to see that unless the European Central Bank decides to cut interest rates (or alternatively the interest rate gap is already set to diminish in the reference scenario), reductions in prices following the expansion in potential output has to rely on sustainable export boost to compensate for the costs of the European integration for a country such as Switzerland.

REFERENCES

Engle, R.F. and Granger, C.W.J. (1987), Co-integration and Error Correction: Representation, Estimation, and Testing, Econometrica, 55, p. 251-276.

Kugler, P. (1998), Price Level Trend-Stationarity and the Instruments and Targets of Monetary Policy: An Empirical Note, Paper presented at EEH Annual Congress, Berlin, September 3-5.

Vaterlaus, S., Himmler, M., Koellreuter, C. and Simmons, B. (1999), Alternative EU-Integrationsszenarien der Schweiz, BWA Schriftenreihe, Beiträge zur Wirtschaftspolitik Nr. 7, Bern.

Whitley, J. D. (1994), A Course in Macroeconomic Modelling and Forecasting, Harvester Wheatsheaf, London.

MONIKA BÜTLER

THE COSTS OF THE EU INTEGRATION FOR SWITZERLAND: ALTERNATIVE SCENARIOS

A Comment

Long-run macroeconomic forecasts are difficult tasks. Not only are even potentially exogenous variables hard to predict, but also does the past offer little guidance in modeling single large shocks, such as an entry into an economic and monetary union. The paper by Banu Simmons-Süer and Margit Himmel compares a possible accession of Switzerland to the EU (and EMU) under two different scenarios, which basically differ in the time of an entry into the EMU. The question of how different time horizons influence the cost of a large policy change is an important one, and deserves a careful analysis. The authors have to be complimented for having attempted this ambitious task.

To conduct such an analysis, a number of choices have to be made. First, one has to decide what policy experiments should be explored. One has to bear in mind that this first decision has been largely out of the authors' control. Second, potentially relevant costs and benefits have to be singled out. Finally, a model must be chosen to quantify the effects derived from the previous theoretical analysis. Consequently, I will focus my comments on these three issues, the choice of scenarios, the costs of an EU accession, and the working of the model.

Scenarios: "Cold Turkey" versus "Transition"

As required by the Secretariat for Economic Affairs SECO, the authors consider and compare two scenarios, which they label "Cold Turkey" and "Transition". *"Cold Turkey"* entails a contemporaneous accession to both the EU and EMU in 2002. *"Transition"*, on the other hand, means accession to the EU in 2002, but amounts to postponing entry into EMU until 2007. At the same time, VAT rates are only gradually adjusted to the required 15% level in the latter scenario. Unfortunately, the gradual increase in VAT hampers a clear assessment of the benefits or costs of a delayed accession to EMU.

So here is a question: Are the differences between the scenarios due to a postponed EMU membership or a stepwise increase in the VAT rate?

My guess is (see also the papers of Müller & Grether, and Bärlocher) that - in the absence of large distortionary impacts - the shift from income taxes to consumption taxes is only of secondary importance, provided the government budget is unchanged. (Note, however, that the contribution to the EU budget is financed by a temporary increase in government debt in the "Transition" scenario between 2002

R.E. Baldwin and A. Brunetti (eds.), Economic Impact of EU Membership on Entrants, 213–215.

and 2004, as the increase in VAT is clearly too small to finance the transfer.) The real difference between the scenarios is, therefore, a 5-year delayed entry into EMU in scenario "Transition". In any case, it would have been helpful to break up the effects into "delayed entry" and "slow increase in VAT".

The aim of the paper is stated to be the medium and long run effects of an EU/EMU accession. A somewhat longer simulation horizon (15-20 years) would have been an asset here (despite the fact that SECO only required a shorter horizon). If the simulations stop barely three years after joining the EMU in "Transition", it is very difficult to compare the two scenarios and explore whether they may lead to different outcomes in the longer run.

Costs of an EU accession

The focus of the study is on costs rather than benefits of a EU accession (although the paper does mention some potential gains from more favorable terms of trade in the results). The advantage of this approach is that no arbitrary assumptions about efficiency gains or the like have to be made. The disadvantage, on the other hand, is that the costs of different scenarios cannot really be compared unless the benefits are comparable in size, which is not a priori clear from the setup. While a postponed entry into the EMU might be less costly than an immediate entry, it might also lead to lower benefits along the transition path.

Having said this, let me briefly comment on the different cost categories that are mentioned in the paper, namely fiscal and monetary costs. The relevance of fiscal costs is undisputed and needs no further elaborations. What needs some more explanation is the low cost (in terms of GDP or consumption) of a sizeable transfer in the "Transition" scenario relative to other studies (KOF). The small decline in output and consumption is consistent with an increase in government debt, but not with forward looking agents who realize that the deficit has to be financed eventually.

Monetary costs are more difficult to assess, but probably also more interesting. The authors rightly distinguish between the costs of losing the Swiss interest rate advantage and losing the right to conduct independent monetary policy, a point made by very few other studies.

In line with most other contributions in this field, the paper assumes that the interest rate advantage disappears upon entry into EMU. To assess the true costs of losing the interest rate differential, one should first know why there is such a differential. Given the reasons - such as an expected appreciation of the Swiss franc, tax treatment, banking secrecy -, one can then try to estimate how much of it will disappear. Any part of the differential due to differences in legislation will probably not go away. Moreover, the interest rate gap has already narrowed considerably during the last 15 year. Maybe it would have disappeared even without Switzerland joining the EMU?

As many other forecasting models, the used model is deterministic and does thus not allow a direct quantification of the loss of monetary independence. An interesting feature of the scenario "Transition", however, is the fact that monetary policy could potentially react to the decline in output due to the fiscal shock in period 2002. Unfortunately the paper does not make clear what the effects of monetary policy are (interest rate, exchange rate, price level?) after 2002, and prior to an entry into EMU in 2007. What really puzzles me, moreover, is the fact that the exchange rate between 2002 and 2007 in "Transition" (table 7) seems to be constant, despite the National Bank's monetary independence.

The working of the model

The model is based on a large scale income/expenditure framework, composed of a large number of structural equations. There are thus no intertemporal adjustments by households and firms, and expectations are formed in an adaptive manner. The advantages and problems of using structural models in forecasting the effects of policy experiments have been discussed elsewhere. I will confine my discussion here on one critical aspect of the simulation model, the importance of expectations.

While the used framework has its merits in investigating the propagation of *unexpected* shocks, it has an important drawback in the context of *anticipated* or even announced policy reforms. In particular, a backward looking model, such as the BAK macro model, makes no difference of whether the policy change is expected or comes as a total surprise to economic agents. Take for example the sharp increase in unproductive government expenditures due to EU membership in 2002. The authors rightly argue that interest rates will converge to EU levels prior to accession, but the model only allows an ad-hoc (and exogenous) treatment of this move in interest rates. The corresponding decline in output would presumably be much larger, if rational forward looking agents took the drop in disposable income into account and saved more prior to accession in order to smooth consumption. As both scenarios assume accession to EU at the same date, this lack of anticipation is a somewhat minor concern.

What is more worrying is the absence (?) of expectation effects – apart from an exogenous move in interest rates - prior to entry into EMU in the "Transition" scenario. The chosen approach misses a huge junk of the interesting adjustment mechanisms that go on before accession, including the working of monetary policy and the potential benefit of still enjoying monetary independence. If, moreover, the policy experiment in 2007 was fully anticipated, the difference in the two scenarios, especially in the paths of macroeconomic aggregates, would probably be much smaller in 2010. As mentioned above, it would also be interesting to know whether the two different scenarios converge to the same levels in the long run, and if not, why?

In sum, the study tackles an interesting and important question of Swiss policy making. It is to be hoped, that further extensions of the paper will clarify some of the issues brought up here. In particular, the benefits and costs of delaying accession deserve more attention in the future.

CHRISTIAN KEUSCHNIGG

LABOR MARKET AND BUDGETARY EFFECTS OF EASTERN ENLARGEMENT IN GERMANY

This paper develops the first intertemporal, computable general equilibrium model combining search unemployment with optimizing savings and investment dynamics. The model is calibrated to replicate the German economy and is applied to quantify the effects of Eastern enlargement of the European Union. The basic enlargement scenario includes trade liberalization, an increase in net contributions to the EU, and some adjustments in common agricultural policy. A separate scenario considers the effects from immigration. Enlargement is found to trigger an investment led expansion. It generates considerable fiscal returns that allow to pay for Germany's share in the fiscal cost to the EU without cutting any expenditure or raising taxes. The expected increase in the wage spread does not materialize. Labor market effects are mainly felt in higher wages rather than lower unemployment. Immigration of low-skilled workers depresses their wages and raises unemployment among them while high-skilled domestic workers gain on both accounts.

1. INTRODUCTION

Enlargement of the European Union (EU) to the emerging market economies of Central and Eastern Europe (CEE) has become a major and contentious policy issue. The CEECs are keen on EU membership and hope that it will help them to catch up more quickly to western income levels. The EU, in turn, has reacted quite promptly by signing the 1990 European Agreements which were intended to facilitate and accelerate integration of commodity markets. Full membership of CEECs, however, is much more controversial largely because of its potential cost to the EU budget and because of its adverse effects on labor markets, especially in the low-skilled segment. Since they are still vastly different from present member countries, the entrants would all be net recipients of EU funds. It is also generally assumed that a significant share of imports from CEECs has a relatively large content of unskilled labor. Basic trade theorems would then predict that trade integration widens the wage gap between high and low skilled labor and, thus, contributes to a more unequal income distribution. In many industrialized countries, policy makers are rather concerned about the decline in employment prospects and relative incomes of low-skilled labor.

Budgetary and labor market effects of enlargement weigh particularly heavily in the case of Germany. In the aftermath of German unification, public sector budgets are heavily strained by the accumulated burden of large scale fiscal transfers to East Germany. To reverse the growth in public debt, now more than 60 percent of GNP, proves to be exceedingly difficult. On top of that, Germany's negative balance with the EU worsened between 1990 and 1995. Germany increasingly considers its negative balance to be too large relative to its wealth and recently insisted on a correction. Its net contribution to the EU in 1999 is estimated at .6 percent of GNP.

R.E. Baldwin and A. Brunetti (eds.), Economic Impact of EU Membership on Entrants, 217–244.

Despite the government's indication that a further EU enlargement cannot take place without a cut in Germany's net contribution, the Berlin summit did not help very much to alleviate the problem.

Germany is also more exposed to potential entrants from the East than most other West European countries. Given geographic and historical reasons, the CEECs figure much more importantly in Germany's trade volume than in many other EU countries. Their share in 1996 German merchandise exports is 6.6 percent, up from 1.59 percent in 1989, while merchandise imports amount to 6.3 percent.[1] By way of contrast, in countries like France or Spain, the 1996 shares are less than 2 percent. Only for Austria is trade with CEECs equally important. A widely held presumption is that imports from the CEECs are concentrated in goods with a relatively large content of unskilled labor. The public debate is rather concerned that Eastern enlargement may be another globalization like trade shock that might not easily be digested by high wage Germany, especially in its low skilled labor market segments. The problem is acute since the German unemployment rate is stuck at 11 percent in 1999 and shows not much sign of a reversal. Given the large number of ethnic Germans still living in Poland and other CEE countries, the immigration pressure poses another threat to the German labor market, on top of the East West migration within Germany.[2]

This paper discusses expected effects of Eastern enlargement on Germany, focussing mainly on labor market and budgetary consequences. Will Eastern enlargement further aggravate the German unemployment problem? Will it hit predominantly low skilled labor? Are there any fiscal returns to public sector budgets that would partly pay for Germany's share in the enlargement cost? There is an established tradition of quantifying the effects of European integration relying on calibrated general equilibrium models [Gasiorek et al. (1992), Haaland (1992), Haaland and Norman (1992,1995), and Keuschnigg and Kohler (1996a), among others]. Regarding the upcoming fifth enlargement towards the CEECs, a consensus view seems to be that large income gains are at stake for CEECs while the efficiency gains for western countries are largely offset and even dominated by the budgetary cost. Using their "internal market model" in conjunction with gravity estimates of the east-west trade potential, Gasiorek et al. (1994) calculate rather small output and welfare effects and even minuscule factor price changes for the west. Similar conclusions arise from Brown et al. (1997). Addressing specific scenarios of Eastern enlargement, Baldwin et al. (1997) calculate a real income gain of up to 18 percent for the group of CEEC7 (Bulgaria, Czech Republic, Hungary, Poland, Romania, Slovak Republic, and Slovenia), and a modest gain of 0.2 percent for the EU(15) countries which is largely offset by the net budgetary burden. Benefits and costs are, however, quite unevenly distributed across EU countries. Arguably, the most

---

[1] The figures have been calculated based on OECD trade data.

[2] According to Layard et al. (1992), more than 3 million ethnic Germans still live outside Germany, many of them in Poland. Sinn (1999) discusses migration in the context of EU enlargement and draws a parallel with German unification. Haisken De New and Zimmermann (1999) discuss the recent German experience with trade and immigration.

interesting countries are those with a particularly high exposure to the east such as Germany and Austria.

This paper is unique in analyzing the consequences of Eastern enlargement with a dynamic CGE model that features fully specified labor markets along search theoretic foundations, differentiated with respect to high and low skilled market segments. Apart from addressing a major policy concern, it is, in fact, an important separate methodological contribution of this paper to develop and calibrate such a model for commercial policy applications. In line with the empirical evidence due to Davis and Haltiwanger (1992), a large part of the literature emphasizes job creation and job destruction as a principal source of unemployment. The core theory of search unemployment was pioneered by Diamond (1982), Pissarides (1990) and Mortensen and Pissarides (1994). The literature was recently reviewed by Mortensen and Pissarides (1998). However, it has proved notoriously difficult to integrate the models of search unemployment with meaningful intertemporal models of savings and investment behavior. When individual unemployment spells are stochastic, agents become heterogeneous with respect to their past unemployment history and savings behavior. In the absence of any analytically tractable aggregation procedure, some form of income pooling assumption is unavoidable. The recent theoretical literature on growth and unemployment [Aghion and Howitt (1994), for example] as well as the recent real business cycle literature [Andolfatto (1996), Merz (1997) and Den Haan, Ramey and Watson (1997), for example] adopt such an assumption of perfect insurance and income pooling within the extended family. While precluding a welfare analysis of explicitly redistributional issues, this approach allows to address the consequences of policy shocks for unemployment rates and average incomes, as well as the 'asset' values of employed and unemployed agents.

Section 2 offers a stylized theoretical perspective on the expected effects on labor market and public budgets. Section 3 gives a brief overview of the computational model and specifies a policy scenario that captures the most important economic aspects of Eastern enlargement as they are relevant for a present member country such as Germany. It then presents quantitative estimates from simulation exercises. Section 4 concludes with a short summary and discusses further research.

2. A STYLIZED ANALYSIS

This section offers a preliminary analysis of budgetary and labor market effects of Eastern enlargement as they might obtain in a small open economy. At the same time, we familiarize the reader with the essential labor market features that are built into the more detailed CGE model and demonstrate some key transmission channels for policy effects. We may thus obtain a flavor of important macroeconomic effects of enlargement and build intuition for the numerical results. The CGE model is described in a separate appendix.

2.1. The framework

2.1.1. Household sector

The household sector is populated by overlapping generations that each face a constant probability of death as in Blanchard (1985). A dynasty born at date υ saves and consumes $C_{\upsilon,\tau}$ such as to maximize expected life-time utility, $\int_t^\infty U(C_{\upsilon,\tau})e^{-(\rho+\beta)(\tau-t)}d\tau$, subject to a dynamic budget constraint, where ρ is the rate of time preference, β the mortality rate. An annuity scheme provides perfect insurance against death. In addition to mortality, agents also face an income uncertainty due to unemployment. We adopt the usual assumption that each dynasty pools incomes of its many family members and provides each one with the same average labor income Y^L [see Andolfatto (1996)]. Perfect insurance against both types of risk allows for convenient aggregation across generations and employment status, giving aggregate savings per capita equal to

$$\dot{A}_t = r_t A_t + Y_t^L - P_t C_t, \; Y_t^L \equiv (1-t_t^Y)W_t L_t + B_t U_t. \tag{2.1}$$

A dot indicates a time derivative. From now on, we suppress time indices for more concise notation. The variables stand for assets A, interest r, consumer price index P, wage rate W, (un-)employment rate L = 1-U, government provided unemployment benefits B, and income tax rate t^Y. All agents have the same marginal propensity $\bar{c}$ to consume out of life-time wealth whence aggregate consumer spending is $PC = \bar{c}(A+H)$. Human wealth, $H = v^L L + v^U U$, is a weighted average of the asset values attached to the employment status. The dynasty attaches a value υ^L to a currently employed member equal to the expected present value of net wage income while υ^U gives the value of an unemployed. These values are determined by basic no-arbitrage conditions

$$\text{(a)} \quad (r+\beta)\upsilon^L = (1-t^Y)W - s\cdot(\upsilon^L - \upsilon^U) + \dot{\upsilon}^L, \tag{2.2}$$

$$\text{(b)} \quad (r+\beta)\upsilon^U = B + f\cdot(\upsilon^L - \upsilon^U) + \dot{\upsilon}^U.$$

An unemployed finds a job with probability f while a currently employed agent is separated from her job with probability s. The separation rate is constant. To account for mortality, the probability of death β is added to the interest rate r. The expected value of being unemployed involves a dividend B, a capital gain of

$\upsilon^L - \upsilon^U$ with probability f in case the agent finds employment, and a capital gain $\dot{\upsilon}^U$ if the agent remains unemployed. Dividends plus capital gains must be equal to the risk adjusted return on the asset value υ^U. Equation (2.2a) lends a similar interpretation to the expected value of being employed.

In merging an overlapping generations model with search unemployment, labor market flows must consistently reflect demographic change in addition to job creation and destruction that occurs for other reasons,

$$\dot{L} = fU - (s + \beta)L, \quad \dot{U} = \beta + sL - (f + \beta)U. \tag{2.3}$$

The aggregate employment rate increases as a fraction f of the unemployed find a job, giving a flow fU. Employment declines, however, on account of job separation, sL, and death among old workers, βL. A similar argument gives the dynamics of the aggregate unemployment rate. A part sL of previously employed workers get separated from their jobs and become unemployed. The mass β of labor market entrants contributes to aggregate unemployment as well since they search for jobs much the same way as unemployed members of old agents.[3] Unemployment declines by $(f+\beta)U$ on account of job finding and death among unemployed agents.

2.1.2. Investment

Investors own capital and rent it to firms at a competitive rental rate. They finance gross investment spending $PI = P(\dot{K} + \delta K)$ by retained earnings and obtain a dividend equal to

$$\pi^K = (1 - t^Y)R^K K - PI. \tag{2.4}$$

Value maximization yields a standard efficiency condition that equates marginal value product with the user cost of capital,

$$(1 - t^Y)R^K = \left(r + \delta - \dot{P}/P\right)P. \tag{2.5}$$

The value of the capital stock is $V^K = PK$ and satisfies $rV^K = \pi^K + \dot{V}^K$.

---

[3] The size of a cohort born at date v is $N_{\upsilon,t} = \beta e^{\beta(\upsilon - t)}$ whence labor market entrants have mass β. The size of the overall population is, thus $\int_{-\infty}^{t} \beta e^{\beta(\upsilon-t)} dv = 1$.

2.1.3. Firms

Output is produced from labor and capital according to a standard neoclassical technology. Firms rent capital K^i on a competitive market for machines, taking the rental price R^K as given. When a firm wishes to add workers to its labor force, it must post vacancies v^i and incurs search costs. Recruitment requires to divert a part κv^i of its labor force to searching activities whence only a part $L^i - \kappa v^i$ is available for production. Multijob firms can eliminate all uncertainty about the flow of labor as in Pissarides (1990). Firms maximize the expected present value of profits, $\Omega_t^i = \int_t^\infty \pi_\tau^{L,i} \cdot e^{-\int_t^\tau r_\mu d\mu} dt$. In symmetric equilibrium, all firms are identical. Suppressing the firm index, and denoting output price by p, profits are

$$\pi^L = (1 - t^Y)[pF(K, L - \kappa v) - LW - R^K K]. \tag{2.6}$$

The stock of workers is accumulated according to

$$\dot{L} = qv - (s + \beta)L, \tag{2.7}$$

where q is the probability that a worker is found in period t for a given vacancy. From the firm's perspective, q is exogenous. By the law of large numbers, q also denotes the fraction of vacancies that a multijob firm is able to fill at any instant. The optimality conditions for posting vacancies and renting capital are

$$R^K = pF_K(K, L - \kappa v), \qquad qJ^F = \kappa \cdot (1 - t^Y) pF_L(K, L - \kappa v). \tag{2.8}$$

The first condition equates the marginal product of capital with its rental price. The second indicates that firms post vacancies until marginal search cost just matches the expected shadow price of a vacancy which is equal to the probability of finding a worker times the value of a filled job. The value that a firm attaches to a filled job is given by

$$rJ^F = (1 - t^Y)[pF_L(K, L - \kappa v) - W] - (s + \beta)J^F + \dot{J}^F, \tag{2.9}$$

where W is the gross wage rate resulting from bargaining between a firm worker pair. Linear homogeneity of technology implies that the value of the firm is equal to the replacement value of occupied jobs, i.e. $\Omega = J^F L$, or $r\Omega = \pi^L + \dot{\Omega}$ for later reference.

2.1.4. *Wage bargaining*

When a firm with a vacancy and a job seeker are matched, a potential surplus is created and to be distributed among the two parties. Filled jobs have higher value than vacancies from the firm's perspective, and gaining employment is valued higher than remaining unemployed from the workers' perspective. Assigning a bargaining power of $0<\varsigma<1$ to the worker, the division of the total surplus created by match *i* may be determined by the Nash bargaining solution.[4]

$$W_\tau(i)=\arg\max\left\{\left[v_t^L(i)-v_t^U\right]^\varsigma\cdot\left[J_t^F(i)\right]^{1-\varsigma}\right\}. \tag{2.10}$$

Integration of (2.2a) and (2.9) yields

$$v_t^L(i)=\int_t^\infty\left[\left(1-t_\tau^Y\right)W_\tau(i)+s v_\tau^U\right]e^{-\int_t^\tau(r_\mu+\beta+s)d\mu}d\tau \text{ and}$$

$$J_t^F(i)=\int_t^\infty\left(1-t_\tau^Y\right)\left[p_\tau F_L-W_\tau(i)\right]e^{-\int_t^\tau(r_\mu+\beta+s)}d\tau \text{ respectively.}$$

Changing the wage rate affects only the value of employment $v_t^L(i)$ and of a filled job $J_t^F(i)$ of match *i* since agents take as given the behavior of other workers and firms. When rejecting the offer, the job applicant expects to remain unemployed for a while and only later to obtain employment *elsewhere* with value v_τ depending on average rather than individually negotiated wages.[5] The threat point v_t^U, thus, does not depend on individually negotiated wages $W_\tau(i)$ in match *i* but depends on average wage rates W_τ in the economy as a whole. In symmetric equilibrium, the optimality condition is

$$\varsigma J^F=(1-\varsigma)\left(v^L-v^U\right). \tag{2.11}$$

Differentiate (2.11), substitute (2.2) and (2.9), and use (2.11) to obtain the implied wage rate,

$$\left(1-t^Y\right)W=\varsigma\cdot\left(1-t^Y\right)pF_L+(1-\varsigma)\cdot\left[B+f\left(v^L-v^U\right)\right]. \tag{2.12}$$

---

[4] Since there is no investment cost to posting a new vacancy, its value is zero in equilibrium with free entry.

[5] The value of being unemployed is $v_t^U=\int_t^\infty\left[B_\tau+f_\tau v_\tau^L\right]e^{-\int_t^\tau(r_\mu+\beta+f_\mu)d\mu}d\tau.$

The net wage rate is thus a weighted average of the net marginal value product of labor and the reservation wage. The reservation rate is equal to the unemployment benefit plus the expected capital gain from finding employment elsewhere.[6]

2.1.5. *Labor market frictions*

Given a matching technology *m(·)*, labor market flows must fulfill the identities $fU = m(v,U) = qv$ such that the transition equations of employment for households and firms are mutually consistent. With large numbers, the individual probability f of an unemployed to find a job is also equal to the fraction of all job seekers that actually do find employment. The same interpretation holds for the transition rate q. Denoting the ratio of vacancies to job seekers by $\theta \equiv v/U$, and assuming a linear homogeneous matching technology, we have $f(\theta) \equiv m(\theta,1)$ and $q(\theta) \equiv m(1,1/\theta)$. The matching properties imply

$$f(\theta) = \theta q(\theta), \qquad f'(\theta) > 0 > f''(\theta), \qquad q'(\theta) < 0 < q''(\theta). \tag{2.13}$$

2.1.6. *Equilibrium*

The government collects revenues from an income tax on capital and labor income, $t^Y pF$, and spends on unemployment benefits and a lump-sum transfer T^U to the European Union. The GBC is, thus,

$$T^U = t^Y pF - BU. \tag{2.14}$$

We now state the equilibrium conditions of a small open economy that is a price taker on world commodity and capital markets. We also assume that the home economy is specialized in an export good. To derive the current account, we start with household savings. Financial wealth is invested in three perfectly substitutable assets that must yield identical rates of return in equilibrium if arbitrage is to be excluded, $A = V + \Omega + D$ where D denotes foreign assets. Using (2.1) and the no-arbitrage conditions on V and Ω, we have $\dot{D} = rD + (1 - t^Y)WL + B(1 - L) + \pi^K + \pi^L - PC$. Substituting the dividend terms and the GBC then gives the current account,

---

[6] Replacing $(1 - \varsigma)(v^L - v^U)$ by (2.11) and using (2.8) as well as $\theta q = f$ [see (2.13) below], we may also write $(1 - t^Y)W = \varsigma(1 - t^Y)pF_L + (1 - \varsigma)B + \varsigma f J^F = \varsigma(1 - t^Y)pF_L \cdot (1 + \kappa\theta) + (1 - \varsigma)B$.

$$D = rD + [pG - P(C + I)] - T^U . \tag{2.15}$$

The trade balance given by the square bracket is the difference between domestic income and absorption. By definition of the price index, spending on home goods and imports amounts to $PC = pC^h + p^m C^m$. The trade balance thus may also be written as the excess of exports over imports, $[\cdot] = p(F - C^h - I^h) - p^m(C^m + I^m)$.

2.2. *Effects of enlargement*

The stylized framework highlights the essential labor market and investment features of the CGE model and also lends itself to a first back of the envelope calculation of some expected effects of Eastern enlargement. The most direct impact will be felt from a mutual reduction in trade barriers between current member states and accession countries and an increase in *net* contributions to finance the fiscal costs of enlargement. Trade integration reduces import prices in the EU but also creates export opportunities as Eastern countries have improved access to EU produced commodities. One may arguably expect an improvement of the terms of trade vis a vis the entrants as well. As Baldwin et al. (1997) have argued, membership may increase the growth prospects in applicant countries much more than in the EU. Regarding the fiscal costs of enlargement, we take a somewhat different view. Rather than analysing an exogenous increase in net contributions, one may ask whether the effects of trade integration creates a fiscal surplus in the current member states that would allow them to pay at least part of the higher net contributions that will become necessary. The stylized model leaves open many questions that we further investigate with the help of the CGE model in the next section.

2.2.1. *Capital intensity*

Removing trade barriers towards CEE countries sqeezes demand prices $p^m = 1 + \tau$ in current member states for imports of Eastern origin. Since tariff revenues directly accrue to the EU, there is not much difference between tariffs and real trade costs. Depending on the import share γ in total investment expenditures, lower trade barriers favorably affect the price index for capital goods [as well as other demand categories].[7] Indicating percentage changes by a hat, tariffs and output prices feed into the price index according to

$$\hat{P} = (1 - \gamma)\hat{p} + \gamma\,\hat{\tau} . \tag{2.16}$$

[7] Given homothetic preferences, the price index is defined as $P = \min\{pc^h + p^m c^m \ s.t.\ C(c^h, c^m) \geq 1\}$.

According to the stationary investment condition given by (2.5) and (2.8), $(1 - t^Y)pF_K = (r + \delta)P$, higher output prices, i.e. an increase in the terms of trade, and lower tariffs improve investment conditions which boosts the capital labor ratio[8] $k = K/(L - \kappa v)$ by $\hat{k} = \frac{\sigma}{1-\alpha}\gamma(\hat{p} - \hat{\tau})$. Labor's marginal product therefore increases by

$$\hat{p} + \hat{F}_L = \hat{p} + \frac{\alpha}{1-\alpha}\gamma(\hat{p} - \hat{\tau}). \tag{2.17}$$

2.2.2. Labor market tightness

Both workers and producers share in the benefits of higher labor productivity. Producer rents are capitalized in the asset price of a filled job which is determined in stationary equilibrium by (2.9),

$$(r + s + \beta)J^F = (1 - t^Y)[pF_L - W]. \tag{2.18}$$

Bargaining results in a wage rate that is a weighted average of the marginal value product of labor and the reservation wage. Rewriting the wage equation (2.12) as in footnote 3 allows us to relate it to net producer rent,

$$(1 - t^Y)[pF_L - W] = (1 - \varsigma)[(1 - t^Y)pF_L - B] - \varsigma f J^F.$$

Equate the two relationships to eliminate net producer rent and replace the asset price by the efficiency condition for vacancies in (2.8). One thus obtains a reduced form equation for labor market tightness as measured by the vacancy/unemployment ratio θ,

$$\frac{r + s + \beta + \varsigma f(\theta)}{q(\theta)} = \frac{1-\varsigma}{\kappa}\left[1 - \frac{B}{(1 - t^Y)pF_L}\right]. \tag{2.19}$$

By the properties of the transition rates f and q given in (2.13), the l.h.s. is upward sloping in the vacancy/unemployment ratio θ. In a small open economy with exogenous terms of trade, the r.h.s. is fully determined by the net marginal value product of labor which is fixed by (2.16). Both a reduction of trade barriers τ

---

[8] The elasticity of substitution in production is $\sigma = -(1-\alpha)f'/(kf'')$ and capital's share in value added is $\alpha = kf'/f$ where $f(k)$ denotes the production function in intensive form.

and an improvement of the terms of trade brought about by a rise in p boost investment incentives and lead to more capital intensive production. Consequently, the marginal value product of labor increases and raises producer rents which, in turn, boosts the value of filled jobs and the incentives to post more vacancies. Labor markets become tighter. If unemployment benefits B are not indexed but kept constant, the r.h.s. of (2.19) increases and thereby boosts θ, indicating tighter labor markets.

2.2.3. *Employment*

In a stationary equilibrium, the level of unemployment is given by (2.3),

$$U = \frac{s + \beta}{s + \beta + f(\theta)}. \tag{2.20}$$

By raising labor market tightness θ, a reduction in real trade costs and an improvement of the terms of trade should contribute to lower unemployment in current member states.

2.2.4. *Tax revenues*

Eastern enlargement tends to reduce unemployment and boost investment in present member states. Output $F(K, L - \kappa v)$ expands both on account of higher employment and larger capital stocks.[9] Real income, $pF(\cdot)/P$, is also magnified by terms of trade gains and a reduction of import prices due to lower trade barriers. Furthermore, the expansion of the home economy swells the tax base and boosts revenues from a preexisting income tax. Given a fixed per capita unemployment benefit B, equation (2.14) points to a further improvement of the public budget that comes from the savings in public spending on unemployment benefits. Such fiscal returns create room to increase net contributions to the EU without raising domestic taxes or cutting other expenditures such as social benefits.

3. A COMPUTABLE APPROACH

3.1. *Model and parameters*

3.1.1. *Structure of the model*

To pin down the likely effects of enlargement in useful detail and to gauge some orders of magnitude, one needs to take account of relevant country characteristics and requires a more detailed *structural model* that is *implemented empirically*. This

---

[9] Appropriate conditions will assure that an increase in employment L results in more labor for both production and search.

section reports the results for the case of Germany based on a numerically solved, dynamic general equilibrium model. The most important addition to the stylised model introduced in the preceding section is that production occurs in twelve different sectors that are connected by interindustry shipments of intermediate goods. Sectoral output is differentiated whence production is subject to monopolistic competition and increasing returns due to specialization. In addition to variable cost, each firm incurs a fixed cost for non-marketable overhead purposes which is covered by a profit margin on variable output. Free entry subject to a zero profit condition determines the equilibrium number of firms and differentiated goods within each sector. The demand for differentiated sectoral output is derived from Dixit Stiglitz (1977) preferences such that different brands are imperfectly substitutable in demand. The composition of investment, government and export demand similarly reflects allocation of expenditure across differentiated, sectoral commodities. The presence of a downward sloping sectoral export demand functions makes the country large on its output markets and endogenizes the terms of trade.[10] The domestic real interest rate reflects changes in terms of trade over time but is otherwise tied to a constant rate determined on world capital markets.

On the supply side, employment and capital stocks are accumulated separately in each sector. Due to convex installation costs, capital is sector-specific in the short-run, giving rise to windfall gains or losses in various sectors in response to policy shocks. In the long-run, capital is intersectorally mobile as accumulation responds to sectoral investment incentives. Furthermore, the household sector and the demand for labor inputs in production distinguishes high and low skilled labor. Consequently, the model features two segmented labor markets along the search theoretic lines introduced in the preceding section. Finally, public sector spending includes the costs of goods and services, output subsidies, income transfers to households, unemployment benefits, interest on public debt and contribution payments to the EU. The government raises revenues through distortive commodity and income taxation. Income transfers to households are endogenously adjusted to support a constant level of debt. In modeling public revenues and expenditures, we are able to rigorously treat the budgetary implications of EU enlargement. The benchmark equilibrium is based on a 1996 data set and reflects the state of the German economy prior to EU enlargement.[11] The model is solved under the assumption of perfect foresight for the complete adjustment paths, treating enlargement as an unanticipated policy shock.

---

[10] Keuschnigg and Kohler (1996a,b) expose the core structure of this model including monopolistic competition.

[11] Several authors have relied on a gravity approach to estimate a quite impressive potential for east-west trade, e.g. Baldwin (1994) and Winters and Wang (1994). In contrast, Gros and Gonciarz (1996) used post-regime-change data from 1992 and found relatively little scope for further increases in trade flows relative to GDP. The use of 1996 trade data thus captures the fact that CEECs have already become increasingly open to trade in the process of systemec transformation.

3.1.2. Parameters

We select certain taste and technology parameters from the econometrics literature and also draw on parameters commonly used in the real business cycle literature [see Andolfatto (1996), Burda and Weder (1998), Mortensen and Pissarides (1998) etc.]. Other parameters are calibrated such that the stationary model solution reproduces a benchmark data set. Due to the fast labour market adjustment, the model has to be implemented quarterly in order to capture meaningful lengths of unemployment spells. We comment briefly on calibration of search related parameters which is, at this stage, somewhat tentative. The unemployment rates of high and low skilled workers are set at 6 and 10 percent, respectively. In accordance with the empirical search literature, we set the transition rates such that the average unemployment duration $1/f$ of high and low skilled labour is 1.75 and 1.25 quarters. Vacancy duration $1/q$ is set at 1.5 and 1.3 quarters. Compared to investment dynamics, this results in extremely fast labour market adjustment. We further postulate that 10 percent of total wage costs result from search activities, implying a value of κ. In the base case, unemployment benefits amount to 40 percent of net wages. Finally, we set the matching elasticity η at .4. Together with a quarterly mortality rate of $\beta = 1/60$,[12] these parameters then imply a quarterly split rate and a bargaining power of workers to replicate the labour market equilibrium. Calibration of the rest of the model is more standard and not repeated here.

3.2. The policy scenario

Accession negotiations are presently under way with five CEE countries. In order to disentangle the implications of different aspects of enlargement, we decompose the scenario into several steps that partly reflect the historic sequence of events starting with the Europe Agreements. Scenario is further decomposed to reflect the key issues in the current public debate: further trade liberalization (scenario B.I), sectoral repercussions from extending CAP (B.II), and budgetary implications of extending EU expenditure policies to new members (B.III).

3.2.1. Europe agreements

Eastern Enlargement of the European Union should be seen in the broader context of opening up of CEECs to world markets. As a first component, **scenario A** in table 1 (lines a and b) considers a bilateral *tariff liberalization* in non-agricultural sectors. Even though such tariff liberalization was already part of the Europe Agreements long before negotiations on enlargement started in 1998, the agreements cannot be properly understood without the eventual prospect of full membership. We therefore treat them as an integral part of Eastern enlargement. Note, however, that the Europe Agreements affect trade with all CEEC1 *and* CEEC2 countries while the first round

---

[12] An expected life-time of 15 years or 60 quarters may seem rather low. This parameter is, however, not to be interpreted literally but rather reflects disconnectedness of dynasties and discounting of future wage incomes. Is is also dictated to generate meaningfull savings behavior.

of enlargement will only extend to CEEC1. Furthermore, the tariffs listed in table 1 are average rates. Table 2 reports considerable sectoral variation in tariff protection.

3.2.2. Trade integration

Internal market access involves both a complete removal of all remaining (agricultural) tariffs on east-west trade and a variety of non-tariff barriers. Baldwin et al. (1997) stipulate a reduction of real trade costs in the amount of 10 percent uniform across all sectors. We improve upon previous attempts to model the costs of real trade frictions by exploiting new information on the frequency of non-tariff barriers in various sectors. This allows us to take account of important sectoral differences in real trade costs (see table 2). Furthermore, we are more conservative than Baldwin et al. (1997) in assuming that the savings in real resource use for cross border transactions is only 5 percent on average for CEEC1.

3.2.3. CAP repercussions

Generally, the CAP implies that eastern farmers will come under the protective umbrella afforded by the EU price support system. Although there is much public concern about the adjustment costs to EU farmers, one may argue that consumers and producers in the CEECs should be more heavily affected than their western counterparts by extending CAP. Regarding imports into the EU, for instance, eastern farm products will simply switch from the external protection regime of CAP to its internal price support scheme. While Eastern farm imports were formerly available to German consumers at threshold prices, they will now become available at intervention prices which effectively provide a price floor for agricultural products in the Union. Under the present regime, import levies raise prices for Eastern farm imports to the EU threshold level, while subsequent to entry the EU domestic price support scheme will increase them to the intervention level. By design of the CAP, the difference between threshold and intervention prices is very small, precluding any significant effects on prices for imports from CEEC1s. The abolition of agricultural tariffs is paralleled by increasing farm prices in the entrant countries (to the level of intervention prices, see line e in table 1). We take the difference in agricultural tariffs between the EU and CEEC1 countries to measure this expected price change.[13] Second, German farmers should similarly feel little impact if the CAP is continued unreformed. Prior to enlargement, they could earn EU prices on exports to CEECs (and rest of the world) since under the CAP price support scheme any difference to lower market prices in those destinations is compensated by means of variable export subsidies. In the wake of enlargement, farm prices in CEECs will be raised to higher EU levels. Consequently, EU exports to the CEECs will no longer need to be subsidized to the same extent (line f of table 1). Again, we use the

---

[13] If t_E and t_U are the external tariff rates of the CEEC1 countries and the European Union, respectivily, then the assumed percentage change for eastern farm prices from the point of view of the German consumer is equal to $(t_U - t_E)/(1 + t_E)$.

pre-enlargement tariff rates to approximate this fall in export subsidization. Third, we assume that, given higher guaranteed farm prices under CAP and also in response to the expected increase in productivity, agricultural output in CEECs will expand. This should put significant pressure on world farm prices. Relying on an estimate reported in Anderson and Tyers (1995), world farm prices are assumed to decline by 2 percent. Assuming that the EU will not raise its variable import levies and export subsidies in order to protect its farmers against this erosion of world market prices, we consider such a price reduction in scenario B.II (line g of table 1) which reduces import prices from all regions and, thus, puts pressure on German farm prices. In the simulations, we consider scenarios B.II and B.III together.

3.2.4. *Budgetary implications*

Apart from being a key issue in the popular debate, the budgetary implications are also a dominant factor in determining the magnitude of the simulation results. Our scenario implements medium term financial projections made by the European Commission in the Agenda 2000 which reflect certain changes in EU policy (see European Commission, 1997 and 1998b). The actual plans of financing EU enlargement are based on the reforms agreed upon in the meeting of the European Council in Berlin (European Council, 1999). Total payments appropriations for enlargement are estimated, for 2006, at Euro 14.22 Billion or 17.34 Billion when including pre-accession aid. With contributions to the EU budget by new members estimated at Euro 3.74 Billion, the net cost of an enlargement to CEEC1 (without pre-accession aid) is Euro 10.48 Billion or .113 percent of EU15 GNP. The major burden of enlargement will lie on Structural Operations, with some adjustment also in revenues. Compared to 1999, the Commission aims at reducing EU15 expenditure in 2006 by Euro 6.76 Billion. Commitments through the European Regional and Structural Funds (ESF), including pre-accession aid, are projected to fall by almost a quarter from Euro 39.025 Billion in 1999 to 30.21 Billion in 2006. By way of contrast, CAP budgets will bear relatively little of the financial burden. The planned reduction of 6.76 billion Euro falls short of the estimated cost of enlargement, implying a need for an increase in own resources of 3.72 billion Euro by 2006, or 0.04 percent of EU15-GNP. To obtain Germany's contribution and return flows implied by an enlarged Union, we rely on an econometric model of EU revenues and expenditures by Breuss and Schebeck (1996). This model estimates contributions and return flows under CAP and ESF programs, both for old and new countries. Our scenario assumes a cut in the ESF return rate (from .245% to .195%) while maintaining the contribution and CAP return rate at previous levels (1.154% and .314%, respectively). Consequently, Germany's net contribution rate will increase from .595% to .645% of GDP (line h in table 1). Since the overall policy scenario is sufficiently decomposed, the reader may easily anticipate the effects of tighter budgetary assumptions.

3.2.5. *Low-skilled immigration*

Germany attracts most of the immigrants from CEE, many of them with ethnic German origin. Naturally, the expectation of increased immigration and the potential negative implications for wages and unemployment leave many Germans severly worried and creates further reservations about the benefits of Eastern enlargement.[14] Somewhat hypothetically, we assume further immigration of low skilled workers equal to 2.5 percent of the total population. In the light of recent experience in Germany, this assumption seems quite realistic. We further assume that immigration is concentrated among low-skilled workers. Since only about 17 percent of the total workforce is classified as low-skilled in our data, the unskilled labor force expands by 15 percent approximately. This scenario also helps to put into perspective the labor market effects of the other aspects of enlargement.

3.2.6. Globalization

It seems interesting to compare the implications of Eastern enlargement for employment and wages with those of a more typical 'globalization' scenario [Sapir (1999) discusses the impact of globalization in Europe]. We thus construct a simple trade shock that involves a reduction of world market prices by 20 percent each in the six most unskilled intensive sectors. Table 2 lists agriculture, textiles and clothing, wood and paper, chemicals, and mining and quarrying as the most labor intensive industries. This scenario holds a rather powerful shock since it affects trade with all regions including the EU, rather than only CEECs.

3.3. Quantitative results

3.3.1. Macroeconomic repercussions

3.3.1.1. Europe agreements

Table 3 reports long-run, steady state effects in terms of percentage differences from the reference equilibrium. The first column displays the effects of the Europe Agreements with CEECs on Germany (scenario A in table 1). Tables 1 and 2 point to the fact that CEE countries, on average, need to cut tariffs by more (6.7 percent for CEEC1 and 11 percent for CEEC2) than Germany (6.3 percent and 7.6 percent, respectively). The agreements are expected to stimulate German exports to the CEECs (especially to CEEC2) by more than imports from those regions, subject to considerable sectoral variation. Since revenues from common external EU tariffs are not part of national government revenues but rather accrue to the Union budget, this liberalization scenario holds no compensating loss in tariff revenue.[15]

The supply and demand reactions are easily pointed out. Cheaper intermediate and capital goods from the east improve supply conditions. Home producer prices similarly get under pressure on the demand side with buyers favoring cheaper imports of eastern origin. On the other hand, the elimination of relatively higher

---

[14] See Haisken De New and Zimmermann (1999) for a discussion of recent German experience with immigration..

[15] National tariff revenues are part of gross contribution payments to the Union which are fixed as a percentage of GDP (1.15 percent of GDP for Germany). Any variation in tariff revenues is thus offset by other parts of contribution payments.

CEEC tariffs creates a vigorous German export boom to the east (about 18 percent in equilibrium) and creates excess demand for home goods. Domestic producer prices increase negligibly by .049 percent on average to restore equilibrium. Higher output prices choke off demand for home goods and at the same time reinforce the supply side expansion by strengthening the incentives to invest. While the reduction of unemployment rates is barely visible, the overall economy experiences an investment led expansion with capital stocks accumulating by .269 percent. The output expansion largely occurs via firm entry and potentially contributes to productivity gains due to increasing specialization and diversification of industrial production. Such productivity gains due to specialization are felt in lower prices indices which further stimulate investment and other final demand and, thereby, magnify the output effects. GDP is up by .117 percent. As the aggregate economy expands, the preexisting tax rates generate additional revenues that are channeled to the household sector in form of higher transfers (i.e., .107 percent). Higher capital intensity boosts wages. Surprisingly, wages of skilled workers gain slightly less than those of unskilled (.289 percent and .304 percent, respectively).

3.3.1.2. Trade liberalization

Further trade liberalization represents the first step of a more comprehensive integration scenario. On top of the tariff cuts relating to the Europe Agreements, it includes a complete elimination of agricultural tariffs as well as a reduction in real trade costs for trade with CEEC1 (scenario B.I. in Table 1). Complete single market access, as is reflected in the mutual reduction of real trade costs, seems much more important than the tariff cuts agreed upon in the Europe Agreements. Since tariff revenues accrue to the EU budget, the economic implications of lower tariffs and lower real trade costs are rather similar since both are felt in lower domestic demand prices for imports of Eastern origin, and both stimulate exports by reducing Eastern demand prices for German products. To the extent that capital goods are imported from CEECs, vanishing trade costs squeeze the acquisition price of capital goods and boost investment incentives. In contrast to the Europe Agreements, however, the reduction of real trade costs is symmetric with respect to imports and exports. In addition to much larger exports towards the CEEC1, substitution towards competing imports is more pronounced. The reduction in real trade costs weighs more heavily than the elimination of import tariffs whence the quantitative reactions reported in column 2 of Table 3 are larger. Home prices increase by .124 percent in equilibrium. The large terms of trade gain vis-á-vis the CEEC1s (7.036 percent) is due to the fact that vanishing trade costs are direct equivalents to a terms of trade improvement while the terms of trade effect of a tariff cut emerges only indirectly through the market clearing condition.[16] Investment adds .529 percent to the long-run capital stock. Wage rates rise by about .57 percent with no clear cut effect on the wage spread between skilled and unskilled labor. In the long-run equilibrium with a fixed interest rate, overall consumer spending (.7 minus .165 percent) and accumulated

---

16 Since cheaper imports reflect savings in resource use on the part of eastern suppliers, there is no offsetting terms-of-trade loss for the east!

savings all increase approximately in proportion to disposable wage income (.535 percent). While unemployment rates move into the direction indicated in the stylized analysis of section 2, the reduction is barely visible. Consequently, unemployment spells become slightly shorter while the expected length of job vacancies increases. If there is any noticeable difference at all, unskilled workers are somewhat favored by the reduction in unemployment rates and the increase in wages. Trade liberalization also implies significant budgetary effects. The overall expansion of the economy considerably swells the tax bases which boosts, for given tax rates, revenues from both direct and indirect taxes. This revenue effect allows for a remarkable increase in transfers (.614 percent) to the households sector.

3.3.1.3. EU enlargement

The enlargement scenario includes, on top of the previous trade liberalization measures, an increase in net transfers to the Union, as well as some special repercussions from extending CAP to CEE countries [see scenario B.II and B.III in Table 1]. Germany's share in the cost of enlargement is reflected in net contributions growing to .645 percent of GDP, up from .595 prior to enlargement. This scenario is ambiguous a priori since the abolition of trade barriers tends to expand the economy while higher net transfers to the EU are contractionary [see Keuschnigg and Kohler (1996a)]. Our results indicate that the mutual reduction of real trade costs stemming from improved single market access clearly dominates the picture. The difference in the second and third columns of Table 3 essentially results from the effects of higher net contributions. The special adjustments in agriculture are hardly of much significance for the aggregate economy although they weigh more importantly in the sectoral reallocation. Disposable income suffers on this account whence domestic demand is depressed and the increase in equilibrium home prices (.05 percent) is less than in the second column. Lower home prices at the same time translate into a lower capital goods price index whence investment incentives $\left(\hat{p} - \hat{P}^I = .17\right)$ are largely retained and capital stocks expand by about the same amount (.5 percent). Germany is expected to benefit from large terms of trade gains vis-á-vis the CEE accession countries (almoust 7 percent) that mainly stem from the removal of trade barriers. As in the preceding partial scenarios, wages for skilled and unskilled workers rise by almost equal amounts (.5 percent) although high skilled workers now gain a shade more. As in the previous case, the unemployment rates for both skill groups decline but the magnitude is hardly of any significance. The fiscal burden of enlargement is passed on to households by cutting transfer income. It seems realistic to assume that government will make up for the lower return flows from structural funds operations by raising its own expenditure, at least partly so. Despite of this additional spending item, the government still affords to raise transfers by .362 percent. The fiscal returns from enlargement are, thus, more than enough to pay for the increase in net contributions. Total consumer spending and disposable wage income (.637 and .388 percent, respectively) suffer somewhat relative to the previous scenario mainly because of this more moderate increase in transfers.

3.3.1.4. *Low-skilled immigration*

One of the most hotly debated issues in Germany are the potentially adverse effects of enlargement on labor markets, especially with regard to low-skilled workers. But quite to the contrary, our analysis reveals that the fiscal and trade related aspects of enlargement are beneficial for Germany's workers, both skilled and unskilled. Given that one of the Union's principles is free movement of labor, Germany could attract a considerable wave of immigration. Whatever the Union's migration policy will be, we now allow for immigration of low-skilled workers equal to 2.5 percent of the total population, or 15 percent of the unskilled labor force.[17] Immigration is considered in isolation from the rest of the enlargement scenario. In essence, the increased labor force, accompanied by an equally large increase in capital stocks (almost 3 percent), results in a supply side expansion (GDP is up by 2.1 percent). The additional output stems from new producers and a larger range of product varieties rather than larger production scale. The resulting productivity gains from increasing specialization and division of labor are reflected in lower price indices despite of the fact that domestic producer prices essentially remain constant. For the same reason, the terms of trade deteriorate whence exports grow by 2.3 percent.

Immigration of low-skilled workers clearly diminish the income and employment prospects of domestic low-skilled workers. The unemployment rate among them picks up by more than one percentage point and swells to 11 percent while wage rates decline by a full 10 percent. By way of contrast, wages of the skilled increase by 2.6 percent, and their unemployment rate falls by slightly more then a tenth of a percentage point. Most of the shock thus translates into wages rather than (un-)employment.[18] The rather strong fiscal returns from immigration boost government transfers to the household sector. Average disposable wage incomes result mainly from the gains in wages and employment of high-skilled workers and from more generous government transfers. On average, real consumption thus expands by more than 4 percent.

3.3.1.5. *Globalization*

Next, we compare the effects of enlargement with a globalization scenario that involves a reduction of world market prices by 20 percent each in the six most unskilled intensive sectors [agriculture, textiles and clothing, wood and paper, chemicals, and mining and quarrying, see Table 2]. Rather than only CEECs, this powerful import price shock affects trade with all regions including the EU. The increased import competition puts downward pressure on domestic prices (-4.458

---

[17] One may doubt that immigrants from CEE countries are low-skilled. The scenario was partly chosen to highlight the model's potential for labor market effects. Is is also motivated by the fact that policy makers are primarily concerned with the fate of low-skilled workers since much of German unemployment is concentrated in the low-skilled labor market segments.

[18] This behavior is most probably due to the low bargaining power of workers that comes out of calibration (around .17 and .26 for high- and low-skilled). Model calibration should be revised to allow bargaining power to enter as an exogenously controlled parameter shich will allow the model to be subjected to sensitivity analysis with respect to this important parameter.

percent). Since the capital goods price index falls somewhat less, investment conditions deteriorate somewhat. Confirmed by the analysis of section 2, unemployment increases, capital stocks decline, and output contracts. The unemployment rate of low-skilled labor picks up by half a percentage point to 10.55 percent while the increase in unemployment among the skilled is more moderate. Deflating by the consumer price index, real wages increase by .374 percent for skilled, but fall by -.81 percent for unskilled workers. Globalization clearly widens the wage spread and deteriorates the employment prospects of the unskilled relative to the skilled. Given the size of the shock, however, the effect seems rather small.

3.3.2. Structural effects

Production sectors differ significantly in cost structure and exposure to Eastern Europe and, thus, benefit quite differently from EU enlargement. Table 4 reports long-run supply and demand effects (compare column ENL in Table 3). The strongest effects are observed in the agricultural, food, textiles and clothing, and chemical sectors. Agriculture is a special case. As CAP policy is applied to new EU entrants, eastern farm products will simply switch from the external protection regime to the EU internal price support scheme. As Eastern farmers are low cost producers, expansion of farm output in the CEECs is expected to depress world market prices by about two percent. We assume that the EU will not raise its import levies and export subsidies to protect its farmers against this decline in world prices.[19] With foreign farm prices lower by two percent, imports flow in from all regions. For the same reason, the increase in home prices relative to world market prices severely retards German agricultural exports, except for exports to the CEECs which benefit from vanishing real trade costs. The elimination of high real trade costs, tariffs and the reduction of world farm prices results in a rather dramatic increase in imports from CEECs. The reduction of farm costs and producer prices in agriculture is rather limited, however, in face of the overall expansion and wage growth. Moreover, since the cost share of intermediate goods is rather low, agriculture benefits less than other sectors from lower import prices, thus being more severely affected by a rise in factor costs. Consequently, the demand shock in agriculture mainly translates into a severe output contraction (by more than 3 percent). The food sector faces the highest cut in EU external protection (see Table 2) which generates an unrivaled import boom in Eastern food (243 percent). Food, however, has a much higher cost share of imported intermediates and, furthermore, is taking advantage of new export opportunities to CEEC markets much like other sectors. Hence, it does not experience the cost pressure and contraction that farmers face (+0.09 percent for food as compared to -3.03 percent for agriculture).

A different pattern is observed for textiles and clothing: strong expansion in result of attracting demand via lower producer prices (-.63 percent). This sector experiences the largest loss in domestic demand (-5.34 percent) since enlargement cuts a rather high rate of tariff protection and also removes the highest non-tariff

---

[19] This implies a reduction in farm import prices. Since we treat farm products as differentiated and imperfectly substitutable to imports, domestic prices are not completely tied to import prices.

barriers (see Table 2). Furthermore, tariff cuts are asymmetric with CEEC1 countries eliminating much higher rates than the EU. Yet the sector expands by a healthy 2.38 percent (which is surpassed only by chemicals with 2.55 percent). The explanation is that textiles is the strongest export performer, on top of an already high initial share of exports to CEECs. A similar pattern is noticed for chemicals, and metal processing, though less pronounced. The textiles and clothing sector is expanding production much more vigorously than the average. At the same time, this industry is much more intensive in unskilled labor (with a factor share of 25.7 percent of sectoral value added) than the average economy (with a share of 15.2 percent). It starts out with the highest share of production being shipped to the CEECs, while being the top export performer in Eastern Europe markets at the time when enlargement occurs (see Table 2). However, it creates less than one percent value added in total economic activity. On the other hand, more skill intensive industries, such as trade and other services, contribute more than average to national value added but expand much less than average in response to enlargement. These observations lead one to expect that enlargement would compress the wage spread as indicated in the first two columns of Table 3 reporting the results from the trade integration scenarios. The fact that the wage spread remains constant in the overall scenarios is then only explained by the relatively larger contraction of agriculture (-3.03 percent) in response to CAP effects. Agriculture is among the sectors most intensive in unskilled labor!

4. CONCLUSIONS

Several objections are often stated against the more optimistic proponents of EU enlargement. Taking in CEECs may create a significant fiscal burden to present EU member countries which adds to an already tight fiscal stand in Germany. With Eastern Europe being strongly specialized in labor intensive goods, it is expected to further aggravate the problems in sensitive industries and, thus, hurt unskilled workers. Relying on a dynamic equilibrium model of the German economy, we find that some of the often heard concerns seem ungrounded. Despite some difficulties in agriculture, the integration of the five CEE countries holds a potential for an investment led expansion of the German economy. Rather than representing a fiscal burden, it contributes to a more healthy public sector budget. Despite of the required increase in net contributions to the EU, the expanded macroeconomic activity swells the tax bases to an extent that allows more generous transfers to the household sector without increasing public debt. Furthermore, the particular scenario of trade integration coming with Eastern enlargement tends to favor equally skill and labor intensive industries. Eastern enlargement of the EU neither affects the wage gap between high and low skilled labor nor does it aggrevate the unemployment problem. More pronounced effects on wages and unemployment are only expected if enlargement triggers immigration from the entrant countries.

A major innovation of this project is the development of a consistent model of unemployment along search theoretic lines. According to the best of knowledge, this CGE model is the first one to model labor markets with this modern approach. Further research is necessary, however, to refine the model. A welfare measure needs to be developed that takes account of the welfare implications of non-competitive wage setting and of search externalities in the matching process. Sensitivity analysis should reveal how the results on unemployment and wages depend on important structural labor market parameters such as bargaining power, matching elasticity, vacancy cost and split rates.

REFERENCES

Aghion, P. and P. Howitt (1994), Growth and Unemployment, Review of Economic Studies, 61, p. 477-494.

Anderson, K. and R. Tyers (1995), Implications of EU Expansion for European Agricultural Policies, Trade and Welfare, in Baldwin, R.E., P. Haaparanta and J. Kiander (eds.), Expanding Membership of the European Union, Cambridge: Cambridge University Press.

Andolfatto, D. (1996), Business Cycles and Labour-Market Search, American Economic Review, 86, p. 112-132.

Baldwin, R. E. (1994), Towards an Integrated Europe, London: CEPR.

Baldwin, R. E., J. F. Francois and R. Portes (1997), The Costs and Benefits of Eastern Enlargement: The Impact on the EU and Central Europe, Economic Policy, p. 127-176.

Blanchard, O. (1985), Debt, Deficits, and Finite Horizons, Journal of Political Economy, 93, p. 223-247.

Breuss, F. and F. Schebeck (1996), Ostöffnung und Osterweiterung der EU, WIFO Monatsberichte, 2/1996, p. 139-151.

Brown, D., A. V. Deardorff, S. Djankov and R. M. Stern (1997), An Economic Assessment of the Integration of Czechoslovakia, Hungary and Poland into the European Union, in Black, S. W. (ed.), Europe's Economy Looks East: Implications for Germany and the European Union, Cambridge: Cambridge University Press.

Burda, M. C. and M. Weder (1998), Endogenes Wachstum, gleichgewichtige Arbeitslosigkeit und persistente Konjunkturzyklen, Humboldt University of Berlin, Discussion Paper.

Davis, S.J. and J. Haltiwanger (1992), Gross Job Creation, Gross Job Destruction, and Employment Reallocation, Quarterly Journal of Economics, 107, p. 819-864.

Den Haan, W. J., G. Ramey and J. Watson (1997), Job Destruction and Propagation of Shocks, University of California, San Diego, Discussion Paper 97-23.

Diamond, P. A. (1982), Aggregate Demand Management in Search Equilibrium, Journal of Political Economy, 90, p. 881-894.

Dixit, A. and J. E. Stiglitz (1977), Monopolistic Competition and Optimum Product Diversity, American Economic Review, 67, p. 297-308.

Gasiorek, M., A. Smith and A. J. Venables (1992), '1992': Trade, Factor Prices and Welfare in General Equilibrium, in Winters, L.A. (ed.), Trade Flows and Trade Policy after `1992', Cambridge: Cambridge University Press.

Gasiorek, M., A. Smith and A. J. Venables (1994), Modelling the Effect of Central and East European Trade on the European Community, European Economy, 6, p. 521-538.

Gros, D. and A. Gonciarz (1996), A Note on the Trade Potential of Central and Eastern Europe, European Journal of Political Economy, 12, p. 709-721.

Haaland, J. I. (1992), Comparative Advantage, Terms of Trade and Welfare Effects of European Integration: Some Preliminary Assessments, Scandinavian Journal of Economics, 94, p. 373-391.

Haaland, J. I. and V. D. Norman (1992), Global Production Effects of European Integration, in Winters, L.A. (ed.), Trade Flows and Trade Policy after `1992', Cambridge: Cambridge University Press.

Haaland, J. I. and V. D. Norman (1995), Regional Effects of European Integration, in Baldwin, R.E., P. Haaparanta, and J. Kiander (eds.), Expanding Membership of the European Union, Cambridge: Cambridge University Press.

Haisken De New, J. P. and K. F. Zimmermann (1999), Wage and Mobility Effects of Trade and Migration, in Dewatripont, M., A. Sapir and K. Sekkat (eds.), Trade and Jobs in Europe: Much Ado about Nothing?, Oxford: Oxford University Press.

Keuschnigg, C. and W. Kohler (1996a), Austria in the European Union: Dynamic Gains from Integration and Distributional Implications, Economic Policy, 22, p. 155-211.

Keuschnigg, C. and W. Kohler (1996b), Commercial Policy and Dynamic Adjustment Under Monopolistic Competition, Journal of International Economics, 40, p. 373-409.

Layard, R., O. Blanchard, R. Dornbusch and P. Krugman (1992), East West Migration. The Alternatives, Cambridge: MIT Press.

Merz, M. (1997), A Market Structure for an Environment with Heterogeneous Job Matches, Indivisible Labour and Persistent Unemployment, Journal of Economic Dynamics and Control, 21, p. 853-872.

Mortensen, D. T. and C. Pissarides (1994), Job Creation and Job Destruction in the Theory of Unemployment, Review of Economic Studies, 61, p. 397-416.

Mortensen, D. T. and C. A. Pissarides (1998), New Developments in Models of Search in the Labour Market, Unpublished paper, Northwestern University.

Pissarides, C. A. (1990), Equilibrium Unemployment Theory, Oxford: Basil Blackwell.

Sapir, A. (1999), The Impact of Globalization on Employment in Europe, in Dewatripont, M., A. Sapir and K. Sekkat (eds.), Trade and Jobs in Europe: Much Ado about Nothing?, Oxford: Oxford University Press.

Sinn, H.-W. (1999), EU Enlargement, Migration, and Lessons From German Unification, Munich: CESifo WP No. 182.

Winters, L. A. and Z. K. Wang (1994), Eastern Europe's International Trade, Manchester - New York: Manchester University Press.

Wong, K. (1995), International Trade in Goods and Factor Mobility, Cambridge: MIT Press.

Table 1. Eastern Enlargement: Decomposition of Scenario

Policy Elements		OLD	NEW
A. Europe Agreements			
a)	German (EU) non-agricultural tariffs removed vis-à-vis CEEC1 and CEEC2 countries	CEEC1: 6,3% CEEC2: 7,6%	0% 0%
b)	CEEC1 and CEEC2 countries non-agricultural tariffs removed vis-à-vis Germany (EU)	CEEC1: 6,7% CEEC1: 11.%	0% 0%
B: Enlargement to CEEC1 countries			
B.I.	*Trade integration:*		
c1)	German tariffs on farm products removed	12,2%	0%
c2)	CEEC1 tariffs on farm products removed	9,8%	0%
d)	internal market: reduction of real trade costs	5,0%	0%
B.II.	*Repercussions from CAP:*		
e)	higher prices for farm imports from CEEC1s		0.61% increase
f)	lower subsidies for farm exports to CEEC1s	8,5%	0%
g)	lower world prices for farm products		2% reduction
B.III	*Fiscal costs:*		
h)	higher net contribution rate (% of GDP)	0,595%	0,645%

Table 2: Structural Information

	Import tariffs	Export tariffs	Real trade costs CEEC1	Output (% of tot.)	Ex-ports/ Output	Exp. CEEC1 (% sect. Exp.)	Im-ports/ Output	Imp. CEEC1 (% sect. Imp.)	H-Skill/ VA	L-Skill/ VA	Capi-tal/ VA
1 Agr/For	12.18	9.77	4.25	1.23	8.12	0.71	32.98	0.91	44.43	17.18	38.39
2 Food	21.65	10.20	5.41	3.93	12.87	0.63	16.73	0.58	53.14	12.84	34.02
3 Tex/Clot	11.22	8.64	9.92	0.96	29.95	4.03	103.25	8.39	57.61	22.59	19.80
4 Wood/ Paper	3.47	4.55	3.86	2.58	18.06	1.21	25.09	1.98	59.15	14.94	25.91
5 Chemic	6.66	5.59	4.45	4.68	39.83	2.12	20.54	0.73	59.28	16.37	24.35
6 Petrol/ Energy	3.50	1.63	3.83	4.79	4.51	0.16	11.60	0.29	44.51	6.83	48.65
7 Min/Quar/ Miner	3.17	2.10	4.56	1.42	12.58	0.75	43.76	2.54	51.43	13.71	34.86
8 MetProd/ Proc	4.03	6.73	3.73	17.47	39.52	2.00	27.95	1.40	66.95	13.48	19.57
9 Constr/ Transpor	0.00	0.00	5.00	12.34	8.31	0.25	14.72	0.46	65.34	10.54	24.12
10 Trade	0.00	0.00	5.00	7.27	9.13	0.39	2.23	0.11	72.21	7.77	20.02
11 Insur/ Othserv	1.73	0.00	5.00	30.85	2.37	0.08	2.27	0.08	55.48	6.40	38.11
12 Public	0.00	0.00	5.00	12.49	0.22	0.01	0.32	0.01	59.36	12.13	28.51
Average/ Total	6.28	6.69	5.00	100.00	15.46	1.03	25.12	1.46	57.41	12.90	29.69

Source: I/O data for 1993, updated to 1996. CEEC1: Czech Republic, Hungary, Poland, Estonia, and Slovenia.

Table 3. Long-Run Macroeconomic Effects

Variables, changes in percent *)		EA	TRA	ENL	MIGR	GLOB
P	consumer price index	-0.091	-0.165	-0.248	-0.220	-5.015
P^I	investment price index	-0.042	-0.049	-0.121	-0.335	-4.372
P^Q	intermediate price index	-0.072	-0.101	-0.179	-0.335	-4.060
$\overline{p}$	dom. producer prices	0.049	0.124	0.050	0.017	-4.458
$\overline{p}_E$	terms of trade with CEECs	-0.042	7.036	6.979	-0.306	-1.050
E_E	exports to CEECs	17.885	45.894	45.479	2.336	-2.566
E	total exports	1.380	2.824	3.037	2.107	1.565
$1-L^s$	unempl.rate, skilled (6) *)	5.986	5.972	5.975	5.877	6.259
$1-L^u$	unempl.rate, unsk. (10)	9.975	9.953	9.960	11.058	10.549
$1/f^s$	unempl.duration, skilled (1.25)	1.247	1.244	1.244	1.223	1.308
$1/f^u$	unempl.duration, unsk. (1.75)	1.745	1.741	1.742	1.958	1.857
$1/q^s$	vacancy duration, skilled (1.5)	1.503	1.505	1.505	1.522	1.456
$1/q^u$	vacancy duration, unsk. (1.3)	1.302	1.305	1.304	1.206	1.249
w^s	wage rate, skilled	0.289	0.567	0.509	2.589	-4.641
w^u	wage rate, unskilled	0.304	0.580	0.497	-10.043	-5.825
z	government transfers	0.107	0.614	0.362	5.574	-6.730
ω	average disposable income	0.173	0.535	0.388	3.848	-5.263
C	average consumption	0.264	0.700	0.637	4.079	-0.257
K	$\sum_j$ capital stocks	0.269	0.529	0.505	2.953	-1.144
$\overline{n}$	number of firms	0.269	0.490	0.515	2.645	-1.016
Y	gross domestic production	0.117	0.346	0.283	2.102	-4.926

(EA) Europe agreements (scen.A in Table 1). (TRA) Enlargement, trade liberalization (scen.A+B.I in Table 1). (ENL) Enlargement including CAP (scen.A+B.I+B.II+B.III in Table 1). (MIGR) Immigration low-skilled labor. (GLOB) Reduction world prices in labor intensive industries. A bar (e.g. $\overline{p}$) denotes weighted averages of sectoral values. *) Labor market variables in absolute terms, initial values in brackets.

Table 4. Long-Run Structural Effects of Enlargement base case, percentage changes

Sectors	p	$\tilde{p}$	y	K	L^s	L^u	v^s	v^u	D^H	D^E	E^E
AGRFOR	-0.03	0.29	-3.03	-3.10	-3.49	-3.48	-3.17	-3.15	-3.51	131.31	18.93
FOOD	-0.37	0.32	0.09	-0.24	-0.78	-0.77	-0.45	-0.43	0.03	242.75	83.85
TEXCLOTH	-0.63	0.41	2.38	1.85	1.18	1.19	1.52	1.53	-5.34	185.36	141.73
WOODPAP	-0.03	0.37	0.43	0.46	-0.13	-0.11	0.21	0.22	0.01	33.44	32.65
CHEMIC	-0.26	0.38	2.55	2.32	1.75	1.77	2.09	2.11	1.07	46.23	40.37
PETROLEN	-0.08	0.22	0.60	0.45	0.16	0.18	0.50	0.51	0.47	26.24	21.36
MINQUAR	0.02	0.31	0.13	0.23	-0.37	-0.35	-0.03	-0.02	-0.02	29.45	25.77
METALS	-0.05	0.42	1.29	1.23	0.72	0.73	1.05	1.07	0.24	34.88	41.91
CONSTRA	0.08	0.38	0.23	0.26	-0.17	-0.16	0.16	0.17	0.22	29.38	28.49
TRADE	0.26	0.41	0.20	0.56	-0.09	-0.08	0.25	0.26	0.11	27.61	25.51
INSUROS	0.16	0.29	0.30	0.57	-0.08	-0.07	0.25	0.26	0.21	34.27	25.94
PUBLIC	0.14	0.36	0.02	0.27	-0.38	-0.37	-0.05	-0.03	-0.01	27.36	25.93

p : price of home goods, $\tilde{p}$: price of value added, y : sectoral output, K : capital stocks, L^s : skilled labor demand, L^u : unskilled labor demand, v^s : skilled job vacancies, v^u : unskilled job vacancies, D^H : final demand for home goods, D^E : final demand for CEEC1 imports, E^E : exports to CEEC1.

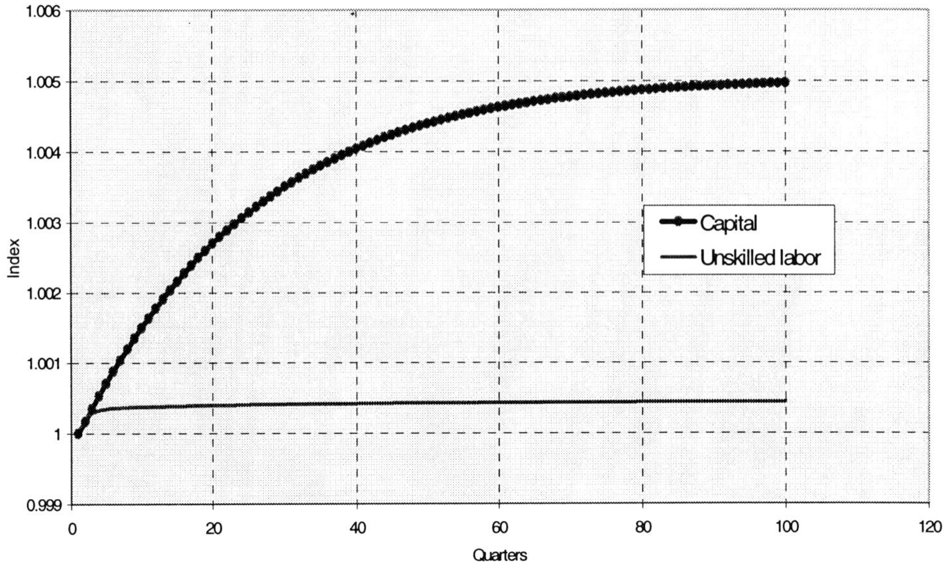

Figure 1. Unskilled Labor and Capital

THOMAS STRAUBHAAR

MIGRATION AND SWISS EU MEMBERSHIP

1. INTRODUCTION

The free movement of persons is one of the lasting and extremely controversial issues in the debate whether Switzerland should take part in the European integration process in one way or another. It was one (if not *the*) reason for the rejection of the EEE-agreement in the voting of December 6, 1992. And again it has become the hottest issue in the parliamentary treatment of the bilateral agreement in the summer of 1999. In the foreground, the trade unions have emphasised their fears of a so labelled "social dumping" (meaning that EU-citizens would be willing to work for lower wages or to accept lower standards of protection and security issues in their work conditions). In the background, however, the prospect of a free movement of EU persons to Switzerland fuels the genuine fears of a small and wealthy population towards a much larger and less prosperous neighbourhood. It is feared that the removal of legal restrictions to migration would lead to mass immigration from the European Union to Switzerland. Both views result in an extremely powerful left-right alliance against the free movement of persons. Due to the fact that the freedom to move is a constitutional right in the understanding of the European Union it also leads to a rejection of a too far reaching Swiss integration into the EU.

How realistic are the left-right-wing fears of "social dumping" and "Überfremdung" (i.e. domination by foreign influences in Switzerland)? Does economic theory give us some arguments for (or probably against) such expectations or does empirical evidence shed some light onto these dark feelings? Could we even "guesstimate" how many EU-citizens might immigrate into Switzerland if they were allowed to do so? These questions are the focus of my contribution. In the analysis, I will concentrate on some extremely rough quantitative estimations of the potential immigration pattern to Switzerland after a free movement of people with the EU has been agreed on. Section 2 presents the assumptions. Section 3 records the estimations. Section 4 evaluates the quantitative results. Section 5 concludes.

2. ASSUMPTIONS

An agreement for a free movement of people within an integrated labour market between Switzerland and the EU will remove legal and pecuniary obstacles to cross-border movements of Swiss and EU citizens. Generally speaking, EU citizens could

R.E. Baldwin and A. Brunetti (eds.), Economic Impact of EU Membership on Entrants, 245–264.

freely enter Switzerland, they could search for work and in case of being successful they could stay as long as they want living on their own financial expenses. How strongly would such a decrease in the costs of immigration quantitatively stimulate the entrance of EU citizens into Switzerland? To answer this question, we could follow different methodological approaches:

1. The most common approach is the extrapolation of historical evidence into the future. Such a procedure is not valid in the case of a Swiss-EU agreement on the free movement of people though. Of course, after a change in the political rules of the game, the *Lucas-critique* is always an argument against an extrapolation of the past. In this special case the change from a more or less fully regulated restrictive immigration system to an "open door" for EU citizens is so dramatic that the *Lucas-critique* prohibits a simple extrapolation of historical behaviour even more than in most other cases.

2. Another approach is to search for analogies that might look similar to the Swiss experience. And indeed, we find other examples where the opening of national borders to European Community (EC) citizens has taken place. Interestingly enough, EC's experience has mostly been a history of fears of the free movement of people. When in 1957 the Benelux countries, Germany and France joined Italy to build the original European Economic Community (EEC), the Germans and French were afraid of being flooded by Italian guest workers. When in 1981 Greece and in 1986 Portugal and Spain became members of the EC, Northern-EC member countries again worried about the south-north-migration potential. Also in the recent and slowly developing EU enlargement process towards the Central and Eastern European countries (CEEC), the free movement of people has been seen as one of the most crucial issues. Especially Germans are afraid of a potential "trek to the West". Thus, a look at the historical evidence of EU's free movement of people and the drawing of an analogy to the potential Swiss experience seems an interesting thing to do.

In my study, I follow the second approach. I first looked at historical evidence with respect to the free movement of people within the EC. The basic idea is to search for the strongest bilateral intra-EC migration flows in the past in order to then transfer this experience to Switzerland's future. In doing so, I will in a first step simulate something like an extreme scenario that indicates an upper limit for the maximal immigration potential. In a second step I will take some more realistic numerical values that have been confirmed by the long term experiences of the intra-EC-migration pattern. Finally, I will do some rough sensitivity calculations by taking into account some potential short run adjustment migration flows.

The "analogy approach" has some strong implications:

1. It is assumed that the European past has some explanatory power for the Swiss future. Of course this assumption has to be discussed further. However, the inner-European migration experience has shown such a stable generalising pattern that there is a rather strong probability that it will not completely change for the Swiss case. One of the clear facts is that intra-EU-migration has been and still is demand-determined (see Straubhaar 1988). Experience tells us that EU citizens

mostly move if an employer abroad offers them a job on a contractual basis. Sometimes (with an increasing tendency) employers are being sent abroad by their own companies, a phenomenon called internal labour market movements. Why should they change their behaviour?

2. The geographically close neighbourhood to Switzerland has rather similar standards of living and employment opportunities. Nevertheless, there are no strong movements from other poorer EU regions towards these rather prosperous areas. Why should people from Greece, Portugal, Spain or Southern Italy move suddenly to Switzerland if they have had the possibility to go to France, Bavaria or Milan for many years?

3. The analogy takes historical EC experiences from the late eighties and early nineties and applies them to the years after 2002. However, there is a strong empirical evidence (see Straubhaar 1999) that an increase of the absolute standard of living (i.e. an increase in *levels*) leads to a decreasing importance of relative income *differences* which normally determine the power of so-called push migration. Empirical evidence for intra-European migration seems to confirm this. Consequently, the more the EU countries will improve their absolute standard of living until 2002 and later on, the more will historical migration propensities between countries disappear. Technically speaking: The migration elasticity is not constant. It decreases with an increase of per capita incomes. However, in all scenarios I have assumed a constant (high) migration elasticity. Thus, the estimations will definitely indicate an upper level.

4. Finally the analogy neglects all business cycle effects. The reference period (i.e. 1986-96) has been characterised by an economically rather positive cycle (with the German reunification as an extreme increase in demand). This might have produced rather strong short run intra EU-migration flows in the "anchor period". Again, this effect has not been corrected for the Swiss case to include the migration pull effects of positive business cycles. In case that Switzerland's economic performance after 2002 is not as good as it was in the EU between 1986 and 1996, my calculations will overestimate the migration flows.

After these more general remarks, I will present the basic assumptions behind the estimations in more detail:

1. It is assumed that Switzerland has to accept the free cross border movement of EU-citizens after 1.1.2002. There are no transitory exceptions. Every EU citizen who can live by his own financial means (either by current income, savings, pensions or family support) can enter and stay in Switzerland.

2. To get an upper border line that indicates the largest potential immigration to Switzerland, I do not differentiate between the motives or the intentions of moving to Switzerland. This means that I look at *people not at labourers*. Thus, all the counter-balancing, migration reducing effects in the labour market (i.e. the impact of unemployment in the immigration country) are being neglected.

3. In a first step the immigration potential from the EU to Switzerland is treated as being dependent on *wage differentials* only. I assume that larger income gaps between Swiss and EU wages will result in stronger immigration flows. Wages

in all regions are proxied by average per capita income at purchasing power parities (see table 1).

4. The average *migration propensities* between each specific EU-country and Switzerland have been calculated from historical migration data. This has been done by taking average yearly bilateral net migration flows from within the EU for the last decade. Out of all these bilateral migration propensities (see table 2), I concentrate on the highest bilateral net migration flows that has been recorded in the last decade. This maximal bilateral flow is related to the bilateral gap in the average per capita purchasing power between the EU sending and EU receiving country involved.

5. Finally, the strongest bilateral *intra-EU-country migration propensity* is weighted by the absolute size of the EU destination country (i.e. the population) to get a standardised "per capita" migration propensity.

The formula to estimate the potential migration flows from the EU to Switzerland can be written as:

$$Mig_{EUi \Rightarrow CH,\,2002} =$$

$$(Mig_{EUi \Rightarrow EUj} / Pop_{EUi})_{1990} * (\Delta Y_{EUi \Rightarrow CH,\,2002} / \Delta Y_{EUi \Rightarrow EUj,\,1990}) * (Pop_{CH}/Pop_{EUj})_{1990} *$$

$$Pop_{EUi,\,2002}$$

where

$Mig_{EUi \Rightarrow CH,\,2002}$	=	migration potential from EU-country i into Switzerland in 2002 (calculated)
$(Mig_{EUi \Rightarrow EUj} / Pop_{EUi})_{1990}$	=	migration propensity from EU-country i into EU-country j in period 1988-1996 (measured as the ratio of all migrants from i to j (=$Mig_{EUi \Rightarrow EUj}$) and total population of the emigration country (=Pop_{EUi}))
$(\Delta Y_{EUi \Rightarrow CH,\,2002} / \Delta Y_{EUi \Rightarrow EUj,\,1990})$	=	ratio of the difference of per-capita income between Switzerland and EU-emigration country i ($\Delta Y_{EUi \Rightarrow CH}$) in 2002 (forecast) to EU-immigration country j and EU-emigration country i ($\Delta Y_{EUi \Rightarrow EUj}$) in period 1988-1996 (measured)

$(Pop_{CH}/Pop_{EUj})_{1990}$ = Demand effect calculated from the ratio of Swiss population (Pop_{CH}) to population of EU-immigration country (Pop_{EUj}) in periode 1988-1996 (measured)

$Pop_{EUi,\ 2002}$ = Amount of population of the EU-emigration country in 2002 (forecast)

For a better understanding of the calculation procedure, it might be helpful to rewrite this formula to:

$$Mig_{EUi \Rightarrow CH,\ 2002} =$$

$$\{[(Mig_{EUi \Rightarrow EUj} / Pop_{EUi}) / \Delta Y_{EUi \Rightarrow EUj}] * [Pop_{CH}/Pop_{EUj}]\}_{1990} * \{Pop_{EUi} * \Delta Y_{EUi \Rightarrow CH}\}_{2002}$$

All parameters in the first { } parenthesis have historical values that are recorded in official statistics. These relevant data are summarised in table 2 (migration data) and table 1 (all other data). The second { } parenthesis includes expected values that have to be forecasted. Table 3 shows the forecast of the few relevant variables for the period 1998 to 2015.

Table 2 makes clear that the bilateral migration flows within the EU were not really strong in the decade 1986-96. Once more: Table 2 records all bilateral migration flows that did not more or less erratically oscillate back and forth from a positive sign in one year to a negative one in the next year. As can be seen there are only a few bilateral migration relationships that exceed a minimal threshold. Furthermore, most of the bilateral migration pattern follow some historical paths and not necessarily economic theory (why do the Greeks move only to Germany but not at all to France or Austria?). Finally, it is worth to mention that some of the most intensive cross-border movements happen in the really integrated labour markets of the Benelux-Germany-France area. Most of them are not recorded as permanent migration (because they include daily or weekly commuters, seasonal workers, project workers, business trips) or they are counterbalanced by an intensive in-, out- and return migration. Again, all these cross-border movements and the back and forth movements, the in- out and return migration do not follow a generalised macroeconomic behaviour that could be explained by traditional (neo-)classical theory (e.g. of the Hicks or Harris-Todaro type, see Straubhaar 1988).

In what follows, I estimate the immigration flows from the EU into Switzerland in three different scenarios:

1. Scenario 1 calculates the potentially highest immigration flows that we could think of according to the historical experience of intra-EU-migration and following the assumptions presented above.

2. Scenario 2 is a more realistic scenario. It takes into account that intra-EU migration flows did not follow economic theory and especially that they were not a reaction to the existing wage differentials between EU countries. In other words, wage differentials have no explanatory power at all. Remember that *the inner-EU migration flows were demand-determined by employment opportunities in the destination area and not supply driven by wage gaps!* This is a clear and empirically well covered fact. Thus, scenario 2 just takes the actual migration rates and it weights them by the size of the destination country relative to the Swiss population.

3. Scenario 3 takes into account that in an initial phase of the free movement of labour regime a short run "hump" could occur (see figure 1). This hump could be an adjustment behaviour, or the consequence that people have delayed their migration decision to make it easier now, or it could be just the case that people like to try out this new opportunity. Whatever reason it might be, scenario 3 estimates the immigration flows from Greece and Portugal to Switzerland with an extremely high migration propensity in the initial phase and the historically immigration propensity (according to scenario 2) afterwards.

3. ESTIMATIONS

The simulation results provide some clear findings which shall briefly by presented in the following:

1. The most important result is that there is no evidence that Switzerland will be flooded by EU-citizens after the free mobility of people has been introduced. In all scenarios it rather looks like immigration will be quite moderate. At its extreme we expect net-migration to Switzerland of no more than 10000 EU-immigrants.

2. The presented scenarios suggest that the strongest migratory movements will occur between Switzerland and its direct neighbours (Germany, France and to a lesser extent Italy). There is no historical evidence that there will be strong immigration to Switzerland from other areas.

3. Scenario 1, estimating an upper threshold to Swiss immigration, provides the following results (compare with table 4):

- At its extreme there will be 10000 immigrants from EU member states.
- Strongest immigration is expected from direct neighbours. The strong immigration from the Netherlands results from the model's assumptions and will probably overestimate future migration flows.
- Strong immigration from southern European countries must not be expected.
- The amount of immigrants goes down to 50% after about 10 years. This result is based on the assumption that EU countries grow more quickly than Switzerland.
- The expected catch-up process of EU-member states (in terms of economic growth) may justify interim periods resulting in immigration taking place at a later point in time. The effects of interim periods are marginal and do almost not have any effect on long term immigration potential at all.
- Scenario 1 considers the expected decrease in population which is expected in the period 2002-2015. It illustrates that population development is not

influential enough to change the expected immigration potential significantly.

4. Scenario 2 considers historical experiences of intra-EU migration. Results change as follows:

- Estimated net immigration goes down to 8000 EU-citizens each year.
- A comparison between Scenarios 2 and 1 displays that mostly immigration from neighbouring countries falls. This is due to the use of more realistic migration propensities. Immigration from southern European countries, Portugal and Greece, remains, in contrast, quite stable.
- There is still considerable immigration from the Netherlands which requires further analysis.

5. Scenario 3 shows that a "hump-effect" has only little quantitative impact on the two poorest EU-countries, Portugal and Spain (compare with table 5). Immigration potential from these two countries doubles though. In the case of Portugal this hump effect could even turn out to be stronger, due to historical ties to Switzerland. On the other side migration flows will fall even stronger thereafter. Over a 12-year period (until 2015) scenario 3 does not differ much from scenario 1.

4. EVALUATIONS

What do these simulation results tell us? We will focus on a quantitative interpretation of the results:

1. The estimated immigration potential from EU-countries into Switzerland is moderate. It differs little from the migration performance in the 1990s. Average net immigration in the period 1988-1997, for instance, accrued to 5000 EU-citizens each year. The estimates do not consider other migration hindering effects, periodical business-cycle effects or migration hindering demand shocks. In other words: the assumed migration propensities reflect some kind of boom period. Germany, at the beginning of the 90s, experienced a demand boom in the construction sector with the resulting immigration as a consequence of the reunification. This German experience has implicitly been transferred to future Swiss expectations. A worse economic development would thus also reduce the demand for EU-immigrants to Switzerland. This justifies the expectation that the quantitative effect of the free mobility of labour will be marginal for Switzerland.

2. The relatively strong immigration potential from neighbouring countries is not so much the result of differing per capita incomes. Income and unemployment do not differ so much between Switzerland and its neighbouring regions (Bayern, Baden-Württemberg, Elsass, Piemont, Lombardia, Vorarlberg, Tirol, Bozano). The mobility rather suggests merging regions and integrated labour markets on both sides of the border. This form of migration between highly developed countries hardly differs from intra-country migration. The word "mobility" rather than "migration" therefore seems to be more appropriate. A lot of immigration from France and Germany is also a result of "pensioners' tourism". Wealthy, elderly people from abroad often wish to live in Wallis or in Tessin.

3. Scenario 1 and 2 calculate high immigration potential from the

Netherlands (NL) and from Sweden. These expectations are likely to be exaggerated. They result from the assumption that migration from the NL to Switzerland is as high as it is between the NL and Germany. Since Switzerland is not a direct neighbour of neither the NL nor Sweden we may expect less immigration. In particular, the Swedish experience suggests that the migration propensity falls with distance (compare with Fischer, 1999).

4. Recent results from a micro-based analysis of the Swedish labour market can be believed to be exemplary for intra-EU mobility. Less than 3% of the population changed residence in the period 1985-1990 (see Fischer 1999). In Nordic countries, intra-country migration was dominant. In hardly any of the analysed countries international mobility accounted for more than 0.5% of the population. In other words, results from scenarios 1 and 2 could be overestimating actual outcomes, since too high migration parameters might have been used. Also distances have been neglected: The larger the distance between Switzerland and a potential emigration country the less will the actual immigration outcome be.

5. South-north migration within the EU has been little in the past few years and is likely to decrease even more. Why should Switzerland, contrary to these observations, have to expect strong immigration from southern Europe? Greek immigration into Germany reduced after a "hump effect". Portuguese immigration into Germany was mainly due to the construction boom after the reunification. This rather peculiar reason for migration should not be existent in the Swiss case.

6. The simulations are likely to overestimate migration from southern Europe into Switzerland. The actual experience from the 1990s teaches us that more people move from Switzerland to southern Europe than vice versa (compare with tables 6 and 7). Nowadays many southern Europeans tend to leave Switzerland going back into their home countries. Why should this trend be reversed as it is being suggested by the simulations?

7. The free mobility of labour between Switzerland and the EU would undoubtedly also enhance the repatriation of EU-citizens. Bureaucratic hurdles in Switzerland still make it extremely difficult to attain a work permit. Leaving Switzerland normally implies the loss of the work or stay permit. Any foreigner owning a Swiss permit would currently not dare to leave the country for the search of another job (not even if he was unemployed) because he knows about giving up his chances in Switzerland. Thus, an integrated labour market with easy access also implies a quick return to the home country.

8. Also the improved working possibilities for Swiss citizens should be kept in mind. After all, they would also be allowed to work in an integrated EU labour market. Especially this issue is likely to play a very important role in the discussion.

9. Switzerland being the host-country of many multinational enterprises has a strong interest for open labour markets which enables the firm-internal cross-border movement of Swiss employees. The unrestricted mobility and use of firm specific know-how and know-why (i.e. knowledge, information, skills etc.) is strategically most important for multinational firms. Firm-specific and firm-internal labour markets increasingly have an international dimension. A rising ratio of highly skilled workers to all migrants provides empirical evidence for this fact. The migration of so

called "Gastarbeiter" is already a historical phenomenon. Putting it differently: migration of blue-collar workers is out, migration of white-collar workers is in. The highly skilled, several languages speaking Swiss workers would benefit a lot from an integrated Swiss-EU labour market.

10. The presented simulation results and their economic interpretation demonstrate that interim periods are neither necessary to prevent vast immigration nor are they in the interest of the Swiss economy. Since the issue is not the prevention of keeping out masses of unemployed EU-citizens but rather the Swiss demand for highly skilled EU-personnel, further postponement of labour mobility will mainly be harmful to the Swiss economy. Additionally, Swiss workers will not be able to move abroad. The current situation of bilateral treaties of Switzerland with EU-countries is a sufficient interim period. Any further prolongation is unnecessary.

5. CONCLUSIONS

Labour market effects are considered as being very important in the discussion about the different integration options of Switzerland. This is mainly due to the immediate repercussions which (suspected) immigration is believed to have such as feared wage falls. According to a popular (populist) assertion, labour market mobility is said to imply: more foreigners, stronger competition, less welfare. This study provides theoretical arguments and empirical proof that these fears are not justified. It is the opposite we should expect: Labour mobility with the EU and a common external migration policy will lead to better prerequisites for growth, employment and wealth than any other political alternative.

A labour mobility treaty with the EU (either as a bilateral treaty or as a consequence of Switzerland's accession to the EU) will not lead to substantially stronger immigration flows.

1. There is hardly any theoretical justification why an integrated labour market between homogeneous economies should lead to strong migration. Economic theory rather suggests that trade and capital mobility will be efficient substitutes to labour mobility. This means to bring machines (capital) to men and not vice versa, particularly since people still prefer to live in their domestic environment to any other country. As long as trade and capital can not completely substitute labour mobility, migration will be necessary in order to ensure economic equilibrium. In this case, migration is a positive rather than a negative phenomenon.

2. Also empirical evidence is missing which might argue in favour of strong migration. The possibility to go and work abroad is the freedom used the least within the EU. Most of EU's citizens are primarily immobile. Only 1.5% of EU's population lives in another EU country.

The little labour mobility within the EU is noteworthy because income and employment differentials are considerable between the economically strong and the economically weak EU member states. If income differentials or unemployment were really to trigger migration, intra-EU mobility should be much larger. Southern Europe would long be deserted and northern Europe over-populated. The opposite is the case: Regions with the highest immigration statistics are regions which also experience a lot of emigration. Hence, migration is not a one-way phenomenon. For some time now labour mobility within Europe has been intra-industrial migration. The traditional blue-collar (Gastarbeiter) migration is nowadays not much more than a historical anecdote.

The German reunification provides an impressive proof that job security is judged to be more important than higher earnings somewhere else (compare with Franzmeyer/Brücker, 1992:92). Those workers who have a job perspective at home are unlikely to move. All 15 EU-member states offer relatively secure job perspectives so that strong migration to Switzerland appears to be unlikely.

Intra-EU mobility increasingly changes being intra-industrial mobility of highly skilled workers and managers. This rather modern form of migration is mainly the result of cross-border links of regional labour markets. To a lesser extent it is therefore an arbitrage phenomenon. It rather is a strategic element in international competition to exploit comparative cost advantages.

Is Switzerland so much different to the EU so that EU's experience is unlikely to be valid? Should we expect a strong magnetic effect on many EU workers due to higher wages and less unemployment in Switzerland? These scenarios neglect the fact that neighbouring regions have economically caught up with Switzerland. Neither income nor employment figures differ much any more.

EU-regions being economically more behind are also further away from Switzerland in a geographical sense. With an increasing distance, however, the propensity to migrate decreases rapidly. This fact has been proved in a micro analysis studying the migration pattern within an integrated economic area (compare with Fischer, 1999). If people decide to move they often stay within the same county. Long distance mobility remains an exception.

The quantitative estimates of potential Swiss immigration presented in this study confirm the expectations of extremely little migration movements. At its maximum only 10 000 EU-citizens p.a. are expected to immigrate into Switzerland. This upper threshold is even likely to be lower if migration propensities from the EU-experience are applied in the calculations rather than unrealistically high other propensity values.

Our results confirm the supposition that strongest mobility can be expected between Switzerland and its equally developed neighbouring regions. Germany and France would be the main sources of immigrants. Still, this kind of migration would rather be mobility within a naturally grown integrated economic area. It would be a sign of converging labour markets. The use of specialisation advantages as well as the adaptation to changed structural conditions would be the rationale.

A north-north form of migration as may be expected in the Swiss case has nothing to do with the traditional form of blue-collar, south-north migration. It rather is the mobility of highly skilled workers. Mobility will mostly take place within the same enterprise and concern mainly management personnel. Particularly for a country like Switzerland, with its attractive prevailing economic conditions for multinational firms, the exchange of know-how and knowledge is likely to be of central importance.

Not only white collar workers may be expected to benefit from cross-border mobility. Also other Swiss people are likely to profit, for instance, from an EU-wide use of services and the unrestricted mobility for educational reasons. In order to ensure the employability of young Swiss an increased international mobility is very important.

International communication, global empathy and teamwork in international networks are central factors for success in the age of globalisation. Young Swiss will be obliged to learn and apply these global elements. Their international competitiveness will otherwise diminish quickly with the corresponding negative effects on their wages and on the whole Swiss economy.

If, as predicted, immigration will be relatively little and if mostly white collar workers come to Switzerland, macroeconomic effects will be weak but positive. EU-immigrants will help to fill supply gaps on the labour market with the following consequences:

1. Those Swiss employers working in jobs which will be subject to increased competition from immigrants will not be able to benefit any longer from the artificially established rents. The growth of wages in these sectors will be increasingly moderate and conditions will normalise. Sectors such as self-employed, law and economic consultants, medical, nursing, education and research service providers will be mostly affected by this development.

2. The rest of the economy will benefit from increased competition in the highly skilled sector. Firstly, services of highly skilled will become cheaper which benefits consumers. Secondly, complementary workers to the highly skilled benefit form the wage fall since it reduces the general cost level and enhances international competition.

3. Especially in the lower skilled labour market it should be remembered that already many foreigners work there. In the construction, tourism and health sector, domestic workers have been in strong competition with foreigners for a long time. Economic rents have disappeared since. Labour mobility is unlikely to change anything in this sector. The question arises who is supposed to be protected by a Swiss type of "Entsenderichtlinie" (a state ordered minimum wage for certain low paid sectors). Could it possibly be that contrary to what is normally argued, the concern is not about low paid, low skilled but rather highly skilled jobs? EU-labour mobility will certainly not protect the Swiss labour market from structural changes. However, labour mobility will not be the cause of structural changes but some kind of support to overcome this challenge. It is important to keep in mind that it is not "employment" but "employability" and not "rigidity" but "mobility" which will be of importance in the next century.

REFERENCES

Fischer, B. and Th. Straubhaar (eds.) (1998), Ökonomische Konvergenz in Theorie und Praxis, Baden-Baden: Nomos.

Fischer, P.A. (1999), On the Economics of Immobility - Regional Development and Migration in the Age of Globalisation, Bern: Haupt.

Franzmeyer, F. and H. Brücker (1997), Europäische Union: Osterweiterung und Arbeitskräftemigration, in: DIW Berlin, Wochenbericht 64, p. 89-96.

Martin, Ph. (1993), Trade and Migration: NAFTA and Agriculture, Institute for International Economics, Washington.

Straubhaar, Th. (1988), On the Economics of International Labor Migration, Bern: Haupt.

Straubhaar, Th. (1991), Schweizerische Ausländerpolitik im Strukturwandel. Bundesamt für Konjunkturfragen (BFK), Strukturberichterstattung, Bern.

Straubhaar, Th. (1996), Schutzzoll auf Arbeit – das neue Gesicht des Protektionismus, List Forum, 22, p. 209-211.

Straubhaar, Th. (1998), Wirtschaftliche Konvergenz: Was, wie, wozu? in Fischer, B., Th. Straubhaar (eds.), Ökonomische Konvergenz in Theorie und Praxis, Baden-Baden: Nomos.

Straubhaar, Th. (1999): Integration und Arbeitsmarkt: Auswirkungen einer Annäherung der Schweiz an die Europäische Union, BWA-Schriftenreihe, Beiträge zur Wirtschaftspolitik Nr. 3, Bern.

Straubhaar, Th. and R. Weber (1993), Die Wirkungen der Einwanderung auf das staatliche Umverteilungssystem des Gastlandes: Eine empirische Untersuchung für die Schweiz, Schweizerische Zeitschrift für Volkswirtschaft und Statistik, 129, p. 505-526.

Straubhaar, Th. and M. Wolburg (1998): Brain Drain and Brain Gain in Europe - An Evaluation of the East-European Migration to Germany, Working Papers 4.16, Center for German and European Studies, University of California, Berkeley.

Table 1. Potential Migration into Switzerland, Initial Values

	Greece	Portugal	Spain	Ireland	Finland	Sweden	Italy	Switzerland
GNP/cap, 1997 in US-$-PPP	13080	13840	15720	16740	18980	19030	20060	26320
in % to CH, CH=100	50%	53%	60%	64%	72%	72%	76%	100%
Population 1998 in millions, mid 1998	10,5	10,0	39,4	3,7	5,2	8,9	57,7	7,1

	United Kingdom	Germany	Netherlands	France	Austria	Belgium	Denmark	Switzerland
GNP/cap, 1997 in US-$-PPP	20520	21300	21340	21860	21980	22370	22740	26320
in % to CH, CH=100	78%	81%	81%	83%	84%	85%	86%	100%
Population 1998 in millions, mid 1998	59,1	82,3	15,7	58,8	8,1	10,2	5,3	7,1

Source: Worldbank (1999)

Table 2. Bilateral Intra-EU Migration: 1986-1996
(Basis for the estimates of potential migration into Switzerland)

TO:	Denmark	Belgium	Austria	France	Netherlands	Germany	UK	Italy	Sweden
FROM:									
Denmark									
Belgium									
Austria									
France	100	2184			817				
Netherlands	200	2683							
Germany	500	2650			3271				
UK	400	533			2343				
Italy	100	356			480	4033			
Sweden	300								
Finland	100								2807
Ireland									
Spain						-1266			
Portugal		1156				6167			
Greece						7533			
Period	1990-1995	1991-1996	1986-1996	1990-1996	1990-1996	1988-1996			1988-1996

Source: OECD-Sopemi-reports, different years
Note: all data are average yearly data (i.e. inclusive of repatriation and reversed migration) Missing data imply that bilateral migration was either insignificant or irregular.

Table 3. Growth Rates 1997 and Forecast 1998-2015

	Greece	Portugal	Spain	Ireland	Finland	Sweden	Italy	Switzer-land
Growth rate of real per capita income (PCI) 1997 in %	3,1	3,3	3,1	7,3	4,3	1,7	1,2	0,7
Forecast of growth rates of PCI, 1998-2015 in %	3,0	3,0	3,0	5,0	3,0	3,0	2,5	2,0
Natural population growth 1997 in %	0,0	0,0	0,0	0,5	0,2	0,0	0,0	0,2
Forecast of natural population growth 1998-2015	0,0	0,0	0,0	0,5	0,2	0,0	0,0	0,3

	UK	Germany	Nether-lands	France	Austria	Belgium	Denmark	Switzer-land
Growth rate of real per capita income (PCI) 1997 in %	3,2	2,2	2,7	1,9	1,9	2,7	3,1	0,7
Forecast of grwoth rates of PCI, 1998-2015 in %	2,5	2,5	3,0	3,0	2,5	2,5	2,5	2,0
Natural population growth 1997 in %	0,2	-0,1	0,3	0,3	0,1	0,1	0,2	0,2
Forecast of natural population growth 1998-2015	0,2	-0,1	0,3	0,3	0,1	0,1	0,2	0,3

Source: Own forecasts based on data from: Worldbank (1999), OECD (1998b)

Table 4. Estimations of Potential Immigration into Switzerland
Scenario 1: Upper threshold (assumption: strong migration, no transition period)

Year	Gree-ce	Portu gal	Spain	Ire-land	UK	Fin-land	Swe-den	Italy	Nether -lands	France	Germa-ny	Aust-ria	Bel-gium	Den-mark	Σ
2002	639	446	474	20	688	206	780	431	3113	1996	2119	178	200	223	**11512**
2003	632	440	465	17	675	200	758	423	2943	1866	2068	173	194	215	**11071**
2004	625	434	457	15	662	194	736	415	2772	1735	2018	168	187	206	**10624**
2005	618	428	448	12	649	188	713	406	2598	1601	1967	163	181	198	**10171**
2006	611	422	440	9	636	182	690	398	2421	1466	1915	158	174	190	**9713**
Σ **2002-2006**	**3126**	**2170**	**2284**	**73**	**3310**	**971**	**3679**	**2073**	**13846**	**8665**	**10087**	**839**	**936**	**1032**	**53091**
∅	**625**	**434**	**457**	**15**	**662**	**194**	**736**	**415**	**2769**	**1733**	**2017**	**168**	**187**	**206**	**10618**
2007	604	416	432	6	623	176	667	389	2242	1329	1864	153	168	181	**9249**
2008	597	410	423	3	610	169	643	381	2061	1190	1812	148	161	173	**8780**
2009	590	404	414	-1	597	163	619	373	1877	1049	1760	143	154	164	**8305**
2010	582	398	406	-4	583	156	594	364	1691	906	1708	138	147	155	**7824**
2011	575	392	397	-8	570	150	569	356	1502	761	1655	133	141	147	**7338**
2012	567	385	388	-12	556	143	544	347	1310	614	1603	127	134	138	**6845**
2013	560	379	379	-16	542	136	518	339	1116	465	1550	122	127	129	**6346**
2014	552	373	370	-20	529	129	492	330	919	313	1496	117	120	120	**5841**
2015	544	366	361	-24	515	122	465	322	720	160	1443	111	113	111	**5330**
Σ **2007-2015**	**5170**	**3523**	**3569**	**-76**	**5124**	**1346**	**5111**	**3201**	**13438**	**6786**	**14892**	**1191**	**1264**	**1319**	**65859**
∅	**574**	**391**	**397**	**-8**	**569**	**150**	**568**	**356**	**1493**	**754**	**1655**	**132**	**140**	**147**	**7318**
Σ **2002-1520**	**8296**	**5693**	**5853**	**-4**	**8434**	**2317**	**8790**	**5273**	**27284**	**15451**	**24979**	**2031**	**2200**	**2351**	**118950**
∅	**593**	**407**	**418**		**602**	**165**	**628**	**377**	**1949**	**1104**	**1784**	**145**	**157**	**168**	**8496**

Source: own calculations

Table 5. Scenario 3: Hump-Migration (only in Greece and Portugal)

	Year	Greece	Portugal	Σ
	2002	1277	841	**2118**
	2003	1263	830	**2093**
	2004	1249	819	**2068**
	2005	1235	808	**2043**
	2006	148	255	**403**
Σ	**2002-06**	**5171**	**3554**	**8724**
	∅	**1293**	**888**	**2181**
	2007	146	251	**397**
	2008	144	248	**392**
	2009	142	244	**386**
	2010	141	240	**381**
	2011	139	237	**375**
	2012	137	233	**370**
	2013	135	229	**364**
	2014	133	225	**359**
	2015	132	221	**353**
Σ	**2007-15**	**1249**	**2128**	**3377**
	∅	**139**	**236**	**375**
Σ	**2002-15**	**6420**	**5682**	**12102**
	∅	**459**	**406**	**864**

Source: own calculations

Table 6. International Migration: Balance of Immigration and Emigration 1988-1997

Citizenship	1988	1989	1990	1991	1992	1993	1994	1995	1996	1997
All EU-countries	12447	12521	22294	16984	1318	1393	5095	-1467	-10094	-11244
Of it:										
Belgium	228	253	233	160	162	108	140	99	61	123
Germany	2274	2116	3620	2670	2560	1477	2545	1779	1887	2132
France	1387	1542	1791	1174	1226	1083	1764	1159	958	1170
Greece	-1	-1	35	-1	-78	-143	-126	-222	-158	-204
Italy	-2136	-2020	-1146	-1429	-6048	-3483	-2407	-4140	-6898	-6091
Netherlands	260	226	567	357	394	98	401	336	101	-165
Austria	634	506	767	569	333	119	301	-70	48	9
Portugal	8209	9724	14755	13793	8502	5922	4669	2678	-1124	-3744
Spain	742	16	596	-1427	-6731	-4290	-2807	-3364	-4593	-4376
UK	357	-97	470	419	467	415	397	330	-66	-2

Source: Statistical Yearbook of Switzerland (1999).

Table 7. Permanent, Foreign Citizens in Switzerland and their Nationalities 1990-1997

Citizenship	1990	1991	1992	1993	1994	1995	1996	1997	**Diff 97-96**
All EU-countries	805 416	823 748	826 636	828 478	833 999	836 170	827 094	817 383	-9711
Of it:									
Belgium	5 935	6 051	6 218	6 343	6 495	6 643	6 771	6 947	176
Germany	84 485	86 132	87 571	88 168	90 129	91 976	93 686	95 737	2051
France	51 729	52 409	53 071	53 418	54 421	55 407	55 974	56 750	776
Greece	8 468	8 386	8 185	7 877	7 619	7 293	7 010	6 682	-328
Italy	381 493	380 458	374 872	370 699	367 074	361 892	352 669	344 591	-8078
Netherlands	12 134	12 460	12 844	12 962	13 434	13 992	14 234	14 204	-30
Austria	29 123	29 185	29 031	28 714	28 658	28 454	28 385	28 297	-88
Portugal	86 035	102 207	113 412	122 068	129 555	135 646	137 848	137 148	-700
Spain	116 987	116 325	110 447	106 853	104 703	102 320	98 516	94 898	-3618
UK	18 269	18 682	18 986	19 188	19 494	20 030	19 755	19 814	59

Source: Statistical Yearbook of Switzerland (1999).

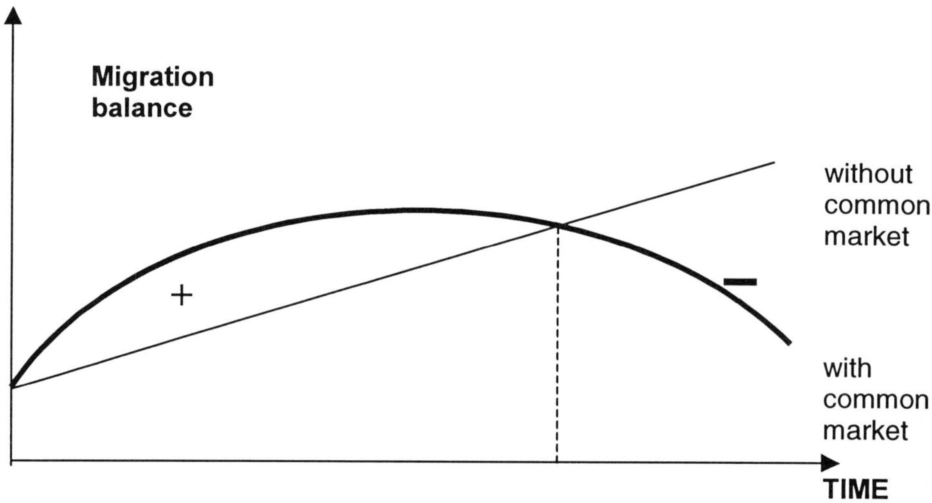

Source: own graph (after Martin 1993:136)

Figure1. Migration-Hump

SLOBODAN DJAJIC

MIGRATION AND SWISS EU MEMBERSHIP

A Comment

On the basis of the 1986-1996 experience of the European Union, this paper convincingly argues that the elimination of existing legal restrictions on the free movement of persons between Switzerland and the EU is not likely to result in a large flow of migrants into the Swiss economy. Citizens of the EU have enjoyed preferential treatment in applying for work permits in Switzerland since 1990, when the *Conseil fédéral* applied the „three circles policy". This policy gives priority to EU and EFTA citizens over other foreign applicants for Swiss work permits. Elimination of the requirement to apply for a permit would result in a modest, further reduction in barriers to migration between the EU and Switzerland. I very much agree with Thomas Straubhaar that this reduction is not likely to trigger large new inflows.

What I would like to do, however, is consider the possibility that we may be underestimating the migration potential from the EU into Switzerland. What are the factors which could contribute to large inflows? Where could the calculations of Thomas Straubhaar's carefully executed study possibly go wrong? I will focus on the possibility that preferences of labour market participants, as well as the costs and benefits of migration within Europe, may have changed considerably over the last few years, increasing the propensity of young Europeans to migrate. This would contribute to an increase in migrant flows from the EU into Switzerland, independently of whether legal barriers are removed or remain in place. In this context, I would like to make four points.

1. The last few years have been a period of poor employment opportunities in a number of EU countries, at least in relation to the late 1980's and early 1990's, which is the reference period for this study. Young entrants into the labour force, including college graduates, have been experiencing difficulties in finding attractive employment. The unemployment rates for the under-25 age group is currently hovering in the neighbourhood of 20%, while young women are experiencing unemployment rates in excess of 25%. Due to lack of employment opportunities, many students are deciding to continue their studies or to acquire additional practical training. At the same time they are becoming more and more open to the idea of working abroad. In France, for example, the prospect of getting a job in Canada, the US, the UK, or high-wage Switzerland, is becoming a frequent topic of conversation among university students. In addition to the scarcity of attractive employment opportunities in their own countries, the continuous decline in the cost of transportation and communication is changing the attitudes of young Europeans towards job search abroad.

R.E. Baldwin and A. Brunetti (eds.), Economic Impact of EU Membership on Entrants, 265–267.

The notion of working in a foreign country, experiencing a foreign culture, getting involved in a new social circle and shaking off what is often perceived to be the boring life style of the home town, is becoming increasingly appealing to young labour-market entrants. And while family connections and networks are still very useful to them in getting their first serious job locally, such connections are becoming less important in an ever more open and competitive pan-European labour market. It means that the gravitational forces keeping young people in their home town may be becoming weaker, while the attraction of moving abroad to benefit from a broader and deeper range of employment opportunities becomes more compelling.

There is also the consideration of perfecting a foreign language and getting valuable work experience with a foreign enterprise. So there is a human-capital element in the potential payoff associated with a move abroad. It is quite different from the blue-collar migration of the 1960s and 70s, where the primary motive was asset accumulation. All of these considerations raise the question of whether a fundamental shift in preferences and costs and benefits of migration is taking place, which makes past intra-EU migration experience less useful than we might imagine in predicting future labour flows into Switzerland.

2. In addition to the international real wage gap, which has been traditionally used as the key explanatory variable in models of migration, I wonder if in the present context of very high youth unemployment rates in the EU, it may be appropriate to focus on the Euro-Swiss differential in the probability of finding a job. With a 20% youth unemployment rate in the EU, a large number of potentially very mobile workers is repeatedly failing to find attractive employment at home. At the same time, the Swiss youth unemployment rate seems to be considerably lower (roughly 6%). An announcement that Switzerland is removing legal restrictions on employment of EU citizens may have, under these circumstances, a larger impact on migration flows than what the historical experience would suggest.

The fact that intra-EU migration flows have been demand-determined by the employment opportunities in the destination area and not supply driven by relatively low wages in the countries of origin, suggests that the probabilities of getting a job at home and abroad may have a more important role to play in explaining migration flows than the real wage differential. From the perspective of projecting future flows, the important question is whether workers are likely to conduct their job search at home or abroad. Improvements in the communications technology and the rapidly growing use of the Internet, implies that job search as well as recruitment across international borders is going to be much more common in the years to come. The Internet has enormous potential for improving the efficiency of matching jobs to workers over international borders. It is only a matter of time before it is fully exploited for that purpose, serving to increase the propensity of EU citizens to migrate in relation to that observed in the period 1986-1996.

3. I also want to mention the role of language in the analysis of international migration patterns, as it may be important in this context. It is true that France and Germany were not flooded by Italian, Spanish and Portuguese workers. The fact that

most of them do not speak French and German may be an important part of the explanation. Foreign workers are preoccupied with two basic activities in the host country. One is the process of transforming their labour and human capital services into income and the other is that of transforming income into utility. If those transformations are to be achieved efficiently, command of the local language is critical. Loss of efficiency due to lack of language skills can easily wipe out any potential benefits associated with the real wage differential between the domestic and foreign markets for labour. Since Switzerland's EU neighbours speak Swiss languages, there is little or no language barrier in the way. This may result in migration flows being relatively more sensitive to the elimination of legal restrictions on migration.

4. The notion that Spanish, Portuguese, and other workers do not dare to leave Switzerland in fear of loosing their work permits, implies that a permit is a valuable asset. It would be interesting to examine how valuable this asset is perceived to be. This is not a simple task, since the asset is not tradable. But even a rough, indirect estimate of its value and the elasticity of demand for it would be very helpful in the process of estimating the potential inflows of labour into Switzerland.

With an abolition of legal restrictions on migration, Switzerland is essentially agreeing to distribute this asset, free of charge, to any EU citizen willing to check out the Swiss labour market. Without additional knowledge of what this asset is worth and its elasticity of demand, it is difficult to venture a guess on how many EU workers will come to claim it.

As a final remark, and to emphasise the principal message of Thomas Straubhaar's paper, even if migration flows are large, they only reflects a large improvement in the efficiency of labour allocation throughout Europe. This is a phenomena that we should not be afraid of.

AUTHORS' AFFILIATIONS

Baldwin, Richard E.,	Graduate Institute of International Studies (GIIS), Geneva, and CEPR
Bärlocher Jürg	Swiss National Bank, Zurich
Brunetti, Aymo	State Secretariat for Economic Affairs, Bern, and University of Basel
Bütler, Monika	HEC, University of Lausanne, and CentER Tilburg University
Djajic, Slobodan	Graduate Institute of International Studies (GIIS), Geneva
Forslid, Rikard	Stockholm University and CEPR
Francois, Joseph	Tinbergen Institute and CEPR
Genberg, Hans	Graduate Institute of International Studies, Geneva
Grether, Jean-Marie	University of Geneva, Laboratoire d'économie appliquée
Haaland, Jan. I.	Norwegian School of Economics and Business Administration and CEPR
Himmel, Margit	Basel Economics Ltd. (BAK), Basel
Kadareja, Arjan	Graduate Institute of International Studies, Geneva
Keuschnigg, Christian	University of St. Gallen and CEPR
Markusen, James	University of Colorado, NBER and CEPR
Midelfart Knarvik, Karen Helene	Norwegian School of Economics and Business Administration and CEPR
Müller, André	ECOPLAN, Bern
Müller, Tobias	University of Geneva, Laboratoire d'économie appliquée
Rutherford, Thomas F.	University of Colorado
Schwarz, Umberto	Swiss National Bank, Zurich
Simmons-Süer, Banu	Basel Economics Ltd. (BAK), Basel
Stalder, Peter	Swiss National Bank, Zurich
Straubhaar, Thomas	President, HWWA-Institute for Economic Research, Hamburg, and CEPR
Tarr, David	The World Bank
Van Nieuwkoop, Renger	ECOPLAN, Bern

INDEX OF AUTHORS